Managerial Leadership for Librarians

MANAGERIAL LEADERSHIP FOR LIBRARIANS

Thriving in the Public and Nonprofit World

G. Edward Evans and Holland Christie

LIBRARIES UNLIMITED™

An Imprint of ABC-CLIO, LLC

Santa Barbara, California • Denver, Colorado

Library of Congress Cataloging-in-Publication Data

Names: Evans, G. Edward, 1937- author. | Christie, Holland, author.
Title: Managerial leadership for librarians : thriving in the public and
    nonprofit world / G. Edward Evans and Holland Christie.
Description: Santa Barbara, California : Libraries Unlimited, an imprint of
    ABC-CLIO, LLC, [2017] | Includes bibliographical references and index.
Identifiers: LCCN 2017035038 (print) | LCCN 2017036676 (ebook) | ISBN
    9781440841712 (eBook) | ISBN 9781440841705 (paperback : acid-free paper)
Subjects: LCSH: Library administration—United States. | Public
    libraries—United States—Administration. | Libraries—Aims and
    objectives—United States. | Public administration. | Nonprofit
    organizations—Management. | Leadership. | Library science—Vocational
    guidance.
Classification: LCC Z678 (ebook) | LCC Z678 .E925 2017 (print) | DDC
    025.10973—dc23
LC record available at https://lccn.loc.gov/2017035038

ISBN: 978-1-4408-4170-5
EISBN: 978-1-4408-4171-2

22 21 20 19 18   2 3 4 5 6

This book is also available as an eBook.

Libraries Unlimited
An Imprint of ABC-CLIO, LLC

ABC-CLIO, LLC
130 Cremona Drive, P.O. Box 1911
Santa Barbara, California 93116-1911
www.abc-clio.com

This book is printed on acid-free paper ∞

Manufactured in the United States of America

CONTENTS

TABLES

PREFACE

The foundation upon which we prepared this book consists of four assumptions. The first assumption is that the reader has become or is becoming familiar with the core concepts of managing any type of organization. That in turn relates to our second assumption—that there is a core set of management concepts and activities that every manager knows and performs. Certainly those concepts and activities are modified, to a greater or lesser extent, depending upon the organizational context and mission, regardless of sector: for-profit, nonprofit, or public. Thus, we make passing references to such core concepts in various chapters, but do not explore them in any depth.

Our third assumption is reflected in the book's subtitle: our focus is on the nonprofit and public sector. The vast majority of libraries exist in one or both of those sectors. Librarian managers must understand how these environments require modifications of the basic managerial core concepts as well as include some managerial issues that do not exist in for-profit sector organizations. Some of the major differences between sectors are explored in chapter 1. The subsequent 20 chapters look at such basic areas such as accountability, budgeting, and leadership, while noting sector differences. Certain chapters contain information that is more sector-specific, such as fundraising and politics.

Finally, the fourth assumption is our belief that truly successful organizational careers arise from someone having a mastery of both managerial concepts and very strong leadership skills. A person may have a useful career being an outstanding manager while being a weak leader, and vice versa. Outstanding organizational outcomes are a result of having senior administrators who excel in *both* areas. Because of our belief we use the phrase *managerial leader* throughout this book.

As has been our pattern in collaborating on other book projects, we make extensive use of sidebars throughout this book. Their primary purpose is to identify resources you can use for further information about the ideas covered in a chapter's main text. To a lesser extent we employ sidebars to provide examples of first-hand experiences of the authors and advisory board members from their "on the floor" practical experiences relate to the chapter context.

We were fortunate to have an outstanding group of advisors/readers on this project. They read draft chapters as we finished each one. Their feedback helped us improve the quality of every chapter. The members of this group were as follows:

DR. CAMILA A. ALIRE—Dean Emerita at the University of New Mexico and Colorado State University. Alire received her doctorate in Higher Education Administration from the University of Northern Colorado and her MLS from the University of Denver. She is past President (2009–2010) of the American Library Association (ALA) and past President (2005–2006) of the Association of College and Research Libraries (ACRL) and also past President of the nation REFORMA (the National Association to Promote Library and Information Services to Latinos and the Spanish-speaking).

DR. JOSEPH MIKA—Professor Emeritus at the School of Library and Information Science, Wayne State University (Detroit, MI). Mika served as Director of the School twice (for a total of 15 years) during his tenure of 25 years at the university. He was also Assistant Dean at the School of Library and Information Science, University of Southern Mississippi (Hattiesburg); Assistant Library Director at Johnson State College (Johnson, VT); and Assistant Library Director, Ohio State University, Mansfield Campus. His teaching areas included administration, customer service, personnel management, and collection development. He is co-owner of Hartzell-Mika Consulting, a firm that has been in business since 1999, providing assistance with library director searches, strategic planning facilitation, facility development and planning, and staff and board training sessions. Mika is a retired colonel in the U.S. Army, having served 29 years in the Army Reserves.

DR. PATRICIA LAYZELL WARD—Semi-retired; currently Ward is Honorable Archivist to the *Festiniog Railway Company*. Ward has worked in public and special libraries and enjoyed a long involvement in teaching and research. This included posts as Director of the Centre for Library and Information Management at Loughborough University and Chairs in Library and Information Studies at Curtin University, Perth, Western Australia, and the University of Wales Aberystwyth. She is Emeritus Editor of Library Management, author of conference papers and journal articles, examiner to a number of universities and has consulted in Europe, South America, Southeast Asia, and Australia. She holds a master's and PhD from University College London.

MARGARET ZARNOSKY SAPONARO, MLS—Head of Collection Development at the University Libraries, University of Maryland (UMD). Saponaro is responsible for providing leadership and vision for the content of purchased and licensed collections across all disciplinary areas and formats in the UMD libraries. She also directs the collection development work of the Libraries' subject specialist liaison librarians, with primary responsibility for content and budgeting of the UMD libraries' general collections. Her prior work experience includes serving as librarian for journalism and for hearing and speech sciences and also as manager of staff learning and development at the University of Maryland; as associate director of learning resources at the Alexandria campus of Northern Virginia Community College; and as librarian for the College of Human Resources at Virginia Polytechnic Institute and State University. Saponaro has also served as an adjunct faculty member for the University of Virginia and is currently a member of the ALA and ACRL. She holds a master's degree in library science from the University of California, Los Angeles, with postgraduate work in the areas of personnel programs and public administration. Her research interests are in the areas of collection management, instruction, and emerging technologies in libraries.

SACHI YAGYU—Reference and Consulting Librarian at the RAND Corporation. Yagyu spent 18 years of her career at a private university as a reference librarian and as head of Public Services.

We also wish to acknowledge three other individuals who read one or more chapters for us and provided valuable feedback—Jackie Chandonnet, Regional Development Officer, University of Minnesota (chapters on fiscal matters); Leslie McLean, attorney (legal issues chapter); and Steve O'Connor, director of Information Exponentials, editor of the journals *Library Management* and *Collection Building*, and an adjunct professor at Charles Sturt University's School of Information Studies (feedback regarding sector variations).

G. Edward Evans
Flagstaff, Arizona

Holland Christie
Flagstaff, Arizona

Chapter 1

WHY NONPROFIT AND PUBLIC SECTORS MATTER FOR LIBRARY INFORMATION SERVICE MANAGERS

[T]he belief that the profit motive is the only reliable motive for welding organizational actions to social needs is wrong. . . . Such empirical evidence as we have on the relative efficiency of private and public organizations shows no consistent superiority of one over the other.

Herbert A. Simon, 1998

There are three broad organizational sectors—that is, categories into which organizations are placed—for-profit, nonprofit, and public. The vast majority of libraries and information services in the United States are dependent, to a greater or lesser degree, on tax monies and thus they fall into the public sector. Most of the other libraries (such as many museum libraries) fall into the nonprofit sector. As discussion in this book will demonstrate, the sector differences do matter in terms of management and leadership.

This is not just another in a long line of library and information science (LIS) books about being a manager or leader of an information service. Existing LIS texts on these topics, including ones by this book's authors, draw heavily on for-profit sector concepts and research. They give too little weight to a critical factor in the successful operations of information services: whether they are nonprofit/public versus for-profit. That factor is the foundation upon which LIS organizations exist and operate (nonprofit/public). This by no means is meant to suggest that all for-profit concepts of management and leadership have no place in LIS operation. Many for-profit concepts are relevant to any managerial situation.

However, without taking into constant consideration the nonprofit and public nature of an organization, libraries are less effective in achieving their goals and finding funding.

Why do we make the claim that there are significant managerial differences between the three sectors? Table 1.1, at the end of this chapter, identifies 25 major managerial differences among the sectors. These differences can and do affect the usefulness of research done in one sector when the results are applied in another sector. Sometimes the impact is slight and at other times have a major impact on how, and even if, you can employ the results. We explore the managerial differences in one or more of the book's chapters.

GENERAL SECTOR DIFFERENCES

For-profit (private) organizations have one common fundamental measure of success: a profit rather than a loss. Two secondary measures are (1) an ever-growing increase in revenue and (2) financial gains for shareholders. Those clear-cut measures of success allow for great freedom in an organization's decision making and actions as well as in comparability. Organizations in the nonprofit/public sector lack such common measures of success. The lack of such measures makes comparing success between nonprofit and public organizations difficult, even when they are engaged in similar activities such as libraries and information services.

Another major difference between for-profit organizations and other types is the nature of their governance. For-profit sector chief executive officers (CEOs) have great latitude in action, unlike their counterparts in the nonprofit and public sectors. In the case of family-owned and privately held organizations, the CEO has almost unlimited power in making decisions and implementing actions (within the law, of course). Nonprofit and public sector CEOs have much more limited powers to act without gaining prior approval from a governing/advisory board. There are few, if any, information services that do not have such boards. We explore governing board issues in chapter 5.

Organizational purpose is another key difference. Profit is the common driving purpose of private sector organizations, or, in some cases, at least having enough income to cover expenses and build a reserve fund. On the other hand, nonprofit and public sector organizations have a host of purposes. If there is a single basic purpose for such organizations, it is the very hard to define purpose of "providing a public good or value." Some years ago, Mark Moore suggested the following:

> Every time the organization deploys public authority directly to oblige individuals to contribute to the public good, or uses money raised through the coercive power of taxation to pursue a purpose that has been authorized by citizens and representative government, the value of that enterprise must be judged against citizens' expectations for justice and fairness as well as efficiency and effectiveness. (1995, 52)

Moore's approach makes it rather clear where the emphasis on accountability and assessment for libraries funded primarily through tax monies has arisen.

For nonprofit and public organizations there is not even something like Moore's statement above to define *value/good*.

Many people working in the for-profit sector hold the belief that only private organizations can operate efficiently and effectively. As this chapter's opening quotation from Herbert Simon (a Nobel Prize winner in Economics) suggests, such views may not be entirely valid. Nevertheless, these views exist and from time to time they lead to, or attempt to lead to, the privatization of some nonprofit or public organizations, including libraries and information services. The reason given for this view is that profit motives are so strong that a for-profit business not only can better manage a public agency, but can do so for less money, make a profit, and provide as good or better service. The Simon quotation suggests the jury is still out as to whether profit and the market are the only way to achieve efficient and effective outcomes. We explore privatization in later chapters, in particular chapters 8 and 9.

As you might guess from the above, there is also a difference in "ownership" between for-profit organizations and the other two sectors. "Ownership," in this context, means who has the basic control of the organization. For-profit organizations are owned by one or more investors, public organizations are owned by the government/citizens, and nonprofit organizations are owned by groups of people with a common value/purpose. Needless to say, ownership and funding sources are not as simple as the foregoing might imply. One way to think about the variations is to visualize them as a nine-cell matrix (nonprofit, public, and profit organizations and three sources of funding—donations, taxes, and investment/sales). A donation-nonprofit example could be a museum library. The obvious tax-public example would be public libraries. One example of an investment/sale for-profit would be a corporate library. Beyond those easy examples are tax-funded but privately owned/managed libraries (such as privatized public libraries) or private organizations that are highly dependent on government grants (the Rand Corporation Libraries is one such example). Many publicly funded libraries also rely on donations to provide the range of programs and services they think appropriate—typically friends groups and library foundations. Ownership and funding sources do make a difference in what a manager-leader can and cannot do.

Public Sector Organizations

There are a number of significant differences between private and public sector organizations beyond their purposes. The most obvious difference is where the money comes from—sales and investments versus taxes and fees. The former came be controlled, at least to some degree, by the organization. For public organizations, raising taxes is a major political issue and not easy to do. Raising fees is easier; however, such revenue is generally a very modest portion of the funds required to operate at even a minor level of effectiveness. Likewise the public sector's annual budget cycle is fixed, with little flexibility, whereas the private sector's budget cycle is, or can be, much more fluid. When it comes to accounting practices the private for-profit sector has one standard approach (we will discuss this in more detail in the chapter on fiscal matters). Public sector agencies can select from several sets of accounting standards—federal, state, and professional. When it comes to procurement, however, public sector agencies have to follow mandatory requirements (often some form of bidding process). (One of the authors of this book once worked in a public academic library in a state that had such a requirement—the annual periodical/serial bidding cycle was a nightmare for the staff.) Even marketing is different, in that private organizations have greater flexibility to enter or leave a market as sales and consumer tastes change. Public sector bodies have a defined service population, a market that is very difficult to change.

Another clear difference lies in the legal basis for an organization's existence. Most of the private sector organizations and all public sector organizations have a legal base. For the private sector, the typical underlying document is the articles of incorporation that spell out the expected areas of operation. Such documents tend to be filled with legal jargon covering many pages of text. However, articles of incorporation they are kept rather vague in order for the organization to quickly adjust to changing circumstances. In the public sector, almost all long-term bodies come into existence as a result of legislation, which is generally rather narrow in its articulation of purpose. For example, most public libraries come into being as result of the state legislature passing a set of library laws.

In many other areas the public sector organizations face constricted freedom to act in comparison with those in the private sector—for example, in response time to changes, operational goals, and adding value. The overarching reason for the reduced freedom to act is that public agencies operate within the framework of laws, codes, regulations, and rules that are much more restrictive than those that apply to those in the private sector. Once a public organization comes into existence its structure is very difficult to change because there are a variety of stakeholders with diverse interests that are not always compatible. The same is true of matters of policy and procedure. (Transparency and "consulting widely" on decisions, as well as on priority setting, as now the public often demands, will slow change.) When it comes to accountability there is no doubt that public sector managers face far greater expectations than do their private sector counterparts. We are not suggesting there is no accountability in the private world, rather, it is more limited when comes to decision making and taking action.

On the "people" side the differences are also rather marked. For example, risk taking is not highly regarded, and even less often rewarded, in the public sector— "Do your job, don't take risks." This is a serious downside for the public sector. In the area of staffing, the differences are stark. Public sector hiring is generally governed by some form of civil service system that often begins with job-seekers taking a test. Those passing the test are ranked and a prospective supervisor must interview the individuals who have the highest scores. Dismissals are also more complex and drawn out in the public sector. Rewarding high performing individuals is far more complicated in the public sector than in the private sector. Finally, turnover of staff is much lower in the public sector, where job security can lead to long-term retention of poor-performing individuals.

Public organizations (almost always some type of government agency) seem to have always had to address a widespread challenge: the citizen's distrust of government. In a sense, you can say that the American Revolution was a massive exhibition of the mistrust government. Levels of mistrust rise and fall with the political tides. There is now a strong undercurrent of distrust of the federal government; distrust may be less strong regarding state agencies, depending on which state you are in. Even local governments are not immune to the distrust virus. Given that distrust, it is not hard to understand why public organizations have managerial-leadership challenges and why, on occasion, the people working in public sector organizations feel frustrated and stressed out when citizens find something to complain about, no matter what is or is not done.

Despite the widespread "mistrust of government," most people expect and demand a variety of government services—fire and police protection, good roads, and an ample water supply, for example. If people are asked in the abstract about the level of trust they have for such services, the results, over all, are likely to be positive. Needless to say, there are times when such basic services are thought of as less than trustworthy. Perhaps one reason for the overall distrust rests on press coverage. Successful, uneventful, cost-effective agency performance is rarely thought of as newsworthy, while failures, cost overruns, "Golden Fleece Awards," and the like make the news. For public organizations, no news is indeed good news. One aspect of the trust issue probably lies in the degree to which an agency is buffeted by political winds. The more the political philosophies regarding an agency's mission or purpose differ, the more people there are who do not trust the agency.

There is good news for publicly supported libraries and information services: they run counter to the general trend of distrust. What is meant by *trust* in this case is better termed *social trust*; however, for purposes in this section, only *trust* will be used to save time and space. One concise definition of *trust* is that people believe in the honesty, dependability, and integrity of others (people and organizations). Libraries appear to be a trusted organization in the United States. In 2007, a Pew Research Center survey found that 50 percent of those surveyed agreed with the statement "You can't be too careful in dealing with people" (Taylor, Funk, and Clark, 2007, 1). Many people are even less trustful of government agencies.

A study by Public Agenda contained an interesting chart showing the results of respondents' assessment of job performance of libraries and selected government agencies in their communities. Libraries were the rated the highest, with "excellent" and "good" performance (library ratings for those two categories was 76 percent). The next closest public agencies were police departments, with a 68 percent positive rating. You will probably not be surprised to learn the local community government took last place, with a positive rating of 43 percent. Only 56 percent of respondents rated their public school system as doing an "excellent" or "good" job (Public Agenda, 2006, 20). Certainly perception of job performance is not the same as a person having trust in a highly regarded organization. However, it seems rather unlikely that an agency thought to be performing marginally is likely to be highly trusted. In any case, if three-quarters of a service population thinks you are doing an excellent or good job, that cannot hurt your creditability. Being very creditable is essential for public and nonprofit organizations.

The Public Agenda report, discussed above, suggests that "public libraries seem almost immune to the distrust that is associated with so many other institutions. People have high expectations of their libraries. Topping their list of priorities is that the basic services they come to expect from libraries remain free of charge to the public" (Public Agenda, 2006, 11). Our local newspaper, *Arizona Daily Sun*, conducts an annual online survey asking readers to rate the "Best of Flagstaff." The "Best" list covers all manner of organizations, including the best public service agency. The Flagstaff City–Coconino County Public Library wins that category consistently. It is difficult to imagine any organization being viewed in such a fashion and not being trusted at the same time. On the issue of trust, in 2011 the OCLC issued a report entitled "Perceptions of Libraries, 2010: Context and Community," which was an update of a similar study conducted in 2005. The 2010 report noted that libraries and Web search engines were trusted equally (Gauder, 2011, 40). That outcome may not be all that pleasing for those who worry about the future of libraries in a digital world; however, it does support the notion that libraries are trusted.

We need to draw upon our library's social trust as we go about our professional duties. We also should have it in mind when thinking about our programs, services, and needs. Trust is a very fragile thing; once trust is broken it is very difficult to repair, much less return to its former level in the community.

Beyond trust, there is the belief that public agencies are naturally incompetent and wasteful or inefficient, at least in the minds of some people. Such views are rather common among those working in the for-profit sector and, as noted earlier, lead to efforts to privatize various public agencies. As we noted above, there is some evidence that libraries have been able to avoid being tarred with such views (see the Public Agenda report cited earlier), but that has not meant that some libraries have not been privatized (a number of federal libraries are privatized; some public libraries have been as well).

Nonprofit Organizations

The concept of nonprofit as a sector is less than 100 years old and encompasses a very wide range of organizations, including public/government agencies. The variability within the sector is clear when we consider that it includes academic institutions, charitable organizations, governmental agencies, libraries in their various forms, and religious bodies. Each of those categories has a number of variations as well, making it impossible to identify a single overarching purpose for the sector.

Nonprofit organizations occupy the middle ground between private sector and public sector organizations. Nonprofit organizations have more flexibility than do public sector entities and less flexibility than organizations in the private sector. Nonprofits exist as a result of having a certain Internal Revenue Service (IRS) status, articles of incorporation, and a set of bylaws. The three sets of documents provide the basis of a nonprofit organization's purpose and structure. There is less flexibility than usually found in for-profit organizations but more than is the case for public sector organizations. The bylaws, including purpose and structure, can be changed more easily than those of public or private as there are fewer stakeholders involved and those that are have less diverse interests than those in a public sector organization.

Robert Glavin (2011) identified five characteristics of nonprofit organizations beyond providing a social good. Nonprofit organizations have an organizational structure but not all of them have articles of incorporation (incorporation is an essential step if the organization wishes to have a tax-exempt status). While they may take some pressure off government agencies in providing a benefit/value for society, they are private in ownership. Their funds may only be dispersed in expenditures that assist in meeting their organizational purpose. Finally, they are self-governed and are voluntary in membership. It is important to note that this does not mean a nonprofit organization cannot have paid staff or that all funds go directly to the organizational purpose. Very large nonprofits do have paid staff as well as covering administrative cost with funds from donations.

AUTHOR EXPERIENCE

Evans was a member of the board of the Friends of the Flagstaff City–Coconino County Public Library. This is a 501(c)3 organization that raises funds that supplement the library's official funding sources. All seven of the board members are volunteers who were elected to the board by the members of the Friends group. Money is raised through book sales, group membership fees, and the sale of library-themed merchandise. This Friends group has no paid staff; however, Evans knows of Friends groups in large metropolitan settings that do have at least one paid staff member. Evans estimates that 95 to 96 percent of the monies raised go to various library units based on formal requests. The remaining balance covers such expenses as accountant and back fees, board insurance, postage, and so on.

From the donor's point of view only the group membership fees and cash gifts are tax-deductible. Donations of items for the group to sell are deductible but the cost of purchasing a "Friends item" is not. This can and does cause some confusion for some people. "You said you are a tax-exempt group?" Under IRS rules the cost or price of any tangible product (magazine subscriptions, coffee cup, etc.) that the donor receives as the result of a gift is *not* tax-deductible.

Such issues will be discussed further in later chapters.

Peter Hall succinctly describes the complex nature of nonprofit organizations:

> It is difficult to generalize about what nonprofit organizations are, what they do, and how they do it. They differ enormously in scope and scale, ranging from informal grassroots organizations with no assets and no employees through multibillion-dollar foundations, universities, religious bodies, and health care complexes with thousands of employees or members. (2010, 3)

Perhaps the clearest distinction is how the IRS classifies such organizations. There are two broad categories of tax-exempt organizations in the IRS Code; however, there are more than 70 subcategories. Knowing an organization's status plays a role in fundraising activities. Without doubt, the overarching characteristic of nonprofit organizations is their special IRS status.

One of the broad categories that almost everyone has seen, if not really noted, is stated on the solicitations you receive in the mail requesting a gift for a group: "This is a 501(c)(3) organization." What that designation means is any money you give that group is tax deductible, and most information service organizations can have this status, but there are limits, as noted earlier. As we will describe in chapter 11, tax-deductible status is a key issue in fund raising. The IRS has another broad category for nonprofit organizations: 501(c)(4). Organizations in this category—civic organizations—are not taxed, as is true for those in the 501(c)(3) category; however, they cannot offer deductibility for any donations or gifts they receive.

There are limits as to what, if any, political activity a tax-exempt organization may engage in. The actual subcategory status determines the level of political activity allowable. As we will cover in chapter 11, the status is critical in fundraising, especially in terms of voter bond issues. There is also the question of what constitutes political activity; where is the line between political activity, lobbying, and advocacy? It does matter. This topic is explored in more detail in chapter 13.

One point that probably runs counter to what many people believe about nonprofit/public organizations relates to staff commitment. What we mean by "commitment" is organizational; that is, how committed do employees feel to the organization. Research, such as that conducted by Laurel R. Goulet and Margaret L. Frank (2002), has shown that nonprofit and public sector employees have less organizational commitment than their for-profit counterparts. Based on the research, including studies cited in the article by Goulet and Frank, it seems that LIS manager-leaders may need to pay even more attention than they currently do to staff morale, providing solid support and engaging the staff as much as possible in planning and decision making.

Another difference of importance to LIS manager-leaders, which did not fit in Table 1.1, is organizational independence. The majority of for-profit organizations are standalone entities. Almost all LIS organizations are part of a larger organization—academic, city, or school district, for example. This has major implications for managerial leaders in such circumstances in that their actions and behavior must take into account the larger organization's mission, policies, practices, and expectations.

WHAT WORKS AND WHAT DOES NOT?

By this point, you undoubtedly understand why it is so important to be both a manager and a leader in the information services field. Essentially, library managers have substantially less freedom of action than do their counterparts in the for-profit sector. While all organizations have some stakeholders, libraries, for the most part, have more stakeholders than most, and those stakeholders often have differing points of view as to what should or should not be done. It takes both managerial and leadership skills to effectively navigate these differences to reach a consensus.

This is a good point to define some terms that will be employed throughout the book. "Senior management" refers to the person ultimately responsible for what the library does and does not do and that person's direct reports. "Managerial leader" can be anyone who has supervisory duties—leadership does not and should not just reside in the upper administrative levels. "Operational staff" includes any person who works for a library—paid employee or volunteer.

The answer to this section's question (what does and does not work?) is straightforward. The fundamental management concepts you learned in a management basics course do apply. However, these concepts work only in the sense that all organizations must plan, create a structure, hire staff, secure funding, and so on. The

Table 1.1.

Comparison of Private, Nonprofit, and Public Management Differences

Topic	Private	Nonprofit	Public
Purpose	profit	social value/good	social value/good
Budgets	flexible	modest flexibility	low flexibility
Set prices	unlimited	modest flexibility	low flexibility
Governance	self-contained	some social oversight	strong oversight
Ownership	self-contained	members/societal	government/societal
Accountability	limited	moderately strong	very strong
Structure	highly varied	flexible	limited flexibility
Market	basically unlimited	defined/possible to change	fixed
Value added	high	moderate/high	moderate/low
Policy action	unlimited	moderate/legal	limited/political
Operational goals	flexible	moderately fixed	fixed/limited
Response time	rapid	moderately fast	slow
Funding	investment/sales	donations/grants	taxes/donations/grants
Accounting	fixed	variable	moderately fixed
Procurement	unlimited	unlimited	highly constrained
Hiring	highly flexible	highly flexible	highly constrained
Staff dismissal	wide latitude	wide latitude	limited options
Turnover	high	moderate	low
Performance reward	unlimited	unlimited	limited
Staff loyalty	moderate/high	moderate/high	low/moderate
Risk tolerance	moderate/high	moderate	low
Decision making	internal	internal with some external	heavy external
Transparency	low	moderate	high (expected)
Priority setting	internal	internal/some external input	external
Legal base	articles of incorporation	IRS status	laws

key difference is the importance of keeping the particular sector an organization is in at the forefront of their thinking while engaging in such common functions. What differs between organizations is their sector and purpose. Libraries trying to apply for-profit "new ideas and concepts" can cause problems; purpose and freedom of action do matter.

This book looks at a variety of management issues from a library information service perspective and from whether they are in the public or nonprofit sectors. We have found it managerially helpful to spend some time reading journals such as the *Harvard Business Review* and *Sloan Management Review* and to balance that with time spent reading journals such as *Public Administration Quarterly* and *Nonprofit Management and Leadership*.

REFERENCES

Gauder, Brad, ed. 2011. *Perceptions of Libraries, 2010: Context and Community*. Dublin, OH: OCLC. http://oclc.org/content/dam/oclc/reports/2010perceptions/2010perceptions _all_singlepage.pdf.

Glavin, Robert. 2011. "The Role of Nonprofits in American Life." In *Nonprofit Management 101*. Edited by Darin Rodriguez Heyman. San Francisco, CA: Jossey-Bass.

Goulet, Laurel R., and Margaret L. Frank. 2002. "Organizational Commitment Across Three Sectors: Public, Non-Profit, and For-Profit." *Public Personnel Management* 31, no. 2: 201–210.

Hall, Peter Dobkin. 2010. "Historical Perspectives on Nonprofit Organizations in the United States." In *The Jossey-Bass Handbook of Nonprofit Leadership and Management*. 3rd edition. Edited by David O. Renz and Associates. San Francisco, CA: Jossey-Bass.

Moore, Mark Harrison. 1995. *Creating Public Value: Strategic Management in Government*. Cambridge, MA: Harvard University Press.

Public Agenda. 2006. *Long Overdue: A Fresh Look at Public and Leadership Attitudes about Libraries in the 21st Century*. New York: Public Agenda. http://www.publicagenda.org /files/Long_Overdue.pdf.

Simon, Herbert A. 1998. "Why Public Administration?" *Public Administration Review* 58, no. 1:1.

Taylor, Paul, Cary Funk, and April Clark. 2007. *Americans and Social Trust: Who, Where and Why*. Washington, DC: Pew Research Center. http://www.pewsocialtrends.org /files/2010/10/SocialTrust.pdf.

Chapter 2

LEADING

The wicked leader is he who the people despise. The good leader is he who the people revere. The great leader is he who the people say, "We did it ourselves."

Lao Tzu, 6th Century BC

There is a growing need for effective leadership. As budgets decline and mission-critical demands expand, employee engagement becomes more critical.

Tim A. Flanagan and John S. Lybarger, 2014

If leadership has a secret sauce, it may well be humility.

The Economist, 2013

It was also important for external stakeholders to feel like part of the greater library community. Because many of the identified areas for change came from input from students and faculty, library managers developed ways to collaborate with each group.

Corey S. Halaychik, 2014

If anything, managers of nonprofit and public sector organizations need stronger leadership skills than do their profit sector counterparts. Why is that the case? The answer lies in the nature of the sectors and their purposes.

Providing a societal benefit or value means that almost everyone has, at least minimally, an interest or stake in how a nonprofit or public organization functions. That, in turn, means, or should mean, before taking action to do or not do something, a nonprofit or public organization almost always goes through consultation, comment, and consent processes. Those processes often involve a number of stakeholders who do not always agree on what should be done. As noted in chapter 1, the various stakeholders often hold widely divergent views on the matter at hand.

Also, as noted in chapter 1, for-profit managers have much greater freedom to act and can even force actions based on little or no consultation.

Leadership focuses on people rather than on the organization. Nonprofit and public organizations (at least libraries and information services) are people-oriented as well. Given the variety of interests that people have about what such organizations do, you can see where people skills and leadership play a key part an organization's success. The opening quotation to this chapter makes the point that great leadership can make people think "we did it ourselves."

Interest in leaders and good leadership clearly goes back thousands of years, as the opening quotation from Lao Tzu illustrates. You might not get that sense from looking at management literature in general or library literature in particular. It is not something new except in the sense that it was only relatively recently that we again took a major interest in the concept of good leadership. A fairly large portion of the leadership literature is devoted to a specific crisis or lack of leadership. One reason for that emphasis may be because the literature focuses on the very top leaders in the profit sector, and scandals as well as prison terms for some of those top leaders offers fodder for some writers. Bill Georges (2007) and Jeffery Pfeffer (1992 and 2010) make an important point regarding organizational leadership: organizational leadership can and does take place throughout an organization, not just at the top. A thought to take away from their point may be that by looking holistically, there is no evident crisis or lack of leadership.

One of our favorite leadership books is Barbara Kellerman's *Bad Leadership: What It Is, How It Happens, Why It Matters* (2004). She makes a significant point, arguing that "[starting] to look at leadership through rose-colored glasses is a mistake for many reasons, not least because we tend to learn more from our failures than from our successes" (221).

ADVISORY BOARD EXPERIENCE

Mika has often mentioned in his library administration classes and workshops that while you do learn by observing good leadership, it is often by examining "bad leaders," their mistakes, and poor management and leadership styles, that you may gain the most knowledge and therefore know what not to replicate in your own administrative style.

Kellerman's book suggests you think of leadership as falling along two axes—ethical to unethical and effective to ineffective. Further, those axes apply to both leaders and their followers. Leaders can and do stay in that role for a long time while being unethical and ineffective, as long as their followers do not object or take action. Emmett Carson (2011) made a similar comment about effective leaders: "I underestimated the importance of effective leadership and believed that strong staff members could still be successful even when led by a weak leaders . . . they cannot achieve their best on a consistent basis without strong leadership at the chief executive level" (29). Perhaps the most striking example of a leader being effective and unethical is Hitler in Germany during the 1930s and '40s. By the same token, it is possible to have a highly ethical but ineffective leader. The point to take away from Kellerman's book is that not all leadership is "good."

In 1998 Hennery Mintzberg commented on the leadership of professional organizations by suggesting "Leadership is clearly a tricky business in professional organizations. . . . I saw a lot more doing than what we conventionally think of as leading" (144). This is an important comment to keep in mind when reading the general leadership literature. The literature tends to focus on the for-profit environment rather than the nonprofit/professional setting. You may recall in the last chapter we made the point that as a manager you engage in less professional work than you did prior to taking on a managerial role, but you will continue to do some. Thus, his comment about "more doing than . . . leading" is spot on in terms of librarianship.

A challenge for public sector leaders is the constantly shifting political winds. The two major U.S. political parties tend to be far apart on many issues; such differences make it difficult for public agency manager-leaders to navigate and maintain the middle ground. Moving too far off-center can cause problems when one party leaves office and the other takes over. Although very rare, it is not unheard of for a senior library manager-leader to lose her or his position due to having taken a strong leadership role on some politically charged issue. (Think about intellectual freedom cases or freedom to read policies as potential pitfalls.) Any library policy formulated along political points of view can generate leadership challenges in the long run.

Political winds are somewhat less challenging for nonprofit organizations— "somewhat" being the operative word. Such winds are more variable for the nonprofits, while public sector organizations face a more constant variety. Political winds are also a little more predictable for the nonprofits. That is, nonprofit organizations know there are certain "hot button" issues that can and do arise from time to time as the political parties in power change. However, leaders in this sector must be just as flexible and responsive to wind shifts as their fellow leaders in the public sector.

It is commonly accepted among nonprofit and public sector managers that their actions revolve around what have been called the "3 Ms" (Mission, Money, and Management). Not that the 3 Ms don't come into play in the profit sector, they do; however, they play a less dominant role—bottom line profits matter most. Essentially nonprofit and public sector leaders must keep the 3 Ms in the forefront of their actions, decisions, and behavior and seek not to generate conflict between the three. Actually, it goes beyond avoiding conflict; the challenge is to assure consistency and strong support for all three.

BASIC LEADERSHIP THEORIES

This is not intended to be a review of the many theories regarding leadership and their uses. Rather, this section will highlight the more common theories and ones you likely already know to some degree. The references at the end of the chapter, as well as the "Check This Out" sidebars, provide citations for those mentioned as well as some that aren't covered that may be of interest to you.

Leadership research began early in the 20th century with a focus on the personality traits of individuals viewed as leaders. Little other work was undertaken until after World War II. While most of the literature labels this research as trait theories, the reality is they only identify what a leader personality is, not how such people lead. You will find that many of the leadership self-tests we mention later in this chapter are personality-trait focused. Most of the trait tests "assess" such things as your social skills, task-related skills, and other personal characteristics.

One early effort to go beyond trait analysis took place in 1939, when Kurt Lewin, Ronald Lippitt, and Ralph K. White published a leadership study based on experiments studying three leadership styles (how a leader acts): autocratic, democratic, and laissez-faire. The article's importance was in defining leadership in terms of behavioral style. Following World War II, leadership researchers focused on leader behavior. By the end of the 1950s, Ohio State University researchers had developed a questionnaire (the Leader Behavior Description Questionnaire). That questionnaire, revised from time to time, is still a widely employed assessment tool.

CHECK THIS OUT

Try the Leader Behavior Description Questionnaire (LBDQ) questionnaire, you can find it at http://fisher.osu.edu/research/lbdq/.
    See how accurate you think it is in identifying your leadership behavior.

Other researchers studied how various situations impact leadership behavior. Ample evidence existed and still exists that indicate a person who was/is effective in one environment may not be as effective in a different environment. Situational leadership affects leaders in all three sectors, although leaders in nonprofit and public sectors tend to have more varied situations to address more frequently. An essential element in a leader's tool kit is the skill to quickly assess and react to changing situations and take the appropriate action.

Charismatic leaders can be thought of as individuals who apparently have exceptional abilities (such as Hitler as an example of a bad leader and Martin Luther King as a good example) who inspire their followers to devote unexpected levels of time, energy, effort, and commitment and achieve major results. A great many "studies" of charismatic leaders are in the form of biographies. As a result, each reader is likely to take away different ideas about what constitutes a charismatic leader. That also means such biographies are of marginal value when it comes to developing leadership abilities because such studies tend to reinforce the idea leaders are born, not made.

"Transformational leadership" was James MacGregor Burns's (1978) contribution to leadership studies. Burns blended behavioral and trait concepts into a single conceptual model. His view was that influence was the key element in leadership; that is, both leaders and followers influence each other in a manner that transforms their relationship. He expanded the concept of transformational leadership into what is referred to as "transactional leadership"—a style in which there is give and take (a transaction) between a leader and followers.

CHECK THIS OUT

A good article about transformational leadership is Doina Popescu Ljungholm's "Transformational Leadership Behavior in Public Sector Organizations" (*Contemporary Readings in Law and Social Justice* 6, no. 1 [2014]: 76–81).

Robert Greenleaf (1977) proposed another theory: servant leadership. He believed people viewed as great leaders were first "servants" and that such individuals took on a leadership role as a result of feeling the need to serve and made a conscious decision to lead (27). Greenleaf also thought followers would grow and develop into servants.

CHECK THIS OUT

The Greenleaf Center for Servant-Leadership website is at http://www.greenleaf.org/. It provides more details about the concept.

An article that provides a sound summary of Greenleaf's ideas is Robert F. Russell's "The Role of Values in Servant Leadership" (*Leadership & Organization Development Journal* 22, no. 2 [2001]: 76–84).

The quotation from Corey Halaychik (2014) at the beginning of the chapter is from an article about the servant leadership concept as applied in an academic library setting. It reflects the importance of collaboration in any truly successful leadership effort—the people focus mentioned earlier. In the case of the library in question, there was strong emphasis on self-evaluation, stakeholder input, and honest straightforward communication in order to identify appropriate changes with built-in accountability. The article concluded by stating, "The servant leadership themes . . . provide library leaders with an easy to follow road map for initiating change in a variety of settings" (12).

LEADERSHIP SKILLS

Just what are the skills you need to become both an effective and ethical leader? There are different many lists of requirements—some are long, some are short. However, almost everyone agrees on a core set. The first skill on most lists of leadership skills is some variation of "vision." Vision is what makes followers want to follow a leader. Without a vision and followers, a person leads nothing.

A second common skill on almost every list is "communication." You may have the world's most compelling vision, but if you cannot communicate that vision, and do so effectively, you will lead nothing. Persuasion is, of course, related to communication. However, just being a good communicator does not always translate into

CHECK THESE OUT

We highly recommend Warren G. Bennis's *Managing People Is Like Herding Cats* (London: Kogan Page, 1998).

A leadership title that focuses on libraries is G. Edward Evans and Patricia Layzell Ward's *Leadership Basics for Librarians and Information Professionals* (Lanham, MD: Scarecrow Press, 2007).

persuading listeners to agree with the message. Being persuasive is essential for a leader. If no one is persuaded, you lead nothing.

Part of being effective at persuasion lies in the ability to develop solid relationships with people/followers. Developing relationships does not mean developing friendships in the common meaning of the word. Rather, it means you deal with people in an ethical manner and there is a trusting relationship. Your followers know what to expect from you on a consistent basis. If there is little trust and consistency, followers will drop away until you lead nothing.

ADVISORY BOARD EXPERIENCE

Alire commented that "One of the best compliments that I could receive and did receive as a leader was that I was 'fair and *consistent*.' It meant that I was predictable because of that consistency of fairness in our leadership style and was not perceived as arbitrary and capricious in my dealing with people."

Other elements in having good leader/follower relationships are a leader's skill in creating collaborative environments, developing/coaching, and sharing power. Effective leaders display all of these skills on a daily basis. The development/coaching aspect is probably the most critical to long-term leadership. Collaboration and power sharing are less critical but still important. As followers gain in skill and ability, many want to have greater empowerment and flexibility in their activities. A good leader knows who those individuals are and provides such opportunities; failure to do so will likely cause those individuals to cease being followers and to leave.

While leaders are known for consistently following the same core values and practices, consistency does not, or should not, mean inflexibility. An effective leader must have adaptability. Striking a balance between being consistent and being adaptable is a challenge. Failing to change is a recipe for disaster, but changing too soon can also cause disasters. There are many examples of organizational leaders who made a change and failed and those who did not change soon enough and failed. Too many failures will result in there being nothing to lead.

Planning, decision making, and risk taking are all essential skills for a successful leader. All three are interrelated. Every decision or plan carries some degree of risk. Having a reasonable degree of risk tolerance is critical for a leader. Risk tolerance may be one of the personality traits that is most difficult for some people to change.

A final skill that most people agree is part of an effective leader's arsenal of tools is having an optimistic outlook. Such an outlook is a key element in motivating followers to strive to achieve the vision and goals of the leader. During difficult times it is a challenge to maintain genuinely optimistic behavior. Faking such a behavior is not recommended. Your staff will quickly see through the facade and become non-followers.

The following are some of key leadership abilities to cultivate:

- Learning from mistakes
- Recognizing and working on weaknesses
- Recognizing and maintaining strengths
- Controlling emotions, at least in the workplace
- Maintaining a balance in life—both personally and professionally
- Understanding when one should step aside or step down

Barbara Kellerman offered some additional thoughts on working with followers:

- Establish a culture of openness in which diversity and dissent are encouraged.
- Bring in advisors who are both strong and independent.
- Avoid groupthink.
- Get reliable and complete information and disseminate it.
- Establish a system of checks and balance.
- Strive for stakeholder symmetry. (2004, 235–237)

After reviewing the theories and concepts regarding leadership, common characteristics of success and failure that impact leadership emerge. *Do not* view the list in Table 2.1 as a definitive list; it does, however, highlight some of the most common factors.

One reason working with a particular leader or manager is enjoyable is a function of the chemistry in the relationship. Two fantastic leaders who influenced our careers and our approach to leadership gave their staff freedom to do their jobs, took a personal interest in staff and their families, and had strong and outgoing personalities. Neither was universally popular; not everyone likes a strong leader.

Table 2.1.
Leadership Characteristics

Leadership Failure Factors	Effective Leadership Factors
Avoiding challenges	Welcoming challenges
Avoiding staff	Being available when necessary
Micromanaging	Seeking new ideas
Demonstrating little trust	Showing trust in followers
Behaving unpredictably	Being consistent
Lacking empathy	Knowing oneself

They allowed their staff to innovate and made things happen; they also "allowed" staff to make mistakes while innovating, as long as those mistakes resulted in learning—and did you learn!

Other bosses that we have reported to didn't have a "presence;" staff didn't see them often or know what they were thinking about the organization or the staff. At the other extreme were the "control freaks" that left staff unsure of their "boundaries," and of their tolerance for innovation or suggestions. We suspect some of the staff who worked under the "controllers" would have been happier working with a less intrusive leader.

TRY THIS

Think of organizations you know and you can probably identify someone at a lower level who takes a leadership role. This is common in libraries where support and paraprofessional staff play a major role in the functioning of the service.

Think of the managers you have known—the good and the bad—both in the work situation and in clubs, societies, sports teams, and so on. Draw a line down a sheet of paper. On one side write down all those things that you think make a "good manager," and on the other write down all those things that you believe define a "bad" manager.

ASSESSING YOUR INTEREST IN BEING A LEADER-MANAGER

Do you want to undertake the time and effort to become a real leader in an organization? Not everyone does. Not wanting to be a leader does not mean you may not want to be a leader in another context. The way to determine your interest is, in part, through an honest self-assessment. Warren Bennis's *On Becoming a Leader* (2003) offers a thorough description of how to begin assessing your leadership skills. What follows is a *very* brief summary of his thoughts reworded to fit the library information service environment. His book focuses on the for-profit sector, thus the need to recast some of his ideas.

A sound starting point is to make some comparative lists. Base your lists on what you hope to accomplish in your professional career. Not everyone aspires to be a library department head, much less a senior leader or director. It is important to think long and hard about long-term career goals before starting your lists. With that in mind, start by listing what you do want from your career, then create a second list of what you don't want. For example, how much time are you willing to devote to work-related activities? The higher you move in an organization, the more time will be consumed by its activities, if you are to be successful. That means some evenings and weekend days may be required, or should be required, by your representing the library at various functions, meetings, and conferences. For public and nonprofit organizations, "showing the flag" is essential and that activity takes ever-greater amounts of time the higher you go administratively. Clearly, such activities will result in less personal time. Certainly, the time commitment for a library managerial leader may be somewhat less than for a for-profit leader.

However, the fact is the more time you commit to such activities, the more your service will benefit.

CHECK THIS OUT

Because of the ubiquitous nature of technology, supervisors and employees alike are feeling the pressure to be "on call" 24/7 via their email, smart phones, and/or texting services. One article that discusses the challenges of managing the demands of technology is "Time Thieves and Space Invaders: Technology, Work and the Organization" by Ian Towers, Linda Duxbury, Christopher Higgins and John Thomas (*Journal of Organizational Change Management* 19, no. 5 [2006]: 593–618).

It is also useful to create a pair of lists comparing your abilities against your actual capabilities. (There is a difference between the two.) For example, a person may have the ability to understand how to do something but for some reason is incapable or unwilling of doing so effectively.

AUTHOR EXPERIENCE

Evans experienced an example of the above when a staff member knew what was required in terms of production quality and what the consequences would be for failing to achieve that output—dismissal. The problem was not just an internal library issue but also an institutional one. This fact limited Evans's options and made the dismissal a given, if the person did not meet the established goal. Even when the person was allowed to keep the production quality data the person was unable to reach the level required. Although he never could learn exactly the reason the person would or could not achieve the necessary quality production, Evans believes it was a matter of principle rather than the person not knowing how to achieve the required quality and quantity.

Making these two lists will not be easy as we often have trouble identifying our own limitations. One way to handle the process is to make your lists as best you can and then ask a work colleague or mentor with whom you are close to review the lists and make additions, corrections, and comments. That process can be uncomfortable; it is never pleasant to look at one's shortcomings. A solid mentoring relationship will be necessary for this approach to work properly. (We address mentors and mentoring in later chapters.)

In some sense, the most significant comparison is the list of your workplace goals, values, and priorities against a list of the organization's goals, values, and priorities. The greater the commonality between the two lists, the greater the likelihood is that taking a leadership role in the organization will be successful for you. Your last task is to consider the differences between the lists and identify those that could be changed through training or developmental activities. Of those differences, how many are there that you are seriously willing to work on modifying? Learning to be a leader takes time and effort. The fewer differences you want to work on, the less the chances are you will be satisfied with and successful at being a leader in your workplace. As Bennis noted, knowing and differentiating between "who you are and who you want to be from what the world thinks you are and wants you to be" (2003, 48) is an important if highly complex process.

Beyond the making of lists, there are a host of leadership self-assessment tools. Most of these are trait-based and thus should only be one component of your self-assessment activities. How valid, useful, and reliable are such instruments? The answer is that they vary. Every psychometric measurement has some limitations. The more abstract the concept one tries to measure, the greater the limitations, thus affecting the accuracy of the test results. Leadership is obviously an abstract concept with many definitions; that means there are many, many leadership assessment tools out there. For example, a mid-2015 Web search using the phrase "free leadership assessment tools" generated about 1,394 results. By the time you read this text the number will probably be higher.

The greater the number of people who use a particular instrument, assuming there is someone monitoring and modifying the analysis of the "test results," the greater the likelihood of reliability. No single instrument will provide the definitive data about your potential and actual leadership abilities. We strongly recommend using a number of tools, particularly ones that assess a variety of aspects related to leadership. The Learning Center offers a 30-point "Leadership Assessment: Personal Satisfaction Survey" (http://www.learningcenter.net/library/leadership .shtml). Some of the areas covered include "making and communicating decisions promptly," "involving others in planning actions," and "believing in and providing training that teaches leadership, teamwork, and technical skills." The test taker responds on a five-point scale from "very satisfied," "satisfied" to " dissatisfied," and "very dissatisfied," with a "neutral" midpoint. Two other sites that offer several free assessment tools are Daniel Kehole's Leadership & Management Shop (http://www.dkmanagementtools.com/free-leadership-self-assessment-tool) and Leadership-and-Motivation-Training.com (http://members.leadership-and -motivation-training.com/quizzes) There are many others to choose.

YOU CAN DEVELOP LEADERSHIP SKILLS THAT MAY NOT BE NATURAL FOR YOU

Mason and Wetherbee (2004) made the point that "the first fundamental assumption is that leaders can be developed. This was long a fiercely debated topic, and is now accepted as true. A second assumption is the belief that management differs from leadership and that managers can be transformed into leaders through training and development" (188). It took some time for the notion that a person was either a natural leader or not to die out. Another long-standing view has been that leadership, regardless of sector type, was the same. We believe that anyone thinking carefully about sector differences will quickly realize that sectors can and do affect leadership behavior and approaches. Certainly there are some individuals who are leaders by nature; however, today there a great many more people who are leaders as a result of undertaking leadership training.

Workshops, seminars, and even short courses all help you develop leadership skills, especially when they are sector focused. However, one or two such training activities do not make a leader; thinking they do would be rather like thinking a recipe that states "just add water and microwave for 3 minutes" will produce a gourmet meal. It takes time, effort, and, most of all, practice to develop leadership skills. (It also takes making mistakes.) Almost the first item on anyone's list of effective leadership skills is "vision." Training cannot provide you with a vision that others will follow. A vision comes from you and your circumstances. Programs may be able to help you identify steps to take in creating a vision, but only you can create it.

A great starting point for identifying training and development programs related to library leadership is the American Library Association's (ALA's) Library Leadership Training Resources website: http://www.ala.org/offices/hrdr/abouthrdr /hrdrliaisoncomm/otld/leadershiptraining. This website lists programs around the country, and it is not limited to those sponsored by ALA. ALA itself has an emerging leaders program. As noted on the Emerging Leaders website, "The American Library Association (ALA) Emerging Leaders (EL) program is a leadership development program which enables newer library workers from across the country to participate in problem-solving work groups, network with peers, gain an inside look into ALA structure, and have an opportunity to serve the profession in a leadership capacity. It puts participants on the fast track to ALA committee volunteerism as well as other professional library-related organizations" (http://www.ala .org/educationcareers/leadership/emergingleaders). Emerging leaders is primarily an online program over a six-month period. Several of the content consultants for this book participated in this program.

Other library leadership training offerings are available through OCLC's WebJunction® website (http://www.webjunction.org). WebJunction® offers a variety of webinars and courses ranging from customer service skills to legal responsibilities and ethics. An example of a library school program is the University of California, Los Angeles (UCLA) Department of Information Studies' Senior Fellows program—a three-week program that requires participants to be nominated by their current employer (http://is.gseis.ucla.edu/programs/professional-development -programs/senior-fellows/). Another professional association program is the Texas Library Association's Tall Texans Leadership Institute. According to its website it "provides advanced leadership and management education in service to all the libraries of Texas and the communities they serve. Participants study strategic planning, risk-taking, conflict negotiation, teambuilding, coaching, ethics, advocacy, personal career planning, and more. This transformational program helps attendees learn and embrace their potential to take new initiative for their institutions, their profession, and their stakeholders" (http://www.txla.org /texas-accelerated-library-leaders).

There are also a variety of general leadership programs you can enroll in, both university-based and commercial programs. Some are very expensive while others are rather reasonably priced. One example of a university-based program is the University of Maryland University College's Leadership Development Program® sponsored by its National Leadership Institute. This five-day on-campus program costs between $7,200 and $8,200, depending upon whether a participant stays on campus or commutes (http://www.umuc.edu/nli/ldp.cfm). Examples of commercial leadership programs are the services offered by SkillPath (http://www.skillpath.com/index.cfm/training/category/cat/Management-Supervisory). Skill-Path offers both in-person and online training on a variety of topics and includes specialized seminars for women leaders.

PITFALLS FOR LEADER-MANAGERS

Everyone makes mistakes both in their work life and personal life, even the most knowledgeable and able leaders. Good leaders learn from their mistakes and acknowledge when they were wrong. There are some individuals, regardless of their leadership roles or aspirations, who have difficulty believing they could be wrong or make a mistake, much less admitting it. Leaders who refuse to accept responsibility, and/or acknowledge they were wrong, are not true leaders. As a friend noted, "You don't have to always be right to be a good manager and leader." However, knowing about the pitfalls as you embark on a management career may help you steer clear of them (or be prepared with a response should you find yourself in the midst of one).

What are some of these pitfalls? It is obvious that there are far too many possibilities to list all of them. The following are some of the more common situations you may want to avoid:

- Forgetting there is a difference between management and leadership.
- Thinking that leaders must always be right; doing so reduces risk taking and risk taking is part of being an effective leader.
- Failing to delegate and properly balancing the amount of delegation you use with the amount of work you take on yourself.
- Thinking gender doesn't matter, especially when assuming a leadership position when the previous incumbent was of a different gender.
- Forgetting to engage in self-assessment from time to time, especially in terms of your leadership style.
- Failing to remember that environmental scanning must be a constant activity rather than a periodic one.
- Thinking that an accurate performance and a perfect performance are one and the same.
- Failing to engage in enough preplanning before acting. (The famous "shoot first and ask questions later" pitfall.)
- Forgetting that users, senior managers, and governing boards may well have different values, goals, and expectations than yours.
- Thinking the unexpected cannot happen to you.
- Failing to address the conflicts that will arise as quickly as possible.
- Failing to take steps to balance your work and personal life—burnout is real.
- Failing to keep your perspective. For the most part, the work we do in libraries is not "life or death." There is generally time to reflect on a situation before acting and

the decisions we make generally are not of the same impact as curing cancer, or fighting a fire—so it is okay to occasionally make mistakes in making decisions.

- Failing to recognize you are not personally holding together the organization and thinking you cannot possibly "disengage" for any amount of time even if health or family commitments require it.

- Failing to remember that communication is primary. *Everyone* on staff, not just the administrative team, needs to know what is happening, what is going to occur, and what will affect them, the library, and/or the public. Not providing information to the front-line staff is a fatal error.

- Failing to keep your boss informed at all times. Just a "heads up" message may suffice. No one likes to be blind-sided on an issue.

- Underestimating the opposition on any matter. You have to always think ahead or strategize for "if I/we do this, then X, Y, Z might happen."

All of us—authors, advisory board, and content consultants—have stumbled into one or more of the pitfalls during our careers. By learning from our experiences we survived and became better leaders. You can do the same.

LEADERSHIP CONSTRAINTS

Earlier in this chapter we suggested that organizational sector has an impact on the leadership practiced in the organization. There have been times when, while we have been attending a leadership workshop or listening to a leadership presentation, our sense was that the presenter(s) believed effective leadership can surmount any challenge. Although that probably would not have been the case if the presenter had been asked directly if that is what he or she meant, nevertheless, there sometimes is the sense that effective leadership is the panacea for all organizational problems. While our take on leadership is that it never hurts and more often than not, it helps, there are sector constraints on just what leadership can do for an organization.

One major constraint for public sector organizations is the multiplicity of stakeholders, far beyond what for-profit leaders must take into account. Many of the stakeholder groups have very different points of view about almost everything the organization does. Beyond such broad differences between stakeholder groups there are also differing points of view within the groups regarding how strongly, when, and in what manner they should push their values. For most libraries there are at least eight identifiable stakeholder categories: library staff (sometimes with several subcategories such as paid and volunteer staff and collective bargaining and non-collective bargaining staff); an advisory/governing board; users/clients (with a variety of subgroups); donors; supporters/volunteers; funding agency; regulators and accreditation bodies; and last but not least, society at large (taxpayers as a special subgroup). Certainly, that list varies among the types of libraries, but whether it is a school, academic, special, or public library there are a number of stakeholders. Effective leaders find themselves challenged by and to some degree constrained in what they do when interacting with the various stakeholders. Essentially compromise is a critical component of what outcomes a leader, in such a diverse stakeholder situation, can achieve.

Another major constraint is the ever-changing environment. Yes, those changes can and do affect for-profit organizations; however, they are able to respond more quickly as for-profit organizations need few, if any, approvals in order to implement their response(s). One common constraint for both for-profit and public organizations is the presence of a union or collective bargaining group. Again, while certainly constraining, the for-profit's greater freedom to act makes this challenge substantially less. Work rules in existing contracts can be very challenging when the changing environment calls for adjusting who does what, when.

Although external environmental changes are not always predictable beyond knowing they will occur, such changes do constrain all leaders. However, as we will cover in some detail in chapter 7, "scanning" the environment can provide some early warning for many changes as well as time to make adjustments. There are occasions when the change(s) may call for revising the organization's mission or vision. Again, leaders of for-profit organizations have the advantage of great flexibility compared with their counterparts in the other sectors. That is, almost all libraries are part of a larger organization—city, school district, academic institution, or nonprofit organization (for example, the Huntingdon Library is part of the Huntingdon Group). Being part of a larger group often entails compromise between the smaller organization's mission and goals and those of the larger body. Time is always a constraint for any manager or leader but for those in the public sector it can be a major issue. Gaining consensus, compromise, and consent all take more time in the public sector and, on occasion, too much time.

What competitors do also affects all leaders; however, leaders in the public sector face one class of competitor that those in other sectors do not—other public agencies within their parent group. What you might like to do for your public library may be constrained by what the parks and recreation department plans to do. Both agencies are competing for tax monies. (We explore the budgeting process and politics in chapters 9 and 12.) The very best leader is likely to lead nowhere in the absence of financial resources.

For libraries, one relatively new competitor is commercial information services. What those firms do or not do can limit what you can do in your library. Providing a "public good," "public service," or "public value" are not phrases that roll off the tongues of e-competitors. Depending on the local politics, there can be challenges for your library and leadership in the area of funding and perhaps privatization.

For libraries, the variety of staffing categories, as well as the organizational commitment of staff (often less than that of for-profit staff), can also constrain leadership behavior. Full-time, part-time, professional, support, and volunteer staff, as well as, for many libraries, student assistants, often present different challenges. Leadership abilities depend in large part on being able to adapt to a given situation. Considering staffing, for example, you have to face the fact that volunteers may be very important in your operations, while at the same time many volunteers have less commitment to the organization, and going too far to accommodate their needs can generate serious morale problems among the paid staff.

Leadership is absolutely essential for public sector organizations to succeed, regardless of constraints faced by the leaders. You can develop the necessary leadership skills with time and practice. Being a good leader does take time; being a great leader is a career-long learning effort. Making the occasional mistake is part of the learning process.

COMMON MANAGERIAL CHALLENGES

There are common challenges that face every manager that are personal in nature. Personnel issues, and how well you handle stress and differing opinions, especially those views that go against your own, will arise with some frequency in a library or information service environment. Perhaps one of the more difficult challenges you will face is your ability to handle the varying expectations of your major stakeholders—senior management, those whom you supervise, library users, and other outside groups. To some degree these are, at times, almost irreconcilable expectations, with all the groups holding incongruent views about a matter, and you are in the middle. Before accepting a management position, you probably thought, at least briefly, about having to deal with downward and upward expectations. You may not have thought about the sideward pressures that can arise at times from people outside the library, most often from users but also from vendors or consortium partners.

An example of three-way pressure happens when trying to identify something that must be cut due to a reduced budget situation—either service hours or a program for a special population (homebound seniors for example). Senior management, staff, and users are likely to have different ideas about what should happen, creating a highly stressful environment for you as manager.

Something to keep in mind is that any manager is not alone in such squeezes. Senior managers, as well as governing boards, experience the same challenge. Almost all libraries are part of a larger organization and the senior manager reports to a supervisor in that larger body. In addition to having a supervisor, most directors have a governing or advisory board that has some greater or lesser power to influence decisions. Directors also must consider and respond to outside stakeholders' interests, wants, or requirements. In a very real sense, the higher up you move in managerial responsibility, the more often you will experience the three pressures that do not match one another. Chapter 5 addresses governing board relationships; these can be "testy" on occasion.

Your always-present challenge is handling the pressure you may have anticipated, that between senior management and your staff's expectations. Your managerial role as communicator, translator, spokesperson, negotiator, and change agent are important to handling the expectations of both groups. It is fairly common for senior management and operational staff to have differences in perspectives, differences that are sometimes minor and sometimes major in character. Balancing different perspectives, finding a middle ground, helping the library move forward, and being viewed by both groups as effective and supportive are significant and an ongoing challenges.

Meeting these challenges requires strong people skills and diplomatic abilities. Diplomacy is not a course offered in most schools. For that matter, it is rarely a workshop or seminar topic. Yes, you can find opportunities to learn customer relations skills or how to handle customer complaints, but diplomacy itself goes beyond customer issues. It involves a great deal of negotiation and trying to reach a resolution that is acceptable to both parties. (See chapter 19 for an in-depth discussion of negotiation and diplomacy.) Like listening, diplomacy requires practice, practice, and more practice as well as some less successful efforts before you get comfortable with the role. A rather common situation where tact and diplomacy skills are necessary is when a user appeals a staff member's decision, such as a fine, and you need to find a way to satisfy the library's needs, somehow make the staff member not look "bad," and leave the user feeling positive about the library.

Managing and Implementing Change

We all know change is inevitable, no matter how much we might wish it wasn't. There is an old saying, "the only people who really like change are babies." As a manager you will have people both above and below you who are resistant to change. Nonprofits, as well as public organizations, ought to be nimble. Being nimble, of course, implies being able to change quickly. Unfortunately, nimble is not a word often associated with libraries and information services or, for that matter, most public and nonprofit organizations. Change in such organizations normally requires going through consulting and approval procedures, which slow the change process. (You will find more in-depth discussion of change management in chapter 7.)

Change is an area where three-way squeezes often occur. When the need for change does arise, the hardest group to assess and work with is the outside stakeholders. You will have some experience in assessing work colleagues in terms of their reactions to a proposed change. Outside stakeholders are harder to assess, in part because of a lack of shared experiences with change. Another factor is, as a group, they may not be in agreement on a position regarding a change. Holding open forums can help you obtain input, but it is rather depressing when, after meeting with a group and thinking there is some agreement, letters to the editor begin appearing in the newspaper suggesting there was or is no consensus. At least in the print world you have a chance of assessing the views. In the digital world of texting, blogging, tweeting, and so on, it is much harder to assess the real views, both because of the volume of information and because people don't express necessarily express real views online. In the print world you can read what people are thinking, with social media you may not have the time to locate where things are being discussed, much less the content.

Training and Developing Staff

Training and developing staff is complex as it touches all aspects of a library's operations. You must ensure that existing staff have the requisite skills to carry out the duties assigned, which involves assessing performance on a daily basis and providing assistance when the need arises. One indicator of a well-run unit is very low turnover of staff. However, some turnover is inevitable, so you will have to work with new staff members in learning your unit's processes. Another aspect of your role is to mentor individuals in your unit to help them develop and grow so they too may move on to greater responsibilities, if they so wish. This aspect is a challenge as you are not likely to want to lose a high performer, but you also know it is beneficial for the individual and very often for the library as a whole. (This topic is discussed in more detail in chapter 17.)

A very sound summary of the basis of all managerial communication is Margaret Macmillan's comment, "To make good connections a library manager needs to identify with others by being willing to take an interest in the other person, finding common ground, recognizing the value the other has to offer and relating to him or her in a way that builds trust and rapport" (2011, 5).

Being an Attorney of Sorts

All staff members ought to have some understanding of basic legal issues that relate to library operations, for example, confidentiality of user records. As a manager, especially in the public service area, you need to become something of an attorney, at least in the sense of having some knowledge of laws that affect library activities. This knowledge is important in part because of your responsibility to orientate and train new staff members but also because you need to be able to anticipate and identify problems that may become legal issues before they become an issue. Public and nonprofits are subject to a wide range of regulations and laws, such as those we mentioned in chapter 1 with regard to the Internal Revenue Service (IRS). (This topic is explored in some detail in chapter 14.)

SOMETHING TO PONDER

Many states have published compilations of library laws, and manager-leaders should be aware of these laws. Two such examples may be found at:

- New Jersey State Library, http://ldb.njstatelib.org/library_law; and
- Web Junction, http://www.webjunction.org/documents/pennsylvania/Pennsylvania_Library_Law_Manual.html

---

Doing More with Less

Doing more with less has been a challenge for nonprofit and public organization managers for some time, and it does not appear to be decreasing. Libraries and other information services face having a static staffing situation while handling ever-increasing user demands. Although not many libraries have had to let staff go, most have had to come to terms with hiring freezes and loss of full-time equivalents (FTEs) when a staff member resigns. Whatever the cause for staff size reductions, libraries have striven to maintain high quality service with their remaining resources. Doing this generates stress for everyone. Again, such environments call upon your best managerial and leadership skills. It often means managers work longer hours or take on additional duties. Maintaining quality service in such circumstances requires creative and innovative thinking. (We look at quality and assessment in chapter 8 and managing resources in chapters 10 and 11.)

Moving Ahead in Management

When you move into a management position you need to adjust your thinking about work. Many of the daily activities you've been doing will have to fade, and new activities will take their place. Essentially, moving into management calls for dropping some activities, or sharply reducing them, and acquiring new skills and activities. The higher you go the less you will exercise the technical skills that you used when you assumed your first library job.

As an operational or front-line staff member, most of your time (85–90%) went into technical or professional practice activities. In today's tight economic circumstances, it is likely you will still need to perform some of those activities (generally much less than 50% of your time), especially if you manage-lead your old unit.

Although your technical performance responsibilities will decline, you must continue to make a significant effort to keep up to date with trends, developments, and any standards associated with professional practice, especially those related to your unit. You are the person the staff will look to for guidance. You will need to study the changes, work with the current head of cataloging to decide what changes your library ought to implement, and assist in planning and implementing the changes. You also will need to develop a vision for your unit/library. Chapter 6 covers the importance and challenges of creating a vision.

One of the more difficult areas of change when taking over a unit where you were once a staff member is your friendships. Those associations must change. It may be tempting to think that outside the workplace such friendships may continue unchanged. That may be possible if, and it is a big *if*, you and your work friend(s) absolutely do not discuss work. That is much harder to do than you may think, especially when the friendship is many years old—perhaps going back to school days. One of your new responsibilities is to say "no" when necessary. Saying no to a friend is difficult in any case; when it comes to the workplace it can be necessary on occasion.

You may think or hope other staff will not notice such friend(s). Be assured, they will. In the case of being the head of your old unit, other staff will know of your existing friendship(s) and may be concerned about what impact those friendships may have on them. Concerns over someone being "teacher's pet" and similar staff concerns will quickly destroy trust—the keystone to effective operations. (Note: The issue of staff favorites is a concern regardless of the type of unit for which you are responsible.) Friendships are possible with former colleagues or new ones; however, discretion is absolutely necessary.

You will have fewer worries about friendships if you move to a different department in the same library. However, even in this situation there can be dangerous friendship "landmines." There is a temptation for friends to inquire if you could influence a decision affecting their department. You may even agree there is need to modify the decision. The best recommendation is, don't do it. You should be cautious about giving too much support, unless you are certain you understand *all* the facts. "But so-and-so said" can come out under the pressure of the moment and lead to difficulties for many parties.

Does moving up mean you can have no work friends? No, it does not, but it does mean those friendships should be more controlled than in the past. A good first step when moving up in the same library is to have a serious discussion with your close work friends, if possible even before you get the promotion, about the issues. Note that the higher you go in administration, the more this issue comes into play. Remember the saying, "it is lonely at the top." However, keep in mind that you may find yourself forging new friendships with peers at your new administrative levels, so do not think that a position in management will force you into a hermit-like existence at work.

Time Management

Great managerial leaders are also outstanding time managers. Prior to becoming a manager you had comparatively great freedom in what you did and when. Yes, you may have had scheduled times at a service point, class sessions to teach, project deadlines, and meetings to attend; however, you could largely decide when to do what. The people you supervise rightly expect you to be available to assist in resolving problems, sorting out issues, and so on. You cannot be certain when such demands may arise. There will also be demands on your time from senior management as well as from a variety of other people. There will inevitably be reports to write, requests to provide input on various library issues to respond to, budget requests and justifications to develop, and performance appraisals to conduct. This list could go on at some length. To effectively meet the constant demands on your time, you must develop your own time management abilities.

In terms of managing and planning your time, a few events are reasonably predictable, such as budget preparation and performance reviews. However even these deadlines may vary by a few weeks or even a month or two from year to year. Such variations almost always arise from changes in the needs of the parent organization over which library managers have little input or control. Danita Johnson-Hughes correctly pointed out that "meeting your employer's expectations becomes increasingly important. Managing your time effectively, however, is often hampered by interruptions at work. . . . A high rate of interruptions can be a serious issue in the workplace and can be a barrier to success" (2011, 13). We agree, but would add to her opening sentence "and your staff's." Both groups have expectations regarding your time and availability. Johnson-Hughes goes on to discuss six strategies for managing your time, which are worth reviewing. The better you manage your time, the fewer "extra" hours you will have to work in or out of the office to meet those expectations.

Conceptual Skills

Conceptual skills include thinking about the future and what that future might mean for your unit (covered in chapter 6). Planning in its various forms is another skill (covered in chapter 7). Looking toward the future and planning for changes that will help your unit achieve success down the road is essential. Being a good steward of the money and physical facilities for which you are responsible are other key skills you will need, and these are addressed throughout this text.

KEYS TO A SUCCESSFUL CAREER

Table 2.2 lists several "keys" researchers have found to be conducive to having a successful managerial career. While this list is not intended to be exhaustive, it may be useful for you as you assess your own strengths and areas for development as a manager-leader.

If the list appears formidable, that's because it is. However, mastering all or most of these skills should help you be successful at any level of managerial responsibility, not just as an upper-level manager. We hope the following chapters will help you down the path to a very successful managerial leadership career.

CHECK THIS OUT

An article of interest to public library managers is Ed Everett's "Today's Local Government Management Model" (*Public Management* 97, no. 2 [2015]: 22–25).

Table 2.2.
Keys to a Successful Managerial-Leadership Career

People Skills	Conceptual Skills
Effectively coaching and training	Creating a vision
Supporting teamwork	Assessing issues
Communicating openly and honestly	Making rational decisions
Collaborating with others	Accepting reasonable risks
Managing conflict	Thinking strategically
Driving cultural competency	Managing funds effectively
Addressing user needs	Employing a big-picture perspective
Creating trust	Writing thoughtfully
Motivating others	Listening with an open mind
Demonstrating flexibility	Developing realistic plans
Championing change	Learning throughout life
Assessing performance fairly	Seeking to improve processes
Recognizing/supporting talents in others	Showing initiative and innovation

REFERENCES

Bennis, Warren G. 2003. *On Becoming a Leader*. Revised and expanded edition. New York: Basic Books.

Burns, James M. 1978. *Leadership*. New York: Harper & Row.

Carson, Emmett D. 2011. "On Leadership in the Nonprofit Sector." In *Nonprofit Management 101*. Edited by Darian Rodriguez Heyman. San Francisco, CA: Jossey-Bass.

The Economist Staff. 2013. "Davos Man and His Defects." *The Economist*, January 26. http://www.economist.com/news/business/21570684-global-leadership-industry-needs-re-engineering-davos-man-and-his-defects.

Flanagan, Tim A., and John S. Lybarger. 2014. *Leading Forward: Successful Public Leadership Amidst Complexity, Chaos, and Change.* San Francisco, CA: Jossey-Bass.

Greenleaf, Robert K. 1977. *Servant Leadership: A Journey into the Nature of Legitimate Power and Greatness*. New York: Paulist Press.

Johnson-Hughes, Danita. 2011. "Managing Interruptions and Your Time." *Supervision* 72, no. 7: 13–14.

Kellerman, Barbara. 2004. *Bad Leadership: What It Is, How It Happens, Why It Matters.* Boston: Harvard Business School Press.

Lao Tzu. n.d. "Lao Tzu Quotes—Page 3." *Brainy Quote.* http://www.brainyquote.com/quotes/authors/l/lao_tzu_3.html.

Lewin, Kurt, Ronald Lippitt, and Ralph K. White. 1939. "Patterns of Aggressive Behavior in Experimentally Created Social Climates." *Journal of Social Psychology* 10, no. 2: 271–299.

Macmillan, Margaret. 2011. "A 'Coach Approach' to Staff Engagement." *Partnership: The Canadian Journal of Library and Information Practice and Research* 6, no. 2: 1–9.

Mason, Florence M., and Louella V. Wetherbee. 2004. "Learning to Lead: An Analysis of Current Training Programs for Library Leadership." *Library Trends* 53, no. 1: 187–217.

Mintzberg, Henry. 1998. "Covert Leadership: Notes on Managing Professionals." *Harvard Business Review* 76, no. 6: 140–147.

Pfeffer, Jeffrey. 1992. *Managing with Power: Politics and Influence in Organizations.* Cambridge, MA: Harvard Business School Press.

Pfeffer, Jeffrey. 2010. *Power: Why Some People Have It—And Others Don't.* New York: Harper-Collins.

Chapter 3

COMMUNICATION AND PERSUASION

We have observed three major contributing factors to the communication barrier: language, culture and personality.

Santoso Sugianto and Dan Johns, 2011

Obviously, the main issue in communications is getting it right, so often the discussion often turns rapidly to what goes wrong.

Hal Rainey, 2014

Listening is . . . the way to make sure that the library is responsive to community needs' and not working from personal, professional or generalized hunches about those needs.

Linda W. Braun, 2015

Hal Rainey's comment about the "main issue in communications is getting it right" (2014, 392) is, in our opinion, spot on. We all know communicating effectively makes our lives easier, regardless of context. Poorly worded or poorly planned statements, and, on occasion, even well-formulated efforts, can create interpersonal problems in both personal life and work life. One of the first thoughts you had after reading the above probably was about speaking and oral presentations. Certainly verbal communication is the most common communication channel, but it is far from the only one. Knowing which of many communication channels to use and when is a hallmark of a great managerial leader.

The fact that there are a number of channels is a significant factor in why there is so much miscommunication. What we mean by miscommunication is that the person on the receiving end of a communication effort will misinterpret and misunderstand the message. Just about any workplace problem can be blamed to some extent on a communication failure (lack of communication, inaccurate statements, poor timing, bad word choice—the list could go on and on).

If asked to quickly name communication channels, the first two on almost everyone's list would be spoken and written. How many other channels would be on the list would vary by how well the person making the list communicates. The better a communicator the person is, the longer the list will be. They would certainly include nonverbal and listening. (We all employ both of these every day but rarely think of them as communication channels; nevertheless, both send messages to others.) Two other channels the great communicators would identify are graphic and feedback. Other issues in communication lie in the mode of communicating the message, such as in person/direct, remote/indirect, paper, electronic, and the communication setting/atmosphere; again, the list could go on and on. We believe it is obvious that effective communication takes time and effort and is truly a life-long learning process, especially if you want to be highly effective. The good news is that taking on this challenge and pushing yourself to continually develop your skills as a communicator will pay off in rich dividends, both professionally and personally.

You probably know other factors that communication specialists often label as "noise" that come into play in effective communication. Our opening quotation from Sugianto and Johns identifies three very big noise factors: language, culture, and personality. Even when people share the same native language there are challenges with interpretations. The shorter the word, generally, the more dictionary meanings you find (look up words such as "fair," "good," and "poor" in a comprehensive dictionary if you doubt the statement). Each person has her or his usual definition of such words, and then when you combine that with the fact that we also tend to associate certain words with past experiences, you can understand why miscommunication is so common.

Leaders in the nonprofit and public sectors face more communication challenges than do their for-profit counterparts. Nonprofit and public sector constituencies are much more varied in terms of language, education, cultural backgrounds, interests, and personality, to name just a few aspects, which contributes to the fact that a single communication effort is likely to miss some of the people it was intended to reach.

ESSENTIAL FOR PERSONAL AND ORGANIZATIONAL SUCCESS

As we noted in chapter 2, leadership is people-focused and, needless to say, effective leaders must be effective communicators. Part of being an effective leader is creating a sense of connection between yourself and others—only then are you likely to persuade them about best options for the organization.

Effective leaders build and maintain connections in part through oral and written presentations. What do we mean by connections and connecting? Connecting is being able, as a leader-manager, to identify with and relate to other people in a manner that makes them listen to you and be willing to follow you. Lacking such connections, you are not likely to be more than a manager. In both your personal and work life, being able to connect with others makes life easier. There are two main categories of people that you will need to connect with on a regular basis—individuals and groups. There are some subtle, but important, differences between groups (for example, your unit, library staff in general, and users) and audiences of individuals (such as a presentation to the Friends of Library membership meeting, or being a participant in panel discussion to a professional group or a keynote speaker).

Oral interactions are often the starting point for building connections with others. However, writing is also a means of creating a connection between yourself and your reader. There was probably a time or two in your life where you said something along the lines of, "I really felt a connection with the author." Think about what made you feel there was a connection. Among your reasons may have been that the person's message was on "you" rather than "I." Another factor may have been that the message was positive, upbeat, enthusiastic, inspiring, and made you feel good. The message might have given a sense of greater worth or value to what you do. Still another possibility is the message was such that you thought, "I've been there, felt that, acted that way; this person has it right"—essentially, that the person was like you. We can learn from such examples and we can improve our skills in making connections and thereby make the work environment more pleasant and effective.

Power of Persuasion

Connecting and persuading are linked. You are less likely to persuade when there is no connection. Through strong connections persuasion becomes easier. Have you ever put together a "message" where your logic was perfect, you marshaled indisputable facts, and you identified correctly all the pluses and minuses of the proposal, yet failed to persuade the readers or listeners? Many of us have had that dispiriting experience at least once in our working lives, after which we faced a big *why*? One very real reason is because we focused too much on content (what) and not enough on the delivery (how), and as a result failed to create a connection and therefore failed to persuade.

Robert Cialdini (2011) suggested that, although some people are naturally persuasive, a person can learn to be a more effective a persuader through developing the appropriate skills. The skills he identifies also enhance our connecting skills. Cialdini identified five "principles" that underlie effective persuasive ability:

1. Liking (individuals tend to like those who like them)
2. Reciprocity (getting and receiving are interlinked—give praise and receive continued or even better performance)
3. Social proof (individuals tend to follow people they perceive as like themselves—find commonalities with others)
4. Consistency (individuals accept and follow messages from a person they believe is consistent)
5. Authority (individuals are more likely to follow directions from a person they believe or know has expertise in the activity)

ORAL AND WRITTEN COMMUNICATION

As noted above, nonprofit and public sector leaders must communicate with a wide variety of constituencies. Effective leaders understand the need to tailor their communication efforts to the needs of the target audience. One way to think about the communication is as a cycle in which there are six Ps—planning, preparing, presenting, perceiving, participating, and thereby ultimately persuading. Great communicators think through (*plan*) what it is they wish to communicate, then *prepare* it in terms that are most likely to be understood by the target recipients, and deliver/*present* it in an appropriate manner. The cycle then continues with *perceiving* how the message was understood by, in the case of face-to-face communication, the nonverbal behavior and the tenor of questions or comments from the recipients. The *participation* aspect is in listening to what recipients are saying and providing feedback. This may lead back to another round of planning, preparing, and so on.

How you plan and prepare to communicate with staff is likely to be slightly different than for your governing board. For example, with your staff you can employ professional jargon, when appropriate, and be almost certain staff members will understand. Using such jargon with other groups, such as your governing board, is likely to cause some miscommunication. The timing of the delivery of a message is part of your preparation—not too soon and not too late.

Communication Groups

There are a number of broad categories of people that nonprofit and public sector managers must communicate with effectively, beginning with library staff and ending with the general public. In between are such groups as other managers, service users, governing/advisory boards, vendors, funding authorities, granting bodies, supporters and donors, regulators, tax payers (as a distinct group within the general public), librarians from other libraries such as consortia partners, and professional associations. Within each major group there are subgroups, each of which is likely to have some special communication considerations.

Examples of such subgroups within library staff are new and existing employees, full- and part-time staff, volunteers, and, in the case of where there is a collective bargaining agreement, those covered by the agreement and those who are not. Even the professional category may contain sub groups such as local professionals with whom you interact rather frequently and may encounter socially on a more or less regular basis. You are likely to be more cautious in what you share as well as how you do so with fellow professionals at the national level. Clearly when it comes to the general public there are numerous subgroups. Tailoring a single message that is effective for all the groups and their subcomponents is almost impossible; multiple messages about the same topic call for the careful implementation of the six Ps.

While the basics of good communication are constant, there are variations for each subgroup. One broad variation is that of technical jargon (terms such as *thesaurus*, *MARC*, *CALM*, *GroupWare*, for example), which has a very good chance of being misunderstood or not understood by people not working in a library. Even within a library, the use of unit-specific short phrases (*MARC field 805* and *encumber*, for example) can be a hindrance to good communication. Use jargon only when you are certain the receiver knows the meaning.

In today's e-world, many of our exchanges with others are electronic, supplemented by a paper communiqué (the latter is very useful in maintaining a solid paper trail for significant matters in terms of managerial activities). An increasing segment of our interactions with others even within the library is "in passing" (in a hallway or briefly before or after a meeting). Such encounters are not bad in themselves; however, when they become more and more the communication norm, problems may arise. Bruce Tulgan, in writing about such situations, said "I call this phenomenon 'management on-the-fly' or 'management by special occasion.' There is no systematic logic to the timing of management conversations, and, in fact, they are random, incomplete, and often too late to avoid a problem or solve one before it grows too large" (2010, 70). Tulgan strongly recommends, as do we, that you hold regularly scheduled face-to-face meetings. (We will address meetings in chapter 20.)

Regular meetings will not solve all your communication problems, but they will help assure more consistency in the process. If nothing else, such meetings let you know that all is going well. Thinking about an upcoming meeting may also trigger thoughts about some small issue that wouldn't come up in a passing conversation. Such "heads up" can assist in avoiding a big problem later. Ron Hess wrote, "Do you really want to make a value-added difference in your organization? If you do, then make improving face-to-face communication a priority" (2008, 48). Hess was commenting on both the randomness of passing conversations and the ever-growing impersonal communications of the e-world. Issues such as nonverbal behavior and tone can and do impact the character of the message and they don't really exist in the electronic communiqués (using emoticons or a bold or italic font, etc., may or may not help convey the true emotional aspect of the message). We explore the impact of both of these factors on communication later in this chapter. Some elements to keep in mind for good communication with others are:

- Take the lead for the process;
- Share good and bad news because people do not like being blindsided, especially senior managers; and
- Remember it is generally best to disagree with someone privately rather than publicly.

We want to emphasize that timely, accurate feedback in both directions is perhaps the most critical aspect of effective communication with people.

CHECK THIS OUT

Although "old" in terms of publication date, the content of this 1991 article by Janet Barnard remains valid today: "The Information Environment of New Managers" (*Journal of Business Communication* 28, 4: 312–324).

AUTHOR EXPERIENCE

As an example of communicating with professional colleagues: Evans once hired an administrative assistant with more than 12 years of experience in the same type of job for a large medical library—clearly someone with substantial experience with library operations—however she was not a librarian. During the performance assessment session (six months into the job), when asked what Evans could do to make her job easier, she responded, "It's taken me a while to get use to your shorthand communication style. I think I'm catching on, but try to fill me in more. It will save us time in future, but for now give me more to work with." Five years later, she still occasionally reminded me to "expand on that." The key point is that timely, accurate feedback from both parties is critical for good communication.

Communicating with Staff

Remember that there are several major subgroups for staff communication, including new and existing staff in your unit, staff in other units, and volunteers. It is not uncommon for you to communicate with staff in other units (in team settings, with cross-trained staff, and with those sharing holiday, weekend, and evening hours, for example). It is a dual communication process—staff often get the message from their supervisor who got it from you. The added layer can, and often does, create a situation where miscommunication may occur. While your message may be fully understood by the other manager, you have little, if any, control over how your message is communicated to the receiving staff members. Direct communication reduces the risks of filtering, but organizational culture and communication style may make direct communication inappropriate.

Keep in mind the major purposes of your staff communication. Conroy and Jones (1986) identified nine major purposes, listed below, along with two additional purposes we have included:

- To inform
- To motivate
- To coach or discipline
- To mentor
- To build teams
- To create a strong service orientation
- To gather information
- To instruct or train
- To counsel
- To develop staff
- To build an organizational culture

One communication challenge with staff that may arise relates to the use of the "official channel." By its very nature, management is to some degree manipulative—accomplishing things through people. As a result, there are times when the staff views official channel messages as manipulative. Such occasions arise when there is little or no trust of management. Effective managerial leadership will build and maintain high trust levels. With that potential hostility in mind, especially when you first take over managing a unit, you should strive to:

- Establish authenticity;
- Reduce the time between work activities and their evaluation; and
- Involve the staff in decision making whenever possible.

These steps will assist in achieving better communication through feedback and shared experiences.

You should take the lead in generating feedback—ask for it rather than waiting for it to materialize. How you make that request, as well as overall manager-staff relations, will determine the accuracy of the feedback. For feedback to be useful, you must make it clear that questions, clarifications, and so on, are welcome and that the goal is to ensure that everyone is "on the same page." With a multicultural staff, you should be aware of possible cultural values that may prevent some individuals from expressing confusion or contradicting the "boss." Listen to staff as much as you talk to them. An old saying that is good to keep in mind is "Feelings are facts; ignore them at your peril." This is particularly true when it comes to your staff.

COMMUNICATING OUTSIDE YOUR UNIT

There are a host of groups outside the library with whom you must communicate; here we will touch on some of the most common categories. Each group will call for an adjustment in how you plan, prepare, and present your messages. Who are some of the major outside groups?

- Vendors
- Maintenance staff
- Service users
- Funding agencies
- Taxpayers
- Politicians
- Architects and consultants
- Governing and/or advisory boards
- Professional colleagues
- Granting agencies
- Parent organization staff
- Donor groups
- Regulators (such as accrediting)
- Society at large

The above is only a modest listing as most of the groups contain two or more subcategories. For example, you might initially think a governing body is a unified group. After your first meeting with the group you'll see there are differences within the group. The worst case is when there are opposing "camps." In such cases, it will require your very best powers of persuasion to achieve consensus and consent. Once again, you can understand why organizational sectors do matter. Your for-profit counterparts have fewer communication groups to consider.

Vendors and Suppliers

Working with library vendors, for example, your Integrated Library System (ILS) firm or database company, is a little like working with staff. This is because any vendor who has been in the business for any length of time has learned library jargon related to their area of business; in many cases they have contributed to that jargon. Many have service representatives who have a Master of Library and Information Science (MLIS) degree and practical work experience in libraries. Also, it is to the benefit of the vendors to make sure their representatives are cognizant of library-related terms and their meanings.

One of the balancing acts when talking with vendors is knowing how much to share (or not to) while trying to maintain honest and open communication. In the authors' experience, there is the occasional vendor representative who thrives on "picking up the latest gossip" about library X and sharing that with other customers. Vendor "reps" can be a useful source of relatively current information about how other libraries are addressing a problem or an issue, or what new product is or isn't working. Maintaining the proper balance between under- and over-communicating information about the library can be a challenge. How relevant is information about funding levels, staffing changes, and so on? Again, time with the various reps and chatting with colleagues will help sort out what to share.

Governing and Advisory Boards

As noted above, overseeing bodies are rarely homogenous in their views about all issues, at least initially, unless you have carefully prepared them prior to the actual presentation. (We will explore governing/advisory board relations in chapter 5.) Certainly most differences are minor and there is quick consensus after a brief discussion. As your experience with the group grows and topics are debated, you will be able to anticipate what topics will generate greater or lesser dissent, as well as which members will be the most difficult to persuade. We are not suggesting that differences should be avoided; strong debate and differences of opinion are a sign of sound consultation and vetting of significant issues. Keep in mind you and your staff may be wrong about a topic—at least occasionally. Your board may well be better attuned to users and community wants and desires than you are. An important element in sound managerial leadership is consultation and consent.

When planning and preparing a board presentation it is best to avoid jargon and technical terminology, even when you think everyone will know what you mean. Leaving one or two board members basically "in the dark" about your meaning has the potential of making them feel left out and perhaps unwilling to ask for clarification. New board members are particularly prone to wanting to fit in and not appear unknowledgeable about LIS issues. One of your priorities should be to orient newcomers to your service's activities and needs.

Maintenance and Service Personnel

Few LIS organizations have service and maintenance personnel on staff. Such individuals are usually employees of the parent organization or a for-profit contractor. Many times they are members of a union that has a contract spelling out, in some detail, what they will and will not do (work rules). A seemingly simple request, at least to you, may have a surprising outcome (e.g., a formal grievance filed against you, the requested work being done and resulting in a large bill, or a demand to rework the contract).

AUTHOR EXPERIENCE

Evans once was responsible for a university library where housekeeping was outsourced by the university. The outside company's employees were diligent in performing their duties, as spelled out in the contract. One of their duties was to vacuum the carpeted floors. Not too long after Evans became the library director, he noticed that the carpeted stairs appeared not to be vacuumed, at least not on a regular basis. The meeting with the company owner to talk about the matter was pleasant and, for Evans, surprising. The owner stated the question of stairs was covered in the contract but only in terms of wet mopping, not vacuuming. Further, if the library staff wanted the stairs vacuumed, the university and the housekeeping company would have to work out a price because the work would be strenuous and not everyone would be physically able to do the work. The university did finally decide to cover the "additional work," as spelled out in the contract ($250 a month plus the direct labor cost). "Vacuuming" become a focal point in the next round of contract negotiations.

A new manager coming into a union environment is well advised to take the time, early on, to read the terms of the contract in order to avoid unexpected consequences. Remember the danger of indirect communication—sometimes all communication regarding work issues must go through a union representative, who usually is not the person who will do the work.

The technology support personnel, especially those who are not library staff, pose another communication challenge. All too often, when information professionals and information technology (IT) personnel get together, jargon seems to be the only language anyone can speak. Part of the issue, at least in the United States, is that many of the "techies" (generally highly focused on system integrity) don't understand that information professionals do have some grasp of technology, and many LIS professionals believe that the techies don't understand the needs of their library (such as the maximum possible open access). When both sides have doubts about the other side's understanding of the issues, many words will be said but little information will be gained by either side.

Professional Colleagues Elsewhere

Communication with other professional colleagues has several aspects—working with other local professionals, collaborating on projects with regional colleagues, and networking with former classmates and other professionals you regard as friends on a national level.

Working with local professionals is similar to communicating in your workplace, but with less shared time or experience. This results in a more formal communication style on everyone's part (especially when individuals know little about each other), more jargon use, and modest feedback, at least on a personal level, until members of the group become comfortable with one another.

Managers, especially newcomers, should develop a support network of professional colleagues, ideally consisting of a number of peers in terms of age, experience, and responsibility, and one or two older individuals who act as mentors. A peer group provides a mechanism for talking through issues outside the organizational framework and addressing concerns about the consequences of what is said. Peer networks can be effective tools for "thinking out loud" without worrying about what people think, for seeking advice when you want it, and for sharing work experiences and "horror stories" as well as personal issues.

Parent Organization Staff

Communicating with staff who are employees of the parent organization (academic, city, corporate, etc.), but not of the library (such as staff in Human Resources, the business office, and the chief administrator's office, for example) can be complicated at times. Human Resources (HR) and business offices are the units that you will most likely have occasion to interact with and thus build some understanding of the communication styles desired or expected. These are also units with which disagreements can arise, especially when it comes to preferences in how to handle a matter and there are official guidelines addressing the "how." Both "sides" will view it from a perspective of "Which way will it cause us less work?" Diplomatic communication is what you need, even when you are not feeling all that charitable. Fighting for a principle may feel good, but it is not too likely to gain support from the other unit(s). Keep in mind these are some of your competitors for limited resources and they may well have better connections during budget approval cycles or have the "ear" of a key decision maker.

Communicating with senior administrators or their staff is difficult. Tact and diplomacy are the order of the day in such communications—factual and tactful. Many libraries have meeting rooms or spaces sometimes labeled "celebratory" (open spaces such as atriums) that can be utilized by senior managers (in the parent organization) that have no relationship to the LIS activities and in fact disrupt operations before, during, and after an event takes place. How to handle such requests is never easy; having a strong supporter in the senior leadership can be very helpful, but not always possible. How do you say "no" to the mayor or campus president? The answer is, very carefully.

AUTHOR EXPERIENCE

Evans had a mentor early in his career who gave him some sound advice regarding how to handle disagreements. He wishes he could say he always followed that advice, but it isn't true. What is true is those times Evans failed to follow the advice, the results were not very pleasant.

The advice was "When you are upset and want to write a nasty letter or memo, do so with all the vehemence you are feeling. When you have finished put it in your desk drawer for at least 48 hours. Then take it and read it carefully. Chances are you toss it away and prepare something more thoughtful and effective. In the meantime, you'll feel better having gotten the anger out of your system."

Evans can say that 99.9 percent of the time, when following that advice, the approach was very sound. He has passed the idea to students and advisees over the years.

AUTHOR EXPERIENCE

One of the libraries Evans managed had a fine atrium—between the original facility and a later addition. Both the university president's office and motion picture and television production companies asked to use it for functions on a regular basis. Most of the times they requested to use the atrium were during library service hours. The other regular part of the requests involved serving food—the faculty committee and the academic vice president had to review frequent requests to do away with the "No food or drink in library" policy.

In these situations, the library staff became something like the ham in a sandwich. You face unhappy users due to disruption who ask, "Why can they have food and drink and we can't?" on one side, and parent organization officials on the other side. (Note that the university received substantial use fees from movie and television production companies when a campus venue was part of the filming.)

After a time, the library avoided filming activities, with the active support of the academic vice president. However, it was never possible to completely keep campus events confined to non-service hours. Diplomacy and reality do have to come into play when working with senior parent organization leaders.

Service Users

Service users are why libraries exist and sometimes we lose sight of that fact as we try to do more and do better with fewer resources. Although we try to not let those efforts drive us to sometimes do things that benefit us rather than the users, it does happen occasionally. Are our OPACs and databases really user-friendly? Are we offering services that users truly want and need? Are our collections, regardless of format, appropriate for user needs? The list could go on, but the point is that we need clear user feedback to answer such questions.

All communication rests on a number of assumptions, several of which have special significance in service provider-user communications. Five of the most significant assumptions are:

- Communication has verbal and nonverbal components;
- Communication has content and relationship components;
- Communication is influenced by context;
- Communication is transactional; and
- Communication requires cooperation (Ford, 1989, 8–9).

Another way to think about those assumptions is the communication process is almost always multichannel; that is, while content is important so too are the relationships between those involved. The environment in which communication occurs can impact how messages are perceived; that is, it requires a give and take on the part of all parties involved to be effective. Feedback is critical in having a successful outcome.

LIS staff members send both verbal and nonverbal messages during a service transaction. When the two are congruent, users easily understand the message(s); however, when they are incongruent the customer becomes confused and tends to believe the nonverbal message(s). Staff also establish content and relationship messages that are informational and attitudinal in character during a transaction. The definition of the transaction arises from the content side of the message, while the interpersonal aspect comes from the relationship-oriented message.

The physical surroundings during a transaction (an open environment with other people present versus a one-on-one office setting, for example) can influence a service outcome. The context is influential in determining the approach to the library—courteous, manipulative, or personalized. Service interactions are highly transactional in character—both provider and customer constantly exchange both verbal and nonverbal messages while interpreting and reacting to messages received.

Research by Tory Higgins, William Rholes, and Carl Jones (1977) indicated that people are most influenced by the first and last information they receive. In our experience, libraries are very good about the way they open a transaction but give less thought to the closing. An important fact to keep in mind is that too much empathic speech can be detrimental to a person's perception of good service, primarily when the speed of the transaction is an important customer value.

Researchers (for example Richard Haase and Donald Trepper, 1972) have found that nonverbal immediacy (eye contact, body orientation, etc.) contributed more to a customer's sense of empathy during the transaction than did verbal behaviors. If there is incongruity between the two, the customer usually will perceive the empathic/courteous speech as false. For example, saying "we" rather than "you" ("Let's see if we can find what you need") can create a sense of psychological closeness. Other more immediate language forms are "here," "these," and "this" rather

---

WORTH CHECKING OUT

There are many books that address customer service and communication:

Mou Chakraborty's (ed.) *Stellar Customer Service: Training Library Staff to Exceed Expectations* (Santa Barbara, CA: Libraries Unlimited, 2016) offers practical advice and models for training your staff to excel.

Victoria J. Farkas's *Customer Relations* (Hauppauge, NY: Nova Science Publishers, 2011) covers all aspects of working with your users.

Kathy L. Middleton's *Yes! On Demand: How to Create Winning, Customized Library Service* (Santa Barbara, CA: Libraries Unlimited, 2017) specifically addresses the library environment.

An interesting article that looks at how you must adjust your library communication style for a particular user group is Adrienne Hannan's 2011 "Communication 101: We Have made Contact With Teens" (*Aplis* 24, no. 1: 32–38).

A large amount of what occurs in a service transaction is nonverbal in character. One of many videos that help you think about the visual aspects of communication is *Communicating with Customers: An Entry Level Guide* (Lake Zurich, IL: Learning Seed Company, 2005).

---

than "there," "those," and "that." One issue in creating and maintaining courteous service is the degree to which you demonstrate responsibility for the transaction. Using conditional statements distance you from the user. Part of the effective process is to share responsibility; for example, saying "Here are some options for handling the fine" is better than "How are you going to pay the fine?"

Personalized service is what most libraries wish they could achieve. Lack of sound funding and limited staff and space make personalized service a rare occurrence in libraries. Surprenant and Soloman defined personalized service as "behaviors occurring in the interaction intended to contribute to the individuation of the customer" (1987, 87). Although our professional standards recommend equitable service to all, in almost every library there are a few users who are "more equal than others." An inquiry from the office of the president, mayor, or school superintendent demands personalized service, followed by some of the "regular heavy users."

There are four communication strategies associated with personalized service: customer orientation, interaction involvement, information sharing, and social support. Without question, the service philosophy of the information professional is to provide customer orientation and to assist with his or her information needs.

Interaction involvement is the degree to which the service provider becomes fully engaged with the user, both cognitively and behaviorally, during the inquiry. Involvement requires full attention (nonverbal cues often indicate lack of attention), perceptiveness, clarification, and finally interpretation.

Social support is a basic element in the "helping professions" that may be a simple extension of empathic speech patterns, or may involve demonstrating sensitivity to customer uncertainty and/or increasing the customer's self-esteem, or providing the customer with a sense of social connection with others.

Funding Bodies

There are two significant times you communicate directly with the agency that provides the majority of your operational funds. (Note: it is very rare for an LIS today to operate on sole source funding. To provide appropriate and effective services an LIS must find supplementary sources.) One of the obvious interaction times is budget preparation and approval cycle; "time" may be a poor word choice as some cycles last for months and occasionally seem to never really stop. As we will cover in chapter 10, there are jurisdictions and funding agencies that use as many as five funding cycles in their planning process—past (two cycles), present, and future (two cycles). The most important part of communication during this process is the "justification narrative" which may be written, oral, or both. This is one of the times when planning, preparation, presentation, and persuasion power really can impact your service's operations.

The other major time for communicating with funding bodies, or business offices, is when you believe you need to shift some funds allocated for one purpose to another purpose. You probably remember from your basic management training that budgets are plans and estimates of what it will cost to carry out a set of activities over a set timeframe. Further, they rest on certain assumptions about the future; those assumptions do not always hold true due to changing circumstances. As a manager, you will face occasions when shifting funds may be desirable. How much, if any, flexibility you have in this area depends on the budget format and funding agency rules. There may be times and categories of expenditure where you are free to shift funds without prior approval. More often you will have to request permission to make such a shift and have some reasonable expectation of obtaining the approval.

In our experience, there is one area where you will not be allowed to make shifts, at least during your current operating year: salaries. Even if you have a staff vacancy for several months, the salary for that full-time equivalent (FTE) can't be touched. Almost all public sector funding bodies, as well as nonprofits, employ a concept labeled "salary savings," or something similar—that is, they expect a certain percentage of staff turnover and thus unspent salary monies. Those "savings" are factored into the planning of how much money will actually be needed for a fiscal year. There are some funding bodies that inform you at the start of the fiscal year what your salary savings target is and it is your challenge to achieve it.

Asking permission to shift other monies and gaining it is a matter of effective communication skills and your leadership/political abilities. An important component of communication is building relationships between yourself and others. Developing a strong, positive, trusting relationship with funding agencies and business offices will pay dividends when it comes to being allowed to shift funds.

Granting Agencies

In many ways, communication with granting agencies is similar to that of funding agencies. They are interested in the facts and the ability of the requester to effectively and appropriately use the monies requested. They are likely to review any history they have of your success in handling any prior grants. Factual straightforward narrative is the order of the day. (We look at securing grants in more detail in chapter 10.)

Donor Groups

Communication with support or donor groups can be tricky at times. It is tricky in the sense that hitting the right balance between being too technical and talking down to the group is not always easy. One reasonable expectation, but not absolute, is the support group is already positively inclined toward the library and its mission. Just as is true of your staff, the more shared experiences you and group have the better you can gauge how technical you can be. The vast majority of the time you can expect support, but not always. There will be occasions when the group does not view an issue the way you anticipated they would. You need to gauge how far you wish to pursue the issue; pushing a relatively minor concern too far has the potential of alienating one or more members. It can also raise doubts about your judgment and perhaps even trustworthiness. In many instances, your ability to the "read" the nonverbals of those present will alert you to losing their attention or support.

Society at Large and Taxpayers

There are two major categories of communication that you must consider in terms of this dual component group: general information communiqués and communiqués that carry monetary implications. Certainly the community at large does include a high percentage of taxpayers (although not everyone) and some of them will be among your most active supporters while others will be active detractors. You are unlikely to craft any message that will please everyone when money is involved. The challenge is to create messages that please far more individuals than they displease—not an easy task, but not impossible. (We will look at the political communication in more depth in chapter 13.)

As you would expect, use of jargon is a killer of effective communication with the general public, regardless of the fiscal issues involved in your message. All of your communication efforts with the group should be concise and to the point, use hard data, and be straightforward and friendly. This is not an occasion to demonstrate the number of six-syllable words you can string together in a sentence, nor is it the time to engage in literary flights of prose or allusions. The old television crime series line, "Just the facts ma'am," is very appropriate for all such efforts. Check and recheck your facts; you can count on the fact that those unfavorably disposed toward you will do so in hopes of "catching you out" and being untrustworthy. In public forums, maintaining control of your emotions can be challenging at times, especially when facing particularly persistent opponents to the issue being considered. Losing control will likely result in more than the loss of your emotions. Even your supporters may begin to have doubts.

Library bond campaigns are one example of when you must communicate with the general public. (We explore bond campaigns as a fiscal issue in chapter 9.) If it is generally important that you and your staff understand how to field questions about changes in the library, it is critical when it is comes to bond drives. Likely questions will relate to why, what, and when, plus the inevitable, "How much will it really cost me, the taxpayer?" Our advice in such cases is to stick to the facts. Any drive that involves asking for more tax money, even when grants and private donors provide almost all of the funding, is very likely to become political. Avoiding getting pulled into such discussions and debates will be a challenge. Having well articulated fact sheets will help to some degree. Your major challenge will be to keep from making it appear that the library is on one side or the other of a debate, especially if the issue becomes politicized. Keep coming back to the idea that libraries, with rare exceptions, are open to anyone regardless of politics, education, economic status, and so on. Failing to do so can have a serious impact on the campaign's outcome.

LISTENING—KEY TO SUCCESSFUL COMMUNICATION

We were given one mouth and two ears, perhaps to suggest that we should listen twice as much as we speak. When people discuss good communication, more often than not there is little or no attention given to the "art of listening." Like any art, listening requires practice, and few of us have truly mastered it. We can hear about four times faster than most people speak; that leaves about three-quarters of our "listening time" free for the mind to wander, and it will, unless we concentrate on listening. Think back to a recent speech or lecture you attended. Can you honestly say that you did not think about such things as where to eat afterwards, errands to run, letters to write, something you want to say to someone in the audience, or a host of other matters unrelated to what the speaker was saying? If you can, then you are one of the few who really practices the art of listening, and you have no need to join the rest of us in practicing that art.

ADVISORY BOARD EXPERIENCE

Mika had a mentor that cautioned him as he left for his first professional administrative faculty position to "keep his ears flapping, and his mouth closed." It was good advice, particularly as a new management member in an established department, where entrenched faculty are not keen on hearing, "at X we did it this way." It behooves new leaders to listen far more than talk, especially in the beginning stages of a new position. By the way, Mika passed along that sage advice to his son when he took a new job as a lobbyist for a major firm where he has been quite successful—maybe the advice helped.

Researchers have established that most of us engage in a process they label "filtering." That is, we may hear and translate a message accurately for ourselves; however, if we pass the message on, some of what we forward will be different. Think about the children's game of telephone where a group of children whisper a message one to another: the final "outcoming" message is different than the original input. There are three major types of filtering: leveling, sharpening, and assimilation. Managerial leaders really must understand the filtering process as receiving and sending messages is critical to organizational success.

Leveling, as you might guess, occurs when we drop parts of the message we received and pass on a modified version to colleagues. We often level messages by dropping elements or qualifiers that either enhance or quell fears that we may harbor. For example, during tight fiscal circumstances staff members are likely to level the message's content in order to match their expectations—either positive or negative. Sharpening is the addition of extra meaning. Just as with leveling, a person may mentally change a modifier such as "may" to "will." Thus, something that "might occur" becomes "will occur." Efforts to tamp down worries can backfire as a result of sharpening. Assimilating is the process where a person retains the full meaning of the original while adding additional meaning when passing it forward. This filter essentially creates a new message in terms of meaning.

We all engage in filtering activities. How often have you read something and your initial thought is very positive or negative, and only later do you realize that reaction was overdone? Some people are unaware of the filtering that is taking place. Some others may be aware of the potential of misinterpretation due to filtering, but only by thinking about that potential. There are a very few who understand the process and try to make use of it to gain some advantage from their perspective. As a manager, it is wise to keep filtering in mind as you plan, prepare, and present your messages, as well as when you perceive how they are translated.

Barriers to Effective Listening

You undoubtedly can recall the old saying regarding the word assume and its impact on people. Assuming is the great barrier to effective listening. Assuming we already know the content of a message. Assuming the content is unimportant to us. Assuming the information is of no interest. The litany of assumptions could go on and on, but you get the point; assumptions are a problem in listening and "hearing."

Keeping an open mind regarding content and meaning is the best defense against making assumptions. Of course, saying that is easy, while doing it is another matter. As a manager, knowing the potential for your recipients to make assumptions when preparing your message (why it is new, important, etc.) will pay dividends in the long run.

Related to assumptions, and very common in occurrence, is jumping to conclusions about what the message is about. Filtering comes into play here as well, especially in stressful situations. We think we know the direction or content of the message and our filters take over in our interpretation of its meaning.

Another very common barrier, and one linked to making assumptions and jumping to conclusions about content, is starting to mentally prepare a response before hearing the full message. One very common situation in which this barrier arises in the workplace is during performance appraisals. Given the fact that few people enjoy being on the receiving or the giving end of the process, it is not surprising the rebuttals and replies are inevitable. Too often the parties involved become more focused on what they will say next rather than thinking about what the process is intended to achieve—the best possible performance.

One challenge some of us have during a presentation is critiquing the presenter's delivery. We begin thinking about style and cease listening to the content. This is not just a matter of negative assessment; it may be due to how well the presentation is being given. We imagine things we might do to improve it. In either case, we have ceased to listen.

All of us have some "hot-button" words and phrases the can create havoc with our listening. They are personal in character, and probably only family, close friends, and long-term colleagues may have any idea what those words and phrases are. Most of them are relatively common but for an individual they are associated with some negative past experience in which the words or phrases played a major role. As a manager, all you can do is to realize such issues exist within your staff. Such words and phrases essentially cut off any hearing and understanding for the individual.

AUTHOR EXPERIENCE

Evans once had an experience where a "hot-button" word played a significant role in the operations of a library department. In that case, it was a single word and involved two individuals. The event took place as a result of a disagreement between a staff member and department head in which the staff member knew a hot word for the department head and used it. What should have been a minor matter blew up into a problem for library operations. The department head went on medical leave for months due to stress. The staff member had to be transferred to a different agency and the department activities were disrupted. All of that because of one hot word for one person. You never know when such an event may happen—probably never as extreme as the above—but don't be surprised when hot-button words or phrases arise and create challenges.

WORTH CHECKING OUT

Three useful books that can assist you in honing your listening skills are:

Chris Battell, *Effective Listening* (Alexandria, VA: ASTD Press, 2006).

Diana Bonet Romero, *The Business of Listening: Become a More Effective Listener*, 4th edition (Rochester, NY: Axzo Press, 2009).

Judi Brownell, *Listening: Attitudes, Principles, and Skills*, 5th edition (Boston, MA: Pearson, 2013).

NONVERBAL COMMUNICATION

Essentially, in face-to-face communication there are three major components to consider: word choice, tone, and nonverbal behavior. All three interact in terms of how the recipient of a message will interpret its meaning. The same is true regarding any feedback based on the original message. When there is any lack of congruity between the three components, the tone of delivery and nonverbal behavior become the basis of interpretation. Clearly managers must be aware of and "read" the impact of tone and nonverbal behavior in all their interactions with others.

Are nonverbal behaviors a significant workplace issue? The answer is, *yes!* Researchers indicate that roughly two-thirds of our interpretation of a message arises from nonverbal clues or cues (Arthur, 1995; Hect and Ambady, 1999; Stubbs, 2003). Gaining an understanding of the various meanings of nonverbal behaviors requires having some long-term shared experiences with work colleagues as well as doing some reading on the topic. Your experience with a person must be over a long period of time because each person employs nonverbals in his or her own unique, personal style, and it takes time to understand the variation from colleague to colleague.

Saying nonverbal behavior is complex is somewhat like saying brain surgery is complex. There are hundreds of variables to try to grasp. We will just list nine of the top most basic nonverbal clues or cues that impact our messages:

- Body posture
- Facial expression
- Touch
- Timing
- Personal space
- Eye contact
- Gestures
- Dress
- Intensity

These "clues" are very much culturally dependent. For example, Western European people tend to view lack of eye contact as indicating someone is untrustworthy.

CHECK THESE OUT

The following are a few titles that will assist you in gaining some understanding of the nature of nonverbal clues and cues and their impact on what you are attempting to communicate.

Peter A. Anderson, *Nonverbal Communication: Forms and Functions*, 2nd edition (Long Grove, IL: Waveland Press, 2008)

Judee K. Burgoon, Laura K. Guerrero, and Kory Floyd, *Nonverbal Communication* (Boston, MA: Allyn & Bacon, 2010)

Judith L. Hanna, *To Dance Is Human: A Theory of Nonverbal Communication* (Chicago, IL: University of Chicago Press, 1987)

Valerie Lynn Manusov and Miles L. Patterson, eds., *The SAGE Handbook of Nonverbal Communication* (Thousand Oaks, CA: Sage Publications, 2006)

Ferando Poyatos, *Cross-Cultural Perspectives in Nonverbal Communication* (Lewiston, NY: Hogrefe, 1988)

Native American cultures generally regard eye contact, beyond a brief glance, as offensive. The above nine clues become hundreds based on various cultural norms. In addition, there are personal variations to consider as well. During a job interview, for example, is a person sitting in an upright posture with his or her back against the chair signaling that he or she is an individual with great self-confidence or is someone who feels the need for solid support of any kind? Only time with the person can begin to indicate which is correct.

LIS organizations are generally diverse in both staff and service populations. That means you must begin to sort out both cultural and personal nonverbal clues you get from those with whom you interact.

E-COMMUNICATION

Electronic communication requires paying at least as much, if not more, attention to the communication Ps (planning, preparing, presenting, perceiving, participating, and persuading) as do oral and paper-based efforts. There are two aspects of e-communication that heighten the importance of planning and preparing your message: speed and length. Without question, social media can quickly help to "spread the word." From an organizational point of view, that speed can be a problem as there is little or no differentiation between good and unfavorable news. In most cases, e-messages need to be short in length, creating a challenge for getting an accurate "word" out, especially when attempting to reach a large audience.

Some years ago Pulley and Sessa (2001) described five paradoxes related to an e-environment. Although their focus was on e-leaders and e-organizations, we think their points also apply to e-communication. The paradoxes were:

1. Swift—Mindful
2. Individual—Community
3. Top down—Grassroots
4. Detailed—Big Picture
5. Flexible—Steady

The first and fourth paradoxes are the first that come to mind when considering your e-communication efforts. However, it is a true challenge to formulate a single message that seems to be both personal and group oriented. From an LIS point of view, finding the proper balance between top-down and grassroots communication is an ongoing process. Organizations as well as their leaders must appear flexible but steady—appearing to flip-flop has been the bane of many organizations and leaders.

Email

Most of us have a tendency to be very casual in our email messages. Such casualness may not be a problem when we are corresponding with friends and close colleagues. However, it can be a major problem when we are trying to connect with other people. Work related emails are presentations and create in the recipient's mind an image (positive or negative) of you and your library.

We believe there are four major challenges when it comes to sending organizational email messages to outsiders. Almost everyone who has an email account receives dozens of such messages every day and even with the best of spam filters, "junk" still gets through. What constitutes "junk" is a personal definition. First and foremost, your challenge is to be as certain as possible the recipient will actually read what you wrote. Second, you want to be certain the person understands the content of the message. Third, you rarely want to unintentionally annoy, upset, anger, frustrate, or confuse the person. Last, and often the biggest challenge, is keeping the message short (perhaps another law for Ranganathan's laws would be "save the readers' time") while assuring understanding. How often have you closed a long message "to read later" only to delete it without reading it later? In some cases, later, assuming it is read, is too late for your purpose.

TIPS FOR EFFECTIVE WORK EMAIL MESSAGES

- Keep it short and to the point
- Get to the point in the first two sentences
- State any actions the recipient should take and the timeframe for such action clearly
- Outline any benefits of taking action
- Keep font and format clean and simple
- Keep questions to a minimum—long lists quickly end up in the "read later" category
- Provide details, if required, in an attachment
- Be friendly but not overly so, unless you know the person well
- Read through the email before sending to catch any glaring errors or misspellings
- Don't use all capitals or "text speak"

Websites

You would be hard-pressed to find a library today that did not have a Web presence. Some libraries may be far down the navigation list for their parent organization, but they are there. Wherever the presence is, it is always the library's home or "landing page." "Landing page" is a term employed by marketing professionals for the first Web page a person sees for an organization.

Your basic goals for the landing page are to hold the viewer's attention and encourage a desired action. The page must be engaging and have a clearly defined action or option. Most marketing professional agree the page designer, whether that person is a staff member or paid Web designer, must think long and deeply about every element of the page. That is, think about how each element will contribute to the goal of holding people's attention as well as work with other elements.

Effective landing pages have headlines that grab viewers' attention. Their messages are clear and to the point. They are easy to navigate with clearly defined options to act. Web pages with fancy fonts, animation, and a variety of colors tend to be visually confusing for viewers. The goal is to keep the viewers' attention and for them to act on choices you are promoting. The best approach is to employ a professional Web designer and assign one or two staff members to work closely with that person.

Blogs

An organizational blog is very commonplace in today's LIS. Some approaches to a blog are more effective than others. Most libraries have three primary blog audiences: staff, professional, and/or advanced readers; the general public reader; and a mix of the two. Needless to say, each audience requires a slightly different approach, even for what is basically the same information.

Libraries have many choices for how to use blogs—for branding and marketing, conducting surveys, and event promotion, for example. Certainly all library blogs have a marketing element to them but some exist solely to promote and market library services and programs, such as life-long learning. A library might decide to use a video and event blog to attract attention to its upcoming book sale. A survey blog can supplement more traditional methods of gathering user information. In a sense, even a library's online reference activities are a form of blog.

Facebook

Libraries have two methods of employing Facebook—groups and pages. Groups are best for gaining user interaction. Pages are most useful in promoting and marketing the library. A group may be created by any Facebook user. The library might set up a group, assuming it has a Facebook account. A Friends of the Library organization could start a group for its members as one way of keeping in touch, of securing volunteers for an upcoming event, and, of course, for fundraising. If the library has a homework assistance program and has the involvement of some school district teachers, a teacher could form a group for the program.

Unlike pages, Facebook groups are *not* indexed by Web search engines; only Facebook users may view groups. The person(s) who creates a group decides between three types of access—open, closed, or secret. As the label "open" suggests, any Facebook account holder may access the site. "Closed" groups set up a member approval process—a Facebook user asks to be given access. "Secret" groups go a step further and limit access or membership to invitation only. There is a limit on how many mass emails a group may do at one time—5,000—however, that limit is unlikely to be a major problem for most libraries.

Library Facebook pages must be developed by the library. Such pages are indexed by search engines and viewable by any online user. One advantage of pages is you may integrate Twitter with the page. Unlike groups, there is no limit on the number of "fans" a page may have.

We believe both options have potential value for the library, as long as someone is charged with the task of keeping them up to date.

THOUGHTS ON THE POWER OF PERSUASION

All of your managerial communication efforts are, to a greater or lesser degree, intended to persuade one or more individuals, whether you are proposing a new desk schedule or trying to secure support for increased funding. As noted in the opening section of this chapter, nonprofit and public sector managers face a wider range of communication constituents than do their counterparts in for-profit organizations. That also suggests managers in the nonprofit and public sectors must employ strong powers of persuasion if they are to be successful. The Ps of communication all play a significant role in how persuasive you are. However, they are not the sole factors.

There are times when your logic is impeccable, your facts 100 percent accurate, and your word choice flawless, and yet you fail to persuade, convince, sell, or gain the requisite support. Why? The answer usually is one or more of three factors—timing, credibility/trust, and audience.

Timing is the most common factor. Just as "location, location, location" is the key factor in real estate, timing is key to successful persuasion. Being too early or too late certainly can cause problems in terms of effectiveness. Too early always carries the danger of being forgotten by the time implementation is required. Too late can create a challenge for the recipient(s) to have enough lead time to be effective.

Two other factors of timing can create problems. When there are competing messages of seemingly equal importance a recipient tends to focus on the message most interesting to them and pay less attention to any other messages. A related factor is that your message may be overshadowed by more important messages. Your message regarding the night schedule arriving at the same time as the message from the HR department regarding salary increases, or lack of, is likely to get little or no attention for some time. By that time it may be buried under many more recent messages.

Your credibility and trust also play a role in the failure to persuade. Both traits are significant factors in almost all of your managerial activities. Clearly, if your trust level among others is low, your powers of persuasion will be almost nonexistent, regardless of how well you frame your message. A more common challenge is credibility. When your message comes across as very different from what people normally expect from you, they will take more time to accept it, if they ever do, than when your messages are congruent. We see this problem on a regular basis with politicians—"flip-flopping"—that the press and opponents are quick to point out. The flexible and steady paradox arises here. Change must take place; that is a given. However, a key factor in achieving successful change is setting the stage by explaining the need to change. Think about your message: could it create a credibility issue? If so, incorporate appropriate phraseology to make it clear this not flip-flopping, but a deliberate and needed change in direction.

Another consideration, primarily in terms of non-staff individuals, to improve your power of persuasion is a thoughtful audience analysis. Some years ago, after successes and a few surprising failures, we read Gary Williams and Robert Miller's 2002 *Harvard Business Review* article, "Change the Way You Persuade." Williams and Miller suggested a model for thinking about the group you hope to persuade. Certainly we thought about who our "target" audience was, but only in a very general way. Thinking back on the failures, it was apparent that if we had given more thought to the audience composition, with the Williams and Miller model in mind, the outcome might well have been different. (This is one of those times when for-profit research works just as well in the nonprofit and public sectors.)

Williams and Miller focused on for-profit decision makers who had to be persuaded about some issue. Their categories were charismatics, thinkers, skeptics, followers, and controllers. While you might want to use labels that differ from theirs, their discussion of the characteristics of each category fits the types of individuals in any sector group. In the case of nonprofit and public sector groups, you are likely to have a mixture of types to consider and will need to focus your presentation toward the most prominent or important type to persuade.

Their characteristics in the charismatic category are somewhat surprising. Charismatics are, in the Williams–Miller model, individuals who often become highly enthusiastic, intrigued, excited by new or different approaches to an issue or idea. They are the "Great Idea" individuals who also quickly move on to something else that catches their attention. Focusing on just those individuals is unlikely to lead to long-term support unless you gain other supporters. So, catch their attention with words such as "action," "results," and "successful," but be aware that support may be short lived.

Thinkers, as the label implies, are logical and want data before they are persuaded. Words such as "cost-benefit" (with hard data), "research results" (with hard data), and "proven effective" (with hard data) will catch the attention of thinkers. A logical, fact-based, structured presentation works well with such individuals.

Skeptics are a challenge. As the label implies, they are hard to persuade and slow to shift their views. They are the group with which you must have the greatest credibility. Lacking credibility, your chances of persuading the skeptics are almost nil. Having the prior support from a skeptic is a key to gaining other skeptics support.

Controllers are the least common group as a percentage, according to Williams and Miller (less than 10% of a group). Individuals in this category dislike or fear uncertainty and are resistant to major changes or new approaches. A structured, fact-based presentation has the best chance of being successful with controllers, especially if you can demonstrate that other, similar organizations have successfully followed the path you suggest. Like skeptics, controllers look to someone they respect or some other LIS organization they deem credible for guidance. They also share with skeptics a negative reaction to a "hard sell."

Followers—not your staff and supporters—are people who view past practices (both theirs and others) as the basis for taking action, including decision making. They do not mind change as long as it fits a pattern of past success.

In a mixed audience you are likely to succeed with roughly 50 percent of a group (thinkers and followers) when employing a fact-based logical presentation that links your idea(s) to success elsewhere. You may even be able to include a few controllers and charismatic individuals.

We've had more success after using this type of approach—focusing on the types of decision makers our audience is composed of—to planning and preparing a presentation than we had prior to doing so. You will probably never have 100 percent success in persuading people (nobody does-but imagining the possibilities that would come with that type of power is certainly attractive). There will be times when more influential individuals will oppose you and be able to override you. Keep in mind persuasion is a process; it takes more than one effort to succeed.

REFERENCES

Arthur, Diane. 1995. "The Importance of Body Language." *HRFocus* 72 (June): 22–23.

Braun, Linda W. 2015. "Listen First: Taking Time to Understand Patron Needs." *American Libraries* 46, no. 5: 58.

Cialdini, Robert. 2011. "Harnessing the Science of Persuasion." In *Communicating Effectively*. Cambridge, MA: Harvard Business Review Press, 29–51.

Conroy, Barbara, and Barbara Jones. 1986. *Improving Communication in the Library*. Phoenix, AZ: Oryx Press.

Ford, Wendy S. Zabava. 1998. *Communicating with Customers: Service Approaches, Ethics, and Impact*. Cresskill, NJ: Hampton Press.

Haase, Richard F., and Donald T. Tepper. 1972. "Nonverbal Components of Empathic Communication." *Journal of Counseling Psychology* 19, no. 5: 417–424.

Hecht, Marvin A., and Nalini Ambady. 1999. "Nonverbal Communication and Psychology." *New Jersey Journal of Communication* 7, no. 2: 156–170.

Hess, Ron. 2008. "Restating the Case for Face-to-Face Communication." *Communication World* 25, no. 3: 48.

Higgins, E. Tory, William Rholes, and Carl R. Jones. 1977. "Category Accessibility and Impression Formation." *Journal of Experimental Social Psychology* 13, no. 2: 141–154.

Hogan, Kevin, and Ron Stubbs. 2003. *Can't Get Through: Eight Barriers to Communication*. Gretna, LA: Pelican Publishing.

Pulley, Mary Lynn, and Valerie Sessa. 2001. "E-Leadership Tackling Complex Challenges." *Industrial and Commercial Training* 33, no. 6: 225–230.

Rainey, Hal G. 2014. *Understanding and Managing Public Organizations*. 5th ed. San Francisco, CA: Jossey-Bass.

Sugianto, Santoso, and Dan Johns. 2011. "Breaking Down the Barriers." *CMA Magazine* 85, no. 6: 24–27.

Surprenant, Carol F., and Michael R. Solomon. 1987. "Predictability and Personalization in the Service Encounter." *Journal of Marketing* 51, no. 2: 86–96.

Tulgan, Bruce. 2010. "Manage Up and Take Charge of Your Workday." *T+D* 64, no. 7: 70–71.

Williams, Gary A., and Robert B. Miller. 2002. "Change the Way You Persuade." *Harvard Business Review* 80, no. 3: 67–73.

Chapter 4

AUTHORITY, INFLUENCE, AND POWER

Establish ongoing connections to the base of supporters to build power for the long term.

Marcia Avner, 2010

It is unusual for a public manager to have authority over every aspect of a program.

Steven Cohen, William Eimicke, and Tanya Heikkila, 2013

Leadership is not determined by rank, responsibilities, or position. Knowing how to build influence and lead others, no matter what your role, is now a workplace necessity.

Nan S. Russel, 2013

In general terms, external accountability is described in the literature as the situation of an agent previously delegated with some powers or authority by a principal bounded by the duty to account for subsequent actions.

Patrizio Monfardini, 2010

The concept of accountability represents an important ethical and moral principle, basic to the concept and exercise of authority within a democracy.

Burt Perrin, 2015

In the workplace, three concepts play an important role in what takes place or does not: authority, influence, and power. There are related concepts that also have an impact on what takes place, such as duty, responsibility, and accountability. However, the first three words mentioned are the basis of managerial leadership. They are also at the heart of the difference between the for-profit sector and the other two sectors. We made the point in chapter 1 that nonprofit and public sector managers face more constraints on their actions than do their colleagues in for-profit organizations. One of those constraints stems from the nature of the authority, power, and influence given to nonprofit and public managers. Public managers in particular are constrained by the authority and power they receive upon becoming a manager.

Authority, influence, and power, while having different definitions, are interrelated in terms of the workplace. When you look up these words in a comprehensive dictionary you quickly see they are indeed interrelated. Each has at least four "sense divisions." *Authority* (Webster's, 1966, 146) has three managerial related senses: "power to require," "right to expect obedience," and "power to influence. *Influence* also shows the interrelated nature of the words; "the act, process, or power of producing an effect," and "the power or capacity of causing an effect indirectly or intangible ways" (Webster's 1966, 1160). Definitions included for *power* are "capability of acting or producing an effect," "legal authority," and "political sway (influence)" (Webster's, 1966, 1778–1779).

These concepts interact in several ways, with political winds adding a layer of complexity to the mix, especially in the public sector. For example, influence can enhance or detract from a person's power. While you may have the authority, you may find you lack the influence and/or power to implement the authority. Likewise, you may have both influence and power but not actually have the authority to carry out what you perceive as necessary. A manager must have all three in order to manage effectively.

Two of the concepts, authority and power, are often contentious and, occasionally, open to conflict, especially for public sector managers. The question is, in the nonprofit and public sectors, how much of each should a person have? Authority resides in a position not a person. People may come and go in terms of being appointed to a position, but the authority itself remains unchanged unless higher authority makes a change. However, that authority must be rather broadly defined so that changes can take place as situations develop or change. Power is both positional and personal in character. Some level of power does reside in the position and is thought to be proportional to authority assigned to the position. However, you can build on that power through your actions. As suggested in the first quotations at the beginning this chapter, garnering power from supporters is possible. Influence and power are often closely linked in people's minds and their perceptions of who is powerful. The great managers accomplish great things by using influence as much as possible and with as little "power" as possible.

AUTHORITY

The assignment of authority comes from a position at least one level above the position in question (senior managers, governing board, and legal documents for example). Authority carries with it a set of rights that relate to the achieving of the responsibilities assigned to a position. One such right is to make decisions regarding what and how to perform those responsibilities. An associated right is to direct those activities. Yet another right is to plan and change activities as circumstances change. There is also the right to give "orders" to staff members as well as an expectation the staff will carry out those orders. Great manager-leaders understand they have such rights but make limited overt use of them. Rather, they employ their leadership skills to motivate staff, and gain staff and others' input in decision making and planning. Being dependent on such rights alone leads to people viewing you as authoritarian, a poor manager and not a true leader.

Essentially, authority is delegated (downward) to a position. Official lines of authority are reflected in organization charts; however, some authority may not be formally "official" because a supervisor or superior manager may delegate authority to a subordinate for a project or short-term purpose and this authority is rarely reflected in an organization chart. Something important to keep in mind about delegating is, in order for it to be effective, you must delegate full authority to carry out the assignment. However, you are always ultimately responsible and accountable for the outcome of such delegation. Yes, you can hold the person on the receiving end of the delegation accountable for the performance; nevertheless, you and only you will be accountable to those above you.

Leaders must be trusted by their followers and the followers must trust their leaders. Delegation is a tangible demonstration of trust. You should not, and are unlikely to, delegate something to a person you don't have reason to trust. More than 20 years ago Charles Handy (1995) published a thoughtful and useful article addressing workplace trust. Although his focus was on the e-work environment, we believe his ideas apply to any workplace. He identified seven key elements for good workplace trust to exist.

- Trust is not blind
- Trust demands learning
- Trust needs bonding
- Trust requires leaders
- Trust is tough
- Trust needs boundaries
- Trust needs touch (Handy, 1995, 44–47)

There are actually three categories of trust that must exist in the workplace in order for the unit to achieve the highest level of performance. We touched on the two that most people think of when asked about work environment trust—leaders trusting staff and staff trusting the leader. The third component is staff trusting one another. In situations where teams are the primary structure, such trust is absolutely critical to successful team performance. It is equally important in any work environment. Workflows require collaboration regardless of the work structure and collaboration requires some degree of trust in your colleagues. When there is a lack of trust, or worse conflict, work becomes disjointed at best and often almost completely disrupted. Whether you are trying to create a team or just a high performing work environment, you must monitor staff interactions and help them build trust in one another.

Certainly, you can be proven to have placed your trust in the wrong person, but you are not likely to make that mistake a second time. There may be a failure in the delegated task that relates to your issues with trust rather than with the person who was given the task. For many managers, they talk about trusting staff and the importance of empowerment, but because they retain responsibility for the task, they never really delegate the necessary authority and power to ensure that it is carried out successfully.

POWER

Power is a word that often generates a negative knee-jerk response; this is especially true when the hearer has had a bad experience with power. It is, in a sense, one of those hot-button words we mentioned in the last chapter. It is also one that you can assume or expect may be a "hot" word for someone on your staff. Why that negative response occurs is somewhat complex. Perhaps one reason is we hear more about misuse of power, regardless of form, than we do about its positive uses. Another factor is that there is inherent in the concept a coercive, punishment, and sanction component. People tend not to respond favorably to being coerced. Yet another factor is some people have had negative experiences with a person holding some power.

Power in and of itself is not bad. What makes the concept of power good or bad is how the person holding power wields it. Power is a part of managing organizations and getting people to carry out activities they might not otherwise be inclined to do. According to researchers (see, for example, Dorwin Cartwright, 1995), managerial power comes in several forms In the workplace, power is, or should be, about influence—getting people to work together to accomplish a defined goal. Jeffery Pfeffer defined power as "the potential ability to influence behavior, to change the course of events, to overcome resistance, and get people to do things they would not otherwise do" (1992, 30). Managers in the nonprofit and public sectors need to keep in mind that for them, the real workplace power is influence. In either sector, it is rather easy to fall into the trap of thinking we are powerless. We may not have the power to force something; however, we have almost unlimited power to try to influence. Influence is essentially our most effective power. More than 80 years ago Chester I. Barnard (1938) suggested that social influence (in the workplace setting) arises from individuals with leadership skills, not just from those people in positions where leadership is expected or desirable. LIS managers must have a desire to increase their influence and powers of persuasion if they hope to lead a successful organization. They must seek it whenever possible; it is most unlikely just to fall into their lap.

Essentially there are three components to workplace power or influence. First, and to our mind the most important, is the person wielding the influence. Second is how that person wields the influence. Third, is the person(s) on the receiving end of the process. A manager's power and influence arise from five sources: legitimate, expertise, referent, reward, and coercive. We noted the "rights" or powers (legitimate) that are associated with a managerial position earlier in this chapter. Those powers are significant and important in how you manage; however, depending solely on those rights is unlikely to lead to long-term organizational success. To our mind, two powers (expertise and referent) are the ones that are more important to long-term success. Rewards come in third place, and coercive a distant last place.

Some of the elements in Pfeffer's definition relate to authority-positional powers. Influence, especially in the nonprofit and public sectors, is the true source of power. Influence is most easily gained through employing your expertise power. People are much likely to follow your lead (influence) when they view you as an expert. Expertise in both knowledge and in doing is necessary. The more areas of expertise you have the greater is your power to influence. We are never experts in every area of organizational operations. However, if we identify our areas of weakness and bring in people who do have that expertise, we demonstrate to our staff another type of expertise—knowing when to seek assistance. That behavior tends to increase staff confidence in our overall expertise and they are more easily influenced in a rapidly changing environment. That is, "We may not know what will happen, but we have confidence you will make the best possible decisions."

 Another aspect of expertise power is that we can gain new areas of competency and thus increase our powers. We all have heard over and over again about the desirability of life-long learning. Here is a place where that activity has tangible results. A side benefit of doing this is it encourages staff to engage in similar activities. Another outcome is it increases the staff's confidence in your abilities and their willingness to follow you.

The life-long learning aspect also helps build your referent power. Referent power arises from people or staff viewing you as successful and wanting to be associated with you and your successes. Expertise and referent powers are linked in the sense that if you lack expertise you are unlikely to have great success and, therefore, have no referent power. The two combined are powerful tools for influencing people and events.

Reward power is a useful tool up to a point. It is a power to employ judiciously, that is, in moderation. Giving too many rewards causes them to be less and less effective as a means of influence. That is, they are so common as to be meaningless. On the other hand, making rewards very uncommon can also reduce your power of persuasion. Staff can begin to doubt they can ever be "good enough" for you. That can start to demoralize the staff and may even lead to a decline in organizational performance.

Your range of rewards is large, from an occasional word of praise to significant salary increases or even a promotion. Public praise is surprisingly effective, but may also have a potential downside. If you doubt you can, at some point in time, publicly praise every staff member for something, you may want to hold off any public praising. Those who do not receive even an occasional "well done," become less and less motivated and are likely to perform at just the barely acceptable level. There is also the danger, when just a few receive praise, that an atmosphere of "teacher's pets" becoming an issue. That atmosphere will also generate poor performance for the organization.

Coercive power is always available to a manager. It ought to be the last resort power you employ. Having to do so is, in a sense, a mark of failure on your part (or at least it may feel that way to you). You are likely to wonder about what went wrong, what might have been done differently, and whether it could have been avoided. While such introspection is an important tool for learning to be a better leader-manager, it does not always mean that you should avoid using coercion. There are times when it is essential for the good of the organization and you know nothing could have been done differently.

Keep in mind the above "powers" exist and operate in two environments—internal and external. Clearly all of the powers are operational internally, if judiciously employed. Externally, only the expertise and referent powers are available to help you influence people and events. So what options, if any, exist that might be helpful to increase your persuasive powers?

There are a number of personal skills and abilities that will be beneficial in gaining external influence. Some of the skills you likely already possess and just need an understanding of how to employ them to enhance your influence. Others you can learn and develop; learning them is a little like learning bridge or chess. That is, you can read about the skill and take some lessons; however, in the long run you must practice, practice, practice, and accept the fact there will be some failures during the early days.

In the previous chapter, we discussed the value of connecting with others as well as how to persuade them. Both of these concepts are components of influencing people and events. One aspect of connecting with others is having an interest in what they think and believe, as well as in their concerns and values. You should not try to fake this interest; trying to do so may fool a few people for a while but most people will quickly recognize your fakery. Recognizing your duplicity will kill their trust and positive opinion about you, as well as any chance of influencing them. We are not suggesting you take a deep interest in the personal lives of staff; what we are suggesting is getting to know a few personal facts about the people you interact with and hope to influence from time to time.

Take the time to review staff CVs (curriculum vitae, similar to resumes) and look for places of connection, such as past employers, educational institutions, hobbies, outside interests, and so on. For non-staff, finding potential connections takes more time; however, today's social media makes the process less difficult that in the past. Being able to start a conversation on a personal level rather than work related goes a long way toward gaining a little referent power. It also tells the person you think about them beyond what they can do for the LIS. Knowing and commenting about the value of some aspect of their work that does not appear in a job description also goes a long way toward making strong connections.

One important group to connect with is the members of your board—either advisory or governing. One obvious fact that you will know without searching is a board member's profession or occupation. A related but unknown fact will be what the person does outside of their work life—hobbies, volunteer activities, and so on. You may, in the case of a governing board, know something about a person's political philosophy but do you know what his or her "pet" political projects are? An obvious area where connections may be created is education—what level, what schools, their children's age and schools. Such information can be helpful in creating and maintaining connections.

AUTHOR EXPERIENCE

One "interested in you as a person" method Evans employed was to send each person a card during the December holiday period. (He knew some managers would send birthday cards to staff members.) Some staff received very religious-themed Christmas greetings, others received Hanukkah cards. Still others received a "season's greeting" and once he had a staff member who enjoyed receiving a "Bah Humbug" card.

   A card in and of itself is fine, but can seem pro forma rather than reflecting a true interest. Evans always added a handwritten note thanking the person for some activity they had performed during the past 12 months and how that effort enhanced the quality of the library's service. Did it work? He has no data on the matter one way or the other. What he does know is the staff took pride in performing the best quality service given the available resources. In one setting, he expected staff members to stay a few years and then move on to bigger and better positions. He was very surprised by how few individuals did so.

ADVISORY BOARD EXPERIENCE

Mika also sent holiday cards to individual staff and faculty members. His belief dovetails with the author's in acknowledging the hard work of the member during the year, not just for a specific event or activity. He also sent birthday cards to the same members, with the hope that the individual realized that he was aware of their work and that it and they were appreciated. Mika also sent holiday cards to key administrators within the organization. This was his way to express gratitude for their support during the year. And, what better way to remind the university president, provost, research dean, university counsel, graduate dean, and so on, that the library and information science program was part of the university and that Mika was a key member of the university hierarchy. When email became more prevalent, cards were replaced with emails during the holiday season and for birthdays to university administrators. Even in retirement he sends emails to some former colleagues and key university administrators that he felt especially close to administratively.

Related to being genuinely interested in people is the ability to empathize. Empathy is the ability to read and understand other's emotions and feelings. (In a later chapter, we discuss emotional intelligence in some detail.) People can be happy, sad, frustrated, and so on, without engaging in overt behavior. We say things such as "Is everything okay?" or "Is something wrong?" to friends and colleagues from time to time because we sense (empathize) that something may be troubling them. Catching such issues early, especially in the workplace, can keep them form developing into a larger issue and can make it easier for you to manage and influence people and events.

Self-confidence also plays a significant role in your power to influence others. Lacking confidence will greatly reduce, if not destroy, that power. Your expertise and self-confidence are linked in the sense that the more areas of expertise you have, the more confident you are likely to feel. You can increase your self-confidence, without adding new areas of competence, by focusing on those areas in which you are good and work on improving those areas from good to great. Taking some additional preparation time before presentations tends to increase confidence for many people. Another technique is to assess what you can and cannot control. Making sure you have solid control of the ones you can do something about tends to increase your confidence.

While you may know or feel you are confident, will others recognize that fact? Perhaps, perhaps not. There a few steps you can take to help convey self-confidence. As stated in the last chapter, nonverbal behavior plays a large role in our communication activities. Nonverbal behavior can add or detract from how people view your self-confidence. Some examples are maintaining a relaxed but upright posture to signal comfort and confidence. When talking to others, keep your arms at your sides rather than crossed in front of you; this will also convey that you are comfortable and open to communication. Dressing appropriately is certainly necessary for many reasons; however, dressing in a modest but appropriate fashion based on the occasion signals confidence. Dressing too formally for an occasion may signal a lack of confidence, while dressing too casually is often interpreted as lacking a sense of the occasion, or worse, arrogance.

Even your style in written and oral communication will suggest how confident you are—the more direct, forthright, and positive your messages are, the more people will think of you as a confident leader. Finding positive aspects to situations and sharing that perspective with others also communicates confidence. Sharing praise with others is also a positive. Accept such praise or recognition modestly; don't duck it, don't seek it. There is a fine line between "tooting your own horn" and being thought of as arrogant, self-aggrandizing, or weak manager. If you can meet conflict head on and diplomatically, people will see you as confident. When you add positive suggestions for resolution and/or compromise, you further advance your positive and self-confident image.

Who Has the Power?

If you think of power as influence, almost everyone has some (assuming they want it and work to acquire it). As noted above, the power to influence is unlikely to fall into your lap; you must seek it. The likelihood of gaining such power by chance is about the same as the odds of you winning the Power Ball lottery when buying a single ticket.

Jeffery Pfeffer made the point that within an organization not all units are equally influential, regardless of the sector in which sector they are located (2010, 58–60). LIS organizations are almost always among the least influential unless

AUTHOR'S EXPERIENCE

What follows is *not* intended to be anything more than a real-world example of how you can, over time, build solid connections, increase library resources, and increase the library's influence. Certainly when staff were engaged in the activities discussed below the authors, or at least Evans, did not think of it in terms of connections and increasing influence or power. Essentially, we generated power, influence, and a more positive public image while just striving to provide high quality service. The following does, however, reflect many of the points covered in the main text.

The scene was an academic library with no real influence and a highly negative image across the campus (among faculty, administrators, and students). One the first things Evans does when taking on a new position is to schedule one-on-one meetings with all the key players who have an interest in how the unit has been performing. For the first three-plus months, he was more often speaking with others outside of the library than in it. The input was more or less what he expected to hear—a lot of negatives (primarily related to the collections) and only a few positives (related to the library staff).

During Evans's conversations with department chairs and deans, he asked about their information needs and for them to get as specific as possible (journal titles, media formats, and the like). Correcting major collection deficiencies takes time and money—both in rather large quantities. Thus, this could not be a quick fix. As a result, he started exploring an idea (courier service) with a nearby research library that he knew had worked for some other libraries. The first step was to develop some type of framework that could be acceptable to both institutions. Then there was calculating the cost of such an effort (people, startup funds, ongoing expenses, and fee to the "host" institution and the like).

With a proposal and cost estimate in hand Evans approached the Academic Vice President (AVP, who was Evans's supervisor) with the idea. He was new to the institution and he and Evans had already made a connection (we had grown up in the same state, had worked at several of the same universities [at different times], shared the desire to make the library a true asset for the university, and had an interest in publishing). Thus, Evans had a good connection, hard data about the need to do something fairly quickly, and a plan. The AVP found the necessary funds and off they went, establishing a three-day courier service for faculty and graduate students. Results were a win for all concerned: both the AVP and library were seen as forward looking, they provided a major new service, and faculty and graduates gained access to desired research materials very quickly.

The library now had connections and some influential allies. Using the feedback from department chairs, deans, and key faculty members regarding collections needs, the library put forward a request for major funding to address those needs. Once those were in place, we made the case for annual increases to maintain those gains as well as to enhance the collection. The outcome was for 17 years (in both good and bad economic times) the library got a 10 percent increase for print and media materials, 12 percent for serial holdings, and 15 percent for e-resources. Needless to say, in a few years those amounts were large and getting larger; to the point that many of the non-academic units on the campus became increasingly antagonistic toward any library request. Nevertheless, the requests were almost always approved (the exception being new FTEs—always a tough sell).

None of the above would have taken place had the library not had solid connections and a great many allies.

their leadership makes a serious attempt to increase their persuasive powers. Even then an LIS is unlikely to be the top unit in terms of influence. The director of a library has little chance of matching the influence of the chief of police, dean of the law school, or the principal of the school; however, that does not mean the director must be powerless or lacking in influence.

There are some tactics that can help you increase the library's influence or at least reduce the disparity. One obvious tactic is to increase the resources of the library. This is easy to state and tough to do, but not impossible to accomplish. You have two basic routes for increasing resources: internal and external. (We cover external resources—grants, donations, etc.—in a later chapter.) Internal resources are the operating expenses (OE) from the library's parent institution. Gaining more than inflationary increases is a challenge in the best of economic times. In tough economic times, it seems almost impossible (and is, more often than not). That does not mean there is no point in trying; what is certain is, if you don't try there will be no increase. The point is that securing even a small increase, beyond inflation, will be noted by others and, as a result, there will be some small increase in the library's perceived persuasive powers and standing.

A key element in accomplishing such increases goes back to making connections. Making the proper (effective) connections can be challenging—who to connect with, making contact, and building and maintaining the connection, for example. An obvious "who" is the person to whom you report. Yes, there must be contact but not necessarily a connection—the two concepts are very different. Connecting involves much more than making reports, being accountable, and the like; connecting requires that more than work issues be part of the relationship. It may not be possible, for a variety of reasons, to make a connection with your supervisor, but that does not necessarily mean you are out of luck in the quest to increase the library's influence. Connecting with some individuals who do have connections with your supervisor may be possible.

Connecting with your supervisor is a little more complex than doing so with your staff. Although you are unlikely to have the CV for your boss, there are resources that can provide at least some background information and clues as to where you might be able to connect on a non-work basis. Sometimes you may be able to offer support with a challenging situation or provide guidance from your knowledge of working directly with support staff. In addition to your immediate supervisor, it is equally important to also establish positive working relationships, if not connections, with other agency or unit leaders (networking is part of the process). Having allies (or at least not detractors) is another key to increasing the library's influence or power.

ACCOUNTABILITY AND RESPONSIBILITY

Use of authority and power does, or can, have consequences; accountability and responsibility are the two most common. In U.S. society there is a general acceptance that individuals with authority and power are answerable to others—sometimes highly, sometimes almost not at all—for the manner in which that authority and power was and is deployed. More often than not managers are also answerable for the outcome of that deployment. When you accept a position it comes with some assigned duties and at least some power to carry out those duties. You also accept the responsibility to perform the assigned duties; failure to do can cost you the position. Likewise, you are accountable for both how you use the power as well for the results of using the power.

It is true that all organizations can be held accountable for actions taken or not taken; however, it is nonprofit and public sector managers who face ongoing accountability pressures. The opening quotation from Burt Perrin highlights the public sector side of the issue. He also noted in the article that "there has been a major shift in the public sector management from a focus on activities and processes to a focus on *results*" (emphasis in the original, 2015, 183). That is more commonly referred to as "outcomes," a topic we explore in a later chapter. It seems likely that the dual interest in accountability and outcomes has arisen, at least in part, from citizens' growing distrust of public agencies (see chapter 1 for more on the distrust issue).

The fact is that the concept of accountability is rather easy to define but very complex to apply. First, accountability is rather like leadership in the sense both are generally thought of as "good." They are also similar in that the "goodness or badness" is a function of the person holding them; neither accountability nor leadership is inherently good or bad. Robert Behn, in his book *Rethinking Democratic Accountability* (Washington, DC: Brookings Institution Press, 2001), made the point that no one knows exactly what it means to hold a person accountable beyond the notion that there will or could be some form of sanction or worse, prison for example, involved at the end of the process.

Why would it be the case that the process is inexact? First and foremost is the fact that authority and power are "chains" of delegated authority and power. Second, exactly where on that delegation chain does accountability come into play? Top, middle, bottom? Rather often it seems as though it is the person at the lowest level who becomes the accountability scapegoat. Another factor is that what to apply the concept to is far from precise in most instances. There is a school of thought, discussed above, that accountability is really best employed in terms of laws, rules, and regulation compliance—maintaining proper accounting records, for example.

One way to view accountability is in terms of four aspects: efficiency, legal, expertise, and political. One of the expectations and obligations of a manager is to operate her or his unit both efficiently and effectively. Thus, part of accountability is "product" outcomes and what it costs to generate those products—collection items borrowed, questions answered, and the like are products in this context.

The rule of law is straightforward—for example, a rule of law may be a regulation stating there must be an annual independent audit of expenditures. Another example of accountability and the rule of law would be how well the LIS and its HR unit comply with equal employment laws. It is straightforward in the sense you know, or should know, what laws, rules and regulations apply to the LIS. From an accountability point of view, "I didn't know" will not work. It might in other types of accountability, but not in this area. Certainly there will be times when it may not be clear if a rule or regulation does applies; do not check later. Seek legal advice as soon as possible; then if there is a problem, you have the fact that you followed legal advice—assuming you did so. That is, you acted in "good faith."

For LIS, expertise is not often an issue, at least in terms of accountability. One area where it does have the potential of coming up is when there is a challenge to collection content (intellectual freedom issues and the like). Another potential area is when the library has a room that outside groups might use (for free or a fee). Public libraries, as government entities, have an obligation to follow the law, including the U.S. Constitution. Separation of church and state is a legal concept that is not clear-cut. Making a professional call regarding room use, either way, can lead to the courtroom, and has. Even having a use policy in place vetted by the city attorney does not necessarily ensure there will not be challenges to your professional judgment, or someone trying to make the library accountable for the decision.

The biggest accountability challenge for nonprofit and public sector managers lies in the political realm, or what is sometimes referred to as "responsiveness." Political winds are constantly blowing as well as shifting. Responsiveness is very much in the eye of the beholder. Joseph Knippenberg made the following point in terms of the public sector:

> ... legislatures—not exactly the most focused or impartial bodies in the world—would be undertaking the oversight. Information would likely be deployed and evaluated in a partisan context. Program administrators would be tempted to evade responsibility and shift blame, something that would be relatively easy to do, given the time lag between data collection and analysis and the relatively frequent turnover in the highest echelons of government agencies. . . . Our political accountability mechanisms are unlikely to work in such a way as to focus on the efficient delivery of effective social services. (2007, 32)

Responsiveness, politics, and personal values are a complex mix for nonprofit and public sector managers. As we have noted from time to time, non-profit and public sector managers have many more stakeholders than for-profit managers, all of whom believe the managers should be accountable to them. The broad categories of stakeholders are not internally consistent in what they believe should occur. These facts help make a manager's life interesting, to say the least. You must come to terms with the fact you are likely to make some stakeholders unhappy about something you've done and they may try to hold you accountable on some basis.

Bryane Michael perhaps summed up the nature of accountability by writing:

> Accountability can be politics, by other means—serving some (e.g. evaluators and managers) at the expense of others (e.g. third parties). Such politics may even be a form of fighting over power, organizational boundaries, image, the value of public sector activities, or the moral values by which activities are undertaken. If such politics is one aspect of a wider social construction of the value of accountability, then prudence is called for in promoting accountability. (2005, 96).

> **CHECK THESE OUT**
>
> An insightful article on accountability is Jane Green's 2004 "Managerial Modes of Accountability and Practical Knowledge: Reclaiming the Practical" (*Educational Philosophy and Theory* 36, no. 5: 549–562).
>
> Another informative article is Andrew P. Williams and Jennifer A. Taylor's 2013 essay "Resolving Accountability Ambiguity in Nonprofit Organizations" (*ISTR* 24: 559–580).

IMPORTANCE OF EMPOWERMENT

A goal for all managers is to have a high-performing unit. The only long-term way to accomplish this is by having a staff that takes pride in achieving such performance. They must also be highly committed to the unit and organization. As Nora Dávila and Wanda Piña-Ramirez noted, "Employee engagement is a business's backbone. It is the result of the psychological contract plus the experiences that exists between employees and employer" (2014, 6). We believe there is link between staff engagement and empowered staff. Empowered employees are almost certainly engaged. It is less clear whether engaged staff are necessarily empowered; in the best instances that is most likely true. "Staff engagement" has been something of a management buzzword since the "Great Recession" occurred and this emphasis is, we believe, misplaced. Empowerment leads to engagement and thus to sound productivity. Keep in mind that the research presented suggests that nonprofit and public sector employees are, more often than not, only moderately committed to their place of employment (unlike for-profit employees).

To have either engagement or empowerment, there must be trust in the environment. Obviously, you are unlikely to empower someone you do not trust. Nor is it likely the staff will believe you are empowering them unless they trust you. Trust is part of the contract that Dávila and Piña-Ramirez mentioned as a part of engagement and shared experiences.

Andrew Marshall and Natalie Elghossian opened their article with "The public's trust in government is near all-time lows, but there is another trust issue that gets less attention and is just as important—trust within government itself" (2014, 58). Their article explores the differences between staff members and supervisors' views of how their agency operates. The data showed there was little staff trust of supervisors and a high degree of thinking the supervisors were poor managers. Given that the data were collected in 2013, and given the recent past history of furloughs, salary increase freezes, and the like, it is probably not too surprising there was little staff trust. What was rather surprising was that supervisors thought the operations were fine, almost as if they were looking at a different workplace. There appeared to be little staff engagement—much less empowerment—in many of the units surveyed. We wonder what the results would be with a similar study on public libraries—we suspect they would be more positive as there is likely to be a connection between working in a public agency that the public trusts.

J. Peter Leeds and Doug Nierle, in writing about staff engagement, noted that it is a matter of "connecting"—when connected there may be engagement; lacking a connection will result in no engagement (2014). Since the emphasis on engagement has come to the fore, so has the criticism of the concept from some people. Given the argument here that engagement and empowerment are linked, the criticism that Leeds and Nierle noted in their article must be addressed. The first, and certainly most common, complaint is that it costs too much and has too few positive results to justify developing staff engagement. That may well be true when an organization hires an outside consultant to try to instill the idea into the organizational culture. It is probably less valid if the organization makes the effort itself. The criticism is invalid if the effort is undertaken by an individual manager as part of empowering her or his staff.

A second complaint is there is no single accepted definition of what staff engagement actually is. While that is certainly true, the same can be said of many management concepts, including leadership. As Leeds and Nierle stated, just an organization's internal definition can produce useful outcomes. Yet another criticism is that even when there is strong staff engagement and better productivity, engagement did not necessarily cause that outcome. Correlation and causation are not the same. While engagement may not be the cause (it could be in some cases—think of the long ago Hawthorne plant experiments on employee motivation when any change led to increased productivity when they knew they were being observed), there is a correlation. Even if it has only a very slight effect in terms of causation, why toss the idea out? It can't hurt and just might help.

A fourth criticism is that the effort to develop or increase employee engagement may not result in better productivity. That is a fact for any new initiative an organization undertakes—the outcome is not certain. Perhaps for some individuals that uncertainty may be an adequate reason to not try something new. Not taking a risk, real or perceived, is a good prescription for an organization's eventual demise. The criticism also ignores the fact you can stop the process at any time if it is not generating the desired results.

The final objection to trying to increase staff engagement is that it assumes leaders must reach out and engage personnel. That notion is correct in one sense and totally incorrect in another. If a leader does *not* reach out and engage people, who will she or he actually lead? To us reaching out is a key aspect of being a leader, not something to avoid.

How do you engage and empower your staff? There are a number of steps that individually will add up to a very empowered, engaged, and committed work team. Perhaps the most obvious step is to allow employees as much latitude as possible in how they achieve a particular outcome. In the not too distant past, libraries had a tendency to create procedures for almost all of their operations. Such procedures allowed employees little or no freedom of action. Part of that tendency probably arose from libraries implementing "scientific management" concepts in an effort to show they were being efficient. Certainly time and motion studies and the like can be useful; however, having flexibility in how employees can achieve a desired outcome often generates higher productivity than that in such studies. Being able to personalize how someone achieves a positive outcome makes them feel they have some power over their work. Such feelings are empowering for the person and the work unit.

Related to employees having the freedom to make the decisions about how to perform the work is employees having a solid sense of the goals or desired outcomes for that work. Sharing your vision for your unit and involving the staff in creating changes, as needed, to create that vision is also an empowering step. It is even more empowering when you include all levels of employees in that activity. Sometimes there is a tendency to think this is really a "professional" issue and to not include support staff. Certainly there are issues that are just that—for example, creating a promotion scheme for professionals within a position based on professional growth and development. More often than not the issue can benefit from input from all staff categories. We were once involved in a research project that looked at identifying desired new services for several public libraries. It surveyed library staff (full- and part-time) as well as the service community. The rather surprising outcome of the project was the part-time library staff's assessment of what the community desired mostly matched the community input. The support staff's assessment was the second closest, with the professional staff coming in a distant third. Our point is, don't assume that only one staffing category can have useful input on decisions.

A step related to decision making and vision sharing is to involve all categories of staff in as many of your planning activities as possible. As noted above, professional judgment alone may not be the best approach to planning in some instances. A fact to keep in mind about involving all staff categories in planning, decision making, and so on, is that not everyone is comfortable doing so; however, that does not mean they will be happy about being left out of such activities. An approach we found useful was to have a private conversation with such individuals (it does take shared experiences to identify them) to give them an opportunity to say "no thank you" in private and allow them the sense they had some control or power. Lacking that option, people may well feel pressured to "take part" (i.e., the boss said I should) in the process as an uncomfortable participant and one who does not contribute much or anything to the process. Providing that option also generally means people are more likely to accept the process's outcome. That in turn means, when change is involved, there will be less resistance to the change.

Another empowering step is to make staff training an important issue for your unit. Again that should be for all categories, not just professional. (We look at staff training in more detail in chapter 17.) One ongoing challenge of LIS manager-leaders is the difficulty in securing training funds. Too many times when there is an opportunity to secure some additional funding there are several higher priorities than training that you have to address. However, in the long-term, not keeping the staff up to date, especially in terms of technology, you risk having your unit less and less capable of meeting current requirements.

Authority, power, and influence are primarily managers' prerogatives. However, nonprofit and public sector managers often have boards (advisory and governing) that can and do try to become managers. The next chapter looks at such bodies in some detail.

REFERENCES

Avner, Marcia. 2010. "Advocacy, Lobbying, and Social Change." In *The Jossey-Bass Handbook of Nonprofit Leadership and Management.* 3rd edition. Edited by David O. Renz and Associates. San Francisco, CA: Jossey-Bass, 347–374.

Barnard, Chester I. 1938. *The Functions of the Executive.* Cambridge, MA: Harvard University Press.

Behn, Robert D. 2001. *Rethinking Democratic Accountability.* Washington, DC: Brookings Institution Press.

Cartwright, Dorwin. 1965. "Influence, Leadership, Control." In *Handbook of Organizations.* Edited by James G. Marsh. Chicago, IL: Rand McNally.

Cohen, Steven, William Eimicke, and Tanya Heikkila. 2013. *The Effective Public Manager: Achieving Success in Government Organizations.* 5th edition. San Francisco, CA: Jossey-Bass.

Dávila, Nora, and Wanda Piña-Ramirez. 2014. "What Drives Employee Engagement? It's All About the 'I.'" *Public Manager* 43, no. 1: 6–9.

Handy, Charles. 1995. "Trust and Virtual Organization." *Harvard Business Review* 73, no. 3: 40–50.

Knippenberg, Joseph M. 2007. "Social Experiments, Accountability, and Politics." *Society* 44, no. 3: 32–34.

Leeds, J. Peter, and Doug Nierle. 2014. "Engaging in Healthy Debate over Employee Engagement." *Public Manager* 43, no.4: 61–64.

Marshall, Andrew, and Natalie Elghossain. 2014. "Trust within Government." *Public Manager* 43, no. 4: 58–60.

Michael, Bryane. 2005. "Questioning Public Sector Accountability." *Public Integrity* 7, no. 2 95–109.

Monfardini, Patrizio. 2010. "Accountability in the New Public Sector: A Comparative Case Study." *International Journal of Public Sector Management* 23, no. 7: 632–646.

Perrin, Burt. 2015. "Bringing Accountability Up to Date with the Realities of Public Sector Management in the 21st Century." *Canadian Public Administration* 58, no. 1: 183–203.

Pfeffer, Jeffrey. 1992. *Managing with Power: Politics and Influence in Organizations.* Cambridge, MA: Harvard Business School Press.

Pfeffer, Jeffrey. 2010. *Power: Why Some People Have—and Others Don't.* New York: Harper-Collins.

Russell, Nan S. 2013. "How Titleless Leaders Use Conflict to Get Workplace Results." *Public Manager* 42, no. 1: 70–72.

Webster's. 1966. *Webster's Third New International Dictionary of the English Language: Unabridged.* Springfield, MA: G. & C. Merriam Company.

Chapter 5

ADVISORY AND
GOVERNING BOARDS

Quite frankly, trustees do not belong to the library "tribe." But that is precisely why they are the most important players in the public library arena.

Will Manley, 2012

Making decisions about the future is an important aspect of nonprofit governance; hence, it is vital that this process should be as effective as it can be. The focal point for governance decisions in nonprofit organizations is the board of directors.

Yvonne D. Harrison and Vic Murray, 2014

In the past 40 years, student demographics and governing boards alike have obviously become more diverse.

Rosemary Gillett-Karam, 2013

You (trustees) have to set policies, make sure they are implemented and set checks and balances.

Larry R. Handfield in Reginald Stuart, 2009

Almost every organization has some type of board. In the case of for-profit organizations, board members are elected by shareholders or selected by the organization's most senior managers. It is, as Gretchen Morgenson noted, "Cozy corporate boards, populated by a chief executive's pals, are an all-too-common hazard of investing in a publicly owned company. But rarely do stockholders get an inside look at the ties between board members and the chief executives they are supposed to supervise" (2015, B1). Nonprofit boards usually are elected by their stakeholders and supporters, either directly or indirectly (elected officers become the board).

Public sector boards are almost always appointed, which means some degree of politics is involved in the process.

A brief look at how for-profit boards are supposed to operate can help in understanding how nonprofit and public sector boards also function. In the United States, corporate boards have narrow but important functions. First, as suggested in the Morgenson quotation above, such boards are supposed to assess how well the chief executive officer (CEO) is fulfilling her or his contract obligations; often that oversight extends to the senior management team. The second aspect involves monitoring compliance with laws and regulations related to the company's activities. Finally, and the primary focus of most of today's boards, is how well the firm maximizes shareholder "wealth." The compliance and wealth or fiduciary aspects are standard components of governing boards, regardless of sector.

There are basically two categories of boards: advisory and governing. Although the two categories appear to be clearly differentiated, the fact is that the basic role for a board can, at times, become contentious between some board members and the organization's managers. Libraries utilize both types of boards: academic libraries generally have advisory boards, school libraries have governing boards (school boards), and public libraries may have either or both types. A major difference for boards in the nonprofit and public sector versus for-profit boards is that members are almost always "volunteers" and are not compensated for their board activities.

CHECK THIS OUT

To learn more about for-profit boards, see Razeen Sappideen's 2011 article, "Corporate Governance and the Surrogates of Managerial Performance" (*UNSW Law Journal* 34, no. 1: 136–158).

ROLE OF BOARDS

Richard Chait, William P. Ryan, and Barbara E. Taylor (2004) suggested nonprofit and public sector boards operate in three "modes." The first mode, fiduciary, is similar to for-profit boards with its focus on money and stakeholders. In this case, a nonprofit or public sector board's focus is on the most effective use of the funds available rather than on increasing and protecting stockholders' wealth. The second mode is strategic—assisting or planning how the organization might move forward in a strategic or planned manner. The third mode is generative—essentially thinking "outside the box" for the organization (vision is part of this mode).

Boards, regardless of sector, have three basic legal duties: duty of care, duty of loyalty, and duty of obedience (Renz, 2010). These duties existed before there were federal laws, rules, and regulations affecting various sub-aspects of the duties. The concept of trustee duty arose hundreds of years ago in English common law (circa 1200 CE). Today there are a variety of legal trust issues imposed and enforced by government agencies such as the Internal Revenue Service (IRS).

Duty of care, at its most basic level, means a board member will attend meetings and participate. It is the latter aspect that is the key component of care. If a member is faithful in attendance but does not participate in the proceedings, the person might as well not be present. As a manager working with a board, you want active board member input—positive or negative. When someone is not participating, you might have a talk with the board chairperson about the situation, perhaps even explore the need to replace the person in question. An important reason for having a board is to gain insight into the organization's operations and activities. If you have a five-member board and one person is not contributing, you have lost 20 percent of the board's potential input.

SOMETHING TO PONDER

Something we may not think too much about, but a reality in terms of governing boards and the organizations they oversee, is contained in the following from John Carver: "Governing boards . . . do not exist to help staff, but to own the business—often in trust for some larger ownership. If anyone is helping, it is the staff. Volunteers on governing boards are expressing an *ownership interest* rather than a *helpfulness interest*" (italics in the original) (*Boards That Make a Difference: A New Design for Leadership in Nonprofit and Public Organizations*, 2nd edition. San Francisco, CA: Jossey-Bass, 1997, 14).

Duty of loyalty relates to board members actions and decisions. That is, actions and processes that are in the best interest of the organization, insofar as the board can determine. In other words, a board member, or members, should not benefit directly or indirectly from their actions as board members. That duty is not always as clear-cut as it might appear. For example, a library needs to have some essential repair work done and does not have the funds to pay for the work. What can the board members do to resolve the problem?

In reality, there is a range of possibilities for board members to employ if they encounter the above dilemma. The first option may be a member may simply say she or he will cover the cost to until funds can be found. That option, of a board member stepping up to pay for the work, is no problem, right? Not necessarily—if that board member is a building contractor and he or she later uses the donation in marketing efforts for her or his firm there could be legal concerns related to the loyalty duty. Not likely, but possible. Many of the possible options could go either way. The point is that often the immediacy of a problem and its possible solution can lead to negative consequences down the road unless some thought is given to long-term outcomes.

One way boards handle some aspects of the duties of loyalty and obedience (see below) is to have a conflict-of-interest statement signed by each member. For boards that must file reports with the IRS there is Form 990, which asks about conflict of interest policies, their monitoring, and enforcement. Where many organizations that have such statements go wrong is in the monitoring and enforcement of them. Most of us have signed a document like this sometime during our careers. How often have you actually thought about what you were signing? For a great many board members, the conflict-of-interest statement is just one more form to sign in order to "get on with the real work." In some ways, it's like renting a car, when we don't read, much less understand, the rental contract. Thus, it is not all that surprising that there is little monitoring and even less enforcement conflict-of-interest statements.

CHECK THESE OUT

Why people volunteer or stand for election to be board members varies. However, an interesting article that sheds some light on the subject is Robin Mueller's 2011 "Seeking Election: Evaluating a Campaign for Public School Board Trusteeship" (*Canadian Journal of Education* 34, no. 3: 213–228). Although the context is Canada and reflects its laws, the basics of motivation, and so on, appear to cross borders in character. The references in the article contain a number of U.S.-oriented resources, including some cited in the main text of this chapter.

Another interesting article is Jason A. Grissom's 2009 "The Determinants of Conflict on Governing Boards in Public Organizations: The Case of California School Boards" (*Journal of Public Administration Research and Theory* 20, no. 3: 601–627).

Related to conflicts of interest is the need to have independent members on the board. Independence in this case means board members do not receive any significant benefits from the organization. For many libraries, identifying independent members can be a challenge simply because they can't find enough individuals willing to volunteer. Finding a person to be a trustee is much easier than identifying a person for the Friends group. In part, finding a trustee is easier because there is a small measure of prestige for the person, and little or none in being a member to the Friends board, and because trustees, at least in the public sector, are appointed or elected, which in turn involves some politics. Thus, others are likely to assist in the search for a suitable candidate.

Duty of obedience is an individual board member concern. It means the person supports the organization's vision of purpose, its mission, and its goals. It is a duty that is not much of a concern during the initial creation of the board, but it can be a factor when replacement members are sought or when there is the board expands. There are occasions when a board member or prospective member has an agenda, perhaps kept secret, which would entail a radical change in goals or other organizational purpose of the board, such as removing some organization staff members or board members. You may have clues to such agendas when a board member or prospective member articulates complaints about some aspect of your LIS activities. The notion that getting on the board is a good way to force change is rather common; the challenge is how that is handled—secretly or openly.

You probably thought of at least one challenge that may arise from the obedience duty. There is a good chance you thought, "I don't want a 'yes' board. I want one that challenges our/my ideas in order to achieve the highest quality service for the community." A pliable board is not what the obedience duty means; in fact, it is just the opposite in the sense that the obligation is to the organization—not a person or persons. A "yes" board is probably a greater danger to the long-term well-being of the library than is the board that is almost always opposed to changes and/or new ideas. At the very least, opposing boards cause more thinking and assessment regarding what really is best for the library. Your goal is to reach a middle ground between always "yes" and always "no" and, most importantly, to reach decisions that are, to the best of your and your board's knowledge, in the long-term interest of the library's service community.

Size plays a factor in how independently a board operates; the larger the board, the greater the likelihood that a majority of its members are not independent. As discussed it can be difficult to find volunteers to serve, and the task gets harder the more people you need. The average board size ranges from five to 11 members; library boards almost always fall within that range. Beyond the independence issue, large boards tend to become unwieldy, find it difficult to convene a quorum, and at best are only moderately productive.

CHECK THESE OUT

The Urban Institute has published two useful surveys of nonprofit governance that address the above discussion. The first is Francie Ostrower's 2007 *Nonprofit Governance in the United States* (Washington, DC: Urban Institute, 2007). The second is a follow-on by Amy Blackwood, Nathan Dietz, and Thomas H. Pollak, the 2014 *The State of Nonprofit Governance* (Washington, DC: Urban Institute, 2014).

BOARD RESPONSIBILITIES

Just what are the activities that boards are responsible for executing? Keep in mind that while there is a commonality between advisory and governing board in terms of responsibilities, there is a major difference: governing boards decide while advisory boards recommend. The following are the primary duties of a board:

- Hire the CEO
- Oversee finances
- Set/monitor policy
- Monitor programs
- Monitor board performance
- Assist with community relations
- Influence public policy
- Raise funds
- Aid in planning for the future
- Assess CEO performance
- Serve as a sounding board
- Assist in educational activities
- Protect the organization from undue outside pressure

Fiscal Responsibilities

We touched on fiduciary responsibilities of a board earlier; however, that concept covers a variety of subactivities. For a public library fiduciary responsibilities include providing support for budget requests—both preparation and justification/defense. They may entail monitoring how the library is expending its funds and/or assisting in the allocation of funds received to various programs and services.

Part of any library board's fiduciary activity (advisory or governing) with the library staff occurs throughout the budget cycle. Perhaps a board's key activity in terms of budget requests is asking questions. "Why do you need a new FTE?" "Do you think this project will be successful?" "Will this request distract from the other requests and thus actually be a detriment?" "What is your top priority item?" "Why is this the top priority?" Questions such as these assist the library in generating stronger justifications to use when responding to pointed questions that may arise from those who will actually decide what will or will not be allocated.

This is where it is necessary to discuss boards and their roles in different types of libraries. Although the above list of duties applies to all board types, there are significant differences in how those duties play out in different types of libraries. While school library media centers almost always have a governing board, and academic libraries generally have advisory boards, public libraries are a very mixed bag.

School boards are district-wide and responsible for all school-related activities, including the library media centers (assuming they exist). In any event, the harsh reality is library media centers are often among the first services to be cut when there is a need to reduce costs and among the last to receive increases when economic times improve. Those in charge of such centers have limited contact with their governing boards and thus limited opportunities to influence outcomes—fiscal, policy, and planning in particular. While opportunities for building connections with board members may be limited, librarians in media centers should still try.

In the academic library environment, the label for the group of individuals who have board-like responsibilities varies, for example, "senate faculty library committee" and "campus library advisory committee." These bodies may not have the final say on matters; however, their views and recommendations on issues do matter. It is a very foolish library staff that ignores such a group's thoughts on policies and planning matters. Listening thoughtfully to such input is essential in terms of community relations. Most academic library bodies are composed of faculty members (if not completely so), and the majority of them are classroom instructors. (All board members regardless of type of library do reflect a library's service community, as we noted in the above list of responsibilities.) Such groups can be a powerful advocate for the library on many issues, not just in terms of financial support, assuming the relationship between the library and the board is positive. (For the balance of this chapter, given the variety of labels, we will simply employ "advisory board," as the bodies do function in an advisory capacity and have the same duties as an "official" advisory board. Additionally, the literature refers to boards being either advisory or governing in character.)

AUTHOR EXPERIENCE AND ADVISORY BOARD EXPERIENCE

As noted above, there are a variety of names for academic library advisory bodies. For example, Evans had "Overseers" at Harvard. At other institutions, there were a faculty senate library committee (faculty only), a campus library advisory committee (representatives from the faculty senate, student senate, support staff senate a trustee, and a member of the institution's community relations group), and a "library committee."

Camila Alire, a member of our advisory board, contributed the following thoughts about advisory such bodies. "In the three university libraries I headed, they were called library advisory committees or faculty senate advisory committees. I did have, however, a library foundation advisory board in two of the three libraries, which were made up of community members (usually of some stature or reputation) and faculty members—all of whom I invited. The library advisory committees, whom I invited, were faculty and a few students. The Faculty Senate Library advisory committee was appointed by faculty senate—advised the library and reported to the senate. We were always very careful not to call the academic library group a board because the faculty would think that they had "governing" power and could dictate to the academic library what to do and not do."

Alire's last point is important as there can be confusion on the part of some individuals on advisory bodies about what their role actually is—advisory rather than decision making.

When it comes to public library boards, the picture varies. Some have governing boards, some have advisory boards, and a few have a combination of the two. The type is almost always a matter of state laws and regulations; for example, a city library can have a board that is part of the local government—in this case the board is advisory—or the board may be independent—resulting in a governing board. In the instance of a governing board, it is the co-requestor when it comes to budget requests. County public libraries are similar and can have either governing or independent boards, again depending on state laws and regulations. In all of the above, library funding is from the general fund of its political jurisdiction. Another variation comes in the form of library districts, where the board is governing and has direct taxing power. Yet another variation is a consortium of libraries in which the consortium has a board (governing in terms of the consortium activities), as do the member libraries.

CHECK THIS OUT

An informative article about getting the best from public library trustee boards is Maria R. Traska's "Building a Better Board of Trustees" in the November/December 2015 issue of *American Libraries* (46, nos. 11/12: 32–37).

No matter the type of board, it is generally the library staff that generates the draft budget. The reason being is that boards are not, or should not be, micromanagers; they do not have the detailed information that is needed to generate a draft request that reflects the actual needs. However, a governing board develops the final request and presents it to the funding body, along with the senior library manager.

Monitoring fiscal activities, or at least making recommendations about expenditures, is a normal ongoing board activity. In academic libraries, faculty/student advisory committees review budget allocations for collection building. In the cases where funds are allocated to teaching departments, the board works out a formula for such allocations. Gaining campus-wide support for the process is best handled by the advisory board, rather than by the library trying to do it independently. Making use of the board's monitoring responsibly is a great asset in terms of avoiding negative outcomes from fiscal audits that are required from time to time. The board may also become aware of stakeholders' concerns about how the library uses the funds it does possess. A board member or two may have picked up on such concerns through interactions with the service community. An early warning allows the library and the board to review the concerns and make adjustments prior to the concern(s) becoming a major kerfuffle.

When a library is looking to raise additional funds through grants, gifts (cash and in kind), and bequests, boards can be very useful in securing additional funds, assuming the library has a strong positive relationship with board members. (Libraries, regardless of type, never have enough allocated funds to do everything they would like to do or do it as well as they would like. This is why donations are important.) Board members may know of untapped resources, act as a sounding board for grant ideas, assist in the preparation of a request, and in some cases even be a source of modest amounts of money. Of course, board members must understand the nature of the Internal Revenue Service (IRS) regulations that apply to their organization (the IRS has a variety of tax-exempt classifications with different sets of requirements).

It is not unheard of for funding authorities to want, hope, or expect that monies raised from "outside" sources result in a reduction from the amount of funding they have to provide. Some business and finance officers in academic institutions reduce the library allocation by the amount of money they expected the library to generate from charges for services (printing and photocopying, for example) over the budget cycle. The biggest challenge is when the library begins to develop a meaningful endowment (something in excess of $500,000) or when there is a major bequest. The individuals who make such gifts generally believe the gift will *supplement* the funding, not act as a *replacement* of normal operating funds.

A key to addressing the above potential problem is the content of the gift agreement document. Most major gifts require such a document to spell out the donor's wishes in some detail. The challenge is to have the terms specific enough to cover the donor's desires and yet flexible enough to handle a changing future environment. This is not easy, but it is possible. The gift agreement document should include clauses that address issues such as the discontinuation of the desired activity, perhaps a summer reading program or bookmobile service. Such events are unlikely but could occur; the problem is once the monies are given they will not be returned in the event of the closure of the intended activity. Based on personal experience in this area, having a clause or two spelling out where the funds might be used in such circumstances is the best protection for long-term donor wishes.

More broadly, when a library endowment is created the best approach is to document legally how the endowment funds may be used. Thus, having a legal document that specifies that funds are only supplemental in nature is the best protection against political winds creating unwanted turbulence. Again, there is no ironclad guarantee funds can't be diverted—what happens if the library is closed permanently? The answer is the funds go to the library's parent organization.

A rare, but important fiscal activity is assisting and planning of a bond or capital campaign. (Today a capital campaign is much more common than it was even 20 years ago; the increase in frequency is a reflection of the economic times.) This is another area where understanding the library's IRS status comes into play, as many categories do not allow for political activity such as using board funds to influence voters. Most boards have members who work as volunteers—can they engage in political activities in support of the organization's bond issue process as a private citizen? The answer is dependent on the organization's IRS status.

Policy Setting

It is a truism that policies are both more and less specific than they could be. As John Carver stated, "No matter how broad a policy is, it is always *more specific* than if it had not been said and *less specific* than it might have been" (italics in the original, 1997, 40). Boards should always start at the highest and least specific level in terms of policy. Becoming highly specific becomes a form of micromanagement—something few boards are capable of doing well.

Policy-setting duties cover the full range of policy activities—from formulation and assessment, to replacement or abandonment. This is an area where boards and library staff may come into conflict. That is, who controls formulation of policy? There are times when advisory boards think they should have that responsibility, at least on certain topics. There are also times when a library director believes the board should leave policy making on certain topics to the library. When there is a positive relationship between board and library, this rarely becomes a critical issue. When it does, it is very often the result of a new person (board member or director) coming into the picture. Again, in the best situations, the notion that a policy may be necessary, or needs to be adjusted or dropped arises from the library staff.

Any policy, as suggested in the above Carver quotation, allows for some range of decision making or action. In other words it is open to interpretation. When board and staff members have differing views of just what that range may be, problems can arise. Even advisory boards can and do raise questions about why this or that did or did not happen.

Perhaps the most common areas in which differences arise are in terms of collection content and collections usage, especially in public and school libraries. Although less common for academic libraries, it is not unheard of to have some faculty members try to have the advisory board change a policy, such as loan period or recall period, to something they favor. In some cases, the person may even manage to become a board member in hopes of affecting the policy.

Why are public and school libraries more susceptible to policy differences in this area? Perhaps the major reason relates to children; that is, protecting them from inappropriate materials. That need seems most appropriate in the general abstract sense. The question is, who decides what is and is not appropriate? From a professional point of view, a key tenant of the profession is stated in American Library Association's (ALA's) document *Freedom to Read* (1953; 2004). A board may believe its duty is to protect children and, thus, find the ALA position unacceptable. In the school library environment, the board is a governing board and entitled to make policy. The same is true for public libraries that have governing boards. When the board generates a strict policy limiting what people can read or what can be in the collection, some professionals may become conflicted. Follow the policy or the professional standard with the unstated but implied issue of employment status.

What services are offered to various classes of users is another policy area that requires thoughtful cooperation between the library and its board. Advisory boards can hold opinions just as strong as a governing board when it comes to what classes of users there may be as well as which class has access to what services. A classic area of concern is interlibrary loan services—do undergraduates have access? What about middle school students? In the case of a public library with reciprocal borrowing agreements, should that agreement extend to "outside" borrowers?

Even in today's digital environment, InterLibrary Loan is a labor-intensive activity from the library's perspective. The more limited that service is means the more time, even a little, the staff will have for other services. Deciding where to draw the line is not as simple as some people might think. There are often political factors to think about when drawing the line: making the library users happy means more supporters at budget request time. Expanding the service may also prove useful in securing outside funding. These are a few of the factors that may come into play and also apply to many of the services a library offers.

There are some basics regarding policymaking to keep in mind, regardless of what type of board with which you are working. First and foremost is to ensure the policy will not conflict with existing policies of the parent organization, and then to ensure it is congruent with existing library policies. It is surprisingly easy to forget to check these potential conflicts before the policy is implemented and problems arise. Next, and seemingly rather obvious as well, is to ensure the policy reflects the library's mission, value, and vision statements. Again, hurrying a new policy through the approval process can lead to overlooking this step. If there is a conflict, something must be adjusted. Related to this is how the proposed policy fits into existing plans and activities, as well as existing laws and regulations. One example of such an issue involved what was a standard practice: public libraries with branch locations employed a base allocation level for all branches, and then provided supplemental funds based on collection utilization (more circulation = more money). It came as a surprise when the courts ruled this approach could be, and in a specific case was, a violation of the U.S. Civil Rights Act and the state constitution. The point is that legal connections and implications are not always readily apparent and some thinking about long-term outcomes may be very useful.

When it comes to long-range planning, decision making, and the like, the activities follow basically the same pattern as policy making. That is, broad-based planning is the prerogative of the governing board with library input and just the reverse for advisory boards.

A final point about polices and planning in relation to governing boards: boards are, or should be, reflective of the library's service community and should not have any library staff as voting members other than the director (often as an ex-officio member), at least on governing boards. Certainly staff members may be called upon to present materials or respond to board members' questions, but they should not vote. Having library staff as voting members defeats the basic notion of independence that was covered earlier in this chapter. On the other hand, advisory boards, especially in an academic setting, may include both a librarian and a support staff member entitled to vote on issues. Having such members can provide a more varied picture of a library issue for the other board members.

The point we wish to make is most board members are not librarians and very often do not share the values of the profession. Thus, you should not be surprised when serious differences of opinion arise from time to time.

CHECK THIS OUT

Board policy making in any organization is a challenge; in the case of libraries, there is the challenge that none of the members have a background in the field they are to help guide. Personal and professional values can collide from time to time. One book that helps address the issue of library policy making is James C. Baughman's *Policy Making for Public Library Trustees* (Englewood, CO: Libraries Unlimited, 1993).

Meetings

Meetings, meetings, and more meetings: meetings are a fact of organizational and managerial life. We suspect that if you ask a dozen or more library managers, regardless of level, to list the three most time consuming activities that they have to engage in, attending meetings would be at least second, if not first, place. Yes, meetings are, at times, necessary, but unfortunately not all meetings are created equal. Goodness knows that boards are compelled to meet. It is the rare board, governing or advisory, which does not have a set of bylaws (or committee charge in the case of academic libraries) that spell out at least a few some mandatory meetings (if nothing more there will be an annual meeting).

If you ask people to rate the value or productivity of meetings on a scale of one to five, with five being highly productive, we suspect the average rating would be around three. Probably everyone has attended a few meetings, even mandatory ones, and come away shaking their heads asking themselves, "Why was that necessary?" Every group or organization has such less productive meetings along with an occasional "What's the point?" type. The discussion that follows, while applicable to all meetings, is focused on board meetings.

Board members are almost always volunteers in some sense. Thus, wasting their time in unproductive meetings is a mistake for several reasons. First, unproductive meetings make a person wonder "Do I *really* need to give my time and effort to this organization?" Second, they may make it harder to find replacements should a dissatisfied member depart (the word does get out). Third, finding a time when everyone can meet (there is that nasty need to have a quorum in order to conduct board business) is often a challenge, and when members have doubts about the need or value of a meeting, the challenge becomes even greater.

There are some very basic concepts regarding having a successful meeting regardless of organizational context. We think the first, and most important, step in calling a meeting is thinking long and hard about whether having a meeting is truly necessary. One pitfall for managers is to have regularly scheduled meetings that lack the option to cancel it when there is no "real" business to transact. Such meetings waste time, build frustrations, and hurt morale. We are not suggesting regular meetings are unnecessary, far from it. A good practice is to have a set time to meet, especially with those who report to you, *if* there is a need. Then, block out a time, just in case.

When it comes to governing boards, there may be mandatory meetings required by state or local laws, or by the board's bylaws. Even mandatory meetings do not have to fill the time available just because there is a stated timeframe. Few individuals object to getting out of a meeting early. A bigger challenge is when the issue is complex and more time is needed. Again, as volunteers, board members have booked other activities starting after the board meeting's stated time period. The reality is such individuals value their time, perhaps more so than library employees.

When a meeting is needed, careful planning and preparation are a must, if the session is to be productive. In our experience, it is better to limit the number of topics to cover in a single meeting. Too many topics may leave participants frustrated because discussions were too hurried or because a topic of interest did not get discussed for lack of time. Either way, the frustration may well carry over to the next meeting. Even the timeframe for the meeting can generate issues. One way to handle the time and topic concerns is to think about the nature of the topic(s), who plans to attend, and what their views may be about the topic(s). The more differences in opinion that are anticipated mean fewer topics and a longer timeframe.

You might think you have full control over who will attend a meeting. You'd be wrong, at least occasionally, especially when it comes to governing boards. Even in the case of advisory boards you may get a request from someone who is not a board member to attend a scheduled meeting. That can also happen with an internal organizational meeting, especially standing committee sessions. In the case of advisory boards and internal organizational meetings you will have the ability to say yes or no to the requests.

When it comes to public library governing boards, you must say yes to a request 99 percent of the time, and you should expect that some individuals may just randomly show up. All states have "open meeting" laws for government bodies, which include governing library boards. These laws specify that a meeting announcement be made available. The notices normally must give the time, place, and meeting agenda. Such laws also specify how far in advance the notice must appear. Most meetings are very boring for anyone who doesn't have to be there—we all know that. As a result, most governing board meetings only have the required people in attendance. However, you might expect a reporter or two along with some citizens to be present when topics such as budgets, director searches, building remodeling, new buildings, cuts in activities, or service hour issues are on the agenda. Open meeting laws require such attendees to be accommodated, with seating, copies of agendas, any relevant reports, and the like. The only exception to the "openness" requirements is when confidential matters such as personnel are covered (executive sessions).

Preparations for a meeting really do not vary because of meeting type—boards or organizational. Preparations do, in fact, add to the meeting effectiveness. Issues such as seating arrangements and climate control play a surprising role in how well the meeting works. Something as simple as how the seating is arranged says something about what is expected even before anyone is present—what does a "classroom" arrangement versus a circle of chairs say to attendees? A room that is too hot or too cold will have people thinking about temperature rather than the issue being discussed. Time spent during the meeting trying to get the temperature to an acceptable level wastes valuable time. Check it out well in advance.

When you have an invited presenter, ask about any possible media or technology needs. Questions at the start of meeting such as "Is there an Internet connection available?" wastes everyone's time. Examine things well in advance in case you have to find a different room. Long meetings often have one or two built-in break periods; if drinks or snacks are part of the plan, check and double check with the supplier and what their needs may be. Not doing so can waste still more valuable time. These are just some of the major preparation activities needed to help assure a successful meeting.

There are other steps in achieving a productive meeting, such as identifying who does what, having an expected timeframe for each issue on the agenda, and sending an agenda out to attendees in advance of the meeting asking for additions or changes. This will allow time for feedback from participants regarding timeframes and topics. If there is no recorder position for the meeting, select someone, with his or her consent, in advance. Trying to get a volunteer at the meeting just wastes time. One effective method for handling board meetings is to split the agenda items between discussion topics and decision items. Doing that can, assuming you establish that a topic is discussed at one meeting and any needed decisions are taken at the next meeting, lead to productive meetings.

There are some dos and don'ts for board meetings, starting with recognizing when the discussion is getting into micromanaging territory. Boards should not manage, much less micromanage. Any meeting, not just a board meeting, can fall into the trap of discussing trivial issues, at times at some length. In this case, meeting chairs need to call a halt to such discussions. There are occasions when a trivial issue gets officially added to the agenda, as normally any board member may add an item. An effective technique to manage meeting time is to have a timeframe associated with each agenda item when the final version goes to attendees.

A danger for boards is they easily become focused on short-term issues and solutions and become reactive instead of proactive. This happens in part because the concerns raised by library staff often tend to focus on the now rather than on the future. Almost any meeting that has an ongoing meeting schedule can fall into another common trap of time wasting; however, boards are particularly susceptible to spending more time rehashing, revisiting, and reviewing past concerns than on looking to the future. Based on our experiences, it is usually only one of the members that cause this to happen; regardless, this one individual can derail the meeting. Also based on past experiences, short of getting the individual off the board or committee, it is hard to keep the person fully in check, and valuable meeting time is wasted.

To summarize, make meetings count and avoid wasting time by being prepared, having an agenda and sticking to it, and being respectful of others' time. Focus on the critical and high priority topics. Spend time planning and preparing for every meeting. Be certain there is an actual need to meet; don't fall into the trap of "we are meeting today because it is the time to meet."

CHECK THESE OUT

There are any number of books and articles related to how to handle meetings. Two titles that we have found useful are:

Charlie Hawkins's *Make Meetings Matter: Ban Boredom, Control Confusion, and Terminate Time-Wasting* (Franklin Lakes, NJ: Career Press, 2008); and

Jeremy Comfort and Derek Utley's *Effective Meetings* (Oxford: Oxford University Press, 2005).

UNDERSTANDING BOARD RELATIONSHIPS

Members of any type of board have several relationships to consider. Each relationship is important but for different reasons. Each one calls for slightly different approaches in order to create and maintain positive relationships for the library. Significant board member relationships include:

- Senior manager
- Funding authorities
- Donors
- Library staff
- Politicians
- Community members

Senior Manager Relationships

Probably the most challenging of the above relationships is the first one in the list—senior manager. In the best of all possible worlds, this relationship is based on trust and respect. That is close to the real-world library environment—perhaps not absolutely perfect but very workable.

As we noted earlier in the chapter, governing boards are expected to assess the senior manager's performance, hire such individuals, and, on occasion, fire them. For governing boards, the end of the hiring process involves establishing the performance expectations and goals for the new director. In many instances, this takes the form of a contract. Such contracts may spell out the timeframe duration—five years is a fairly common time period. That is long enough for the new person to establish herself or himself and a reasonable period for the board to decide if the fit is still appropriate.

Part of the challenge in assessing a senior manager's performance by a board lies in the question of who has what power to do what. At what time does proper board oversight activity cross the line into managing and/or micromanaging? The reverse also can occur when the senior manager attempts to take over the board's authority. One of the important mechanisms for avoiding such issues is the document that was, or should have been, signed by both parties when the director was hired. You see examples of such relationship issues rather frequently in organizations that own newspapers and magazines.

One such example of the above occurred in Arizona in 2015 when the Superintendent of Schools (an elected office) tried to fire two employees of the Board of Education (appointed) because she had differing views about basic educational policy for the state. Eventually the case ended in court when a judge ruled that it is the Board that sets policy and controls those individuals it employs, not the Superintendent (*Daily Sun*, 2015). You'll find more than a few news articles in the library press on board–director differences of opinion escalating into lawsuits and occasionally the firing of a director.

Mary Moore, in her book for library trustees, made an important point about the assessment of directors by trustee boards: "Many people in library administration received only cursory management training in library school. They need additional training and professional development on the job" (2010, 13). Moore is more or less correct in the sense that not all accredited schools require a basic management course. She is less correct when suggesting many have cursory management training. Like many other managers in the nonprofit or public sector, most librarians learn to manage on the job.

In a report on middle management training for academic librarians, Michael Rooney concluded that "Overall, the current state of management preparation, training, and development . . . is quite strong in several areas, but lacking in some ways as well" (2010, 392). His first table (385) delineated categories of "formal management training" that a department head received when first being appointed to a middle management post. Most unit heads, 77 percent, had taken at least one management course in a library science program. While that percentage is encouraging, it also means that 23 percent had no such background. Perhaps those individuals were part of the 58 percent who reported that they had participated in a management workshop or seminar. Ten percent indicated they had taken coursework in a business or public administration program. Just 4 percent had been in a management internship or fellowship program.

Because Rooney's study focused on academic libraries, the data may be more positive than had he studied public or school librarians. However, it would be most unlikely that any person selected for a directorship had had no front line or middle management experience. Why does it matter if the library director has formal training in management? There are two main reasons. First, while some people do succeed in managing without a formal background, the people they manage may pay a high price in terms of stress and burnout, resulting in a high staff turnover rate (the main responsibility of management is being able to relate to and manage people, not things). The second reason is that most of the management literature you encounter focuses on for-profit organizations. You may well hear something like, "Management is management regardless of organizational setting." As this book suggests, the sector setting does matter in very significant ways.

The challenge for library directors and governing boards is to realize the management sector does matter. It is rather often the case that library boards have at least one member who is a business owner with years of experience. In the best instances, those individuals recognize sector issues do influence how managers operate and do not assume their managerial background will translate well in a nonprofit or public sector organization. This matters when it comes to both setting performance expectations and when assessing directors' actual performance.

CHECK THIS OUT

A lighthearted but to-the-point book about the relationship between library trustees and library directors is Will Manley's book *For Library Directors Only: Talking About Trustees; For Library Trustees Only: Living With Your Director* (Jefferson, NC: McFarland, 1993).

Relationships with Library Staff

The second most challenging relationship is that with the library staff. Depending on the community's size, the chances are moderately high that one or more of the staff members know someone on the board in some context outside the library. If there is friendship involved, the relationship becomes, or can become, problematic. Discretion by both parties is, of course, essential.

There are often complaints from staff to the board. The common type is about a supervisor or the director, in the case of governing boards. Keep in mind, such boards only have oversight of the director, thus, supervisory issues are not within the board's purview. A more serious type of staff concern, and one that is delicate to handle, is when the staff raise concerns about their lack of input in terms of board decisions, which, in almost all cases, have the director's input. There is a very fine line between oversight and micromanaging. The obvious answer is for you to be proactive and gather staff input prior to providing the library perspective to the board. That is just good leadership, board or no board.

Another delicate situation is when the board receives a complaint from the user community regarding a staff member. You should take ownership of the issue and do your best to keep the board out of how you resolve the matter. A few board members can challenge your right to handle the matter and/or require you to report on how you settled the issue. Public employee policies, union contracts, and the like, may limit your options for handling the situation to options that a board member may object to and he or she may demand something else be done. This is a time when solid board–director relationships are essential.

Relationships beyond the Library

Members of any type of board can and should be a voice of and for the library in the greater community. That community is composed of a number of subgroups as suggested above—some as users, others as actual and potential sources of financial support.

Relationships with funding agencies are very important for boards, as they have a fiduciary duty. There is always the body that grants the basic operating income for the library—the group that approves the annual budget. The board may be the requesting body, in the case of a governing board, or supportive, in the case of an advisory board. In either case, the board may engage in "lobbying" throughout a fiscal year; we suggest that this should be done in a coordinated effort with the library director. Library directors and board members working in a joint fashion are much more likely to be successful in gaining needed resources than if they operate independently.

Boards, advisory or governing, have three broad types of relationships with non-library groups: advocacy, lobbying, and outreach. These three terms, although connected to a small degree, are very different. Those differences are significant for libraries and their boards. One example is that the IRS has very strict rules regarding the difference between advocacy and lobbying activities of any organization with nonprofit status. Lobbying is making an effort to influence the outcomes of some legislation, law, regulation, rule, and so on, whether it is a matter of adoption, modification, or implementation. Advocacy, on the other hand, relates to efforts to influence how policies, programs, activities, and the like are interpreted.

IRS rules relating to lobbying and advocacy apply to both library staff and board members. Everyone needs to understand the difference in the two activities, including where those activities may legally take place. Gaining that understanding is not always straightforward. Is proposed legislation that would change an existing policy being approached from an advocacy or lobbying perspective? The only safe answer is to seek legal advice before taking any action.

Outreach is both a marketing activity and programmatic for a library. The line between advocacy and marketing outreach can be blurry at times. Keith Simmons and Kent Oliver, in writing about the role of library trustees as a means of connecting with the library's service community, noted "The library can serve only if it understands the needs of the community, and the engaged trustee must be the eyes and ears of the library in the community. The trustee who has maximum commerce with the community is the trustee that can best inform the library's role and the performance of that role" (2012, 25).

We certainly agree with the basic sense of the above statement—trustees can inform the library about its service community. However, in our view, that information must supplement the library's proactive efforts to understand the community, not be the sole source. There are several reasons for that view. First, not all trustees are in fact engaged beyond their meeting attendance. Second, in almost all cases, trustees are not paid but rather volunteer their time—such people have a variety of obligations and not all of them relate to the library. Third, trustees may not be aware of the library's full capabilities or what is taking place in libraries elsewhere. (In chapter 7, we explore in some depth how the library must actively monitor its service community and operational environment.)

Everyone, board members and library staff, can and ought to follow some basic communication steps when interacting with politicians and the public. First, and most basic, don't assume the individual you are communicating with knows very much about the library. Second, a few people are impressed by statistics (collection size, number of borrowers, etc.); many more are not. The reality is, numbers do little to convey what the library does and its impact on its service population. Use such information sparingly and with caution. Needless to say, be certain about such data; some people, especially politicians, have an impressive ability to remember earlier statement and numbers. Their long memory, particularly when they believe they have been misinformed, misled, and so on, can come back to haunt the library. A good way to communicate such data is on the library's website, assuming you keep it up to date. When appropriate, merely refer people to the page(s), should they be interested.

Regardless of the communication situation—one-on-one, small group, social, or formal presentation—be certain of exactly what your message should be and prepare it thoughtfully. The communication Ps discussed in chapter 3 are the starting point. You might want to consider adding another P—personalization. Connecting is a key factor and personalizing a message, when appropriate, helps maintain connections.

When communicating orally with officials and politicians it is wise to have something in writing as well. Paper trails are very useful for a variety of reasons; one reason is to establish what was covered and said. Memos such as "To summarize our discussion of—" or "Attached are the documents we discussed" help establish a document trail that counteracts miscommunication. One element that helps solidify their value is an ending sentence along the following lines: "If there is some misunderstanding about what we covered, please let me know by [date]."

Being upbeat, positive, and enthusiastic is generally a good idea, but especially when discussing library programs, services, and activities. Being defensive, or suggesting anything less than enthusiasm for the library, will generally "lose the day" in terms of influence or ensuring positive outcome. When it comes to budget requests, spend some time looking for weak points that might be raised by the funding body, especially those that might put you on the defensive. Develop ideas about how to handle such an event and even try to find ways to go on the offense.

Keeping in touch (connected) with key people outside the library is important for several reasons. First, doing so helps keep the library in the mind of key players with political influence and funding authority. Second, it helps maintain connections already made and often strengthens them. Third, it can assist in fundraising by developing current and potential donors. One approach we found useful was to invite such individuals to significant library events, including holiday parties. Most of those individuals did not attend more than one or two events; however, some rarely missed an event. Did their attendance increase library resources? There is no way to know that it did; what is rather certain is that their attendance did not hurt. We are on the board of a public library friends group that gives an annual award (Copper Quill) to a local author. Among the invitees to the award ceremony are local political figures. Has that helped the library? Again, who knows with any certainty—but it probably has not hurt.

AUTHOR EXPERIENCE

The Flagstaff City–Coconino County Public Library holds its Copper Quill event annually to honor a local author. This is a great opportunity to connect with local politicians and to advocate for the library. Held at a local restaurant, the event also provides a chance for attendees to socialize and network in a low-key environment. Many well-known authors, city and county officials, and library staff attend the event and get to see firsthand how important the library is and how influential the library can be.

ASSESSMENT

Library boards should engage in at least two types of assessment: library performance and board performance. For example, academic library advisory boards can assist the library in documenting positive library "outcomes." Outcomes have become a major concern for regional accreditation agencies as part of their interest in institutional accountability. Almost every academic institution (private and public) seeks regional accreditation and libraries are almost always a major component in the assessment of institutional quality. Many members of the board, if not all, are faculty members who may be able to identify, plan, and implement activities that will aid in the library's efforts to document outcomes. As noted earlier in this chapter, governing boards have a duty to assess both the director (hire and fire) and library operations. Their assessments can play a role in the outcome of their library's budget requests, among other things.

Effective boards also engage in self-evaluation. In our experience, this is something some board members have difficulty doing and often don't perceive as necessary. (We should point out that 99 percent of G. Edward Evans's board experience as a director was with advisory boards.) Yvonne D. Harrison and Vic Murray (2014), in writing about board self-evaluation made the following point, "One of the practices that have been linked to improvement of governance effectiveness is board evaluation" (see Gazley and Bowers, 2013; Herman and Renz, 2004, 2).

Assessment techniques for boards are the same as for other assessment activities (see chapter 8 for a detailed discussion of assessment). What is somewhat different is why such efforts may be necessary as well as useful. One obvious reason is when there are "issues" between board members, such as mistrust or factions. A related reason is when there is a sense the board is underperforming or performing poorly.

When the political environment is volatile or highly complex, it may be time to assess board skills in order to navigate effectively in such a turbulent environment. Then there is a very sound reason that solid boards engage in self-assessment— "let's see how well we are doing." Highly effective organizations engage in self-assessment as it helps assure that all is well and on the desired track.

There are a number of board assessment tools on the market. One such tool is the "Nonprofit Board of Directors Assessment Tool" (http://www.joangarry.com /board-assessment-tool/). The Nonprofit Association of Oregon has also posted a PDF of a board assessment tool on its website, www.nonprofitoregon.org. Another resource is Board Source, a membership association of nonprofit organizations (https://www.boardsource.org). It provide three types of board assessment tools:

- Board Self-Assessment (BSA) survey gathers feedback from individual board members and measures the collective performance of the board.
- Peer-to-Peer Assessment (P2P) survey asks board members to evaluate their individual performance and that of their peers to learn how the performance and culture of the full board is affected by the style and engagement of its individual members.
- Diversity and Inclusion Assessment (D&I) educates and assesses the board's progress in implementing diversity and inclusion practices and policies.

A cursory search can turn up many more online resources that provide assessment templates. The key is to evaluate and assess often, regardless of the tool used.

CHECK THIS OUT

A relatively recent book that addresses board governance and relationships is Cathy A. Trower's *The Practitioner's Guide to Governance as Leadership: Building High-Performing Nonprofit Boards* (San Francisco, CA: Jossey-Bass, 2013).

In 2013, Mary Rzepczynski published an article that reviewed the public library trustee environment, "The Survey Says" (*Public Libraries* 52, no. 5: 10–12).

REFERENCES

American Library Association. 1953; amended 2004. *The Freedom to Read Statement*. http:// www.ala.org/advocacy/intfreedom/statementspols/freedomreadstatement.

Carver, John. 1997. *Boards That Make a Difference: A New Design for Leadership in Nonprofit and Public Organizations*. 2nd edition. San Francisco, CA: Jossey-Bass.

Chait, Richard P., William P. Ryan, and Barbara E. Taylor. 2004. *Governance as Leadership*. New York: Wiley.

Daily Sun Staff. 2015. "Douglas Loses Board of Ed Control Suit." *Daily Sun*, Wednesday July 15: A3.

Gazley, Beth, and Ashley Bowers. 2013. *What Makes High-Performing Boards: Effective Governance Practices in Member-Serving Organizations*. Washington, DC: ASAE Foundation.

Gillett-Karam, Rosemary. 2013. "The Future-Shaping Function of the Governing Board." *New Directions for Community Colleges* 162: 37–44.

Handfield, Larry R. 2009. In Reginald Stuart, "Assignments Getting Tougher for Trustees." *Diverse Issues in Higher Education* 26, no. 14: 28–30.

Harrison, Yvonne D., and Vic Murray, 2014. "The Effect of an Online Self-Assessment Tool for Nonprofit Board Performance." *Nonprofit and Voluntary Sector Quarterly* 43, no. 5:1–23.

Herman, Robert D., and David O. Renz. 2004. "Doing Things Right: Effectiveness in Local Nonprofit Organizations, A Panel Study." *Public Administration Review* 64, no. 6: 694–704.

Manley, Will. 2012. "Trust in Your Trustees: Politicians Prefer Your Board's View on Library Needs Over Yours." *American Libraries* 43, nos. 11–12: 64.

Moore, Mary Y. 2010. *The Successful Library Trustee Handbook.* 2nd edition. Chicago, IL: American Library Association.

Morgenson, Gretchen. 2015. "Dish's Chief, and Buddies On the Board." *New York Times, Sunday Business* July 12: B1.

Renz, David O. 2010. "Leadership, Governance, and the Work of the Board." In *Jossey-Bass Handbook of Nonprofit Leadership and Management.* 3rd edition. Edited by David O. Renz. San Francisco, CA: Jossey-Bass.

Rooney, Michael. 2010. "The Current State of Middle Management Preparation, Training, and Development in Academic Libraries." *Journal of Academic Librarianship* 36, no. 5: 383–393.

Simmons, Keith, and Kent Oliver. 2012. "Library Trustees as Community Connectors." *National Civic Review* 101, no. 4: 24–26.

Chapter 6

VISION, MISSION, PLANNING, AND STRATEGY

When writers have tried to divine the future and how it will affect the library's role in society, a number of strong forces have come together. Their notions of the future have been shaped by how they understand the past, what gains they believe they had won, and what dreams remain unfulfilled.

Hal B. Grossman, 2011

A vision statement, a leader's articulation of where the plan should take the organization, is also pivotal to a strategic plan.

Michael A. Germano and Shirley M. Stretch-Stephenson, 2012

Because politically driven policy processes define the goals of public organizations . . . managers have no choice; they must establish and instill a vision and operational path for their organization.

Steven Cohen, William Eimicke, and Tanya Heikkila, 2013

You have probably read Lewis Carroll's *Alice in Wonderland* or have come across a reference to it in a discussion about planning. Such references relate to Alice's quest for direction; because she lacks a specific goal, she is told that any direction will do. Most of us have probably worked in at least one organization that, if not directionless, was doing no more than drifting along with the changing tides. Any organization like that may survive but it will not prosper; a library doing that will fail to serve its users effectively. A good leader will have a clear idea or vision of where the organization ought to go. Library directors and their boards are the keys to establishing the best direction for the library. The topics we cover in this chapter, while different, are closely linked—mission and vision will drive the planning and goal setting processes in any effective organization. Those in turn should drive strategic activities and plans.

Something to keep in mind is vision, mission, and plans should not be static; they must evolve along with their environment. Thus, today's direction is likely to become different tomorrow. Mission statements may periodically be revised, but the purpose that was identified when the library was created does not change very often. Keep in mind almost all libraries exist on the basis of a legal document that specifies a purpose. Library missions are, or should be, directly linked to the mission of the organization that created it. Vision statements must change relatively often as the environment evolves and as people come and go. As suggested in the first quotation for this chapter, they are also, in fact, shaped to some extent by how we view the past.

Unlike their for-profit counterparts, nonprofit and public sector managerial leaders have constraints on their range of vision and mission. Those constraints in turn impact their planning and goal setting activities. As Hal Rainey in writing about strategic management noted, "The public organizations followed a 'vortex-sporadic' decision making process. This involves more turbulence, more shifting participation by a greater diversity of internal and external interests, more delays and interruptions, and more formal and informal interaction among participants" (2014, 197). Indeed, public sector agencies have a wide variety of stakeholders, all of whom, from time to time, seek to have a voice in decision making. For libraries, most stakeholder groups want a voice in almost all decisions related to services and programs.

The need to involve a number of "participants" constrains library staff and library boards in what the library vision and mission will be. Sometimes the discussions of what should be in a final document can be a tad chaotic, if not vortex-sporadic. John Bryson, in his classic work *Strategic Planning for Public and Nonprofit Organizations*, has a figure illustrating government agency stakeholders (2011, 134) that shows 14 different groups. His list covers the "usual suspects"—governing boards, politicians, taxpayers, staff, suppliers, citizens, financial groups, interest groups, future considerations, service recipients, unions, media, competitors, and other governments. For public libraries, that number could easily be increased by groups such as consortia members, subgroups of users, and professional groups.

An important, if not primary, constraint is that almost all libraries are just one component of a larger organization—an academic institution, a city or county jurisdiction, or school district, for example. Thus, any library statement about directions or documents that are central to its planning activities must be congruent with those of the parent body. It seems self-evident that the parent body created the library with a purpose in mind, thus limiting the library's options regarding its mission and, to some extent, vision.

Another constraint is almost every library has a board of some type. Both advisory and governing boards have a greater or lesser role in determining a library's mission and vision. In one sense, boards function as a control mechanism for the parent organization in terms of making certain the library "stays on mission." As noted in the previous chapter, governing boards have a duty to direct and oversee

ADVISORY BOARD EXPERIENCE

As library consultant, Mika has helped a number of libraries create vision and mission statements. He has also included the importance of the visioning process in his "introduction to the library profession" course. Most call the process strategic planning; however, he prefers to see the process as one of visioning a future for the library.

The visioning process:

- Identifies where the library is going;
- Identifies how the library will get there;
- Identifies areas of success and obstacles to overcome for the library;
- Reveals how the library meets community needs;
- Focuses on a three-year to five-year time frame;
- Uses environmental trends as guides; and
- As a result creates a plan that becomes a guide for the library director, board, and staff to follow.

The process leads to creating a strategic plan that lets libraries allocate resources wisely, and allows the library to make better decisions. As part of the process the library visioning (strategic planning) committee, made up of library board of trustee members, key library staff, and community members (hopefully including the city manager, school superintendent, mayor or other key city officials) a few library users (especially parents of users), and teen users, explores how the library is affected by what is happening in the world; in the United States; in the library's home state; locally; and in or to libraries.

The committee first needs to decide upon the most important roles that the library should adopt for itself. For public libraries this involves deciding among the 18 service roles (illustrative, not prescriptive nor fully inclusive) that the Public Library Association has identified (see http://ryepubliclibrary.org/wp-content/uploads/2012/05/ALAserviceresponses.pdf). While a library usually performs all or at least most of these service roles, it is important for the library to identify which roles it can undertake based on its resources—staff, time, budget, and expertise.

The library next needs to decide what core values the library holds. Core values are the principles and standards by which the library operates. A library adopts values that reflect its community, but also usually includes at least some of those identified by the American Library Association (see http://www.ala.org/advocacy/intfreedom/statementspols/corevalues).

Once the service roles and core values have been identified, the library creates and adopts a vision statement. In creating a vision statement the committee words the statement for the board, staff, and community that depicts the library as a model of excellence, becomes a guiding image and an ideal, and stretches the imagination.

Mika has encouraged committees to keep vision statements short and mission statements longer (although some libraries have adopted statements that are the reverse). Well-known vision statements, that often become slogans, include the following.

- Quality is job one (Ford Motor Company)
- I have a dream (Martin Luther King Jr.)
- We bring good things to life (General Electric)

For libraries, some of Mika's favorite vision statements are:

- Anchored in excellence . . . unlimited horizons (Chesterfield Township Library, Chesterfield, Michigan)
- Treasured past—vibrant future (Moline Public Library, Moline, Illinois)
- Where community and knowledge meet to connect, create, imagine, and inspire (Boyne District Library, Boyne City, Michigan)

A library's mission statement provides a framework for its services, core values, and activities. The mission statement specifies:

- What the library's business is;
- Who the library's customers are;
- How the library serves its customers; and
- Where the library serves (if relevant).

Again, some of Mika's favorite library mission statements include the following:

- The mission of the Hackley Public Library (Muskegon, Michigan) is to inform, inspire, and delight our diverse community by providing information, knowledge, literature, new technologies, and traditional and innovative programs.
- The mission of the Traverse Area District Library (Traverse City, Michigan) is to support the District's diverse and changing population in its lifelong search for intellectual, recreational or vocational information and enrichment.
- The East Lansing Public Library (East Lansing, Michigan) provides a place and resources where people gather to share information and ideas to enrich lives and foster community.

Finally here is one mission statement that embodies belief and values of libraries in general:

We believe that libraries change people's lives. They are cornerstones of democracy. The Bridgeport Public Library (Bridgeport, Connecticut) provides opportunities for residents to learn, enjoy and achieve. To accomplish that mission, the Bridgeport Public Library offers free and open access to a relevant collection, staff knowledge, and modern facilities.

the library's operations that, in most cases, are linked to the vision, mission, and plans that exist in an "approved" form.

A third constraint relates to the varied participants associated with decision making in the public and nonprofit sectors that Rainey noted. Today's libraries seek to operate, to some degree, in a participative manner. That is, they actively involve the service community in decision making. Given the diversity of these communities, Rainey's "vortex-sporadic" term for public decision making is apt on occasion.

Although nonprofit and public sector managers are constrained by the above factors, they actually have a surprising amount of freedom, often, more than some believe they have. Much of that freedom arises from the fact the parent organization's mission is usually very broad and driven by a variety of interests. Thus, its subunits have flexibility in their actions while remaining under the larger umbrella mission statement. This is particularly true in the public sector where policies, goals, and so on, are politically driven and move left or right as the political winds shift.

Another basic fact is a library's mission is set, at least in broad terms, by the legal documents that established it. There is some latitude to be sure, but the foundation for a library's purpose has been set in a legal document.

VISION STATEMENTS

A vision statement looks to the future. How far into the future that is depends on a person's confidence in foreseeing what the future holds. Given that much of today's environment is driven by technology—and indeed, that is certainly the case for libraries—you ought not to think much beyond a few years (even five years is a long time in terms of technology). While vision statements are future-focused, they need to be grounded in reality. For both vision and mission, a challenge is finding the right words to make a concise statement that reflects your unique library (and not one like hundreds of other libraries). One way to accomplish this is to create three statements: a vision statement is future looking, a mission statement is purpose focused, and a value statement is what drives the service philosophy.

What we found works reasonably well is to start this process by spending some time alone thinking about each concept and then drafting several variations. The next step is to consult with your immediate stakeholders (staff) by giving them the drafts to review and make comments. A good leader proposes, listens to followers input, and then generates a final version. Once there is a final draft they should go to the library's board for input. When writing about library strategic visions, Deborah Gaspar noted, "In many ways the opportunity to imagine a future of their own design also provided members with a chance to address frustrations with legacy processes and patterns" (2015, 383). In this case, she was referring to the library staff; however, the sentiment can apply to all the stakeholders.

One way to begin thinking about the library's vision is in terms of aspirations. For the vast majority of the time, the preparation of vision and mission statements has already been done; you are not starting without a context. Thus, the "past" will play a role in your thinking (as suggested in the Grossman quotation in the beginning of this chapter). The past will also be in the minds of those who will approve and implement any proposed changes in the documents. Thinking about what has changed, what have we already achieved, and what we may be able to achieve in the future will play a role in any new vision or mission statement. Good vision and mission statements will inspire both stakeholders and staff. For example, a public library vision might be "We will be the community's most people-centered public agency." While it would certainly be aspirational, it would probably not be particularly inspirational (but then few organizational statements convince, much less inspire, 100% of the people reading them).

Another approach is to seek out people's values in what the library does and incorporate some of those in a statement—"The library will provide resources that allow individuals to achieve their potential." Such a statement is grand sounding and hard to achieve and measure in terms of success or failure. Good vision statements go beyond the here and now and are often hard to measure directly; the goals and objectives that arise from the planning process are what lead to direct assessment.

COMPONENTS OF A STRONG VISION STATEMENT

- Future oriented
- Matches organizational values
- Reflects professional standards
- Generates enthusiasm
- Distinctive

- Idealistic
- Matches mission
- Clarifies organizational direction
- Short and easy to understand
- Challenging

COMPONENTS OF A STRONG MISSION STATEMENT

- Is specific to institution
- Clarifies stakeholder groups
- Reflects institutional values
- Reflects institutional capabilities

- Clarifies institutional purpose
- Brief and easy to understand
- Identifies institutional benefits
- Aids in addressing accountability

A value statement is less common among libraries; however, we believe generating such a statement for your library is a good idea for several reasons. One reason is that each of us has a personal set of values that we develop during our childhood. Some we outgrow, some we drop, and some may remain hidden even from our own awareness. Others have a direct and obvious influence on what we do. Also, we don't disregard those values when we arrive at work; they are constantly there and affect how we do things. In the absence of an organizational statement of values, we operate on our personal set and do not really think too deeply about the issue. Having an organizational statement provides an opportunity for staff to assess their personal values in a broader context.

AUTHOR EXPERIENCE

Evans started his career in libraries as a page in a public library working for the branch librarian whose story times he had attended. One of the aspects that made that work experience memorable was the librarian had strong views about what people should and should not read. Evans never knew why the librarian had such a strong aversion to fiction, but it was there and users—adults and children—heard the lecture more than once. "You really ought to read non-fiction rather than these novels." This is an extreme example of personal values coming out in workplace behavior and affecting other people. It seems less likely that such a blatant act would occur today; however, values and biases can and do arise in more subtle forms.

In addition to personal values, you can add professional association values to the mix. Such values may or may not lead to some tension between librarians and other staff members (an issue addressed in chapter 15. There may be a clash between some librarians' personal values and the association's. Achieving a blend of staff members' personal values and the association's values can be challenging; however, there are still other values that come into play.

Library board values—both personal and board duty aspects—also impact the workplace. You may well offer a draft values statement to the board that reflects a blend of staff, personal, and professional association values. However, the board's mix of personal values and board responsibilities can create a situation where no statement can gain approval or endorsement. A typical area where difficulties arise is around professional association values, especially the topic of intellectual freedom. There are times, albeit rare, when a governing board makes the case that community values *must* override any professional association positions. This is a time when your leadership skills will indeed be tested. Only through strong leadership is it likely there will be an approved statement.

So what are the components of a good value statement? One component is that the statement provides an accurate reflection of the principles and ethics that govern the library's activities. The statement should serve as a staff guide to behavior with both the public and one another.

GOOD VALUE STATEMENTS

- Represent true organizational values
- Are easily understood
- Reflect organizational character
- Are clearly stated/unambiguous
- Reflect organizational beliefs

- Are straight forward
- Motivate positive staff behaviors
- Clarify professional values
- Are guides for staff behavior
- Are visible in organizational actions

A reasonable question is, just how common are such VMV (vision, mission, value) statements in libraries? There is not much research data to answer that question. One clear answer is VMV statements are not universal among libraries. Rebecca Nous did look into the matter in terms of ARL library mission statements (2015). Her research base was 114 ARL directors. Even with this select group of libraries, 7 percent had no formal mission statement. An earlier of Canadian academic libraries by William B. Calder looked for evidence of all three statements on the Web study (2011). His results may well reflect a general pattern, but not necessarily the actual percentages for libraries. He found that 81 percent of academic libraries had mission statements, 70 percent had vision statements, and 55 percent had value statements.

CHECK THIS OUT

An older, but still very useful book, that will in aid thinking about and developing VMV statements is Cynthia D. Scott, Dennis T. Jaffe, and Glenn R. Tobe's *Organizational Vision, Values, and Mission* (Menlo Park, CA: Crisp Publications, 1993).

STRATEGY AND PLANNING

Strategy, strategic management, and strategic planning are related but separate concepts. Strategy is about how you think you can achieve the library's mission—it is not in itself a plan. Roger L. Martin noted, "In this worldview, managers accept that good strategy is not the product of hours of careful research and modeling . . . Instead, it's the result of a simple and quite rough-and-ready process of thinking through what it would take to achieve what you want and then assessing whether it's realistic to try" (2014, 80). Assuming you think your mission and vision is realistic, the question becomes how to do this—a plan of attack. When the planning relates to your mission, vision, and strategy it becomes strategic planning. When you base your managerial leadership actions on that plan you are engaging in strategic management. Cohen, Eimicke, and Heikkila make a case for strategic planning and management: "Public organizations are often buffeted by conflicting interests and political signals. Effective public managers must impose order on this chaos, and strategic planning is a key tool for doing that" (2013, 208).

John Bryson, in his classic book about strategic planning in nonprofit and public sectors, noted the differences by stating, "Strategy formulation often involves free-wheeling creativity and the give-and-take of dialogue and deliberation while formal adoption of strategies and strategic plans can involve political intrigue, tough bargaining, public posturing, and high drama" (2011, 219). While strategy formulation can be freewheeling, for libraries the freewheeling can be constrained by the mission and vision statements of their parent organizations. A library's VMV documents certainly play a major role in formulating strategies and plans. Such documents, if nothing more, set some limits on the options to consider. For example, using our above public library mission statement ("We will be the community's most people-centered public agency"), a strategy might be "Build on our public trust to generate greater support." An educational library's mission statement, "The library will provide the resources that individuals need to achieve their potential," might have a strategy such as "Expand collaborative and cooperative activities with teachers and other libraries to enhance student learning."

Although a nonprofit or public sector organization can exist without any of the above, the key word here is "exist." To thrive, an organization must have an idea of what it hopes to achieve and how to go about doing so. Anne Marie Casey (2015) looked at academic library strategies and priority setting. Her research provided three case studies from the Carnegie master level institutions in five states. The interesting aspect of her research was 14 of the 45 institutions selected showed no indication of engaging in strategic planning (33%).

"Planning" is a word that raises concerns in the minds of some individuals. Planning implies something may well change, and change is uncomfortable even to think about for some people. There is also an element of risk in planning—you are looking into the future to some degree. There is a chance you may not accurately predict that future and the plan may fail. While no one likes to fail, the reality is life is full of risk and sometimes failure is inevitable. For strategic planning and management to succeed there must be trust (both of and among managers, staff, and board). Another requisite for success is all the parties must be willing to engage in change when called upon to do so. A third component is all the parties must recognize that the processes take time to do properly—a rushed plan is not likely to be a sound plan. Yet another element to good strategic planning is to not only engage staff and board members but to also include some of the stakeholders (perhaps not in the initial phases but doing so during the early drafts stages will result in greater acceptance).

You may remember from prior reading about organizational change the name Kurt Lewin. He proposed a three-stage process for organizational change: Unfreezing, Change, and Freezing (*Field Theory in Social Sciences: Selected Theoretical Papers*, 1951). Later researchers and scholars expanded on Lewin's basic three by more finely dividing each of the three stages. One of the most common models now used is John Kotter's eight-step change process (1990). No matter what model you use, the first step or activity is getting people to recognize there is a need to change. Strategy formation and planning can help people begin to think about such a need.

We recommend the following as techniques to assist in strategy formulation, planning, and goal setting: attempt to reduce the risk stress factor and help staff to be more comfortable with change. The method begins by involving the staff in the early stages of the process with the objective of generating a draft proposal to present to the library board. Depending on the library type, we also recommend gaining some feedback from the service community about the documents before everything is finalized.

CHECK THESE OUT

Margaret Brown-Sica and Rice Majors published an interesting article in 2014 about making time for strategy: "Getting Around to Being Strategic" (*Library Leadership & Management* 28, no. 2: 1–7).

Tony Horava wrote a thought-provoking article in 2014 about risks and managers: "Risk Taking in Academic Libraries: The Implications of Prospect Theory" (*Library Leadership & Management* 28, no. 2: 1–13).

The core elements of the techniques to assist in strategy formulation, planning, and goal setting consist of creating a matrix based on SWOT (strengths, weakness, opportunities, and threats) and a variation of PEST (political, economic, social, and technology) analysis. While SWOT is an assessment tool you may know and may have used before, PEST has many variations and labels—PESTL, PESTLE, PESTLEE, PESTLED, and PEST-G, for example (there are at least a dozen variations). The addition of the "L" stands for legal, and the additional "E" is for environmental.

Both PEST and SWOT methods are easy to understand, making them good for using in group brainstorming efforts. These methods help you and others better understand the operating environment. The downside to them is they may lead to quick and easy responses and result in a failure to explore a topic fully. Like everything related to management, such assessment should not be done only once—PEST and SWOT must be reviewed and rethought on an ongoing basis. To provide the best results, you, or if not you, someone, need to engage in serious research, which will take time. We have been involved in some such exercises where little research was done prior to a group effort; the results were rather superficial.

At times, however, even a superficial effort can be helpful in thinking about possible strategies. The process will make you, and others, think about possible dangers for the library. Such an assessment will also encourage you to consider risks and what might be done to avoid or mitigate the impact should these risks arise. Thinking about potential challenges also can help individuals understand why changes may be necessary and help them become more willing to adapt to change when that becomes a necessity.

The matrix we like has five columns: topics, strengths, weaknesses, opportunities, and threats. What topics you place in your rows is up to you; you can use some variation of the basic PEST approach or create topics highly specific to your library. We offer an example of a mixture of topics in Table 6.1.

Not every cell must contain data; however, you should spend some time thinking about each cell before moving forward. One of the benefits of employing such matrixes is that it can help reduce risk; certainly not all risks, but there may be fewer events that arise that are total surprises.

Goals

Your next step in this process is to generate a list of possible goals that would aid in realizing the agreed upon vision and mission statements as well the resultant strategy. When engaging in this activity, it is very important to do so with what management writers refer to as "organizational capacity" in mind. There are a variety of goal options for most organizations; however, some are unrealistic in terms

Table 6.1.
Sample Library Planning Assessment Matrix

Topics	Strengths	Weaknesses	Opportunities	Threats
Library management				
Library board				
Library staff				
Community relations				
Finances				
Collaboration/consortia				
Community politics				
Community demographics				
Technology				
Library programs				
Library services				
Library support groups				

of what are realistic resources in the current and likely future. One such example would be a research library having a goal of never having to borrow material from another library. In some universe that might be possible, but not in ours; no library has, or is likely to ever have, the organizational capacity to accomplish such a goal. We are *not* suggesting goals should not be challenging; far from it. We believe sound goals are challenging, but also within the realm of potential capabilities.

Library operational capacity is a mix of what exists in terms of resources, relationships, people, organizations, and so on, and what may be realistic enhancements. Michael Allison and Jude Kaye (2015) identified eight broad capacity categories; we have modified their labels for the categories to better fit the library context (see sidebar).

LIBRARY ORGANIZATIONAL CAPACITY

- People (staff, volunteers, board)
- Operating budget (allocated funds)
- Physical facilities
- Assessment activities
- Organizational structure and culture
- Supplemental funds (endowments and grants)
- Technology
- Service community relations

Rather like the matrix discussed above, you should think about each potential goal against all of the capacity components.

There is a concept related to setting a goal that we have found effective—SMARTER. It may require a little more time to develop such goals, but in the long run your library will be better for taking the additional time. A SMARTER goal is specific, measurable, acceptable, realistic, time-based, extending, and rewarding. A SMART goal will aid in demonstrating accountability, provide a push to be ever better, and inform the community of what you really mean to accomplish. What is an example of a SMARTER goal for almost any type of library? The library will provide a 50/50 ratio of physical books to e-books by the year 2020. Such a goal is specific, time-based, and measurable. Assuming you get board approval or support, as well as from the staff, it would be an acceptable goal. Chances are rather high the goal would be extending. From a reward point of view, who knows; young users are likely to see this as positive while others, older individuals, may not view it that way.

Objectives

Goals usually require greater specificity than you can incorporate into a goal statement, if it is to be useful operationally. The typical organizational approach is to have some very specific tasks (objectives) identified that will achieve the stated goal. Like goals, objectives can and ought to be SMARTER in character. Examples of some objectives related to our above hypothetical goal, assuming the current ratio is 75 percent spent on print titles, are:

- Goal 1, Objective 1
  - Increase e-book expenditures by 10% by 2017
- Goal 1, Objective 2
  - Increase e-book expenditures by 5% by 2018
- Goal 1, Objective 3
  - Increase e-book expenditures by 5% by 2019
- Goal 1, Objective 4
  - Increase e-book expenditures by 5% by 2020

Priorities

What you will identify from the matrix process is a number of issues (eventually in the form of goals)—some you will want to address while others you can ignore. The process is also likely to result in more goals than the library can handle simultaneously. This means you should prioritize the issues and goals from "must do" to "sometime in the future/nice to do." Also, many library goals and objectives are dependent upon securing the requisite additional resources. Thus, prioritization becomes a key component in how you manage and lead your library.

Setting priorities is a surprisingly time consuming activity, unless you do this by yourself (something we do not recommend). Keep in mind that part of establishing priorities is the political process; this is very common in public sector organizations and only somewhat less so for nonprofits. As such, having some type of open process related to the priorities is essential. That also means it will take time, a fair amount of bargaining, and, of course, compromise.

The word "political" covers several types of "political" behavior, all of which can surface during the prioritization process. For public sector organizations (less so for nonprofits), there is the partisan way of governing. In addition, there are internal organizational politics (internal to the library and external with competing organizations). Finally, there are personal politics within the workplace. Your challenge as managerial leader is to assess these politics and make sure they do not undermine the prioritization process.

One element in successfully meeting such a challenge is to understand the art of bargaining and compromise. What you want as an outcome is the strongest possible consensus regarding the priorities. Getting to that point can be time consuming and quite frustrating at times. However, achieving that outcome will pay dividends later in terms of support for the library as well as its performance. (We look at political skills in chapter 12 and negotiating and bargaining in chapter 17.)

You can structure the prioritization process in a number of ways. Regardless of your approach, a first step, assuming you are involving stakeholders in the process, is to review your vision, mission, value, and strategy documents. Doing so will ensure that you have everyone working with the same set of premises and may well help you identify some differing views among the participants, especially stakeholders who were not involved in the creation of those documents.

One method to use to begin the prioritization process is to seek agreement on broad categories of goals. For example, you might use a four-category approach such as essential, important, needed, and desirable. Doing this can get your group quickly to a rough priority list, then you can move on to setting priorities within the categories.

A different approach is to sort the goals in terms of expected time frames for achieving them. For example, you can use categories, such as 1–2 years, 3–5 years, or 5 years or more. Again, such rough sorting creates a type of priority—what needs attention now versus later. Yet another approach is to do a quick sort by how challenging the goal is likely to be to achieve (easy, complicated, challenging, or difficult, for example). This approach, more often than not, will require more time to complete. However, it can provide a better (workable) prioritization of the goals.

No matter how you begin to sort the goals, at some point each one will require detailed consideration. This is one of the times when the extra effort to create SMARTER goals pays off. Asking "is this goal more important than that one?" can move the process forward faster than suggesting "let's discuss the first goal" would. At times, this approach can even get the goals sorted without the detailed discussion of the goal. Certainly, at some point, the details of the goal will be a topic for discussion. However, if you can get the group to determine relative importance without long debates about merit, you will save time.

Another tactic is to not only look at how challenging a goal may be for the library to achieve, but also what it will take to achieve it. This approach may become bogged down in discussions of how realistic the goal is. If you generated the goal as a SMARTER one, then you will be well prepared to address the concern(s) (we are not suggesting that there will not be differences of opinion; in fact, such challenges generally make a goal stronger).

Having specific, measurable, and realistic goal statements, assuming you get consensus that they are such, means there will be more time to handle the more nebulous aspects of SMARTER goals. All of the remaining elements are less clear—the time frame, level of acceptability, and how rewarding are among the most debatable. Perhaps achievability is the most risky aspect of goal and priority setting. These aspects are very future oriented and there may be little consensus as to what that future will be like.

It is relatively easy to rank objectives, assuming you do not involve the stakeholders. The primary reason for not involving stakeholders is that objectives relate to operational activities of the staff. Stakeholders, even those with library experience, do not have the detailed knowledge of how your library operates on a daily basis and rarely are they in a position to question how an objective might be best achieved. At most, you might discuss with the library's board chairperson whether or not the board would want to have a presentation about the objectives. Chances are good that the response will be negative, especially when the board members know they have little voice in operational activities.

You might think the foregoing only applies to organization-wide concerns. Certainly for an organization we believe the above processes are essential; however, much of this material can be applied to your unit regardless of its organizational level. Although we have no research evidence to support our belief, we suspect many, if not most, highly successful managerial leaders employ some variation of the above, whether they think of what they are doing as strategy and strategic planning or not.

STRATEGIC MANAGEMENT

While it is possible to keep a library operational without a strategic plan, doing so will be much more challenging than need be. Effective public sector managers, as well as nonprofit managers, must engage in strategic management with or without a strategic plan. William Brown noted, "For many nonprofit professionals strategic management is the same as strategic planning. It is not" (2010, 206). He might well have included public sector managers in that statement and be correct. Brown went on to point out that one important difference between the two concepts rests on the fact that managing strategically is a daily activity rather than an occasional one, albeit one based on at least an unstated strategy. James Perry and Robert Christensen offered a description of what constitutes strategic management:

> Strategy content has two dimensions: strategic stance, the general approach that describes the organization's position and how it interacts with its environment, and strategic actions, which indicate the specific steps the organization takes to operationalize its stance. (2015, 277)

Brown suggested that strategic managers base their actions on three key ideas: differentiation, competitive advantage, and positional considerations. Differentiation in the context of strategic management relates to how the manager views her or his organization as differing from other organizations. This differentiation is done in terms of competitors, both of a like type and others seeking funds from similar sources. Thus, a public sector library manager leader would seek differences between the library and other libraries. She or he would also look for how the library differs from the other public agencies seeking public monies. Even libraries of the same type do have differences such as service population demographics and the level of community support for the offered activities.

Needless to say, differentiation is not, in itself, the only thing to consider in strategic management practice. A second key component in the process lies in the ability to take the identified differences and turn them into competitive advantages. For example, a school district library media center might see its service population (students and teachers) as an important difference. A potential competitive advantage for the center could be the parents of the students, who could be very strong advocates for the programs and services.

The third key component of the strategic management is how a manager positions her or his organization to take advantage of situations. Positioning relates to organizational position vis à vis other organizations as well as to the organizational resources. For a library, one of the most challenging issues in strategic management is access to resources to be able take advantage of an opportunity. Identifying such opportunities is a time when having strong donors and/or friends groups can pay off.

Some years ago, Raymond Miles and Charles Snow published a book that labeled the basic premises of strategic management. One of the elements they identified in *Organizational Strategy, Structure, and Process* (1978) as reflecting a strategic management environment is the style of such activity. (Their styles have been validated by many researchers since their idea was first proposed.) They suggested a four-category typology—an approach that researchers have identified as reflecting actual practice. The four categories are prospecting, discovering, analyzing, and reacting. What most of the research suggests is that very successful strategic managers employ all of the approaches from time to time.

Prospecting managers base their strategic management tactics on actively seeking opportunities. From a library perspective, we believe that only those libraries with very strong community and/or donor support can effectively employ this approach. Few libraries have slack resources of any kind and without very strong support they are seldom in the position to take advantage of the opportunities a manager may identify. This is not to suggest prospecting is a bad thing for a library manager to do; rather, you must realize that being able to take advantage of situations may require time and patience due to resource issues.

Defenders are managers who find their biggest challenge is keeping what they have rather than reaching out for something new. Being a defensive manager leader is something that too many library managers have had to do over the years. Defense is a strategic option, if one you may wish you weren't forced to employ.

 Engaging in ongoing analysis is always a good strategy and most often employed in conjunction with another strategy. Analyzers focus on their successes while monitoring their environment for signs of threat and opportunities. This strategy, along with defense, is an effective approach for most libraries. Focusing on what is successful and adjusting successes to be even better, while correcting those activities that are less successful, is a sound approach for most libraries.

A reactive strategy may be an all-too-common approach to strategic management in public and nonprofit sectors. Although waiting to see what an enemy will do next may be a reasonable strategy from a military point of view, it is too limiting a strategy to be a basic approach for a library manager.

All of the material in this chapter relates to assessing the operational environment. In the next chapter, we explore the major methods of such assessment activity. The good news is libraries have been engaged in such assessment activities for a long time.

CHECK THESE OUT

The following articles provide some perspective on the nature of strategic planning in several types of libraries (academic, public, and special):

Reinhold Decker and Michael Höppner, "Strategic Planning and Customer Intelligence in Academic Libraries," *Library Hi Tech* 24, no. 4 (2006): 504–514.

Patty Harding, "Planning and Change Management: A Strategic Partnership," *Public Library Quarterly* 20, no. 2 (2001): 3–16.

Judith A. Siess, "Strategic Planning for Hospital Libraries," *Journal of Hospital Librarianship* 5, no. 4 (2005): 37–49

Rashad Young and Susan Benton, "Strengthening the Library's Strategic Role," *Public Management* 97, no. 8 (2015): 6–10.

REFERENCES

Allison, Michael, and Jude Kaye. 2015. *Strategic Planning for Nonprofit Organizations: A Practical Guide for Dynamic Times*. 3rd edition. New York: Wiley.

Brown, William. 2010. "Strategic Management." In *The Jossey-Bass Handbook of Nonprofit Leadership and Management*. Edited by David O. Renz and Associates. San Francisco, CA: Jossey-Bass.

Bryson, John M. 2011. *Strategic Planning for Public and Nonprofit Organizations: A Guide to Strengthening and Sustaining Organizational Achievements*. 4th edition. San Francisco, CA: Jossey-Bass.

Calder, William B. 2011. "Institutional VVM Statement on Websites." *The Community College Enterprise* 17, no. 2: 19–27.

Casey, Anne Marie. 2015. "Strategic Priorities: A Roadmap through Change for Library Leaders." *Library Leadership & Management* 29, no. 2: 1–16.

Carroll, Lewis. 1865. *Alice's Adventures in Wonderland*. London: Macmillan.

Cohen, Steven, William Eimicke, and Tanya Heikkila, 2013. *The Effective Public Manager: Achieving Success in Government Organizations*. 5th edition. San Francisco, CA: Jossey-Bass.

Gaspar, Deborah B. 2015. "Strategic Vision: Navigating Change." *College & Research Libraries News* 76, no. 7: 380–383.

Germano, Michael A., and Shirley M. Stretch-Stephenson. 2012. "Strategic Value Planning for Libraries." *Bottom Line: Managing Libraries* 25, no. 2: 71–88.

Grossman, Hal B. 2011. "A Comparison of the Progressive Era and the Depression Years: Societal Influences on the Predications of the Future of the Library, 1895–1940." *Libraries & the Cultural Record* 46, no. 1: 102–128.

Kotter, John P. 1990. *A Force for Change: How Leadership Differs from Management*. New York: Free Press.

Lewin, Kurt. 1951. *Field Theory in Social Sciences: Selected Theoretical Papers*. Edited by Dorwin Cartwright. New York: Harper and Row.

Martin, Roger L. 2014. "The Big Lie of Strategic Planning." *Harvard Business Review* 92, nos. 1/2: 78–84.

Miles, Raymond E., and Charles C. Snow. 1978. *Organizational Strategy, Structure, and Process*. New York: McGraw-Hill.

Nous, Rebecca. 2015. "Building Cathedrals: Mission Statements in Academic Libraries." *Library Leadership & Management* 29, no. 4: 1–12.

Perry, James, and Robert Christensen. 2015. "Leading Public Organizations Strategically." In *Handbook of Public Administration*. 3rd edition. Edited by James Perry and Robert Christensen. New York: Wiley.

Rainey, Hal G. 2014. *Understanding and Managing Public Organizations*. 5th edition. San Francisco, CA: Jossey-Bass.

Chapter 7

CHANGING ENVIRONMENT—
WHY IT MATTERS

Libraries and librarians have always had a certain relationship with the users. This relationship has been changing due to the introduction of emerging technologies in recent years.

> Linh Cuong Nguyen, Helen Partridge, and Sylvia Edwards, 2012

Organizations everywhere are struggling with an environment of nearly continuous change. . . . forcing agencies—and employees—to be more creative, flexible, and adaptable than ever before.

> Walter McFarland, 2015

Environment scanning is not only a tool for business. Every organization, whether it is a for profit or a nonprofit, needs to be aware of its environment if it wants to be competitive—and you must be competitive if you are going to survive.

> Patricia Katopol, 2014

What lesson might there be in the theory of evolution for a manager? You've probably not spent much of your time, in your managerial role, thinking about that theory. Given this chapter's title, you might guess that the lesson from evolution is "survival of the fittest." That's close but not entirely correct; the survival phrase is shorthand for much more complicated processes. The actual lesson here is the need to adapt effectively to survive. Species that go extinct do so not because they are unfit, but rather because they are unable to change along with the changing environment. No organization, no matter how well endowed with resources, will survive long term if it is unable to adjust and adapt to its changing operational environment.

Libraries have a substantial history of being adaptable—well over 4,000 years of adaptation, in fact. They have changed what they provide, who they provide it to, and how they provide their services, over and over again. The notion of monitoring what is taking place in society is not new for librarians. Librarians use terms such as "community survey," "community analysis," "market analysis," and "needs analysis" for the process of looking at the service community. Many library efforts are more or less single focus—for example, what new services does the community desire, how has the service population changed in terms of information needs and wants, or where to locate a new service point. There is nothing wrong with such an approach other than it is piecemeal rather than broad-based. Certainly a larger scale effort will require greater staffing and probably cost money, at least the first time. Today there is a process that can be both broad-based and incorporated into a library's ongoing activities: environmental scanning (ES). We believe such an effort is well worth the associated costs.

Why do we suggest engaging in a detailed monitoring process that requires a substantial amount of a library's resources given how tight resources are for most libraries? The answer is that the data and information derived from such an effort have a variety of uses and after a first effort it is relatively easy to make the monitoring process ongoing. One obvious use is in strategic planning for the library. As noted in the last chapter, even the vision for the library may change over time, as does its environment. The monitoring data can also inform your decision making—have the community's demographics changed in such a way that you should rethink allocations for collection formats? Should you relocate or close down a service point? These are just two questions that can be answered with such a process. The generated information is also very useful in marketing and public relations (PR) activities. From a leadership perspective, you will glean information that will help you create, build, and maintain connections throughout the service community.

A changing environment forces an organization to at least consider making adjustments, assuming it wishes to have long-term viability. Making adjustments requires making decisions. Making decisions requires you to accept some degree of risk. The more you know and understand about the situation the less risky the decision. A key to that knowledge and understanding is the quantity and quality of the available information. Some years ago, Detelin Elenkov noted, "In practice, perceived environmental uncertainty exists when decision-makers do not feel confident that they understand what the major events or trends in the environment are, or when they feel unable to accurately assign probabilities to the likelihood that particular events and/or changes will occur" (1997, 288). One important step to address this concern is careful ongoing scanning of the environment to reduce uncertainty.

Before we describe the hows of environmental scanning we will expand on our discussion of the change process in the prior chapter. If a library is going to respond to its environment fluctuations, it must engage in a change process. Such activities require managerial leaders to understand the process and how to manage it.

MANAGING CHANGE

Change is inevitable. We know this, and on occasion wish it were not true. One way to think about ongoing change is in terms of three types: desired, likely, and unexpected. Organizations must handle all three types. All organizations work on desired (planned) changes. There is a somewhat surprising fact about organizational planned changes: a very high percentage of them partially or completely fail. In 2015, Robert M. Tobias began his article with "The brutal fact pointed out by Michael Beer and Nitin Nohria in their May 2000 *Harvard Business Review* article is that about 70% of all change initiatives fail. This is true, they explain, whether the efforts involve installing new technology, downsizing, restructuring, or trying to change corporate culture" (35).

Another interesting article by Marlen Jurisch, Christian Ikas, Petra Wolf, and Helmut Krcmar describes their examination of 128 published case studies of organizational change projects. They found that the complete success rate was less than 50 percent for both private and public sector organizations. They did not differentiate between partial and total failure (certainly partial success would be at least somewhat positive for the organization). However, when was the last time you read about a library project failing? Most people do not publish articles about their failures. One of the authors' conclusions was, "the ratio between intended verses achieved improvements appears higher in the public sector. . . . However, public BPC projects are more likely to be exposed to strategy or political/regulatory volatilities due to a highly politicized environment" (2012, 23). BPC is the authors' shorthand for what they labeled business process change. That is, changing some aspect/element in an organization's operations—cost reduction, quality, and customer relations, for example.

Whatever the actual full or partial success rate is, it seems clear that the change process can be a challenge for managerial leaders. If those rates are anywhere near correct for planned change, what must it be for other efforts to change (such as an unexpected development) with little or no real planning time?

Likely or probable developments in the operating environment are the reason organizations should have some contingency plans ready for implementation. For example, public sector organizations know that from time to time the political party currently in power will lose power. It is a wise managerial leader who thinks about what such a change may entail for her or his agency. Such "pondering" may not lead to a planning document but should result in some ideas about what might be done when the shift occurs. One typical type of contingency plan that many libraries have is an emergency response plan (covering such issues as water damage and fire events). As we noted in the previous chapter, sometimes an organization engages in strategic planning or, in this case, a possible event, and neglects to periodically review and adjust the plan. Changes take place in organizations—staff, services, physical layout, and the like—and such changes can cause at least a partial failure in the handling of an event if plans have not been updated to reflect those changes.

CHECK THESE OUT

Three excellent titles that address handling potential emergencies or disasters are:

Camila A. Alire, ed., *Library Disaster Planning and Recovery Handbook* (New York: Neal-Schuman, 2000).

Emma Dadson, *Emergency Planning and Response for Libraries, Archives and Museums* (London: Facet, 2012).

Julie Todaro, *Emergency Preparedness for Libraries* (Lanham, MD: Government Institutes, 2009).

What can a manager leader do to enhance the chances of full success for a planned change process? All managers are aware that there can be resistance to the process. They are aware of models of the change process that start with creating an environment where participants involved recognize the need to change (see, e.g., Kurt Lewin, *Field Theory in Social Sciences: Selected Theoretical Papers*, 1951; John Kotter, *A Force for Change: How Leadership Differs from Management*, 1990; and many others who write about change). Something to keep in mind is that not all resistance is bad. A wise manager listens to the opinions of the resistant party; this is particularly true when the "opposition" comes from staff or library board. A "knee-jerk" negative response may well be a bad mistake on your part. Sergio Fernandez noted, "Resistance to change can play a useful role, serving as a source of vital information and feedback that change agents can use to modify and improve change initiatives that are underway" (2015, 383).

One of the first assumptions people have about resistance to organizational change is that it arises from one or more staff members. While that is often the case, resistance to change can arise from a variety of sources. Experienced managerial leaders know this from having been surprised at least once when resistance came from an unexpected source. There are three basic categories from which resistance might come: individuals, groups, and outside organizations or bodies. However, if it were just that simple, change would not be such a challenge. The fact of the matter is each category has a number of subcategories.

You can encounter individual resistors in all of the broad categories. However, that does not mean you can overcome the variations of individual resistors using a single approach. The approach you can use with a staff member is not likely to be appropriate or effective with a board member. When you meet resistance from a stakeholder or someone from another organization, you can be certain the staff approach will not work. Even if two staff members resist, their concerns may be different, thus making a single approach ineffective.

Group resistance is actually somewhat easier to address in the sense that you may only need to develop one approach. However, group resistance can be hard to surmount. For example, when the resistance is from a collective bargaining body, there is likely to be considerable parsing of the bargaining agreement, especially when the specifics of the proposed change are somewhat abstract. In the case of resistance from a board, you may have an advisory body that believes it is, or should be, a governing board. Stakeholder opposition is a mixed bag. For example, operational changes (hours, service locations, etc.) are decisions for the library and board to make. Certainly they will want to listen and take into consideration users' views, understanding that there is a public relations aspect. Other outside organizations may overrule a library's change process, especially a regulatory body. Such rulings are not always the correct decision; there are times when a regulatory body has not yet adjusted to the "new normal."

While you will need to adjust your approach for each category of resistance, there are some general steps that are useful regardless of where the resistance lies. We mentioned one above: make it clear you are ready to listen, and attempt to understand why there is resistance to the proposed process. A second step is conveying that you will consider alternatives that will, or could, meet the goal for the proposed change process. Just taking these simple steps can reduce the level of resistance.

Other steps to take include setting aside some time to develop a factual and logical "case" for why a change is necessary. You will need to employ all of the communication Ps we discussed in chapter 3. Your "resistor audience" will at a minimum be concerned and will probably be skeptical. There may be times when the person(s) may be hostile; such individuals and groups tend not to be great listeners. In those instances, it is important to defuse the hostility enough that the rest of your message has a chance of being heard. You may want to review the Williams and Miller article about assessing your potential audience that we cited in chapter 3.

Something to consider adding to your change rationale is what benefits are likely to accrue from a successful change—both for individuals and for the organizational. It is equally important, when you are "selling" these benefits, that you acknowledge any negative aspects. Staff and others have almost elephant-like memories when it comes to what was "promised" in the way of benefits and even greater recall about negative outcomes that were not mentioned. This is where trust can be badly damaged; do not state positives as promises and do make certain to list the potential negatives. Once trust is lost it is hard to rebuild.

Some changes, such as technological ones, generate legitimate concerns about skills needed as well as how transitions will take place. Emphasize your confidence in the staff to handle the changes and go further, if possible, by outlining the support there will be for transitioning and skill development. Think through how you will provide support before even putting forward the idea of making a change. Outlining the support will provide people with a degree of "psychological safety." For most people, the unknown is frightening to some degree, and reducing some of the unknown will assist in gaining their acceptance of the change.

Overcoming resistance is never easy, but with effort you should succeed more often than not. Critically, attempting to get everyone on board with a proposed change should improve the overall success rate.

We now turn to one of the major sources for the change process—organizational operating environment.

ENVIRONMENT

Don Sager made the case that libraries should engage in environmental scanning (ES) and he outlined a broad approach for doing so. "Libraries need to scan their environment in order to understand external forces of change, so that they may develop effective responses that secure or improve their position in the future.... Scanning can also be accomplished at different organizational levels in a library, involving different levels of detail" (1999, 283–284). His last point is worth emphasizing: too often, ES is viewed as the obligation of senior managers (assuming it is practiced at all). An effective ongoing ES program should involve all levels of the library structure.

One way to think of the library environment is as a two-level sphere—the inner sphere being the library's direct contacts and the outer sphere consisting of everything else. The inner sphere may seem complex enough to monitor (borrowers, library board, staff, funding authorities, vendors, consortium partners, regulatory agencies, donors, and all other stakeholders), but the outer sphere is even more complex. The bottom line is you should monitor both spheres on an ongoing basis.

Inner Sphere

There are a number of inner sphere concerns. One concern that is sometimes overlooked, unless there is a crisis, is a library's organizational environment or culture. There are a host of potential crises that can make focusing on the organizational culture (OC) very important. Three areas where the need arises to focus on the OC are interdepartmental conflict, conflict between several staff members, and a conflict situation involving staff and the service community. Keep in mind OC does play a surprisingly strong role in how a library performs, especially in service activities.

What are some of the symptoms of a problematic culture? Where the environment is one of low or limited trust, service and performance quality will suffer. When the relationship between professional and support staff is poor, service and performance quality will suffer. With limited policy training or when there is widespread assumption of what a policy may be, service and performance quality will suffer. Where there is a difference between espoused values (on the wall) and workplace behavior (on the floor), service and performance quality will suffer. When staff morale is low, regardless of the cause, service and performance quality will suffer. Those and many other factors are components of organizational culture that impact organizational performance.

Essentially OC is a mixture of elements—people, the staff's interaction with the service community, physical facilities, funding levels, morale, policies, values, boards, parent organizations, decision making, and diversity, for example. The list could go on but the idea is clear: OC is complex and important to quality service. All the components can interact with one another in myriad ways. In addition, there may be several subcultures in place. Toss in past history and technology and you have a true "Mulligan's Stew" at a slow boil to sort out.

Some years ago, Tom Burns and G. M. Stalker suggested there were two basic types of organizational structure—mechanistic and organic (1968). These concepts can be helpful in sorting out your OC environment. (Researchers over the intervening years have validated Burns and Stalker's concepts; for example see Sine, Mitsuhashi, and Kirsh, 2006). The major factor in the usefulness of their ideas is the fact that the organizational structure is the skeleton to which everything else about the organization is attached. Researchers have shown that an organic structure is most effective in dealing with a dynamic or changing environment. A mechanistic structure is best for creating a stable environment, something that few organizations have today.

What are the fundamental differences between mechanistic and organic approaches? When the environment is in flux, organizations with tightly integrated units are more successful, due, in part, to better communication and information sharing. Mechanistic organizations tend to have very weak linkages between units. As you might assume, organic organizations have a highly decentralized decision-making approach. This allows those close to the situation to act more quickly. Likewise, procedures are minimized, standards are guides, and an atmosphere that provides the freedom to fail or to act prevails in the organic organization. All of these factors facilitate a rapid response to a changing environment. Another aspect of the organic model is that it encourages teamwork, builds skills, and intensifies cooperation, which all enhance the organization's viability.

Something to keep in mind is that in a reasonably placid environment it is easy to slip into an increasingly mechanistic structure. A small change here and another small one there and a library becomes more and more like a bureaucracy—something that public agencies are frequently accused of being. We are not suggesting that having a mechanistic structure is necessarily bad or that it creates a bureaucracy; the model is simply more effective than an organic structure in a placid environment. Our point is you need to monitor your library's structure as well as its operational environment in order to make appropriate adjustments as circumstances evolve.

Another aspect of OC, as suggested by the word "culture," is how it handles diversity among staff and its service community. As a public or nonprofit organization, a library has an obligation to provide equitable service to all components of its service population. Most of today's libraries, primarily medium and large libraries, have at least some cultural diversity reflected in their staffing patterns. Cultural background impacts both how a person communicates (eye contact, personal space, etc.) as well as how the individual interprets a message. It also affects how people react to interactions with others (teamwork and competition, for example). Such factors do play a role in the organizational atmosphere, which in turn impacts overall organizational performance and service quality.

Edgar Schein, a prominent researcher in the field of OC, suggested that once established, organizational culture is hard to change (1992). He identified three key components that a managerial leader must focus on to create a change: artifacts, espoused beliefs and basic values, and underlying assumptions. Artifacts are the physical aspects of an organization such as the building, where a staff member is located physically, and what people wear to work. Espoused beliefs and basic values are reflected in both speech and behavior (not always synchronized). Staff members do not always share the same basic assumptions, which can lead to very different approaches to how they perform their duties.

Sound organizational cultures are ones in which morale is high. Staff members see themselves as part of a strong organizational team that performs at a high level. Staff and overall organizational performance is consistent and efficient. It is also a situation in which staff members know that change is inevitable and accept that notion, if not wanting to embrace it. We offer the following as elements for creating a healthy organizational culture:

- Clarify policies and provide training in their implementation.
- Decentralize decision making as much as feasible.
- Create collaborative workspaces that are conducive to quality performance and a sense of belonging.
- Make information sharing the norm.
- Ensure stated values and behavior are congruent
- Celebrate diversity in all its forms
- Provide as many growth and professional development opportunities as possible for all staff.
- Celebrate group and individual successes.
- Have clearly defined goals for both the organization as a whole and each worker within it.
- Make sure your management team is on board and agrees on the direction to go.

CHECK THESE OUT

This 1979 article by Andrew M. Pettigrew's is generally accepted as the origin of the concept of organizational culture: "On Studying Organizational Cultures" (*Administrative Science Quarterly* 24, no. 4: 570–581).

A more recent article, from 2006, is by Davide Ravasi and Majken Schultz: "Responding to Organizational Identity Threats: Exploring the Role of Organizational Culture" (*Academy of Management Journal* 49, no. 3: 433–458).

An article that provides a good review of the literature on OC is this 2008 article by Raduan Che Rose, Naresh Kumar, Haslinda Abdullah, and Goh Yeng Ling: "Organizational Culture as a Root of Performance Improvement: Research and Recommendations" (*Contemporary Management Research* 4, no. 1: 43–56).

There are, of course, more components to the "inner sphere" than the library's culture. One such component, library boards, which we discussed in chapter 5, also evolve in views and have changes in membership. Such factors must be monitored and taken into account when considering your operating environment.

Another component of the inner sphere consists of vendors and suppliers. Like any viable organization, they too monitor their operational environment and make appropriate adjustments. Your library is one element in their environment that they attempt to monitor. Those "service rep" visits are certainly intended to maintain and improve good customer relations; however, they also have a second purpose—to determine how their customers are changing. Questions about funding and new or changed services are not meant to pry into library operations; they are part of the vendor's efforts to monitor the environment. You should view such visits as a segment of your environmental scanning activities. They are opportunities to learn about what changes the firm may be planning. It is also a chance to learn about what its other library customers are doing, changing, or thinking. Another very good time to assess developments among your suppliers and vendors is on the exhibit floor of conventions such as ALA's annual and mid-winter meetings. At these times you have access to almost all your vendors in one place and time. Take advantage of the opportunity.

Clearly the library's primary funding source is part of the inner sphere. You want to look for signs of shifting priorities and determine if the upcoming shifts will be beneficial or detrimental. Related to the funding source, straddling the line between the inner and outer spheres, is political sentiment, which may impact funding priorities and perhaps the composition of the funding body.

AUTHOR EXPERIENCE

The following is an example of a library identifying a political priority and gaining a benefit. For many years at one public library, the director often conveyed to her bosses how busy the library was and how many people from all over the world walked through its doors daily. During one tough fiscal year, this information came in very handy: the library was able to receive funding from Bed, Board, and Beverage taxes (a city tax on motel and hotel rooms and restaurants) that was earmarked for the local Visitor's Center. This funding came in very handy and felt like a small victory after many years of advocating that the library served more than just the local citizenry.

For some libraries, there is a need to monitor any collective bargaining groups associated with the library. This is particularly important when the library's collective bargaining group is affiliated with a larger organization. The larger organization has agenda issues that are often broader than any local concern, but may be imposed on the local group. Keeping an eye on both local and broader concerns can be beneficial when it is time to negotiate a new agreement—the expression "Forewarned is forearmed" applies here.

Outer Sphere

The outer sphere has far too many components for us to address in a single chapter. (There are a variety of publications that provide such depth. We offer a few suggestions for resources later in this section.) Nevertheless, there are several broad categories that we will cover; one such component is past history. We have found that past events can interact with new developments in occasionally unexpected ways. Thus, we suggest keeping historical milestones in mind as you consider the data and information collected from your monitoring activities.

Two related components to consider are geography and transportation. Even academic libraries sometimes must think about these two—a commuter campus and distant education are examples of when a need for such considerations may arise. In the case of a library that encountered potential legal challenges, geography played a major role—an ever-expanding urban sprawl. The library met the expansion issue but gave too little thought to what was left behind (see chapter 5 discussion and a sidebar later in this chapter).

Legal changes are always a concern and require monitoring. Incorporating this area into a scanning program helps ensure that the task is done on a consistent basis. Major legal changes are likely to come to your attention in any case. It is the small tweaks, additions, deletions, and so on, to laws and regulations that are rarely deemed "newsworthy" that can slip by unnoticed.

Any experienced managerial leader understands the need to monitor politics—organizational and party. Both types of politics play a bigger role in nonprofit and public sector activities and operations than is true of the for-profit sector. A key question to ponder is, "Is the library now, or likely to become, a political issue?" We believe organizational politics have the greatest impact on libraries, largely as a result of tight economic conditions. School districts are quick to reduce or shutter library media centers and there is always competition among academic units for resources (as is also true of public libraries). It is not uncommon to hear "the library is getting too much [money, technology, staffing, take your pick] for too little value" or "our unit is more important to [fill in the blank] than the library." Organizational politics play a huge role in the resulting answer. We have discussed "connecting" as a significant tool in a managerial leader's skill set. Connecting and collaborating (see chapter 18) are key factors in the political process. We explore other approaches to addressing questions like the above in chapter 8 (assessment and controls) and chapter 10 (money matters).

As you might expect, economic factors are part of an effective scanning program. As with politics, there are two major elements to think about: the service community and the overall economic picture. A question to ponder when looking at economic issues is where does the major funding come from—taxes, tuition, user fees, and the like—and are there signs of a change in such sources? Funding stability, or lack thereof, is critical to planning and decision making activities.

Competition is always a concern for any organization and libraries are no exception. Questions regarding how the competitors are changing and if there are any new competitors become focal points of interest. You may have the only library in town but that does not mean you have no local competitors. Social service agencies and nonprofits are competitors for dollars and volunteer support, for example. Needless to mention, there are also the ever-growing number of virtual information sources that are major competitors. How the service community communicates with one another—when, where, and so on—can be important considerations in your planning, especially in a public library setting. Are there opportunities to play a role in the community's communication network?

For public libraries, there are three broad categories related to their service community to monitor. One is cultural activities and groups in the community (music, arts, theater, for example). Such groups tend to have a strong influence within the community and it is wise to provide support to such groups. A second category is social groups, such as garden clubs, outdoor clubs, and, of course, book clubs. The third category is social service groups, such as the Lions, Kiwanis, or Rotary. Collaborating with all of these groups can be mutually beneficial; however, it does require good connections and knowing how they are changing as their environments change.

ADVISORY BOARD EXPERIENCE

Mika is a firm believer not only in collaboration, but also in participation. At each institution where he was employed, Mika sought out a group in which he could be a participating member. This served not only to help him know what was happening in the community, but also to make the group aware of what his library, institution, or program was doing. Membership provided access to key leaders in the community and sometimes support for his organization's goals.

The last category to monitor, demographics, is at the center, or should be, of all library planning and decision making. It is an activity (monitoring) that libraries have engaged in for at least 100 years, in the United States. Because of its importance we have included an extended discussion of the topic.

Learning about the Service Community

The library's service community, like its vendors, straddles the line between the inner and outer rings of a library's environment. Library users fall into the direct contact category, while the overall community does not. In some ways, the non-users are more important to understand than are the users. We are *not* suggesting you don't put an effort into understanding your users—you should—however, the support of your nonusers may play a substantial role.

Today's proactive library managerial leaders put an effort into creating an engaged service community. There are several reasons for such efforts; perhaps the primary driver is social media, which can provide solid connections between users and the library. (Note that social media can be a problematic tool for organizations. We believe it is probably better not to engage in social media activities if the library cannot devote adequate resources to doing it well.) A second driver is that by gaining engagement the library can more effectively monitor changes in its active service community populations. Linh Cuong Nguyen, Helen Partridge, and Sylvia Edwards provided a concise statement about the notion of library engagement: "The 'participatory library' is an emerging concept that has captured the attention of the library community . . . It refers to the idea that a participatory library as a truly integrated library system must allow users to take part in core functions of the library like the catalogue system but not the periphery" (2012, 335).

CHECK THIS OUT

An interesting article that touches on the issue of gaining user engagement as well as the topic of branding your library is Rajesh Singh and Amber Ovsak's 2013 essay "Library Experience Matters! Touchpoints to Community Engagement" (*Journal of Library Administration* 53, nos. 5/6:344–358).

Service populations, regardless of library type, are diverse in their demographics. Such demographics do and should play a role in what libraries do, how they do it, why they do it and, ultimately, if they succeed or fail. Yes, a few libraries are not as successful in addressing their service communities as they might be and they don't

---

CHECK THIS OUT

For readers interested in learning more about the above situation of an unintended consequence from not fully analyzing demographic data, see G. Edward Evans and Margaret Zarnosky Saponaro's *Collection Management Basics*, 6th edition (Santa Barbara, CA: Libraries Unlimited, 2012), 43–52.

COMMON LIBRARY SERVICE COMPONENTS: A SAMPLE

- Age
- Address
- Politics
- Social trends
- Education level
- Technology access
- Religion
- Community interests
- Income
- Ethnicity
- Language(s)
- Health
- Users ownership of electronic devices (tablets, e-book readers, etc.)

CHECK THESE OUT

The following are a sample of classic works that you may wish to employ to explore community analysis in more detail.

In 1976 Larry E. Bone edited a volume of *Library Trends* (24, no. 3) entitled "Community Analysis and Libraries" that provides an excellent overview of the concept of library community analysis issues and techniques.

A later publication that provides references to the literature about library community analysis is Herbert K. Achleitner and Edward W. Neroda's *Methods of Community Analysis with an Emphasis on Libraries* (Chicago, IL: CPL Bibliographies, 1980).

Richard E. Klosterman's book *Community Analysis and Planning Techniques* (Savage, MD: Rowman & Littlefield, 1990) provides good general coverage of the methodology of community analysis.

Thomas G. Johnson, Daniel M. Otto, and Steven C. Deller's book *Community Policy Analysis Modeling* (Ames, IA: Blackwell, 2006) provides insights into how you can translate community analysis information into actionable activities.

disappear. The reason most such libraries are what they are, in our opinion, is they failed to change as their environment changed for whatever reason.

An important point, one mentioned over and over, is that just being aware of developments and changes is not enough, you must act on that knowledge. Not only must you take action, but you must do so only after very careful analysis. Earlier in chapter 5 we mentioned an instance of a library system that was aware of changing demographics and expanded its services geographically as a response to some of the changes. Later it learned that by not carefully studying the available information and acting on a detailed assessment, it found itself in violation of several important laws.

Methods for Assessing Demographics

There are a number of ways to gather demographic data; some are easy to identify and others require serious effort on your part. A scanning process requires planning as well as implementation. Part of the planning involves assuring that your data are accurate. You may have had to take a required research methods course at some point in your educational past and wondered "Why do I need this?" Gathering sound demographic data is one of the occasions when knowing and understanding research techniques is essential; or at the very least, having access to someone who does. Data-gathering sources include:

- Published data
- Reading the literature
- Surveys
- Focus groups
- Interviews
- Community leaders/gatekeepers meetings
- Observation
- Transaction logs
- "Secret shoppers"
- Questionnaires

CHECK THIS OUT

There is a series (22 volumes) created by Sage Publications (Thousand Oaks, CA) that offers concise guidance for conducting sound research projects: *Applied Social Research Methods Series*. There are volumes on such topics as survey methods, interviewing, focus groups, observation, and sampling.

A substantial amount of useful demographic data is available from published sources such as those produced by the U.S. Census Bureau. Many municipalities also have community demographic data they employ when seeking firms to locate in their community. They are also often willing to share such data. Academic institutions collect demographic data that may be useful for some purposes. The Registrar's office at a university or college can usually provide data about current and former students that goes beyond years attended, graduation year, and courses completed. Some campuses have an institutional research unit that has data that go beyond current students. School districts often collect data similar to what the public library would like to have and are willing to share the non-confidential data. A key point to keep in mind about data collected by others is the age of the data—how long ago it was collected. Newspaper and journal reading is another method for identifying useful information about the environment. Here you must consider any known biases of the publication you are reading, such as political and economic.

Surveys, interviews, and focus group data collecting requires an understanding of proper research methods. Yes, you can "just" interview people, send out a questionnaire, post a request on the library's social media platforms and the like and get responses. The problem is such data lack reliability and validity—both of which are essential to having sound data upon which to base plans and decision making. Survey and interview questions should be pretested and tested again before beginning the formal collection process. You really do need to know what answers you will receive based on the respondents understanding what you thought the understanding would be; you accomplish this through pretesting the questions.

Interviewing may appear easy to employ as a data collection method. Actually, interviewing requires skills and practice to do it in a manner that provides valid data. The biggest challenge for the interviewer is to avoid giving the respondent clues as to what you like or dislike in their answer. Most people do not want to offend someone unnecessarily and when asked a question usually try to respond in the way they think the questioner will like. We discussed the importance of non-verbals in chapter 3. The slight head nod, smile, grimace, and the like, can and do affect the answers the respondent gives you, which in turn affects the validity of the answers and the data.

Focus groups are not just a group interview process. As Krueger and Casey stated, "A focus group isn't just getting a bunch of people together to talk. A focus group is a special type of group in terms of purpose, size, composition, and procedures" (2000, 4). It is not a town hall meeting or an interview session. Groups are small and led by a moderator or recorder who has one or two specific topics for the group to discuss. The typical purposes of a focus group include to assess possible new

---

CHECK THIS OUT

In our opinion, the best resource for understanding when and how to employ focus groups is *The Focus Group Kit, Volumes 1–6*, edited by David L. Morgan, Richard A. Krueger, and Jean A. King (Thousand Oaks, CA: Sage Publications, 1997). The six volumes cover everything from planning focus groups to analyzing results.

Graham R. Walden published a useful bibliography about focus groups, *Focus Groups: Selective Annotated Bibliography* (Lanham MD: Scarecrow Press, 2008). The first volume covers the humanities and social sciences, including librarianship.

services or programs, a component in a Strengths, Weaknesses, Opportunities, and Threats (SWOT) analysis effort (sometimes referred to as "positioning" analysis); how people use a product or service; attitudinal studies; marketing effort assessment; idea generation; and staff motivational studies. The authors have employed focus groups for several of the foregoing purposes. Results can be useful, if you follow the standard model for employing such groups.

Certainly talking with community leaders and noted "trendsetters" is a less formal way to keep tabs on what is happening in the service community. You might think of such individuals as key informants (using "informant" in a positive sense). These individuals have the pulse of the community. They set trends and understand how the community functions. These are individuals well worth the time and effort necessary to create and maintain a connection.

Observation, both within and outside the library, can provide clues to a changing environment. Direct observation (the observed know there is observer present) has a major limitation: your presence will affect the behavior being observed. What that effect may be is almost impossible to determine. Thus, we suggest caution in the use of such data as there is doubt about the validity. Indirect observation will produce more reliable data but will require more planning. Commercial firms have employed the "secret shopper" approach to assess their services. To employ this concept in a library setting is easy in theory but rather time consuming and requires outside assistance. Another limitation is that it really is more a means of assessing your public service performance than it is for scanning the operational environment.

One indirect method, which provides both assessment and environmental shift data, is the use of transaction logs. Certainly the data are from library users and thus perhaps less a true reflection of the entire service community; nevertheless, such data can provide hints about changing interest among library users. OPACs and database systems generally have transaction logs as part of their software package. Examining such logs on a regular basis will provide insights into what users are looking for as well as how they do so.

CREATING A SCANNING PROGRAM

By this point you realize that environmental scanning is time consuming and, if to be useful, ongoing. No library can afford to dedicate an FTE to such work, and, in fact, it is more than a single person can handle. Most public and nonprofit organizations are in similar positions of limited staffing. One solution many have opted for is a scanning program and following Donald Sager's advice about different organizational level and level of detail.

There are two words you will encounter frequently in the literature regarding scanning: scanning and monitoring. Often the two are employed interchangeably; however, researchers in the field make a distinction between the two. Researchers view scanning as the overall process and monitoring as an activity of a scanner. They suggest some variation of multistage scanning program—for example, creating a scanning team, assigning areas or topics to team members, monitoring, gathering data, interpreting, assessing impact, deciding to or not to take action, and implementing any action.

As you might expect, there is a link between team size and monitoring topics. Not every library needs to monitor all the topics we have described. Even within a library type the topics vary—public libraries serving a homogenous population probably have less of a need to closely monitor demographics. We are not suggesting such a library should ignore demographics; rather, there may be no need to monitor the topic constantly. Clearly, deciding what topics to monitor is a key factor in the success of the program. No library has the resources to monitor everything. The goal is to select those areas that are the most important for the library. Another goal is to have a team size that is large enough to adequately carry out the monitoring and yet small enough to allow for rapid decision making. It is obvious that topics ought to be assigned that are at least somewhat related to an assignee's ongoing job responsibilities.

Monitoring involves looking for issues with the potential to affect library operations, followed by collecting information about what is taking place with that issue. The person doing the monitoring engages in some interpretation and assessment when deciding what to bring, or not bring, to the team's attention. The full team does further interpretation and assessment as to what, if any, action the library should take. Following such a process usually produces the best outcome for the library, even if it takes some time and effort.

What might team assignments be in the case of medium and larger libraries? Senior management might look at the parent organization, consortia, and society in general. The IT department would keep an eye on technological development. Public services would handle the demographic areas, while technical services would handle the vendor and economic topics.

CHECK THESE OUT

The following are some resources for exploring the scanning process in more depth:

Kendra S. Albright, "Environmental Scanning: Radar for Success," *Information Management Journal* 38, no. 3 (2004): 38–45.

Martha M. Lauzen, "Toward a Model of Environmental Scanning," *Journal of Public Relations Research* 7, no. 3 (1995): 187–203.

James L. Morrison "Establishing an Environmental Scanning/Forecasting System to Augment College and University Planning," *Planning for Higher Education* 15, no. 1 (1987): 7–22.

We will conclude with a quotation from Tom Kwanya, Christine Stilwell, and Peter G. Underwood's 2012 article that explores how libraries have changed throughout their history:

These library service models confirm that libraries have always adapted to their environments in an effort to meet the dynamic users' needs. Each model of library service represents a response to a prevailing pressing need in the library environment. . . .

Whereas librarians are advised to consider their environments when choosing which model to apply, they should be brave enough to change or discard services or resources which do not meet the needs of their users. (157–158)

REFERENCES

Beer, Michael, and Nitin Nohria. 2002. "Cracking the Code of Change." *Harvard Business Review* 78, no. 5: 133–141.

Burns, Tom, and G. M. Stalker. 1968. *The Management of Innovation*. London: Tavistock Publications.

Elenkov, Detelin S. 1997. "Strategic Uncertainty and Environmental Scanning: The Case for Institutional Influences on Scanning Behavior." *Strategic Management Journal* 18, no. 4: 287–302.

Fernandez, Sergio. 2015. "Understanding and Overcoming Resistance to Organizational Change." In *Handbook of Public Administration*. 3rd edition. Edited by James L. Perry and Robert K. Christensen, 375–401. New York: Wiley.

Jurisch, Marlen C., Christian Ikas, Petra Wolf, and Helmut Krcmar. 2012. "Key Differences of Private and Public Sector Business Process Change." e-*Service Journal* 9, no. 1: 3–27.

Katopol, Patricia. 2014. "Managing Change with Environmental Scanning." *Library Leadership & Management* 29, no. 1: 1–7.

Krueger, Richard A., and Mary Anne Casey. 2000. *Focus Groups: A Practical Guide for Applied Research*. 3rd edition. Thousand Oaks, CA: Sage Publications.

Kwanya, Tom, Christine Stilwell, and Peter G. Underwood. 2012. "Library 2.0 versus Other Library Service Models: A Critical Analysis." *Journal of Librarianship and Information Science* 44, no. 3: 145–162.

McFarland, Walter. 2015. "Mastering Change Management." *The Public Manager* 44, no. 1: 23–24.

Nguyen, Linh Cuong, Helen Partridge, and Sylvia L. Edwards. 2012. "Towards an Understanding of the Participatory Library." *Library Hi Tech* 30, no. 2: 335–346.

Sager, Donald J. 1999. "Environmental Scanning and the Public Library." *Public Libraries* 38, no. 5: 283–288.

Schein, Edgar. 1992. *Organizational Culture and Leadership*. San Francisco, CA: Jossey-Bass.

Sine, Wesley D., Hitoshi Mitsuhashi, and David A. Kirsh. 2006. "Revisiting Burns and Stalker: Formal Structure and New Venture Performance in Emerging Economic Sectors." *Academy of Management Journal* 49, no. 1: 121–132.

Tobias, Robert M. 2015. "Why Do So Many Organizational Change Efforts Fail?" *The Public Manager* 44, no. 1: 35–36.

Chapter 8

ASSESSMENT, COORDINATION, AND QUALITY

Tasking any kind of library with program assessment is a challenge. Whether the library in question is public or academic, measuring effectiveness, satisfaction, or any other performance indicators such as service quality involves a thoughtful consideration of what it is that needs measuring.

Catherine Haras, Richard Moniz, and Annie Norman, 2010

We need to show more effectively that libraries are not only busy and efficiently run institutions, but that public libraries have multiple direct and indirect impacts on communities.

Carolyn A. Anthony, 2014

Recently, questions about the role of government have become the center of national debates. These questions have prompted some government officials to search for options to deliver services. . . . Experience has shown that privatization of public services has not necessarily produced substantial cost savings.

American Library Association, 2011

Symphony orchestras and organizations share some commonalities, as writers on managerial leadership have noted on occasion. Both start with a number of people skilled at various tasks. Both organize those individuals in groups based on the individuals' skills. Both employ their "groups" to carry out distinctive functions. Both require that those distinctive functions come together as a unified performance while the groups play distinctive roles. Finally, both require someone undertake the role of assessing and coordinating the groups' activities in order to achieve a high quality performance.

Part of being "the person in charge" is to constantly assess and coordinate the actions of both individuals and the groups in terms of achieving quality outcomes.

Library managerial leaders have a challenge that symphony conductors do not face. That is, there are multiple daily performances involving the public and "library groups," and the public makes assessments regarding performance quality of every transaction. There are no "do overs" in private for the library, much less private practice sessions.

Making the situation more complex is the fact a library's supporters or users are vastly more diverse, regardless of library type. That can, and at times does, translate into variations in the user's evaluation of transactions that are identical. Yes, there can be differences in opinion among concert goers about just how good the performance was and if the interpretation was the best one. But, unlike the concert attendee, a library user who may decide not to patronize the library due to poor performance will, in almost all instances, still have to pay something to support the library. Paying for something you don't use or don't think is worthwhile rarely translates into anything but opposition, at times highly active in nature.

Unlike their for-profit sector counterparts, public and nonprofit organizations must engage in assessment and prove their value to their stakeholders and supporters over and over again. Certainly any organization in any sector needs to be assessed, at least in terms of its internal operations. Needing to "prove one's worth" is almost unique to the public and nonprofit sectors. Yes, there is something slightly similar for publicly traded commercial companies as traders buy and sell stock, at least theoretically, on the basis of a sound knowledge of a firm's "value." In our view, that is not "showing one's value"; rather, it is a short-term assessment of what a trader may gain or lose and not a statement about the firm's value to society. When a public or nonprofit organization is asked to prove its value, there is at least an implicit threat to its ongoing support and at worst a threat to its viability. For many libraries, there is always the threat of privatization if there is widespread doubt about the library's performance.

There is at least one other significant dimension to the challenges for the public and nonprofit sectors: they usually have many more stakeholders, with differing agendas, who demand accountability, cost-effective performance, and high quality, and of course doing so with fewer and fewer resources. Even the same topic—financial matters, for example—often requires different approaches for the primary funding authority, a donor group, and library users. Thus, monitoring, coordinating, and adjusting activities as needed becomes a part of the managerial leader's daily life. While there are many linkages in the various group's interests, there are also major differences.

Kathryn Newcomer commented on one rather recent type of stakeholder expectations: "evidence-based assessment" (2015). The underlying assumption of such an assessment is it arises from rigorous evaluation studies. (Needless to say, such studies take time, thought, and effort that have to come from the time, thought, and effort you have to give to all your managerial duties.) Such studies do require some expertise in order to design an appropriate project that generates valid and reliable data. Another assumption, not often stated, is that the recipients of the data will be able to accurately judge the rigor of such studies and their resulting data. In our view, that may not be all that a common skill in the political sector environment.

CHECK THIS OUT

The journal *Evidence Based Library and Information Practice* focuses on evidence-based research and libraries and is an open access title. Volume 1 appeared in 2006; it is well worth checking out from time to time (http://ejournals.library.ualberta.ca/index .php/EBLIP/).

"Transparency" is another word that has become part of the managerial lexicon over the past 20–30 years. It is a concept that generally affects public and nonprofit sector managers more than it does for-profit managers. Essentially, transparency relates to informing stakeholders about an organization's activities, policies, plans, and so on. And, just as with assessment, transparency expectations differ from one stakeholder group to another. Gregory Porumbescu and Tobin Im made the point, "Much of the discourse linking transparency to improved public management centers on the idea that increasing transparency fosters effective public sector accountability" (2015, 120). Assessment, coordination, outcomes, transparency, and quality, although they are different, interconnect in an organizational setting. (You will find an extended discussion of accountability and responsibility in chapter 4, which, of course, also relates to the above.)

ASSESSMENT

Kathryn Newcomer, mentioned above, provides a good explanation of why "assessment" is important for the public sector. "Stakeholders have increasingly called for public agencies not merely to measure workloads and accomplishments under their control, typically referred to as outputs, but to measure outcomes, or impact, of the government efforts" (2015, 334). Libraries, regardless of type, have faced the same demands. In 2013, Claire Hamasu, Betsey Kelly, and Bernard Becker began their article about assessment with "The authors love assessment and evaluation, and we believe it should be integrated into all aspects of library programming . . . Reaching this point in our relationship with assessment and evaluation has definitely had its ups and downs, and we still struggle with it" (85). The authors are not alone: most librarians face the love-hate relationship with those two concepts, along with their related concepts of outcomes, transparency, and effectiveness.

Assessing is, or should be, a perpetual activity for a managerial leader. Top managers engage in the activity constantly and often without being fully aware they are doing so; it becomes a natural part of their workday. They observe their environment and evaluate what they see in terms of what they expect to see.

Your assessment activities should apply to all the activities that occur in your unit. How well is each staff member performing her or his work? Are there any issues—big or small—that need attention? What is the staff's interaction with non-library people, such as users and vendors? Are there signs that quality is slipping? Are there changes on the part of users, vendors, and/or general public that suggest something is not quite right? Are you seeing the best approach to handling the situation or work? Could things be done better and not increase library costs?

These are but a small sampling of the type of assessment questions good managers ponder as they go about their daily activities.

Engaging in ongoing assessment takes practice, practice, and more practice before it becomes second nature. There are multiple assessment goals within the two broad categories of internal and external reasons and purposes. Like everything else, it starts by having an understanding of the techniques, purposes, and tools for "doing" assessment. It is also important to understand why assessment is necessary in the first place. Assessment for assessment's sake is pointless. Quality assurance, effective and efficient service, getting the most from the funds available, and, importantly, demonstrating that you are accountable for the resources entrusted to you, are just some of the reasons you should engage in ongoing assessment.

Being vigilant in your assessment activities is a key component in how well you handle one of the constants of being a managerial leader—accountability. Accountability is a rather complex concept in the real world, as noted in chapter 4. Each of your staff members is accountable to you for what they do, or don't do, as well as how well they do what they do. At the same time you are accountable to senior library leaders and outside authorities for everything that takes place in your area of responsibility. Your staff is not accountable for your area's performance as far as others are concerned, even though their performance is a major contributor to that performance. By the same token the senior leaders are accountable to all library stakeholders (boards, funding authorities, general public, etc.) for everything the library does and doesn't do. The point to keep in mind is, accountability is individual in character—not group based. It is akin to a sports team in that success or failure ultimately rests on how well each player performs and responds to coaching. However, when things to do not go well, it is just a few individuals who are held accountable for the failure. As we stated, accountability is complex in the real world.

All libraries, whether public or private, are accountable to their parent organization. In the public sector, governments may impose performance standards with penalties for failing to reach the established standards. In the private sector, outsourcing services may be an alternative to an internally provided service that is not seen as meeting the needs of the organization at an acceptable cost. Such pressure places a considerable burden on managers to meet standards set for their library by outside stakeholders. There can be, and often is, a very fine line between success and failure. Ongoing assessment helps you avoid failures.

ENGAGING STAKEHOLDERS IN ASSESSMENT PROJECTS

There are occasions, for both internal and external reasons, when involving stakeholders in our assessment efforts is a sound practice. Very often it is users that are the people you want involved in the project. Libraries in the public sector have found user involvement a valuable key in handling assessment and for transparency reasons. Such involvement can provide the type of "evidence" that many external bodies seek when making decisions regarding libraries. It is also an important component in creating a "participatory library" we mentioned in the last chapter.

Essentially, there are five reasons for involving stakeholders in your assessment efforts:

1. To inform
2. To consult
3. To involve
4. To collaborate
5. To empower

As noted above, the "to inform" aspect relates to the need for transparency. The consultation element relates to being an attentive listener to stakeholder "voices" and seriously considering those concerns or views into your assessment analysis. Involvement takes the process further by working with the stakeholders in a manner that assures them that their input actually does matter. Collaboration means involving some stakeholders in considering what the assessment data means and what it might imply in terms of adjustments. Empowerment is the ultimate in stakeholder involvement: the library presents options and allows the stakeholders to make the decision. Most libraries employ the three middle level approaches.

ASSESSMENT, OUTCOMES, AND CONTROL

Assessment and outcomes are important components of your managerial leadership responsibility for controlling and coordinating library operations. Both activities can be challenging and you will need to adjust your approach to fit the individuals involved; that can mean, in some instances, two or more approaches for the same situation.

Earlier, we said that you must constantly monitor operations—people and processes. You assign people to certain duties based on your assessment of the person's skill set and sometimes forget that skill sets can and do change over time. It is only from monitoring activities that we can see the issue; at that point there may be a hard decision to make. "How can I adjust the situation to assure the best possible organizational performance?" "Best possible organizational performance" is your ultimate duty as a managerial leader. Technology and its rapidly changing nature is today's most common cause for staff and manager's heartaches in terms of performance challenges.

Performance expectations clearly need to change as the operating environment changes. When that takes place, you may face the fact it may be necessary for staff to acquire new skills in order to effectively carry out the new performance needs. Providing the requisite training can be a challenge. Few libraries have more than marginally adequate funds for staff development and major retaining efforts usually require seeking outside funding. The good news is that you can usually incorporate such costs into the cost of major technological projects. This tactic puts the responsibility on staff to learn the new skill(s). That might seem to be an obvious statement; however, the authors have encountered several instances where a staff member refused to participate and/or made no effort to understand the importance and need to learn the new skill.

With the exception of technological challenges, you can achieve good control and coordination through setting clear and realistic performance expectations. Needless to say, such expectations must be effectively communicated as well as understood. You need to employ all the communication skills covered in chapter 3 if you hope to have everyone on the same page when it comes to expectations. Consistently applying those expectations is also a key. Certainly there may be times when there are exceptions, such as when a staff member faces health or serious family issues. Even in those circumstances you should not completely ignore performance expectations for a long time. Other staff may well have sympathy for the person, but a long-term lack of good performance can affect the performance of both the unit and the organization.

One challenge, especially in the public sector, when it comes to new skills and existing staff, is most public sector personnel systems have tight rules and regulations. They have limited options when it comes to transferring a person from one position to another, even when the person no longer has the requisite skills to handle new duties and does not wish to acquire those skills. "Passing probation" (a period of time at the start of employment before a new hire is "permanent") is common in almost any organization in the United States. Given the political nature of public sector organizations and agencies, it has become common that employees have a high degree of job security. That "security" is intended to avoid wholesale firings each time there is change in political control of government provide continuity in services and programs. That type of security can create some major barriers when shifting staff to new tasks and developing new skills as the operating environment changes. The existence of a collective bargaining unit will only increase your challenges.

Before you can fight the personnel system battles you have to have a realistic plan to propose. Can you really find a place to transfer the person who may not be capable of learning the new skill in a timely manner? You are unlikely to have a vacant FTE to use in a restructuring process. So, who on the existing staff might be willing to change job duties and gain the necessary skills? Do you have the time to address a grievance process that may arise? Handling the need for new skill sets and changing job duties to assure the best possible organizational performance, without additional resources, is one of the conundrums of managerial life. There is no answer beyond careful thinking and having a very sound relationship with your staff.

Another aspect of good control and coordination is learning from your mistakes. Effective managerial leaders engage in life-long learning in general and, specifically, attempt to learn from their mistakes. What worked? What errors occurred? What could have been done differently? Would more time pondering the matter have produced a notably different outcome? Public and nonprofit managers are well served by using a concept, if not the label, from the military: after-action assessment.

ADVISORY BOARD EXPERIENCE

In addition to his library career, Mika spent 29 years as an officer in the U.S. Army Reserve, retiring as a colonel. As part of his basic officer training, the process of after-action reports became ingrained in him and he utilized it throughout his military and civilian careers and in his managerial style. Whether serving as company commander, faculty member, library school director, or garrison commander, Mika utilized the after-action process to assess what was successful in whatever he was assigned to accomplish or that he assigned to others. After-action assessment allows not only the manager, but also the staff to analyze what actions are successful, what actions could be improved, and what actions are responsible for failure. Knowing these allows the manager to make changes to improve and enhance upon future actions leading to success and to avoid those steps that hinder achievement.

Coordination is both an ongoing concern and a challenge. Like control, it is a people issue more than anything else. One significant reason for this is unit heads do monitor unit operations and outputs. They tend to be less focused on how their unit's output affects other units. It is natural and reasonable to want to be certain your unit performs effectively and efficiently—an internal focus. Those factors do play a major role in how your performance gets assessed. A big issue arises when there is *no* concern about how the unit's activities affect other units. One common factor that leads to overall performance difficulties is unit head rivalries and/or competition. (We explore office politics in chapter 11.) Competition is inherently neither "good" nor "bad"; from an organizational perspective, its usefulness lies in its value in promoting solid coordination and high quality user services and programs.

The nature of most public and nonprofit sector salary systems can play a role in how well coordinated unit performance is and the quality of service the public receives. In today's economic environment, salary increases are rather rare. Cost-of-living increases, when they occur, are modest at best and any pools for merit increases are very small (if they even exist). Somewhat ironically, coordination may suffer when there are merit pools. In the hope of securing a merit increase, staff members may focus more on their own performance at the expense of thinking in terms of group performance. Finding a valid realistic measure of high level cooperative or coordinated personal workplace performance is not easy. Trying to sort through the performance factors that you are comfortable with when having to give very few merit increases is stressful. An easy option of rotating such increases through the staff over time may seem "fair," but rather defeats the notion of "merit" as well as ignoring the fact that there may be several years between having merit increases available.

Does how you structure work activities play a role in how easy or difficult it is to achieve great coordination? The structure in itself is not so much the issue as is the individuals you assign to the units in your structure. Certainly the structure can and does play a role in overall service performance. That means you ought not to think of the current structure as being permanent. It pays to periodically consider a reorganization of personnel in order to achieve better outcomes. For a variety of reasons, people change and so does their work performance. Person A may have performed reasonably well in a unit but in time the performance suffers—a new unit head or new hire may be the issue. Once again the nature of the public and nonprofit sector personnel rules may limit your transfer options.

OUTCOMES AND MEANINGFUL MEASURES

As noted earlier, outputs (such as items circulated and questions answered) are one form of outcomes, but there are others. More often than not, the other types of outcomes are of greater interest to library stakeholders. For example, how effective are library operations? Are they efficient? What is the cost-benefit of the operations or the return on investment? Yes, the library may have efficiently and effectively acquired more collection items this year, made them available to the public, and people may have used those resources at the highest per capita rate than any time in the library's history. So what? What is the social value or outcome of all that? You can ask these questions of any library activity and finding a meaningful answer is why assessment and meaningful measures are such formidable and valuable undertakings. Being able to produce *evidence* is the key. Essentially, it is about gathering solid data on a variety of levels and subjects and compiling them into a compelling narrative answer.

Keep in mind that efficiency and effectiveness are not the same thing. Efficiency is doing something at the lowest possible cost, be it time, money, equipment, or other resource. Effectiveness is doing the right thing at the right time. Thus, your unit may be effective but inefficient or efficient but ineffective. Your obvious is goal is to be both effective and efficient. That is not always easy to do.

In the following sections, we discuss some of the more standard measurement resources that library leaders can employ to generate solid data.

Cost Analysis

Knowing what your operations cost is important both for internal and external reasons. Costs play a major role in determining how efficient your operation may be and point to potential areas to change. A number of elements go into a cost measurement effort. Whatever the system you employ, the process will involve (a) observing staff engaging in the work; (b) asking unit heads to provide the data, or asking staff to self-report data; and (c) comparing your data with other libraries. Each of these methods has its advantages and disadvantages. No matter what approach is taken there will be staff concerns about what is being collected, why it is being done, and how you expect to use the data. It is natural that collecting any type of workplace data will cause some staff anxiety.

James Kusack was correct when he wrote, "Cost finding is not hard, and it certainly doesn't involve higher math. A bit of simple arithmetic and a dollop of logic will suffice. Basically, all the task requires is to add up each of the costs and then divide that total cost by the number of people served or the number of transactions performed" (2002, 152). It is slightly more complicated than the quotation suggests, but it is not all that complex.

There are a number of decisions to make before you engage in the summing and dividing process. The major decision is figuring out what costs you are going to include and why. If it is just something you wish to do for your unit, then some discussion with the staff about what and why should be sufficient. On the other hand, if it involves other units or is library-wide, the discussions of what and why will involve many more people and take time.

Next, identify the elements to include in the cost categories. A common method is to use three categories—labor, supplies, and overhead. Supplies such as pens, paper, books, files, and printer ink cartridges are easy to identify, but what about the upgrading and maintenance of computers, license fees, and so on? Are they supplies or overhead? Do you depreciate equipment (chairs, desks, printers, etc.) costs over a fixed time period or just their acquisition cost in a single year's cost? Do you use the original purchase price or the replacement cost? There are various methods and rationales for deciding these and other related questions. If you overlook such issues, you may ignore some real organizational costs as well as the point of the study. Keep in mind that how you categorize expenses impacts your ability to compare your budget with other units or libraries. You will almost always want to use all the direct costs, such as salaries and supplies. The major question is whether you should include indirect costs such as equipment, equipment maintenance, utilities, physical space, and senior administration, and if so, how many categories and in what amounts?

Another issue is what is a reasonable timeframe for the study? Just focusing on a single budget cycle is probably not useful, unless you are doing it just to check your unit's performance and you have some prior cost data. A key element in assessing the accuracy of data is the sample size. In most cases, it is neither feasible nor necessary to have a 100 percent population sample. Once again, those pesky research methods course elements come into play. Sampling sizes can be relatively small, given the proper selection method; that is, the sample is statistically random.

CHECK THESE OUT

There are a number of books on statistical methods and research that focus on the library environment. One such title is Arthur W. Hafner's *Descriptive Statistical Techniques for Librarians,* 2nd edition (Chicago, IL: American Library Association, 1998).

Another excellent title is Lynn Silipigni Connaway and Ronald R. Powell's *Basic Research Methods for Librarians* (Santa Barbara, CA: Libraries Unlimited, 2010).

We also provided suggestions for more general books on research method topics in chapter 7.

When engaging in a cost-accounting study, you are gathering data that is useful in setting standards and vice versa. A standard serves as a target for performance; to be useful, it should be measurable. The typical measures of quality, quantity, time, and cost are useful individually and even more so in combination: cost-benefit, unit cost, and time-quantity. The key question becomes, how does one establish the standards? Four broad data categories exist that can assist in establishing standards: historical, comparative, engineered, and subjective.

CHECK THIS OUT

In 2011 Mott Linn published a useful article that will help you understand the ins and outs of cost studies: "Cost-Benefit Analysis: Examples" (*Bottom Line: Managing Library Finances* 24, no. 1: 68–72).

Where to place the concept of return on investment (ROI) was a point as authors we debated at some length. Is it a cost benefit analysis? Somewhat, but not exactly. Is it an outcome? Not really, although it has outcome implications. In the end, we decided to place a more detailed discussion of it in the chapter on budgets and money management. The basic ROI method rests on placing a money value on library outputs and services and comparing such values against the library's total expenditure. In the public and nonprofit sectors the concept is most often labeled social return on investment (SROI).

Work Analysis

Work analysis can assist in making effective use of physical space, choosing a sequence for doing work, and finding ways of performing tasks more efficiently. Most work-analysis techniques relate in one way or another to time or money, and, as a result, they provide much of the data needed for budgeting and planning. Work-analysis techniques will help you determine what needs to be done—establish realistic workloads (standards) and compare them to actual performance.

Not all of the work analysis techniques require sampling. Some help you visualize the interrelated nature of unit work activities and perhaps improve coordination or establish that the present system is, in fact, the best. Others help you control complex projects that may not be part of the normal activities. All of them serve in assisting you in assessing, controlling, and monitoring work activities.

A block diagram is a basic form for engaging in work analysis. It provides a picture of the interrelationships that exist between work units or activities. A flow diagram digs deeper into such relationships and provides a graphic view a work area and the "flow" of people or things within work space. Another tool is the flow process chart, which can illustrate the movements of an item without linking those movements to a physical space. You can also chart how decisions impact work activities; such charts are frequently employed when working on technology-related activities.

Such charts and diagrams allow you to track every step or process that an activity goes through. This, in turn, permits you to accurately assess the process and determine if this is the best sequence or if steps could be combined or altered.

The above are but a small sample of the work analysis techniques that you may employ to enhance your unit's work performance. Richard Dougherty summed up the need for librarians to engage in constant work analysis as such: "And even when and if the budget pendulum swings back, there will never be 'enough' money. One way to free up staff time and dollar resources is to streamline processes and procedures, or better yet, get rid of existing operations that are redundant or unnecessary" (2008, ix). We highly recommend his book *Streamlining Library Services: What We Do, How Much Time It Takes, What It Costs, and How We Can Do It Better* (Lanham, MD: Scarecrow Press, 2008). It provides a wealth of useful information and ideas for improving our library operations.

TOOLS FOR ASSESSING PERFORMANCE

There are several useful tools, some from commercial firms, which aid in assessing your library's performance. The key to using them effectively is understanding their strengths and weaknesses. Just because library X used tool Z is not sufficient reason for you to do so, even when outsiders suggest you do. A frank discussion of costs, benefits, and what the information might be used for should be the first order of business.

Benchmarking

With funding agencies and other organizations growing ever more concerned about cost containment, there is an increasing use of benchmarking—a tool for comparing operations for either internal or external purposes. The goal is to provide data that can help managers answer the following questions:

- How well are we doing compared to others?
- How good do we want to be?
- Who is doing the best?
- How do they do it?
- How can we adapt their practices to our organization?
- How can we be better than the best?

While there are four basic types of benchmarking—internal, competitive, industry, and best in class—the first two are the ones most commonly used in publicly funded services. In the corporate sector, industry or best in class is generally used more often.

As the name suggests, internal benchmarking looks at the internal practices of an organization, such as the cost of creating a purchase order in various departments. A competitive benchmarking project might collect data on the cost of creating purchase orders in various departments in a number of institutions. Industry benchmarking would collect data from all or a representative sample of all organizations within an "industry." Best in class benchmarking collects information across industries and seeks the most cost effective practices.

Internal benchmarking may vary between vertical and horizontal projects. A vertical project seeks to quantify the costs, workloads, and productivity of a defined functional area—for example, handling accounts payable. A horizontal study analyzes the cost and productivity of a single process that crosses two or more functional areas—for example, database searching in acquisitions, cataloging, and document delivery.

When developing a benchmarking project, make certain all the participants have a clear understanding of what each benchmark will measure and what data to collect (time, staff salaries, equipment costs, staff benefits, etc.). A common problem on first-time projects is misunderstanding what staff costs should be included—just salary, salary and directed benefits such as health insurance, or all of those plus vacation and sick leave costs. The data will be essentially useless for comparative purposes unless there is a single, clear standard.

CHECK THESE OUT

Patricia Keehley and Neil N. Abercrombie's *Benchmarking in the Public and Nonprofit Sectors: Best Practices for Achieving Performance Breakthroughs*, 2nd edition (New York: Wiley & Sons, 2008), provides in-depth information about using benchmarking.

Frankie Wilson and J. Stephen Town's 2006 article "Benchmarking and Library Quality Maturity" (*Performance Measurement and Metrics* 7, no. 2: 75–82) provides an example of library benchmarking.

Another library-based article is Carol Simon's 2011 "An Examination of Best Practices and Benchmarking in Corporate Libraries" (*Journal of Management Development* 30, no. 1: 134–141).

User Surveys

To assess quality with user surveys, U.S. libraries have drawn upon an approach developed by Parasuraman, Berry, and Zeithaml (1988), known as SERVQUAL. SERVQUAL was designed to measure service quality in the retail sector. Raja Parasuraman (2002) described how this series of empirical studies developed, tested, and refined a scale for measuring service quality as perceived by customers. Today, SERVQUAL is a two-part instrument that measures services along a range of attributes grouped into five dimensions:

1. Reliability,
2. Responsiveness,
3. Assurance,
4. Empathy, and
5. Tangibles, e.g., appearance of the physical facilities, equipment, etc.

There are two levels of expectation: desired service level and adequate service level. The difference between the two levels indicates the levels of service performance a customer would consider to be satisfactory.

Libraries adapted SERVQUAL and developed LibQual+ ® (http://www.libqual .org/home). Journals have published special issues focusing on this approach, describing its use and outcomes in U.S. academic libraries (see, e.g., Kyrillidou and Heath, 2001; Cook, 2002).

ADVISORY BOARD EXPERIENCE

Alire's experience with LibQual occurred at both of the ARL libraries she led. Using LibQual was instrumental in developing objectives to adjust and improve services for the next fiscal and academic year(s) and was tied directly to the strategic plans in place. However, this data was coupled with data gathered from focus groups and other instruments. Each year LibQual was used to evaluate whether or not services identified the previous year and adjusted had actually improved in the eyes of the specific group of users who were identified the previous year.

Alire used the LibQual data to demonstrate to campus decision-makers and stakeholders (i.e., faculty and student governance) that the library was using quantitative methodology to identify areas of service concern; to improve those service areas; and then to show results in improvement.

Some libraries are using another service, similar to LibQual, for assessment purposes—Counting Opinions (http://www.countingopinions.com). The organization's statement of purpose and service is "comprehensive, cost-effective, real-time solutions designed for libraries, in support of customer insight, operational improvements and advocacy efforts." Its list of customers includes both academic and public libraries. Two of the company's products are LibSat™ ("the means to measure customer satisfaction") and LibPAS™ (library performance assessment).

Six Sigma

Six Sigma is both a philosophy and a technique designed to eliminate waste and improve performance. Using statistical analysis (six sigma), it aims to bring down defects in processes and services to near zero. At the same time, it fosters a culture that focuses on creating value for the user and eliminating any redundant processes.

An example of an academic library employing the Six Sigma (or Lean Six Sigma) method can be found in an article by Sarah Murphy. Most markedly Murphy discussed the applicability of the concept to one service element at the Ohio State University (OSU) libraries. Library service is a fleeting transaction and presents challenges as to when and how often to assess such transactions. As she stated, "Services are both intangible and heterogeneous, inviting variability in processes as customers and providers contribute to the inputs and outputs of the service product" (2009, 216). The focus of her project was OSU libraries' process for managing and answering users' email questions. She concluded her article with the statement:

> Libraries can customize and borrow a number of quality management systems and tools from the business community to both assess their service process and continuously

improve their operations. By adopting an approach like Lean Six Sigma, a library can respond better to changing customer needs and desires by creating an infrastructure that supports, nurtures, and sustains a culture of assessment and change. (224)

For more examples of libraries employing the Six Sigma method, see Michael Thomsett (2005), Brett and Queen (2005), and Kumi and Morrow (2006).

Balanced Scorecard

The Balanced Scorecard was developed by Robert Kaplan and David Norton as an approach to strategic management based on a measurement system. It provides feedback on the internal operations and the external outcomes to assist organizations to continuously improve strategic performance (Kaplan and Norton, 2006). The approach views the organization from four perspectives for which metrics are developed and data is collected and analyzed. The perspectives are the learning and growth perspective, the business process perspective, the customer perspective, and the financial perspective (www.balancedscorecard.org).

Alfred Willis interviewed two library administrators who were lead figures in using the balanced scorecard at their library. Jim Self, in responding to a question regarding the value of the technique, said, "It can focus the library. It makes the library as an organization decide what is important. It can be used to improve organizational performance. It broadens our perspective in a structured way, and gives us a more balanced view of our work" (2004, 66). Lynda White's response to the question was "Our balanced scorecard is so user-oriented, it fits really well with what we value. Many of our metrics focus on the results for our users whether or not they are technically in the user- perspective" (66).

CHECK THIS OUT

A book that explores the Balanced Scorecard as it relates to library environments is Joseph Matthews' *Scorecards for Results: A Guide for Developing a Library Balanced Scorecard* (Santa Barbara, CA: Libraries Unlimited, 2008).

Quality Service

Every library attempts to provide the best possible service given available resources. A managerial leader plays a major role in how well the library achieves that goal. In that role, you monitor the daily interactions between library staff and outsiders, be they users, vendors, or other library stakeholders. Your constant assessment of those interactions should serve as an early warning system if something isn't quite right.

There are internal library reasons (mission, vision, and goals, for example) and external (user satisfaction and accountability are two major issues) for seeking high quality. Knowing when you have achieved quality is not always easy or straightforward. How exactly is quality defined, for example? It is important to start any discussion of institutional quality with definitions of goals and objectives and create standards for how the staff is to achieve them. It is also difficult to define quality when there is no physical product. What standard defines quality library service? Is it user satisfaction or something more complex? A person may be satisfied with the information provided and not be aware that the information is incomplete, or even incorrect. In time, the person may determine that the information was less than satisfactory. When should we measure user satisfaction?

Many library services are intangible. Research on service quality, such as by Parasurman, Zeitaml, and Berry (1987) reveals 10 dimensions that, to a greater or lesser degree, determine the quality of a service and also apply to library services. (Their research served as the basis for much for later assessments of what constitutes quality.)

1. Reliability or consistency,
2. Responsiveness or timeliness,
3. Competence,
4. Access or approachability,
5. Courtesy,
6. Communication,
7. Credibility,
8. Security (including confidentiality),
9. Understanding the customer needs,
10. Tangibles (such as physical facilities, appearance of personnel, and tools or equipment).

Understanding users is the key element in assessing quality services. Librarians have a firm understanding of their services and products, as well as what constitutes their primary user groups. What they may not fully understand is what constitutes the total service population. W. Edwards Deming (1986), a well-known scholar in the area of quality management, emphasized that the reason for quality is the customer (whether actual or potential).

CHECK THIS OUT

A solid article that looks at library assessment is Larry Nash White's 2009 essay "Aligning Library Assessment Process to the Library's Service Environment: A Conceptual Model" (*Library Review* 57, no. 7: 499–513).

WHY OUTCOMES ASSESSMENT?

In the last 15 to 20 years, library stakeholders have demanded more than statistics on input (such as items acquired) and outputs (such as items borrowed). They have demanded hard evidence that the use of resources resulted in a positive benefit or outcome. "Did we get anything of value from giving you X?"

A variation of that question is "Prove your worth." Without ongoing assessment data that focuses on the right questions, providing a meaningful response is almost impossible.

The stakeholders' new questions are harder to answer from statistics alone. For example:

- How does the library collect and *analyze* data on its collections, staff, budget, etc.?
- Does the library identify *learning goals* for itself, and are they linked to institutional learning goals?
- Are satisfaction surveys regularly conducted and *used*?
- How does the library *assess* accomplishment of its learning goals?
- How are *assessment results* incorporated into planning and improvements?
- How are library learning goals *linked* to community learning goals?

The above are examples of the ever-growing importance of "proving one's worth" to the community and to those who provide the funding. In the not-too-distant past, libraries in the United States were right there with "the flag, mom, and apple pie" in terms of overall public sense of societal value. Today, a great many people see social services—including libraries, archives, and even education—as too much apple pie, and think that perhaps the country needs to cut its calorie intake. Peggy Rudd succinctly summed up the thoughts/feelings of many information professionals about "outcome assessment":

> For those of us who work in libraries, who educate those who work in them and who use and support them in a variety of ways, the value of libraries goes without saying. We believe they are a public good. . . . But no matter how fervent our beliefs about the value of libraries, our belief system offers the weakest of responses when presented with the classic evaluation question: What difference does it make? (2001, 17)

Having an answer to such questions will become increasingly critical to the long-term viability of publicly funded services, including almost every nonprofit organization.

Denise Davis and Emily Plagman identified four key reasons why any library should put an effort into measuring outcomes. Although their article relates to the Public Library Association's "Project Outcomes" initiative, the basic concepts apply to almost any type of library. The reasons they identified are "To better measure and improve upon the impact in the community, . . . To support planning and assessment over time, . . . To help better manage services and resources, . . . [and] To justify funding requests" (2015, 34). Davis and Plagman describe the elements of Project Outcome; one result of the effort is a series of surveys that a library may sign up to use (www.project outcome.org).

Perhaps there is at least one more reason for measuring outcomes—to avoid being privatized or outsourced. Libraries have outsourced many activities for years. However, they use outsourcing services for internal operations. There are some U.S. libraries (public or nonprofit in purpose) that are operated by for-profit corporations. A number of federal government agencies have, for some time, used for-profit firms to provide their library services. There are also a few "public" libraries that are privatized. Perhaps the most widely known is the library in Riverside County, California. Heather Hill published an article that looked at privatization of public libraries. She identified two approaches to the process: temporary outsourcing of senior management positions and the outsourcing of all library staff (2012). (We should note Hill's doctoral dissertation was a study of library privatization.)

Discussions about privatizing are almost always driven by questions of finance and value for money expended. The reality is the largest portion of a library's operating budget is salaries. The basic source of profit comes through reducing personnel costs—primarily by lowering salaries. In the case of public libraries, that would include changing the retirement plan to one primarily funded by the individual employees (IRAs and the like). Has it worked out as supporters hoped? As of 2012, 18 libraries had made the decision to outsource personnel between 1997 and 2012; only two communities have ceased using outsourcing (Hill, 2012). A more fundamental question that has not clearly been answered is "has service quality declined?" There are many opinions but little, if any, hard data to support a pro or con position.

We believe privatization is yet another reason to have solid outcome or value data available to present at such discussions. The data will also provide a baseline for judging the performance before and after privatization, should it occur. Assessment and outcomes are critical to the long-term viability of libraries of all types.

CHECK THESE OUT

Two books discussing outcomes assessment and service quality that we recommend are Peter Hernon and Robert E. Dugan's *An Action Plan for Outcome Assessment in Your Library* (Chicago IL: American Library Association, 2001); and Peter Hernon and John R. Whitman's *Delivering Satisfaction and Service Quality: A Customer-Based Approach for Libraries* (Chicago IL: American Library Association, 2001)

A title we highly recommend that covers almost every topic in this chapter is Joseph S. Wholey, Harry P. Hatry, and Kathryn E. Newcommer's *Handbook of Practical Program Evaluation*, 4th edition (San Francisco, CA: Jossey-Bass, 2015).

Yet another excellent title to review is Theodore H. Poister, Maria P. Aristigueta, and Jeremy L. Hall's *Managing and Measuring Performance in Public and Nonprofit Organizations: An Integrated Approach*, 2nd edition (San Francisco, CA: Jossey-Bass, 2015).

A relatively recent book that will be very useful for smaller libraries that wish to engage in assessment is Peter Hernon, Robert E. Dugan, and Joseph R. Mathews's *Getting Started with Evaluation* (Chicago, IL: American Library Association, 2014). What makes this so useful is it is a workbook with exercises that walk you through key steps. Very much worth a careful read.

REFERENCES

American Library Association. 2011. *Keeping Public Libraries Public: A Checklist for Communities Considering Privatization of Public Libraries.* Chicago, IL: American Library Association. http://www.ala.org/tools/sites/ala.org.tools/files/content/outsourcing/REVISEDSEPT 2011_ALAKeepingPublicLibraries%20PublicFINAL2.pdf.

Anthony, Carolyn A. 2014. "Moving Toward Outcomes." *Public Libraries* 53, no. 3: 5–7.

Brett, Charles, and Patrick Queen. 2005. "Streamlining Enterprise Records Management with Lean Six Sigma." *Information Management Journal* 39, no. 6: 58, 60–62.

Cook, Colleen. 2002. "The Maturation of Assessment in Academic Libraries: Performance Measurement and Metrics." *International Journal for Library and Information Services* 3, no. 2: 40–42.

Davis, Denise, and Emily Plagman. 2015. "Project Outcome: Helping Libraries Capture Their Community Impact." *Public Libraries* 54, no. 4: 33–37.

Deming, W. Edwards. 1986. *Out of the Crisis.* Cambridge, MA: MIT Press.

Dougherty, Richard. 2008. *Streamlining Library Services: What We Do, How Much Time It Takes, What It Costs, and How We Can Do It Better.* Lanham, MD: Scarecrow Press.

Hamasu, Claire, Betsey Kelly, and Bernard Becker. 2013. "Assessment and Evaluation Is Not a Gut Feeling: Integrating Assessment and Evaluation into Library Operations." *Journal of the Medical Library Association Bulletin* 10, no. 2: 85–87.

Haras, Catherine, Richard Moniz, and Annie Norman. 2010. "Listening to the Customer: Using Assessment Results to Make a Difference." *Library Leadership & Management* 24, no. 2: 91–99.

Hill, Heather. 2012. "A Look at Public Library Management Outsourcing." *Public Libraries* 51, no. 3: 42–47.

Kaplan, Robert S., and David P. Norton. 2006. "The Balanced Scorecard: Measures That Drive Performance." *Harvard Business Review* 83, nos. 7/8: 172, 174–180.

Kumi, Susan, and John Morrow. 2006. "Improving Self Service the Six Sigma Way at Newcastle University Library." *Program* 40, no. 2: 123–136.

Kusack, James M. 2002. "Understanding and Controlling the Costs of Library Services." *Library Administration & Management* 16, no. 3: 151–155.

Kyrillidou, Martha, and Fred M. Heath. 2001. "Measuring Service Quality." *Library Trends* 49, no. 4: 541–799.

Macikas, Barb. 2015. "Language Matters." *Public Libraries* 54, no. 6: 7–8.

Murphy, Sarah Anne. 2009. "Leveraging Lean Six Sigma to Culture, Nurture, and Sustain Assessment and Change in the Academic Library Environment." *College & Research Libraries* 70, no. 3: 215–225.

Newcomer, Kathryn E. 2015. "Evaluating the Performance of Public Programs." In *Handbook of Public Administration.* 3rd edition. Edited by James L. Perry and Robert K. Christensen. New York: Wiley.

Parasuraman, Raja A. 2002. "Foreword." *Performance Measurement and Metrics: The International Journal for Library and Information Services* 3, no. 2: 37–39.

Parasuraman, Raja A., Valarie A. Zeithaml, and Leonard L. Berry. 1984. *A Conceptual Model of Service Quality and Its Implications for Future Research (Report No. 84–106).* Cambridge, MA: Market Science Institute.

Porumbescu, Gregory A., and Tobin Im. 2015. "Using Transparency to Reinforce Responsibility and Responsiveness." In *Handbook of Public Administration.* 3rd edition. Edited by James L. Perry and Robert K. Christensen. New York: Wiley.

Rudd, Peggy D. 2000. "Documenting the Difference: Demonstrating the Value of Libraries Through Outcome Measurement." In *Perspectives on Outcomes Based Evaluation for Libraries and Museums*. Washington, DC: Institute of Museum and Library Services. http://www.imls.gov/assets/1/AssetManager/PerspectivesOBE.pdf.

Simon, Carol. 2011. "An Examination of Best Practices and Benchmarking in Corporate Libraries." *Journal of Management Development* 30, no. 1: 134–141.

Thomsett, Michael C. 2005. *Getting Started in Six Sigma*. New York: Wiley.

Willis, Alfred. 2004. "Using the Balanced Scorecard at the University of Virginia Library." *Library Administration & Management* 18, no. 2: 64–67.

Chapter 9

FISCAL MATTERS

For the effective public manager, the issues of resource acquisition, distribution, and management are critical.

Steven Cohen, William Eimicke, and Tanya Heikkila, 2013

Budgeting and fiscal administration require public administrators to resolve a variety of operational, managerial, and strategic issues.

James L. Perry and Robert K. Christensen, 2015

The major emphasis in business is for profit to exceed cost by as much as possible. In nonprofit managerial accounting, cost containment is import, if the nonprofit organization is to remain viable.

G. Stevenson Smith, 2002.

More than 100 years ago George Bernard Shaw wrote "Money is indeed the most important thing in the world; and all sound and successful personal and national morality should have this fact for its basis" (1905, xiv). We are not certain it is the *most* important thing in the world. However, there is little doubt that without money most, if not all, of modern life would grind to a halt. Since the "Great Recession," libraries have learned to live with less money and fewer other resources. The only slightly bright spot in that dismal picture is that libraries share that environment with almost all other public and nonprofit organizations. Misery loves company! (We hope not.)

The opening quotation from Cohen, Eimicke, and Heikkila concisely summarizes the components of public and nonprofit fiscal management. "The budget" underlies almost every aspect of library operations, either directly or indirectly. We grouse about inadequate funding, we are often unable to engage in a service we know the users would like, and we all too often make tough decisions to reduce this or that activity due to lack of money. In this chapter, as well as in chapter 10, we look at ways to reduce the stress related to funding.

It is easy to forget that a budget is one of the organization's most powerful control tools and to think of only a small part of the budget—the operational expenses (OE)—when we refer to "the" budget. While OE is the one we think about most often because of the constant interaction with its limits, it is only one type of budget. There are capital budgets, project budgets, and personnel hour budgets, for example. Beyond those, there are the familiar budget formats that you probably know from your management reading (line item, program, performance, zero-based, flexible freeze, priority based budgeting, etc.).

A budget is in fact an estimate of what it will cost to perform certain tasks over a specified timeframe. The funding authority expects the manager to "live within the budget." Failure to do so repeatedly will cause the manager problems and perhaps even lead to dismissal. Certainly there is some leeway as the unexpected does happen, but even a single major overrun can become a career-damaging situation. This is another difference between managing in the public and nonprofit sector versus the for-profit sector, where budget overruns are less critical. How often have you read about contractors having major cost overruns when working on a public sector project? Compare that to how often you read that contractor had any consequences for the overage.

PUBLIC AND NONPROFIT BUDGETING VERSUS FOR-PROFIT

When it comes to money matters and its management there are sharp differences between the for-profit sector and the public and nonprofit sectors. While almost all organizations have some form of operating budget, for-profit managers are less constrained by that budget. Those managers can, within limits, have a reasonable expectation that should something cause an overrun in their operating budgets, additional funds may become available. About the only hope public and nonprofit managers have in such instances is a willing donor—even then the amount likely to be available will be modest at best. An important point to keep in mind, especially for libraries, is that generally salaries represent over 50 percent of the operating budget. Further, that expense category is off limits to shifting monies from to another category. One reason is many jurisdictions employ the concept of salary savings as part of the budgeting process. The concept rests on the idea that there will be some staff turnover, unpaid leave or other absences, and so on, that will result in salary costs being unspent. The authors have worked in organizations where the managers are given a percentage for what they are to "save" at the beginning of the budget cycle. That is a much better situation, if no less frustrating, than being told you must have such savings during the budget cycle. You have less time to achieve the results and that in turn can generate a loss of funds in some other category should you not have staff turnover (often from the acquisitions allocation). To achieve such saving usually means you must leave a vacancy open longer than desired.

People in the public and nonprofit sector organizations know, or should know, that their budget process is more than merely setting dollar allocations for various activities. Budgets are a reflection of organizational priorities and policies. They are also, especially in the public sector, political documents. They are more transparent than for-profit budget documents—which are often not available outside of the company.

Broadly, there are four major differences between the for-profit and public or nonprofit sector budgeting processes: purpose, process, decision making, and accounting. The obvious major difference lies in the purposes of the organizations, as highlighted in Smith's opening quotation—profit versus cost containment. Costs are much less important in the profit sector as long as the revenue earned is greater than costs. We are not saying costs are irrelevant in the profit sector, just that they are less important than in the public and nonprofit sectors. Profit organizations can change their pricing structure with a high level of freedom. Public organizations' source of revenue is primarily taxes and fees, which are not easily raised. Nonprofit organizations depend on donors and grants for the bulk of their revenue; again, increasing revenue from these sources is neither quick nor easy. Thus, both of these sectors must make the most of what is allocated. The bottom line, in terms of purpose, is budget managers in the public and nonprofit sectors must focus on achieving the highest possible effectiveness and/or outcomes from their expenditures.

How the budget process is handled between the sectors is also very different. For-profit budgeting is strictly an internal matter for the organization. The public sector process is rather open; perhaps not as open some individuals might like it to be, but very open in comparison with the for-profit process. Nonprofit organizations are somewhere in between the other two sectors. Some are as open as the public sector process while others are very private (senior managers and the board making the decisions with little outside input).

As implied in the foregoing discussion, budget decision making, especially in the public sector, often involves input from a diverse group of stakeholders who may not always agree with one another. One area where there is often disagreement is between the politicians who control the "purse strings" and the active users of library services and programs. Also, a rather typical approach in the public and nonprofit sectors is a bottom-up system in which unit heads put forward a budget request that passes up the authority ladder until the final budget is approved. Naturally, at each step of the upward progress there is a blending and modifying of the amounts requested—modifications are almost always a reduction in the amount first requested. This aspect of the process means you, as the original requestor, must have rock solid justifications and evidence to support the amount requested. You may still get less than originally requested but more than you might have without such data.

Certainly accounting is another area of differentiation. It might be a little surprising to know that for-profit organizations are more tightly controlled in terms of accounting and financial reporting than are the two other sectors. For-profits must employ the "Generally Accepted Accounting Principles" (GAAP), whereas public and nonprofits have the option to use GAAP or not. In our experience, most of them follow a modified version of GAAP. The purpose behind GAAP is to provide uniformity regarding organizational financial health. For any investor in a for-profit company, having uniform financial reports across companies is vital in decision making.

Such uniform comparative data for public and nonprofit organizations is somewhat less important. One obvious reason is there are so many variables among such organizations that those comparisons would be almost meaningless. However, state agencies do need to follow the Government Accounting Standards Board (GASB) requirements. How they go about doing so is up to the state, and there are variations. Some of the sources for the variations are Government Finance Officers Association (reporting, accounting guidelines), American Institute of Certified Public Accounts, and state auditors and comptrollers. There is commonality in what is reported by public and nonprofit organizations as one major concern is credit rating. Public agencies often turn to issuing bonds to finance major capital expenditures and their credit rating determines how much interest they have to pay. The higher the credit rating is, the lower their interest rate. This does come into play at times when a library seeks a bond issue for a new building or similar. (We look at bond issuing—referendums—and libraries in chapter 10).

This is not the place to delve into the details of accounting codes, nor do you need in-depth knowledge to be an effective budget manager. One reason you don't need in-depth knowledge of GAAP or GASB or their variants is that because libraries are almost always part of a larger organization, the financial officers of the larger body will decide what accounting system to use and inform you of how you should report your financial transactions. There is one aspect of the accounting practices that is significant for libraries; that is, when a transaction is "expensed" or recorded.

There are two basic methods for recording income and expenses: accrual and cash basis. Because libraries generally do not generate significant amounts of income, that aspect is of minor importance for you. For libraries, it is the timing of when either income or an expense is recorded that can affect operations. Under the accrual system, both billings and purchase orders are immediately recorded as a credit or debit. With a cash system income is not recorded until the money is in hand and expenses are recorded when you actually pay the invoice. How do these come into play in a library setting?

Primarily the method used for recording income and expenses matters in the library's acquisition activities. When the acquisition department places an order for an item there is a degree of uncertainty about what will be the final cost of the order. Discounts and shipping charges are two big areas of uncertainty; you can make reasonably accurate estimates, but that is all they are—estimates. Another factor is timing—you may not know when the item will arrive, or even if it will arrive. (Publishers may announce a publication date for a book but for a variety of reason the release is delayed or, on occasion, canceled.) "Encumbrance" is the method for handling the uncertainty for accounting purposes. This approach is a middle category, if you will, between available funds ("free balance") and funds paid out (expended). The encumbrance is your estimate of what you will pay upon receipt of the item. It helps you keep from overspending while awaiting delivery.

Why does it matter which method the financial officers select, especially if both the accrual and the cash method allow for encumbrances? This is where the budget period comes into play. Under the accrual system, when the budget period ends everything recorded becomes zero—including encumbrances. Yes, you can carry forward those encumbrances, but whatever that amount is becomes a debit from the next year's allocation. For example, if you want to carry forward $10,000 worth of encumbrances and your acquisition allocation for the coming year is $100,000, your available funds would be $90,000 with $10,000 encumbered. With a cash system, using the above example, you would "carry forward" the encumbrance while still having $100,000 in available funds.

AUTHOR EXPERIENCE

Evans once took over a library that was operating under the accrual system. A few days prior to starting, he met with the financial officer he would work with during an ALA meeting. Over breakfast the person said, "You should know that you will have no operating funds for the coming year beyond salaries." Disbelief is too mild a word for the reaction; the reaction was closer to "Come on. It's not April Fool's Day." Upon confirmation that it was no joke, the reaction was almost "I'm outta here, find some other fool." That did not happen, but as Wellington is reputed to have said after Waterloo, it was a very near run thing.

The culprit for the zero funding was encumbrances—needless to say, they were huge. It took several months of operating on good faith to cancel enough outstanding orders (some more than five years old—it was a research library environment) to have operating funds. Yes, canceling an order requires paperwork—a purchase order is a legal contract.

So, yes; accrual and cash methods do matter for libraries.

ADVISORY BOARD EXPERIENCE

Mika, while serving as head of acquisitions, was approached about three quarters into the budget year by the college budget officer to return all unspent funds. While impossible to return the amount expected, this situation became a teaching point for the budget officer as he learned about the process of encumbrance. Mika informed the officer that he could return some funds, but not the total that was expected. While unhappy with that response the budget officer did finally understand the library acquisition process. Funds were returned, but as the end of budget year approached, the same officer came to Mika and informed him that all of his funds were being returned, and with additional funding. The kicker was that the funds had to be spent and paid, not just encumbered within the month. Fortunately Mika and another staff member were able to arrange to visit a large book vendor's warehouse to select materials (with the agreement that any materials that were duplicated in the collection would be returned to the vendor). After spending three full days selecting materials they were able to return with invoices that were paid by the college, thus meeting the budget officer's deadline.

Table 9.1.

Public/Nonprofit Sector vs. Public Sector Budgeting Process

	Public	**Non-Profit**	**Private**
Purpose	Set by law	Set by a board	Set by a firm
Focus	Community	Narrow group	Bottom line
Revenue	Taxes	Donations/grants	Sales
Flexibility	Limited	Moderate	Substantial
Transparency	Substantial	Moderate	Low
Accounting System	Varies	Varies	Fixed
Decision Making	Interactive	Moderate interaction	Internal
Control Function	High	Moderate	Low

BASIC BUDGETARY PROCESS

As noted above, public and nonprofit organizations employ several different budgeting formats. However, whatever the format used, the approach to handling the preparation and implementation of the budget for any given cycle is fairly standard. First, there is some projecting or estimating what revenues are likely to be for the upcoming cycle. Second, an announcement regarding the need to formulate a request along with a timeframe and preparation guidelines is dispersed. Third, the budget request is made. Fourth, one or more sessions are held in which justifications and/or defenses of a request occur and a final request is formulated. Next is a final approval on the part of the appropriate governing authority. Last, but far from least, is the implementation of the budgeted allocation.

The first step of the process, for most libraries, starts several levels above the individuals who first set down budget figures for the coming budget cycle. The typical process for public sector agencies is for the overall governing body to make an estimate of likely revenues for the next budget period, set an overall budget expansion or contraction level (usually a percentage range), and decide upon the deadline for submitting requests. That document goes to the next highest body—the governing board or the senior library manager, for example. That office modifies the document at least by shortening the submission deadline if nothing more. In the vast majority of libraries, when the senior manager gets the "guidelines," she or he normally passes them on to department heads, again with a shortened timeline—the end of the line.

When the guidelines reach the people who start putting numbers down for a request the timeframe is usually rather short; you are lucky if you have four weeks to complete the task. Normally, you have a general idea when this process might occur, as budget cycles do not change all that often. (Note: although somewhat rare, budget cycles can and do change; sometimes they change with little advance warning, as the authors can attest to.) One idea for reducing the stress that may arise (while the request is your priority, your other responsibilities do not disappear) is to have a file of "budget thoughts." Such a file might contain ideas for improvements in unit activities that would require some new funding, any information about possible price increases (those announces may not match up with your budget preparation cycle), and justifications and/or data to support request. Once you have created your request the process described above goes into reverse.

Unit head requests go to senior managers who must put together the library's single request. This is the stage where the justification/defense process starts. The upward progress of the requests is almost always reductive in character. A fairly typical example for a library might be where all department heads limit their increase requests to the stated guidelines of no more than a 3 percent increase. When combined into the library request, the amount asked for would fit the guidelines. Would that be a problem for the library? The most probable answer is yes, it would be a problem. It has been a very long time since libraries have not had some price increases (3% or less, and sometimes much more) for database access, journals, and so on. Often these prices increase far exceed the consumer price index (CPI) increase that financial officers frequently use to set the overall budget, assuming they are willing to allow one. In most scenarios such as above, a 3 percent increase in the materials acquisition allocation would, most likely, result in a reduction in buying power. Someone(s) must decide what is the best option—let all units have a 3 percent increase or have some units get less in order to assure maintaining the current year's buying power and still comply with the guidelines. This is the first in a series of sessions in which conflict, compromise, concession, and hopefully, in the end, consensus comes about regarding the new level for the request.

The unified library request goes up to the next level where again it may be impossible for all requesting agencies to receive a flat 3 percent and still maintain their mandated activities. Essentially, the process becomes one of priorities and "whose ox gets gored." The best way to avoid getting gored is the have solid justifications and hard data to bolster your request. Also, as we will address in a later chapter, this is a time when your understanding of the politics of the process are invaluable. Sometimes a strategic concession now will pay big dividends later.

Needless to say, failure to follow stated guidelines almost always results in rejection. Upper level decision makers rarely tolerate such failures of procedure. However, just "following the rules," by itself, is not likely to win greater support. What you need is solid data, evidence of significant and valued outcomes, and real returns for monies allocated. In chapter 8, we covered assessments, evidence, hard data, and value for monies allocated (social return on investment, SROI).

Some years ago Patti Phillips and Jack Phillips wrote about some of the myths and realities of return on investment (ROI) in the public sector (2004). Their realities are even more real in today's competitive world of public and nonprofit sectors funding. One of the major myths they addressed was that ROI is inappropriate for such sectors because ROI is a for-profit concept. In truth, it is an updated version of a public/nonprofit sector method—cost-benefit analysis. Organizations in those sectors have long had to prove value for expenditures made. Some people believe, incorrectly, that SROI is a replacement of other measures of value. The truth is, although it supplements other metrics of performance and value, SROI does not replace anything. Of the myths the Phillips cover, perhaps the one with the most validity is that organizations in such sectors have such a diversity of stakeholders that a single measure is inadequate. That is true; however, SROI is rarely used alone. It is just one more tool libraries and other such organizations may employ when confronted with "Prove your worth" demands.

A fundamental assumption of SROI, for library usage, is that in the absence of a library people would fulfill their information and recreation needs from an alternative source. Further, that such fulfillment would generate a cost (direct or indirect) for the individual. For example, suppose a person wanted a particular e-title (e.g., *When Breath Becomes Air*, by Paul Kalanithi) and there was no library. There are at

Table 9.2.
Market Value Method for 2017

Media Usage	Output Value (per unit)	Usage	Direct Values
Hardback	$17	423,243	$7,195,131
Paperback	$13	7,714	$100,282
Video	$2	423,270	$846,540
Audio	$10	88,572	$885,720
E-books circulated	XXX	XXXXX	XXXXXXX
Audiobooks circulated			
In-house usage			
ILL borrowed	XXX	XXXXX	XXXXXXX
ILL loaned			
Computer sessions	$12	190,286	$2,283,432
WiFi sessions			
Early Literacy Station sessions			
Laptop lending			
Adult program attendance			
Youth program attendance (0–5)	XXX	XXXXX	XXXXXX
Youth program attendance (6–11)			
Youth program attendance (12–19)			
One-on-one tutoring			
Job search help			
Adult book club			
Teen book club			
Tween book club			
Community meeting room usage	$150	241	$36,150
Notary services			
Reference questions answered	$5	98,778	$493,890
		Grand Total	$13,173,861

Note: In essence, you fix a value for the service based on local commercial costs or a widely employed standard for such service. You then multiply that value by the documented usage of that category.

least two common alternative sources for gaining access, Amazon ($12.99) and Barnes and Noble ($12.99). Had the person gained access through a library the person's benefit could reasonably be thought of as $12.99.

There are two methods for calculating SROI—contingency and market values. The contingency method employs users' input to indicate their use of various library services and programs. Market valuations use library statistics and market values and estimates of values to calculate SROI. The contingency approach depends upon individuals accurately reporting their usage. Thus it is not always a full picture of library service and program usage, but does have the advantage of community input to the process. We suggest using both methods. There is a method for gaining user input on an ongoing basis (contingency) and the library could undertake the market approach every few years as a broader assessment of SROI. ALA has a commonly employed user-generated data that links usage to a dollar value (see "Library Value Calculator," http://www.ala.org/advocacy/advleg /advocacyuniversity/toolkit/makingthecase/library_calculator). Table 9.2 provides an example of the market valuation approach.

CHECK THESE OUT

A good source of both general and specific information about SROI in libraries is *Public Libraries—A Wise Investment*, by Nicolle Steffen, Zeth Lietzau, Keith Curry Lance, Amanda Rybin, and Carla Molliconi (Denver, CO: Library Research Bureau, 2009). A similar study about Texas libraries can be found at https://www.tsl.texas.gov/roi.

Two articles that illustrate ROI usage in other types of libraries are "Return on Investment for Collaborative Collection Development: A Cost-Benefit Evaluation of Consortia Purchasing," by Denise Pan and Yem Fong, both members of the University of Colorado library system (*Collaborative Librarianship* 2, no. 4 [2010]: 183–192) and "Using an Automated Tool to Calculate Return on Investment and Cost Benefit Figures for Resources: The Health Sciences and Human Services Library Experience," by Aphrodite Bodycomb and Megan D. Del Baglivo (*Journal of the Medical Library Association* 100, no. 2 [2012]: 127–130).

SROI is just one piece of a library's budget request justification tools, but one that is very useful. As we noted above, the justification process can be time consuming as the budget request moves up the organizational hierarchy. Each level becomes even more demanding, thus, you will need to strengthen your presentation accordingly.

MANAGERIAL LEADERSHIP IN BUDGETING

From the above discussion, you can understand why managerial leadership is so important in terms of a library's financial support. Effective leaders understand that fiscal management is a year-round, multi-year activity. It involves more than generating a budget request and monitoring the use of funds received. Not to imply that monitoring is a minor matter; however, it is only part of the entire management picture.

To be effective in handling library finances you really need to keep a minimum of three budget cycles in mind throughout the year: last year, the current year, and next year. Last year's because it may become part of the need to justify the upcoming budget request. It is not uncommon to have someone during the justification/defense process to ask questions about not only your current spending pattern but of the prior year's as well. However, the primary reason for knowing last year's performance is because it is best to maintain a smooth flow of activities throughout the year, especially in the backroom operations such as acquisitions and cataloging. Having a sense of last year's performance can inform your decisions regarding the current year expenditures. Another reason is you do not want to over-spend your allocation (or, for that matter, underspend).

Earlier, we noted that a budget is one of several managerial control tools. While it is a tool it is more like a sledge hammer than a scalpel—very blunt. You can feed a desired program or starve an undesired one, at the extreme ends of the control spectrum. In between those extremes money has a limited control impact.

Some form of a financial control system is a key component for monitoring ongoing expenditures—the system tracks funding obligations and expenditures. Good systems provide both monitoring and reporting capabilities. Very often the system you use is the one mandated by the funding authority. One example of how such systems operate is how a library invoice actually gets paid. You place an order for something and upon its arrival you verify it is exactly what you ordered. If it is, you "approve" the invoice (usually with the date approved, appropriate code number, and your initials or signature) and forward it to the next level in the fiscal control system (perhaps the library business, organization's business office, or treasurer's office). That unit verifies there is an appropriation for such a purchase and that adequate funds are available. If both factors are correct, a check is issued to the vendor. (Libraries rarely have the authorization to issue a check.) As you might guess, this approach to paying bills takes some time. It is not unheard of for the process to take weeks, or, at times, several months. Any discount for payment in 30 days is almost never realized. The good news is that vendors doing regular business with libraries understand the payment process. It is the vendor who rarely does business with a library that has trouble understanding why it takes so long to be paid.

Some of the systems generate monthly reports showing current year expenditures, last year's expenditures, and current year's allocation. The reports are in terms of expenditure categories such as office supplies, OCLC charges, telephone, and so on. That type of information helps you monitor where you are in terms of budget and, importantly, where the funding authorities think you are. (Financial control systems have codes for classes of expenditures across the overall organizations. Supplies, postage, telephone, etc.—each has its own unique code number that allows the funding authority to determine expenditures by type across the organization. Funding authorities can and do decide that negotiating an organization-wide contract for a service is the best approach and you are expected to use that vendor for that service.) Coding errors do occur, on both ends of the payment process, so knowing what each end thinks is the current state of the budget is rather useful in controlling the annual allocation.

AUTHOR EXPERIENCE

Although it is not always set in stone that you are confined to an organization-wide vendor, certainly it is often the case, and more often than not the "price" of that vendor's service is lower than you would get elsewhere.

Evans once had a budget assistant who also ordered the library's supplies and was great at getting the best price on items. (Evans often has said he wished he could have that person buy his next car because he might get the new vehicle and some cash just to end the negotiations.) When the overall organization set up a contract for office supplies with a single vendor, Evans's budget assistant claimed and proved she had been getting lower prices on most of the items offered by the new vendor. It took some time but at the end of the day the organization's business office allowed the library to use whatever vendor provided the best price. That occurred because the library had hard data to support the claim. It probably also helped that the library's track record for handling budgets was solid—never going over and ending the year with a dollar or two surplus. (We never left more than $5.00, but always a little on the plus side. That did help us when we had to justify our budget request. We always under-promised and over delivered, a useful tool in a budget defense.)

Budget Leadership

As a managerial leader, you will need to demonstrate some of your best personal skills and behaviors regarding budgets. Perhaps the most important behavior is to be optimistic, especially when economic times are difficult. A negative perspective will quickly spread through the staff and morale and performance are likely to suffer. Should that happen, you may lose the backing of some of your stakeholders, who might otherwise have a positive influence during the budget justification process by actively supporting the request. It also helps when you demonstrate knowledge of the budget process as well as a grasp of fiscal details.

On the personal side, you will need energy, endurance, and patience, as the budget process can be long and tiring. Knowing and supporting your supervisor's budgetary needs and interests can be significant in achieving your own budget goals. Communicating clearly and often about budgetary issues with supporters, especially your board, is another element in achieving your budget goals. You may find it necessary, on occasion, to remind everyone (even yourself) that budgets are for supporting rather than driving the mission. That is, what does it require in the way of money to effectively achieve our mission and goals? Not, how do we modify our mission and goals to fit the funds available? Yes, there are bad times when the funding is low; however, that ought not change what we do but rather make us do a little less of what we do for a while.

Sometimes the library hopes that cutting back on a popular program will generate a user demand, which will then influence budget authorities and that will generate additional funds. That result does not happen very often. A common outcome is the stakeholders become upset with the library rather than the funding authorities, even when they are aware that lack of funding is the cause. One reason is they interact directly with the library and rarely, if ever, with funding authorities. When budget shortfalls do occur, seek out the low use activities to curtail or even suspend rather than reduce the popular programs and services.

One possible strategy for handling shortfalls is to build an endowment fund and use half of the annual "payout" as a rainy day fund, returning such funds to the principal when there are no rainy days. Accomplishing this is never easy and carries a risk in terms of appropriations. Even without trying to establish such a fund, there is a good chance of the library receiving a memo along the following lines:

> The X [fill in the blank with president, treasurer, mayor, city council, etc.] requests the library supply detailed information about the sources of supplemental funding, especially the endowment, with the objective of utilizing such funds as replacements for operating allocations.

We look at various sources of supplemental funding in some detail in chapter 10.

Another tactic for reducing "budget process stress" is to create a generic budget preparation document. This can assist anyone who has to develop a request. Such a document identifies individuals who are to create the initial requests and provides a general timeline for completing the work. Of particular help is having templates for how to develop the request and sources of information and guidance on how to formulate an effective justification. An example might be resources regarding anticipated price increases and other costs, as well as useful outcome information.

ASSESSING AND SETTING REALISTIC FINANCIAL NEEDS

Something to keep in mind when assessing budget needs is that you almost never start with a "clean slate." There is a budget format known as zero-based budgeting, which, in theory, always starts from a zero base. Almost every organization that has tried to implement this format has found that to produce such a budget, keeping in place all the required theoretical steps, is simply too time consuming (see, e.g., Jimmy Carter's effort to implement zero-based budgeting at the state and federal level). All budget formats, other than line item, if carried out strictly according to their theoretical base, are incredibly time consuming. In today's world of limited human resources and the expectation for public and nonprofit organizations to do more with less, the budget process simply cannot be allowed to consume vast amounts of staff time.

The fact of the matter is, regardless of format, almost all budgets are, to a greater or lesser degree, incremental in character. That is, past allocations are the base for the request. That baseline exists whether the guidelines allow for an increase or mandated cuts. A first step in assessing budget needs is to thoughtfully examine this year's experience as well as last year's. Did we distribute funds to the best or most cost-effective categories? Based on our ES (environmental scanning) activities what, if any, changes are likely to occur next year, especially in terms of services and programs? Would shifting monies from category A to category B allow more flexibility? What is our highest priority that must have an increase, since we are unlikely to get everything? Answers to questions such as these help you think through realistic budget needs.

An equally important part of the budget planning activity is to establish realistic appropriation funding levels. It is good to be optimistic, but creating unrealistic expectations can have a demoralizing impact on staff and users if the results fall short. Part of that thinking should include realistic estimates of what, if any, supplemental funding (donations, endowment payout, etc.) is likely. When there is a strong likelihood of such monies, think about how to best use those funds without generating an expectation on the part of the funding authorities. We have found that once you use such funds more than once for some program or activity, there is expectation that that program or activity no longer needs an allocation from the funding authority. It is a fine balance and one not always easy to achieve. You also need to have a clear understanding about restricted and unrestricted funds.

Although you are much less likely to face funding authority requests or pressure to use restricted funds for operational needs, there are times when it could happen. The funding authority can say it is facing a financial emergency, which allows it the power to "sweep up" funds to address the crisis. There are methods for avoiding such dangers, but only at the time when establishing a restricted gift fund. The donor, or you, can propose "fallback positions" in case the primary purpose is not available for some reason. Creating a restricted gift almost always requires a deed of gift—a legal document—which in turn requires honoring the wishes of the donor. In some cases, the deed specifies that the gift be returned if none of the purposes are possible (closing of the supported program or even the library, for example). In the absence of alternative uses being specified, you could have the restricted fund swept up by your funding authority.

One of your roles, as a senior managerial leader, is to ensure the library's budget request is realistic. A realistic budget is not as easy to create as you might think or hope. You may have solid information about needs, a reasonable understanding about potential price increases from your major vendors, and a sense of what the guidelines are likely to contain. However, guidelines are just that—guides—and there will be times when you need to ask for more than what the guidelines suggest in order to have a realistic allocation to carry out the library's mission without reducing service quality.

In order to hope to exceed the guidelines you must have a well-crafted request, solid supporting data based on demonstrate positive outcomes, and a very strong sense of the direction in political winds. There are two types of such requests that have a chance of being successful. Both types are based on reflecting organizational-wide priorities (an infusion of funds to enhance an existing service or program or starting a new program or service—perhaps labeled a pilot effort).

Starting a new program or service, if it is linked to organizational-wide priorities, is most likely to succeed, especially if others view it as innovative. Innovative is a word we see rather often in the professional literature, both in management and librarianship. Rarely is the "innovation" something entirely new, inventive, or creative in character; rather it builds on existing knowledge and/or applications. Even Albert Einstein's Theory of Relatively rested on his, and others, prior work. Applying an existing concept or idea in a new location or manner is innovative in practice.

Thinking "outside the box" and frequently asking yourself, "What if—?" is one of the hallmarks of a strong leader-manager. Doing so can lead to increased financial support on occasions. (In chapter 4, we described how a courier service was seen as innovative and addressed an institutional priority, resulting in increased funding and even additional staffing.) We are not suggesting this approach always works; however, it has a good track record of succeeding.

CHECK THIS OUT

There are a number of books that can help you "think outside the box." One such book that Evans used when teaching management courses was *A Whack on the Side of the Head: How You Can Be More Creative*, revised edition, by Roger Von Oech and George Willett (New York: Business Plus, 2008). The title contains exercises that assist you in thinking more broadly, reducing your self-imposed limits in thinking, and asking "What if—?"

Another fun book is Maynard Frank Wolfe's *Rube Goldberg Inventions: The Legendary Works (A) of America's (B) Most Honored (C) Cartoonist* (New York: Simon & Schuster, 2000). This title gives strategies for creating outlandish solutions for common problems (watering the lawn, getting up, and opening an door, for example).

A somewhat similar concept to innovation is social entrepreneurship (SE). SE is a label that has come into use over the last 20-plus years. There is no consensus on a definition of what that label entails. Essentially, SE is viewed as an effort to further society's goals in new or more effective ways. A reasonable question to ask is, "How does this differ from what public and nonprofit organizations have always been about?" Perhaps the best answer is found in a definition of SE by Gou and Bielefeld: "(SE is) the pursuit of societal objectives with innovative methods, through the creation of products, organizations, and practices that yield and sustain social benefits" (2014, 7). Another element that helps differentiate between past practice and SE is SE often involves cross-organizational collaboration.

Innovation, creating something new, and collaborating with other organizations all entail some risk. None of those actions are highly regarded in the workplace, at least within the public sector where predictability, stability, and continuity are the traditional values. Thus, engaging in social entrepreneurial activities may not be career enhancing in some situations. But the social value realized from such endeavors exceeds the dangers.

There are additional factors that challenge public and nonprofit managerial leaders in terms of becoming social entrepreneurs. Generally, such managers have less autonomy in terms of shifting or creating new activities and resources. In addition public sector managers often face political interference, even when the proposed activity does reflect a general organization-wide priority. Both public and nonprofit managers have a duty to seek wide input from their stakeholders, which slows down implementation and, at times, stops the effort. The decision-making process in both sectors is more convoluted than in the for-profit world. Nevertheless, SE has a role to play in the world of information work regardless of the challenges.

Many libraries are addressing serious social issues (literacy, latchkey children, and unemployment, for example); however, more often than not they are doing so with little or no collaboration with other organizations that have similar interests. A component of SE is cross-organizational efforts; perhaps we need to think more broadly and also gain more financial support.

As you may have sensed by this point, fiscal managerial leadership is both challenging and a never-ending responsibility. You may not have to address a money matter every day; however, if you are effective, concerns about costs, needs, and so on, are never really out of your mind.

BUDGETING POLITICS

You cannot leave a discussion of fiscal matters without some mention of politics. (In chapter 12, we explore the topic of politics in some depth—both partisan and workplace.) Every organization has its "culture" (see chapter 7), and one element of that culture is that of money or budgets. Everyone understands that almost nothing, from an organizational point of view, happens without access to funds. Everyone also knows that public and nonprofit organizational funds are finite. Every unit wants to maximize its share of that finite "pie." And everyone recognizes there will be overt or covert competition over the size of the slice each unit will receive. The result is one form of workplace politics.

The first financial obligation of a managerial leader is to the secure funds necessary to carry out a unit's work activities. A related obligation is, when necessary for unit's performance, to seek funding beyond its current level. To meet these obligations, the first step is to understand both the budgetary process and the organizational budgetary culture. Lacking such knowledge you will be lucky to retain the current funding level. When joining a new organization, don't be surprised if it takes at least a year to begin to understand the nuances of budgetary culture.

There is no single approach to gaining and mastering those nuances, as every organization is different in character, if nothing more than in the staff and how they interact with one another. However, there is a good book to read and ponder and that provides useful information about budgetary processes and strategies— Aaron Wildavsky's *The New Politics of the Budgetary Process* (2004). His first edition appeared in 1964 without the "new" in the title. The book focuses on the federal government's budgetary process. However, by substituting the positions and agencies you interact with during the budgetary process for the positions and agencies in the book, you will gain a basic understanding of how the politics take place. Certainly there are differences, but you get a solid grounding about the process. You can gain a sense of how generic the content is from the fact it has been in print for over 50 years—sales to federal budget personnel are unlikely to have carried it through that many years. Another piece of evidence is the fact it has been translated into other languages. Finally, and perhaps the least significant, is the fact the authors have found it useful in non-federal organizations as well as in teaching management courses.

BUDGETING IN MULTIJURISDICTIONAL ENVIRONMENTS

There are times when public libraries are involved in multi-jurisdictional systems that involve budgeting. Other library types, while not often so involved, do have commitments to one or more consortia that involve sending funds to another jurisdiction that handles the payment for the services to the group members. (There can be legal issues when it comes to sending funds to another jurisdiction that does not provide the service. It is a good idea to understand the legal implications before joining a consortium.) In this section, we look at the situation in which there is a pooling of jurisdictional funds to provide a service—in this case a library.

At the statewide public sector level there are a variety of multijurisdictional entities (special districts) across the country—air quality management, schools, transportation, and water, for example, and many library districts. These entities all have a legal base—legislative action that allows for the creation of special districts and/or joint power authority (JPA). (A joint power authority is "a contract between a city, a county, and/or a special district in which the city or county agrees to perform services, cooperate with, or lend its powers to, the special district" (http://legal-dictionary.thefreedictionary.com/joint+powers+agreement).

As only a few states have authorized JPAs, while almost every state allows for the creation of special districts, we will focus on the district approach. As you might guess creating a special library district is sometimes rather complicated and even more so when attempting to modify an existing district. One rather obvious reason for the complexity is a special district requires funding to operate. The usual source is taxes. (There are a great many legal aspects to library operation and we explore those in some detail in chapter 14. Here our focus is on the money aspect.)

The state legislature normally sets limits on many aspects of public and school library operations, less so in the case of public academic institutions. One of the limitations is on the library district's taxing power. For example, Oregon library laws set the limit as one-quarter of 1 percent (0.0025) of assessed property evaluation (http://www.oregon.gov/osl/ld/pages/resources/laws/statutes/357/libdist.aspx). Arizona's law specifies the maximum as 1.5 mils. (A "mil" is a term public bodies often employ when describing property tax rates. One mil is 1/000th of a cent—so $1,000 in assessed value at 1 mil would generate a tax of $1.) Just because there is an upper limit does *not* mean the library will be able to go that high. In today's environment, any tax rate is often viewed negatively, no matter how small. How high the mil rate will be is a partisan political matter. Essentially, the only real increase in revenue for the library comes from increase evaluations or in the number of evaluations upon which to base the assessment. Increasing the mil rate is always a challenge.

So what happens when a city and county decide to have a unified library system? The answer is the rather common response, "It depends." Often, one of the jurisdictions contracts with the other to provide the service for a fee or agrees to a certain mil rate. Such contracts often contain a clause specifying what, if any, annual increase in that fee is allowable. Or they have a clause that outlines a process for seeking such an increase—occasionally requiring a vote by the jurisdiction(s).

Sometimes the existing systems decide to merge one or more of their activities—a mobile service or joint purchase (office supplies, database access, etc.), for example. The normal approach is a contract spelling out how the funds are generated and who handles what tasks.

There are a great many variations in what goes into a multijurisdictional library system; however, there is usually some form of tax assessment to generate the funds. When you have two or more jurisdictions trying to secure funding on mil basis you have a complex budgeting process.

We opened this chapter with a quote from George Bernard Shaw to the effect that money is the most important thing. From a library's point of view, we believe money is the second most important thing. In first place, by a considerable distance, is a staff of collaborative people who are committed to providing the best possible service using the available resources.

CHECK THIS OUT

An interesting article that relates indirectly to budgets and funding in today's economic times is Aimee Fifarek's 2014 essay, "Thriving in the New Normal: Strategies for Managing the Scarcity Mindset" (*Library Leadership & Management* 29, no. 1: 1–11).

REFERENCES

Cohen, Steven, William Eimicke, and Tanya Heikkila. 2013. *The Effective Public Manager*. 5th edition. San Francisco, CA: Jossey Bass.

Guo, Chao, and Wolfgang Bielefeld. 2014. *Social Entrepreneurship: An Evidence-Based Approach to Creating Social Value*. San Francisco, CA: Jossey-Bass.

Perry, James L., and Robert K. Christensen. 2015. *Handbook of Public Administration*. New York: Wiley.

Phillips, Pattie, and Jack J. Phillips. 2004. "ROI in the Public Sector: Myths and Realities." *Public Personnel Management* 33, no. 2: 139–149.

Shaw, George Bernard. 1905. *The Irrational Knot*. New York: Bretano's.

Smith, G. Stevenson. 2002. *Managerial Accounting for Libraries & Other Not-for-Profit Organizations*. 2nd edition. Chicago, IL: American Library Association.

Wildavsky, Aaron B., and Naomi Caiden. 2004. *The New Politics of the Budgetary Process*. 5th edition. New York: Pearson/Longman.

Chapter 10

FUNDRAISING

Inspiring visions rarely (I'm tempted to say never) include numbers.

Tom Peters, 1987

The ongoing discussion of fundraising in all sectors makes one thing abundantly clear; libraries need to advocate clearly and articulately for themselves in order to secure their territory in this evolving scene.

Lisa Peet, 2016

But few librarians have been prepared, either by training or by temperament, to undertake an ambitious development program.

Victoria Steele and Stephen D. Elder, 1992

Customized gift options that don't necessarily require the biggest investment up front are attractive for other reasons.

Debra E. Blum, 2016

"Gold is where you find it." This old saying is very true for libraries. We all know that in today's world the primary funding sources for libraries allocate barely enough money to maintain basic services. Monies to go beyond the basic level commonly must come from other sources. Librarians must learn prospector skills and do so quickly, as libraries are not alone in the need for gold. As with looking for gold to mine, librarians' options for prospecting are rather restricted "by the lay of the land." For example, academic libraries face a challenge regarding who they may even approach to ask for support. The authors have experienced the situation that is reflected in the following: "For development purposes at Duke, alumni are 'assigned' to the college from which they graduated. Because no one graduates from a library, we cannot solicit alumni until they have given to us" (Hadzor and Cuniskey, 2014, 19). What that means for academic library development (fundraising) is that the prospectors must explore different approaches to finding the gold. Other types of libraries rarely face the constraints that academic libraries do when it comes to fund raising; their operating environments rarely have competing agencies when it comes to seeking supplemental funding.

Basically there are two broad options: individual donors and granting agencies. Both exist in several variations, especially the individual donor category. There is a third, albeit limited, possibility for the public sector libraries and some in the nonprofit sector—a referendum for either bonds or a tax increase. We touched on this in the previous chapter, primarily in terms of increasing the tax base for the operating budget. In this chapter, we look at that process in terms of a major capital investment fund (library remodeling, new facility, an added location, etc.).

As the opening quotation from Lisa Peet suggests, there is competition and librarians need to stake their claims quickly and effectively. The "Great Recession" caused an increasing use of fundraising to supplement the basic budget allocation. Today, such efforts are almost essential to maintain library services and programs. Nonprofit organizations are always dependent upon fundraising for their existence. In the past, public sector organizations engaged in such activities from time to time, especially in the case of libraries. There were and are variations of library support groups ("Friends" is a common label) that provide modest amounts of money. As the library building needs to expand or be replaced, a fundraising campaign is almost always put into place. In today's world, there is a significant amount of competition between public and nonprofit sectors for what is a finite pool of money and donors.

Many librarians wish there was less need to go prospecting. (Indeed, those who work full-time in fundraising use the term "prospect" for potential donors, thus making our analogy to gold prospectors less of a stretch). Asking for money, outside of the budget process, is not something many people are all that comfortable doing. Few of us were taught anything about fundraising during our degree programs. Learning "on the fly," as many of us have had to do, is difficult and, at times, discouraging as well as embarrassing. There are workshops on fundraising and grant writing that are worth attending, but they are normally short and very general in order to attract an audience large enough to offer the program. Most librarians have had to experience a good deal of trial and error when it comes to fundraising.

Although fundraising has become an ever more essential activity for libraries, few libraries—except the very largest ones—can afford to devote even a half-time full-time equivalent (FTE) to such duties. What that means is either someone on the staff gets yet another duty or there is almost no fundraising. It also means something will get less attention than before. The "someone" on the receiving end of the new duties is almost always a senior manager, if not the senior person. Keep in mind, fundraising, to be effective, is rarely a "one-off" effort; it requires time and repeated efforts.

Like with so many other managerial duties, you need to assess your strengths and weakness for engaging in fundraising (another term employed for the activity is "development"). Perhaps the starting point for that assessment in to ponder your personal thoughts, impressions, and reactions to being asked to donate to this or that cause as well as the people who are asking. Steele and Elder (1992 and 2000) discussed several concerns and fears newcomers often have regarding the activity. A common concern is that asking for money is a form of begging and something a library should not have to do. A related concern is that to be effective you may have to set aside some personal and professional values. That is, you are unlikely to only interact with people who share all your values. That, in turn, could require you to either agree with a person's value statements or risk not getting the money. Should this happen, the best advice is to say nothing and try to steer the conversation to neutral ground. This is a time to practice your diplomatic skills (see chapter 19 for more about diplomacy).

One rather common concern or fear associated with becoming a fundraiser is the subconscious thought that receiving a "no" to an "ask" is a personal rejection. There are a host of reasons for a no, beyond yourself: wrong time, wrong project, wrong approach, and so on. Any fundraiser who has a batting average above 75 percent in getting a "yes" is doing very well indeed.

FUNDRAISING BASICS

One way to increase the yeses is to follow basic fundraising principles. First and foremost, keep in mind there are a variety of money raising methods, not all of which require substantial amounts of managerial time. We will look at such activities before discussing more complex and time-consuming fundraising undertakings.

Libraries have had support groups that raise money for their service activities and programs for many years. Such groups operate under a variety of names, but for the purpose of this discussion we will use the two most common labels for the two distinct categories of support groups: Friends and Foundations (both public and academic libraries of all sizes have one or both such groups). Both categories have had admirable track records of raising money for library operations over the years. For the vast majority of libraries, the dollar amounts are modest at best. Only the larger libraries have support groups that are able to raise big number dollars. However, that is not to say the modest amounts are unimportant. In many ways, those funds are often more significant for the smaller libraries in term of percentage of total budget. Smaller libraries are more likely to have endured more severe reductions in their budgets than larger ones, making supplemental funds ever more critical to ongoing operations.

From a managerial leadership perspective, Friends and Foundations generally require only modest attention. In the case of Friends, the group operates rather independently with a board normally elected by membership. There is some debate that exists over the use of the term "Friends member"—are they truly members or are they donors? For other nonprofit groups that have memberships, a person becoming a member receives some tangible benefits from paying the dues—free access to the facility, a discount on purchases, invitations to special events—even if those events are fundraising in purpose. Free access is a moot point for most libraries. Discounts on book sale items or library "merchandise" are nominal at best, and fundraising events are the same for a member or a donor. Regardless of the label, Friends groups commonly engage in ongoing fundraising activity with book sales—a long-standing activity—as well as variety of other fund raising efforts (see the sites listed below to gain a sense of the varieties possible). Monies raised are usually expended with 12 months of their being raised. Certainly the group needs some occasional interaction with the library, especially about any modest cash needs. However, library managers rarely try to "manage" the group's operations.

CHECK THIS OUT

You can learn more about the issue of member thinking versus donor thinking regarding Friends groups in Liz Boyd's 2013 article "Members or Donors? Weigh the Options" (*Public Libraries* 52, no. 4: 22–24).

The website "Fundraising Ideas & Products Center" offers a host of ideas for fundraising activities that fall within the capabilities of most Friends groups: http://www .fundraising-ideas.org/DIY/notalent.htm.

The American Library Association has a number of resources for Friends and Foundation functions on its website, for example, Friends groups: http://www.ala.org/united /friends; and for foundations: http://www.ala.org/united/foundations.

Foundations are different in several ways. First, they have donors, in the true fundraising sense, rather than a membership. There is a board that handles the oversight of an endowment or other major fundraising activity. The initial board may have been established through the appointment of some prominent community individuals or active library supporters. After this, the board identifies potential new members as the need arises. Most Foundations engage in an annual fund drive for the purpose of enhancing the endowment. They are also likely to play a role in soliciting and formulating those personalized giving opportunities mentioned in Debra Blum's opening quotation—annuities, bequests, and so on. Such activities do require a more active role of one or more senior library managers. Certainly a library Foundation will be a part of any major fundraising effort—a major remodel, a new branch, a building replacement, or a new ILS, for example. Here the basics of fundraising come into play.

Who Gives?

As we noted above, fundraisers are constrained by "the lay of the land" in the sense that the sources of funding for a given cause are finite. An understanding of the demographics is an important aspect for any fundraising effort. Who are the potential sources of support—individuals and/or foundations? Any significant fundraising endeavor, anything beyond the modest amounts generated by Friends efforts and most library endowments, should draw upon basic fundraising practices. Those practices begin by understanding of who gives, why they give, and when they give.

As you might expect, there is demographic data regarding the "who" aspect of giving. Such data is general in character and based on surveys that reflect national tendencies. The sidebar below lists some of the most common giving demographics.

COMMON GIVING DEMOGRAPHICS

• Gender	• Age
• Race/Ethnicity	• Education level
• Marital status	• Household income
• Current employment	• Former employment
• Nationality	• Children at home
• Home ownership	• Health

The demographics in the sidebar are drawn from broad-based averages. The demographics interact in complex ways (see Wilhelm, 2007, and Irwin-Wells, 2002 for in-depth information about the above and other giving tendencies); nevertheless, they provide some insight into what you might expect is typical in your service community.

Some of the typical giving traits may be a little surprising. For example, males tend to give more than females, older individuals (over age 65) tend to give less than those in their middle years, and those who have children at home give more than those who do not. Less surprising is that as educational attainment increases so does the giving amount, and married people tend to give more than do unmarried individuals. The foregoing are broad categorizations based on all giving not just giving to library types.

As a library manager, you probably have solid demographic data for your service community, assuming you have engaged in ongoing environmental scanning. What you may not have done with this data is analyzed the community in terms of potential donors or financial supporters. One method to assess how close your community comes to national giving averages would be to ask if organizations, such as United Way, would share some of their giving patterns. They might not do so, but you will not know unless you ask; should they share the information, you will be better able to plan your prospecting efforts.

Why They Give

Giving is much more complex than simple demographics, and giving and demographics interact in complex ways. An obvious non-demographic factor is the motivation for giving. There are several common motivators that, combined with demographics, illustrate why having a very high rate of "yeses" is so rare. Some reasons are related to ego and self and others are emotional in character.

One common self-benefiting motivator that many understand is the *tax deduct-ibility* of donations to public and nonprofit organizations that have 501(c)(3) IRS status. As you might guess, while such deductions do play a role in a gift, tax deductibility is usually third or fourth in terms of importance in the donor's deci-sion making. What it may do is increase the size of the gift; other factors actually decide the yes or no of giving.

James Andreoni identified three broad categories of motivations for giving: public good theory, exchange theory, and "warm glow" (2001). There any number of variations within each category. *Public good* is very broad and people can and do disagree as to what is a public good. You might hope or expect there would be no difference of opin-ion regarding the notion that a library is a public good. In the very broadest sense, there is a strong consensus that libraries with public access provide a societal good. However, keep in mind our earlier discussion of various efforts to privatize public libraries. Also, there can be differences in views regarding specific library services or programs.

From an *exchange* perspective a donor may feel or believe she or he is obligated to give. Perhaps the person was on the receiving side of help from the organization asking for money. There may be a sense that if they give to an organization, the organization may, in turn, respond positively in some way to an ask from another public or nonprofit organizations. There is cross- organizational support of special fundraising events such as galas, for example, between a literacy organization and various businesses. (You sometimes see a reflection of this in published "thank you" advertisements naming supporters of a large-scale fundraising event.)

A *"warm glow"* can, and often does, arise from giving a gift of any kind for any reason. From a philanthropic perspective, a strong "glow" often arises from giving to a cause that the individual believes is a societal imperative. Another form of giving that generates warmth is establishing an endowment for a loved one. Probably most often a "warm glow" is in combination with other factors and somewhat secondary in importance.

Emotions and motivations are entangled and very time consuming to sort out from one another, if at all. Without question, professional fundraising efforts know how to play on such emotions as pity, empathy, and even worries and fears. How often have you seen television ads with hungry children or sad-eyed animals that are a bid to get you to give? Advertisements seeking funds to support research on a serious health problem can generate at least some concern, if not fear, that the viewer may need a cure sometime in the future. Emotional motivators are of limited use for library fundraising, although empathy may be of some value in terms of gaining sup-port for literacy and employment seeking assistance programs. Academic libraries are not too likely to find emotional issues that will work in their fund raising efforts. Any time they can link their efforts to a cause such as social justice, they will have a strong motivational appeal element at work, at least for many potential donors.

When Do People Give?

Professional fundraisers often identify three broad categories of when a person gives. *Impulse* giving is typically a source of a small amount of support, but the cumulative impact can be significant. Think about how often you've dropped a few coins or a dollar bill into the red kettles of the Salvation Army during the holiday season. Retail companies often encourage such impulse buying by placing modestly priced items by their checkout stations as well as donation boxes to local and national causes. Perhaps library Friends groups might employ similar tactics.

The second broad category of gaining support is *appeals* (solicitations). For libraries, the most common appeal is the Foundation's annual appeal letter. Success of such appeals rests upon the effectiveness of the appeal document. Most library Friends and Foundation groups are voluntary and volunteers often have limited time for such activities. Given time constraints, some such groups recycle last year's appeal letter with minimal changes. Such efforts tend to be less effective than a fresh approach highlighting the library's recent successes.

Creating a compelling "case" for why a person should make a contribution is the key to any appeal effort—such as an annual or capital campaign for a new facility. Since the Great Recession, the case statement has become ever more important in terms of having a successful outcome. Great case statements are a combination of facts and a vision. While the opening quotation from Tom Peters is correct about organizational visions, when it comes to fundraising cases, there is a monetary target conveyed in some manner and usually near the end of the statement. "We hope to expand the library's endowment to $750,000 this year. Your gift will help us reach that goal," or some variation, is often found in annual fund drive solicitations. A case provides a logical presentation of the goal and why a person should seriously consider making a gift.

Being able to cast the appeal (case) more broadly than just supporting the library enhances the chances of having a very successful drive. There are a number of options for doing so; for example, a fund drive to provide library services to group senior living facilities on a long-term basis (endowment fund enriching the residents' lives) or, in an educational environment, expanding accessibility for disabled students (a form of public good). Our advice is, think broadly. A solid case statement covers the current situation and how the solicited funds will significantly improve that environment.

The third broad category is *planned giving*. This form of giving normally requires an extended amount time to bring to fruition. Planned giving is almost always a rare event for the vast majority of libraries. Only the larger libraries have a staff for development and have time to prospect for and "cultivate" potential planned giving donors. An endowment for library collection development purposes is probably the most common planned gift. Most such endowments are modest in size; nevertheless, they can be important for creating an ever stronger collection.

Library endowments are almost always restricted in some manner (see chapter 9 for coverage regarding restricted funds.) A major concern with such gifts is to have a carefully written gift agreement. If the language of a gift agreement is too open there is a danger the funding authorities will view any income as a reason to reduce their allocation. The authors of this book, in an academic library setting, once had a development officer suggest that if the development office could secure a $1 million endowment for collection develop purposes the institution would not need to fund that activity any further. If the language is too tight the library may not always be able to employ the "payout" (a percentage of the earned income) and comply with the donor's expectations. For example, a donor might endow a fund for the acquisition of items exclusively dealing with Southwestern Native American basketry. That is an interesting topic for some individuals, but there are not new titles on that subject to acquire every year. (Note: there can be institutions where the policy is the annual payout must occur and any unused monies are "swept up" into the funding authority's general fund.)

There is no reason that library's endowed funds must be for collection building purposes just because that has been the traditional approach. Almost any library service or program is a candidate for such support—summer reading program, technology upgrade fund, and student award for the best library-based research paper, for example. We covered the issue of properly worded agreements in the prior chapter.

Long-term gifts are rare, if nonexistent, for the vast majority of libraries. When they do exist they are most often the result of an unexpected bequest. (Certainly large, and increasingly medium-sized, libraries have a staff member or use a fundraising professional on retainer to help secure long-term gifts.) Many of the long-term giving methods are revocable. Even a bequest may be revoked under most conditions. Like an endowment, bequests may come with strings attached regarding how the library may use the gift (money, stock, or property, for example). If the library does not know that such a provision exists, the donor may include terms for the gift's use that are beyond the library's ability to meet—monies for a program that no longer exists when the estate is settled, for example.

If a library has a strong Foundation, and the ability to assign at least some staff time to fundraising, there are a number of options for securing a gift in the future. For example, a charitable gift annuity, a charitable remainder trust, and life insurance gifts may be possible. These are the types of gifts that Debra Blum refers to in the quotation from her at the beginning of this chapter. Research on why donors select some form of deferred gift is not definitive. However, two obvious strong factors are the tax advantage and the ability to retain control over personal finances for as long as possible.

AUTHOR EXPERIENCE

Evans recently established three endowed scholarships. What motivated those gifts? As we noted in the main text, most such gifts arise from a number of factors rather than just one. This was certainly true in Evans's case.

Two of the scholarships were motivated, in part, as memorials for his parents. However, there are many ways of memorializing a person other than with a scholarship. Probably the driving factor was and is a concern about the ever-growing debt load college students carry, even at the undergraduate level. Another factor was the strong belief that both the person and society benefit from earning a post-secondary degree.

The third scholarship came about for professional reasons and some sense of obligation. On the professional side was and is the conviction that our field better serves society the more closely it reflects the diversity of communities. Again, a concern regarding debt loads factored into the decision to create the endowment. The obligation aspect arose from the fact that a major portion of the monies funding the endowments was from text-book royalties that a significant number of graduates had to buy over the years.

And, of course tax deductibility was an added attraction, which also affected the timing of the gifts.

Donor motivations are complex and, for planned gifts, require time to fully ascertain.

Planned gift intentions are not "money in the bank" until the money *is* in the bank. As noted above most such gifts are intentions that can and do change from time to time. Assuring those intentions are realized takes time, effort, and sound donor relations.

Donor Relations

Good donor relations are essential to fundraising success, regardless of the nature of the gift. Professional fundraisers know very well, just as retail outlet own-ers know, a current customer takes much less time, effort, and money to retain than it takes to secure a new customer. A common label for the process of maintaining donor relations is "stewardship."

Clearly stewardship is critical in terms of a positive outcome for intended gifts. An unhappy donor can revoke the intention at any time. Even a "fully funded" endowment (most organizations require a minimum amount for a fully funded endowment—often that minimum is $25,000) requires stewardship. Yes, the money is in the bank, but could there be more to come? The answer is perhaps. Many such donors want to see how well the organization handles the endowment—Are the terms met? How did the fund perform in terms of growth? How much money was available for use? And so on. Answers to such questions are important to most donors and they expect the organization to provide such information without being asked for a report—it is a normal part of good stewardship.

Effective stewardship goes well beyond a thank you note and any required IRS documentation (not that these are unimportant, but future gifts are likely to require more than the basics). Essentially stewardship is about creating a stronger relationship with a donor. In many ways, this process does not differ greatly from what we discussed in earlier chapters with regard to staffing and community relationships and connecting. From a fundraising perspective, donor cultivation and stewardship are almost identical in the sense of what a fund-raiser does. In the first instance (cultivation), it is about creating a relationship and, in the second case (stewardship), it is about maintaining and strengthening that relationship. As with creating and maintaining stakeholder connections, involving the donor in library's activities is a good tactic, as is asking for input about this or that change in which the person may have an interest. Bottom line: stewardship matters!

Fundraising Ethics

Although chapter 15 provides an in-depth discussion of ethics—both personal and professional—we believe a brief mention here about fund raising ethics is worthwhile. Perhaps the most significant point to keep in mind about fund raising ethics is that from a public and societal perspective, fundraising activities may be the sole sense of what the organization is and does. Certainly fundraising is very much a public event, regardless of the size of the effort. That in turn relates to public trust, a topic we explored in chapter 1. Needless to say, any material produced for fundraising activities must be factually accurate. When the case addresses plans for future actions or use of monies raised, the ethical issues become less clear. What happens to monies raised if the target goal is not reached; for example, with raising funds for a new branch location that is dependent upon donations?

Certainly most major fundraising efforts require looking ahead for the organization, and long-term forecasting is not a perfect science. As the saying goes, "stuff happens." As with most plans—both professionally and even personally—having a contingency plan can be valuable and can help the organization be resilient when obstacles or unforeseen developments arise.

Finally, trust is an important factor to consider in fundraising efforts. Donors will not be readily forthcoming with their hard-earned money if they feel the organization or even the individual making the request isn't being entirely transparent. Building trust with the community and stakeholders is an ongoing process and should be an essential consideration in all aspects of library operations. If the library's reputation is already solidly in place and the organization practices good stewardship on a daily basis, it will make asking for funds that much easier when the time comes. Another important factor in building trust is how the fundraisers use the data they gather regarding a prospective or actual donor. Issues of privacy and data sharing are a significant concern—we explore library privacy/confidentiality issues in chapter 14.

While fundraisers may not have legal fiduciary responsibilities, there should be a sense of obligation not to encourage a donor to give beyond that person's capabilities or to go against his or her long-term financial interests. This is particularly true when seeking a differed gift.

CHECK THESE OUT

For several years (2011–2015) the journal *Public Libraries* published at least one article per year that focused on public library fundraising. Articles covered topics such as how to solicit funds, going beyond the traditional book sale, conducting major capital campaigns, and so on. While the focus is on the public library, most of the ideas presented can translate into any library setting.

Two very useful books about the ins and outs of library fundraising are:

Victoria Steele and Stephen D. Elder's *Becoming a Fundraiser: The Principles and Practice of Library Development*, 2nd edition. (Chicago, IL: American Library Association, 2000).

Successful Library Fundraising: Best Practices. Edited by M. Sandra Wood (Lanham, MD: Rowman & Littlefield, 2014).

A book about fundraising in any context, though perhaps its 652 pages will be more than you want to know, is *Fundraising Principles and Practice*, 2nd edition, by Adrian Sargent, Jen Shang and Associates (San Francisco, CA: Jossey-Bass, 2016).

The fact is there is little about fundraising that is not covered in this book, other than a library context.

GRANTS

The reality of the economic environment for today's library is that securing significant amounts of money for a new program or service must go beyond fundraising from individual donors. Grants from foundations of various types are part of the supplemental funding mix. A caveat is such funding is rarely a long-term operational commitment, unlike in the past when there were such opportunities. (Even private donors are seldom interested in providing money for "light bulbs and toilet paper," to use a phrase often repeated by fundraisers.) Rather, you need to think of grants primarily as a source for a one-time need or project or as "seed" money to start a new program or service.

Identifying appropriate potential sources of funding starts with knowing your goal for the funds and which sources might have an interest in your project. Granting agencies exist in several forms (public and private)—federal (Institute of Museum and Library Services—IMLS), state agencies (such as the state library), nonprofit foundations (Bill and Melinda Gates Foundation), corporation foundations (for example, the Arizona Power Service Foundation), and community groups (Community Foundations, for example).

Grants also come in several varieties. Research grants support research on both theoretical and applied topics; these are rare for libraries but may arise in the case of collaborative projects between graduate library and information science programs and libraries. Demonstration grants fund efforts to show the feasibility or application of a concept. Libraries often secure such grants, especially public and school libraries. Very often multi-type or consortium library projects have an edge in securing funds to demonstrate the value of a concept. Project grants support a single effort that a library wishes to undertake, such as digitizing a local history collection or upgrading library technology. Such grants are the most common type of library grant. Finally, there are block grants that are given to states by the federal government for further distribution within the state, often on a competitive basis. In the case of libraries, the block grants go to the state library.

Start-up money, one-time projects, and demonstrating how an idea or service can provide real benefits are the meat-and-potatoes of granting agency activities for libraries. How do such grants supplement the operational budget? There are three common ways this can happen. Many grants include money for equipment or storage units (for preservation purposes, for example) that have a useful library life long after the grant activity is completed. There can be physical facility work that either was the purpose of the grant or was associated with a grant's intention—funds that the library had been unable to secure from its primary funding authority.

A third possibility is "overhead" income. Almost all grants involve some administrative expenses as well as use of workspace and existing equipment. Many funding agencies include some funds to offset such costs. In practice, the parent organization of the library takes such funds for its overhead costs. However, it may be possible to secure a share of such funds. If the library is very successful in securing grants, it may even be allowed to retain the majority of those funds. It will take some of your best negotiating skills and connections to gain some share of a grant's overhead income.

When you have a clear notion of what your request is for and the type of agency that might have an interest in your project, you can begin your search for the most likely agency. The good news is there are thousands of such agencies. The bad news is you must find the right needle in a rather large haystack. Where to start?

There are some solid starting points for your search. One of the most frequently mentioned places to start is the *Catalog of Federal Domestic Assistance* (CFDA, www.cfda.gov). This database provides information about all federal domestic programs, which includes grants, eligibility requirements, application procedures, and deadlines. Another commonly mentioned Internet resource is grants.gov, which provides data for more than 900 grant programs.

In terms of nonprofit guides, a great place to begin is GuideStar (http://www .guidestar.org/Home.aspx). This website allows you to search more than 1 million U.S. nonprofits by subject, category, keyword, state, and more. Yet another resource is Funding Sources through The Grantsmanship Center (https://www.tgci.com/funding-sources). One of the Foundation Center's services is Foundation Directory Online (http://foundationcenter.org/products/ foundation-directory-online).

Agency websites provide information about application procedures, deadlines, and the like, but often they only identify very broad areas of funding interests, such as education or children's health care. The reality is most funding bodies target some areas within the broad topic(s) to actually fund. For some groups, those target areas remain in place for a very long time; for other groups, targets change annually. Often the latter group posts a list of the grants given in the past year or two. Doing so helps both the organization and those who might submit a proposal by reducing the number of out-of-scope proposals. Most granting agencies are very open to getting inquiries about a specific topic's fit with its interests; again to save time and effort for both parties. A few agencies will entertain a pre-proposal or, if reasonable, a meeting to discuss more fully the potential funding request.

James Raines and Michelle Alvarez outlined four very useful principles for achieving good "grantsmanship": "The first and most surprising principle is that grant writing should be not only about money. The ultimate goal of grant writing is to build a relationship with grantors so that they become stakeholders in the organization" (2006, 46). Making connections and building positive relationship are clearly interrelated.

Their second principle was that a team effort in preparation of the proposal is generally more effective than a "Lone Ranger" effort. There are at least two reasons for this principle. First, by having a team, assuming you're bringing on individuals who have expertise in some aspect of the proposed project, each person can concentrate on developing the narrative in their area of expertise. Doing that helps create a more compelling narrative and one that indicates the requestors understand and are capable of implementing a successful project. Using collaborative software, the team is able to easily interact without the need for frequent face-to-face meetings while still building a strong case for support. The second reason is such a process tends to reduce the chances of one person having to do everything related to a project in addition to their regular duties. There will be some additional administrative tasks associated with grants you receive, especially when the project is government funded (such as progress reports and detailed final reports). The administrative side of a successful proposal is sometimes overlooked by beginners.

Their third principle may appear to be counterintuitive: "Grant writing should not be about fulfilling unmet needs. . . . Good grant writing is about capitalizing on capabilities" (Raines and Alvarez, 2006, 47). Almost every granting agency's ultimate goal is to make society a better place, no matter how indirectly. Explaining how your library's capabilities will be enhanced by the funding, and will thereby benefit the community, will be a large plus when the reviewers assess your proposal.

Their fourth and final principle is straightforward: break the proposal writing process into small segments and the task will not seem so monumental. This is relatively easy to do as most granting agencies have a specific proposal format that has required sections, beyond the basic narrative, such as institutional background, budget, and personnel. Doing each section with at least a few hours in between, away from the proposal, moves you forward, but in a way that makes the work seem less daunting. Obviously, if you also apply the second principle—team writing— the task will be even easier on you.

TIPS FOR GRANT WRITING

- Ask your coworkers for ideas. They may have insight regarding projects that have been on the backburner for years or they may see areas within the library that are in dire need of help.
- Do look at niche needs that your library is a position to fill for the community.
- Do look at projects that resonate with you personally. It's much easier to write a grant for a project that you're passionate about than one for which you have to feign enthusiasm.
- Select your topic.
- Gather information on the topic or problem.
- Isolate the topic or problem.

- Pick the most feasible alternatives for solving the problem—get reactions from others on staff.
- Select a grant foundation or agency.
- Get the guidelines from the granting agency.
- Carefully match your proposal with the granting agency's current interests.
- Write and organize the proposal to make it easy for agency reviewers to read and understand.
- Follow instructions exactly.
- Use clear language and text that is well structured, and make sure there are no errors.
- Avoid using professional jargon unless you are *absolutely* certain the reviewers will understand the usage.
- Recognize that your proposal hints at your being able to manage the grant.
- List the goals and objectives of the project.
- Avoid using personal pronouns.
- Include outcome assessment measures.
- Include a detailed budget.
- Include a detailed timeline.

CHECK THESE OUT

Online resources that help in grant writing include:

- Basic Elements of Grant Writing (http://www.cpb.org/grants/grantwriting)
- Nonprofit Guides: Grant Writing Tools for Non-Profit Organizations (www.npguides.org)
- Proposal Writing Short Course (http://foundationcenter.org/getstarted/tutorials/shortcourse/index.html)

ALA also has a useful site on this topic:

- Writing Grant Applications http://www.ala.org/offices/ppo/resources/writinggrant.

MANAGERIAL LEADERSHIP CHALLENGES AND REFERENDA ISSUES

Public agencies can, and, from time to time, do, attempt to increase their available funds through a referendum. These efforts are not undertaken lightly as they require the public to vote on the issue. There are two basic types of library referenda—a bond issue or an increase in the library tax levy (mil rate). Either one means citizens will pay more in some manner; thus, the need for a vote.

An important fact about issuing bonds is they pay interest to purchasers. A common life span of public bonds is 20 to 25 years. What that means is when the voters approve the bond, the library or parent organization has an annual obligation to pay the bond holders the required interest, throughout the bond's lifetime. That is, there is a debt burden to pay every year and that, in turn, may impact the library's allocation for other obligations. How much the interest will be depends a jurisdiction's bond rating. A third party determines the rating. (There are three firms in the United States that do this, Standard & Poor's (S&P), Moody's, and Fitch Ratings.) The agencies base their rating on their assessment of the jurisdiction's credit worthiness, rather like your personal credit score. Needless to say, the higher the rating the lower the interest rate will be. The downside of a low rate is it is very hard to sell the bonds and it can take some time to realize the authorized level of funding. Just because the issuance passes does not necessarily translate into library funds—the bonds must sell. Just as you hope to get the maximum return on your personal investments, so do bond buyers. Increasing a library's mil rate (tax levy) is a means to secure an ongoing increase in its allocation, which will assure funds. Such increases are more often than not permanent, but voters can, at some point, take back the increase.

Just as with other fundraising efforts, success on a referendum begins by creating a compelling case for why a "yes" vote is appropriate. There is a major difference between these two efforts, however. A fundraising drive, of whatever type, is rarely a political matter in the partisan sense. A referendum is very much a political matter. Understanding the political climate is a central issue for deciding the time when to go or not go with an effort. Another consideration is gauging the level of trust the community has in the library. In this regard, most libraries are highly regarded, as we discussed in chapter 1. Referenda outcomes depend partly on voters' beliefs about the library's overall performance and value for the money. Once again, the social return on investment (SROI) data can be very valuable in demonstrating such value. Based on recent data, covered below, the amount of money sought does not play as big a role as you might expect in the success or failure of a referendum. A strong case, high trust, and sound library performance appear to the most important factors in having a successful referendum.

Given the fact that such efforts require an election, the rules of engagement for staff and library supporters when it comes to election activities become very important. (We explore the political aspects of all types in chapter 13; we look at the issues of advocacy, lobbying, and marketing all of which play a role in any referendum.) Before embarking on a referendum, we recommend having some meetings—one for staff and library board members, one for volunteers (they are not employees yet they work in the library), and perhaps one with support group members—with a legal advisor regarding what each may or may not do in relation to the referendum.

The fact is the number of library referenda undertaken each year is relatively small. There are over 9,000 public libraries in the U.S. Of that number only 283 held a referendum between 2013 and 2015 (see Rosa 2016, 2015, 2014). Since 2014, *American Libraries* has published an annual "Referenda Roundup" article that provides data about the successes and failures of such efforts in the prior year. The overall average of success, for those three years, was just over 77 percent. Given the general economy and the public's attitude about public agencies the success rate is notable. The funds sought range from just over $1 million to over $100 million. One example of a high dollar amount approved was in South Carolina, where nearly 74 percent of the voters in Charleston accepted a $108.5 million bond undertaking (Rosa, 2015, 68–69).

Referenda can raise substantial dollars; however, you need to think long and hard before committing to such an effort. They are intense, time consuming, and their cost is not inconsequential.

CHECK THIS OUT

Denice Rovira Hazlett's 2014 article "Homegrown Fundraising" (*Library Journal* 139, no. 1: 42–44) describes how the Holmes County, Ohio, public library gained voter approval after several failed attempts. We believe if you are thinking about embarking on a referendum, it's well worth your time to read this piece.

Securing funds beyond the amounts allocated to the library has become an essential part of a managerial leader's job description today. Learning the art of raising supplemental funds for the library takes time, effort, and, more often than not, some failures. Don't let a few failures stop you from trying again and again—when it is successful, it results in more than just monetary pay offs; the professional rewards are exceptional as well.

REFERENCES

Andreoni, James. 2001. "Economics of Philanthropy." In *International Encyclopedia of the Social & Behavioral Sciences*. Edited by Neil J. Smelser and Paul B. Baltes. New York: Elsevier.

Blum, Debra E. 2016. "Personalized Philanthropy." *The Chronicle of Philanthropy* 28, no. 6: 24–27.

Hadzor, Thomas B., and Kurt H. Cumiskey. 2014. "Crazy Smart: Creative Approaches to Developing Your Donor Pipeline and Increasing Support." In *Successful Library Fundraising: Best Practices*. Edited by M. Sandra Wood. Lanham, MD: Rowman & Littlefield.

Irwin-Wells, Suzanne. 2002. *Planning and Implementing Your Major Gifts Campaign*. San Francisco, CA: Jossey-Bass

Peet, Lisa. 2016. "The New Fundraising Landscape: Budgets and Funding." *Library Journal* 141 no. 1:42–45.

Peters, Tom. 1987. *Thriving on Chaos: Handbook for a Management Revolution*. New York: Knopf.

Raines, James, and Michelle Alvarez. 2006. "Cash Through Collaboration: A Relational Approach to Grant Writing for Social Workers in Schools." *School Social Work Journal* 30, no. 2: 45–63.

Rosa, Kathy. 2014. "Referenda Roundup: An Overview of How States Performed on 2013 Ballots." *American Libraries* 45, nos. 1/2: 44–49.

Rosa, Kathy. 2015. Referenda Roundup: An Overview of How States Performed in the November Ballots." *American Libraries* 46, nos. 1/2: 64–69.

Rosa, Kathy. 2016. "Referenda Roundup: An Overview of How States Performed on Library Measures in 2015." *American Libraries* 47, nos.1/2: 54–59.

Steele, Victoria, and Stephen D. Elder. 1992. *Becoming a Fundraiser: The Principles and Practice of Library Development*. Chicago, IL: American Library Association.

Wilhelm, Mark O. 2007. "The Quality and Comparability of Survey Data on Charitable Giving." *Nonprofit and Voluntary Sector Quarterly* 36, no. 1:65–84.

Chapter 11

MANAGING PROJECTS

As work in libraries continues to become more project-driven, formal project-management training for librarians and other library staff is not necessarily keeping pace.

Amy Stewart, 2015

When the headlines and hearings and second-guessing begin, we usually find that failure is rooted not in the way a particular program or project was conceived, but rather in the way its implementation was *managed*.

Ron Sanders, 2014

All projects are risky. By definition, projects deliver unique services and products, distinguishing them from routine operations.

Stanley Emelander, 2014.

Many of us have received an email from our supervisor along the following lines: "Good morning, I hope you had a restful weekend. I'd like to get together with you today. While I know you are very busy, there is a project that I believe you are best qualified to handle. How about coming to my office at 10 a.m.?" The first reaction is almost always "Why me?" That is especially the case when the request comes with some acknowledgement of your heavy workload. For a good many of us, the second reaction is a reflection of the above Amy Stewart quotation—"I've never dealt with managing a project! Where would I start?" Ira Revels, a librarian and consultant/trainer in project management noted when writing about his workshop participants, "By the end of the exercise, it was clear that what these 'accidental' project managers needed was to understand basic elements of project management" (2010, 49).

A very broad definition of a project is a relatively short-term activity with an anticipated end date rather than something that is ongoing. As a result, people tend to use the word with a very wide range of meanings in terms of complexity—managing a Mars landing effort to organizing my office. Both extremes fit the general definition of project; however, their complexities are worlds apart. In this chapter, we focus on managing organizational projects and their associated complexity in the public and nonprofit worlds.

Libraries employ projects as a means of accomplishing their mission and goals on a regular basis today, although they have few, if any staff with project management background. Jenn Anne Horwath reported on her research into librarians managing projects in Ontario; of the 151 respondents 92 percent indicated they had been involved at least one "project" in the past year (2012). All types of libraries were represented in her sample. Formal training in project management was not indicated as a background for any of the respondents. Forty-two individuals said "they read a book" while 37 said they had attended a project management workshop. In her literature review section, she noted that less than 4 percent of the U.S. and Canadian accredited LIS programs listed the topic in their curriculum (7). Even on the job training in project management (7–8) was very uncommon despite the increased employment of the methodology in the workplace.

The good news is, managing a project successfully rarely requires acquiring new skills; your managerial leadership skills are more than adequate. The bad news is you *must* employ them in a different manner. That requires an adjustment in how you think about the activities, people, resources, time, and when and how to use your skills to manage those issues. Such an adjustment can be a little jarring; however, with a bit of reading and guidance you will be able to make the shift and be successful.

So, what is it that requires a managerial thinking reset, at least in a library environment? The one word answer is "time." Another factor, but less significant is the "one-off" nature of the project. Yet another factor is projects are rarely "Lone Ranger" efforts, most involve a team created just for the project. Often members have not had prior work experience with the other team members.

Successful project outcomes arise from the initial detailed planning. It is not uncommon for none of the team members to have prior experience with the purpose of the project. That means planning slows as they learn what is involved and how to achieve the desired outcome(s). That lack of knowledge can also lead to poor planning. Problematic planning in turn makes accurately estimating the resources required to complete the project can be suspect and subject to revision. Such issues slow progress and we are back to time.

More often than not a project will involve at least one other person ("project team"). All of Horwath's respondents had a team of at least two people. The use of a team, in the formal meaning, may not be part of the library's basic operating structure, which raises additional issues for the project.

Another factor in the need to reset thinking is managerial leaders, over time, develop a "style" for their work behavior activities. For example, their approach to achieving control and coordination of their unit's activities was worked out over time. They have preferred communication and decision-making styles. It is very likely some of these characteristics will not be fully effective or perhaps appropriate for managing the project's team.

PROJECTS IN THE PUBLIC SECTOR

Project management in the nonprofit and public sector is rather different than project management in for-profit organizations. The opening quotation from Sanders highlights the very large difference for public sector project managers, regardless of agency type—changing priorities, politics, tons of stakeholders, and so on.

The overarching difference for the two sector's projects is there are many stakeholders who may have an interest in the effort—its purpose, its timing, its process, and its implementation, for example. In the case of a public sector project, the media may be interested in any or all of the foregoing topics. Such interest can occasionally become a distraction and perhaps cause delays. Media issues are almost never present in terms of internal library projects; however, when it comes to public access issues, collaborative or cross-jurisdictional efforts (perhaps a joint ILS acquisition) and the like, the situation is different.

One of the major stakeholders, at least in their minds, are the political leaders who more often than not have rather different agendas. Again, the impact of such agendas rarely directly impact library project management. However, on those rare occasions when they do arise it can play havoc with the project. An example is differences of opinion about what to or not to include in a new facility or renovated space.

It is the indirect effects that can and do cause the most common problems. That is, the rules, regulations, policies, and so on, that politicians impose on the agencies that they govern that create problems. Generally, such issues revolve around securing the required resources to carry out the project—temporary staffing, one-off funds, hiring a consultant, and the like. There can be, and are, methods for getting around such issues; however, those methods commonly take time and effort, which in turn affects the project's progress. A related issue is a change in the politics due to an election and a resulting change in policies and priorities.

Public administrators tend to focus more on compliance than on performance. Strict adherences to compliance guidelines and expectations can, at times cause delays as a result of having to get prior approval to deviate from the standard. It may in fact jeopardize the project. For example, it is not that uncommon for a vendor, say an ILS, to guarantee a price for a fixed installation date, after which the price will change. That does not mean the vendor will not install the system at a later date, but at a higher price, which may be beyond the library's ability to meet. In addition to such concerns, budget cycles may come into play and the library may lose access to funds for the project's temporary staff or consultant services. Again, most of these concerns can be overcome, but at some cost (time and even dollars). If nothing more, the library staff assigned to the project will have less time for their normal duties.

MANAGERIAL SKILLS AND PROJECTS

There will be times when you are called upon to manage or lead a project. No matter the time scale, short or long, character of the project, one common feature, as we noted above, is the creation of a project team. While project teams require many of the same skills as managing other types of teams there are some special aspects to project teams.

Project teams, especially in libraries, are likely to have a rather different composition than ongoing work teams. More often than not, members are there as a representative of some library interest or unit rather a particular skill set. What that means is, as leader, you will need to put more effort into building member buy-in and team chemistry. Mary Feeney and Lisle Sult noted in their description of their project, "At the project's start, there was not enough time invested in teambuilding to ensure that all team members understood their roles and responsibilities" (2011, 758)

Another difference is you may have very limited shared work experience with team members. Related to limited shared work experience is a rather big managerial "no-no"—dual "bosses"—that is likely to come to play. For most people such duality generates stress. That stress may be multiplied when the person is supposed to represent a special interest of one supervisor while trying to be an effective team member for a team leader. Thus, your job, as team leader, is to find a way to achieve effective team outcomes without appearing to be "The Boss." Yes, that is something to strive for in any supervisory capacity, the difference with a project is you have a timeline that often requires tighter control and direction.

When the project cuts across institutional boundaries the challenge is even greater. An example of such a project might be a public library working with the school district and a local school of education to develop an after-school public library–based tutoring-homework assistance program. A related difference is there may be substantial differences in the managerial level of the members. This can result in problems of dominance or timidity on the part of some members. All of these issues will be a challenge calling for more than your usual people skills.

Your people skills are ultimately what will make or break the project, just as they will in terms of your career success. When you review the following list of necessary people skills most commonly listed in project management literature, we believe you will conclude they are necessary for any management activity.

TEAM MANAGEMENT SKILLS

Listening effectively	Developing shared ownership
Being supportive	Being a buffer between team and outside issues
Effectively delegating	Demonstrating leadership
Fostering mutual respect	Showing technical skills
Clearing roadblocks for team	Demonstrating fairness
Building a strong team	Displaying flexibility
Knowing one's limitations	Exhibiting open-mindedness
Providing timely feedback	Making sound decisions
Providing or suggesting solutions	

PROJECTS METHODOLOGIES

There are a variety of approaches for managing a project. They are often complex and many people have little background in how handle a project. The good news is there are some tools you can employ to help with the complexity. Many of the tools you employ to analyze workflows in your unit are also useful in managing and controlling a project. For many people, project management means scheduling. It is true that scheduling is part of the leader's task; however, it is far from the only one. Although you may have experience with staff work scheduling, project scheduling is a very different beast. One the first questions that arises when a project is announced is, when will it be done? Related questions are "can't it be done quicker?" "why will it take so long?" Those questions are scheduling issues. A question you will hear more than you might like as team leader is "Are you on schedule?"

While there a number of project management approaches, many are designed for research and development (R&D) efforts. In terms of the public and nonprofit sector, there are three methodologies that we will discuss—Traditional, PRINCE2, and Critical Chain Project Management. All methodologies involve the stages of the traditional approach to handling a project and then add various features reflecting a certain type of project goal(s).

TRADITIONAL METHOD

Traditional is the "tried-and-true" method for handling a project, regardless of type. The traditional approach consists of five stages: initiation, planning, implementing, controlling, and closing.

Initiation

Initiation involves gaining a full and accurate understanding of the scope of the project, including the timeframe. Once you have that in hand, you and others may select team members, assuming the project will require a team. One example might be you are charged with moving 125,000 items to a remote storage facility. Such a statement might be the short version (public understanding) of what the project is about. However, there are a host of details to identify, clarify, and verify, verify. For example, what constitutes an item—bound volumes, media, government documents, archival material, and so on What are the environmental conditions in the storage facility, are they subject to modification, if so are they a part of the project? Are the arrangements for transporting the "items" part of the team's responsibility? If so, what monetary limits are in play? Is there an official position regarding who should be involved in the selection of items and is there the need to allow for vetoes of a transfer? There are other such concerns, but we think you get the sense that the initiation stage is more involved than you might think.

Planning

When you have all the answers regarding the scope and limits of the project, you and the team can begin the planning process. For newcomers to project management, this is the stage at which the first big mistakes can occur. In terms of scheduling and a successful outcome, the level of detail in planning will make or break the project. Most of us get projects assigned to us that we have little or no background in, which means we have vague ideas about what is involved. What do you do in such cases, especially if none of the team members have prior experience with the project's focus? Being information professionals we fall back on our skills, in this case, doing research on the topic. Thank goodness for the Internet, in days gone by the search and research might have taken longer that the project would. Emails to professional friends, online searches, and posting on various forums will likely generate information on what is involved and perhaps a few contacts at libraries that did such a project.

Such research information gives you and the team a foundation upon which to build, or in this case, to break down the project tasks. What you need to do is break down project activities into smaller and smaller components. There is an experienced project manager's rule of thumb that is helpful to keep in mind during this stage—if an activity, at the lowest level, takes more than 80 hours to complete, there is still room to further divide what has to be done. There is a project management technique known as Work Breakdown Structure (WBS, see http://www.project managementdocs.com/project-planning-templates/work-breakdown-structure -wbs.html#axzz4CnWkPqRy for more information) that is also useful in reducing a project into its component parts. Once you have that in hand you can then create a realistic sequence for engaging in the activities.

One of your challenges in the above storage project example is that you are unlikely to want or expect that the selection decisions be the sole responsibility of the project team. There will likely be several interested parties, some of whom may oppose the storage of anything remotely related to their interests. (Based on the authors' experience with such projects, this issue can *really* slow things down.) Even if the decision makers are willing to store items, they will have their own timelines for selecting items. The team, during the planning stage, needs to think through how to handle the "my time" situation should it arrive and still keep to the project schedule.

Once you have the tasks identified, at the finest level of detail possible, you can start to create a sequence and schedule. Again, there are some tools that are useful in laying out the project schedule. One such tool is PERT (Program Evaluation and Review Technique), which is a method of looking at how to sequence tasks. A component of PERT is the Critical Path Method (CPM). Its usefulness resides in identifying what "must be done before" relationships of project tasks. Essentially PERT data can generate a chart such as in Table 11.1 or graphically as a form or flowchart.

Another widely used tool in managing a project is a Gantt chart. This tool has been in use for more than 100 years. Henry Gantt, a time-and-motion specialist in the

Table 11.1.
PERT Example

Task	Sequence	Best Time	Worst Time	Average Time	Estimated Time
1	1	2	5	3	3.5
2	1	3	5	4.5	4.0
4	2	5	7	6	6.0
7	6	24	39	32	36.0
8	5	55	96	79	85.0
9	7,6	12	22	16	14.0
10	8,9	10	16	13	12.5

Table 11.2.
Gantt Chart Example

1	▓▓	▓▓							
2	▓▓	▓▓	▓▓						
3					░░	░░	░░	░░	
4					░░	░░	░░	░░	░░
7									
8									
9									
10									

tradition of Frederick W. Taylor (scientific management) started using the technique in 1917 as a means of graphically showing a project's timeline and associated activities. Table 11.2 shows a portion of a Gantt chart based on the data in Table 11.1.

The schedule you develop is not set in stone, especially when the project is new for you and team members. However, even knowing that the timing and sequencing may change sometime during the project's lifetime means you know that the initial plan can get you underway. If nothing else, vacation and sick days can have an impact on the timing. When you have a project such as the storage project that brings others for some activities, you must think through how to handle their work priorities versus what you need.

Implementing

Implementing is a bit more involved than just saying to team members, "Let's get to work." One reason is members need to know who is to do what, when, and how. Yes, the planning stage will have established the whats and whens, but not always who and how. Some of the assignments may be clearly based on a person's experience or background. This also sets the stage where a team member's regular responsibilities are worked through in terms of project needs. Needless to say, this is the time when the team leader clarifies what access there is to resources and gains an understanding of how that process will operate—with or without someone else's approval.

It is also the time when senior management's support for the effort is made clear to all concerned. As we noted earlier, most library project teams consist of individuals who retain their other duties (dual reporting). That is why having top management's position about priorities becomes critical for the sake of both teams members and their supervisors. Additionally, as in the case of our phantom remote storage project described earlier, the project may require participation of other staff for one or more of the project activities. Again, senior managers must make it clear just how important such participation is and its priority vis-à-vis other duties.

Then there is the matter of stakeholders with real or imagined interest(s) in the project's processes and outcomes. This is an area that highlights the difference between public and other sector project management activities. Stakeholders play a constant role in how public sector agencies function. Their views are ignored at the risk of having long-term negative consequences. Thus, during the planning or at the start of the implementation, there should be an opportunity for interested parties to learn about and make comments regarding the project. It is rare, but not unheard of, for stakeholder input stopping a project, especially in libraries; however, their thoughts can lead to modifications.

Control

Managerial control is a concept that ranges between very good and very bad work operations, depending on the context. Where the application of workplace control falls is dependent, in part, upon the manager's view of employees. You probably remember from your Introduction to Psychology or Management coursework Douglas McGregor's Theory X and Y continuum. The X end of the continuum is where people dislike working and need to be driven to do so and the Y end is where people enjoy work. Needless to say, a manager who believes in the X side tends to be highly controlling, often with a result that reinforces the person's belief that people are lazy and need to be driven. That is, unit performance is just adequate at best, as the staff members resist and resent the control and demonstrate their attitudes by giving a minimum level of work effort. Thus, most managers and all effective managerial leaders operate on the Y side of the continuum.

When it comes to project management control is another place where preferred approaches are best left on the shelf or at least substantially modified. To keep on schedule, or nearly so, you may need to ramp up your use of control with team members, often beyond what your customary workplace style may be. Group decision making and problem solving are not efficient or appropriate for a large scale project as those activities require time-often large amounts-and as with most projects, time is of the essence. A project leader should make decisions and resolve problems as quickly as possible, often with little or no consultation with team members.

A project manager must continually monitor progress and be "directive" occasionally. (There is a mantra for project managers that goes "measure, evaluate, and correct constantly.") Such behaviors will call upon your best diplomatic skills to gain the performance necessary and also retain team members' best efforts. Part of your success in these efforts will rest on the respect the team has for you and your expertise.

A good way to start earning that respect is during the planning and implementation stages, in which you emphasize collegiality and group process as well as explain the need to be more "authoritative" during the operational stage of the project.

Closing

The final stage—closing—involves activities, as you would expect, that range from thanking team members and others who assisted in the work, to reviewing what was done and what could be improved in the future, to handling the settlement of money issues. Rather often there are some other closing tasks when it comes to library projects. Many library projects arise from getting a grant for the project. Almost all granting agencies require at least a final report that documents what was done with the funds granted. (Many such bodies, for grants lasting a year or more, often require quarterly reports. Generally, a simple combining of quarterly reports is not adequate from the funder's point of view. The funder expects an in-depth report and assessment.) In some cases, the project is not really completed, even with the implementation activities finished and successfully operating. It is rather common for a granting agency to require an assessment of the project's outcomes and effectiveness. Such assessments often take months or a year to complete. Often non-team staff members may well have the responsibility for collecting the assessment data.

CHECK THESE OUT

The following are a few examples of the traditional approach in a library/information service setting:

Nancy J. Burich, et al., "Project Management and Institutional Collaboration in Libraries," *Technical Services Quarterly* 24, no. 1 (2006): 17–36.

H. Frank Cervone, "Standard Methodology in Digital Library Projects," *OCLC Systems & Services* 23, no. 1 (2007): 30–34.

Jennifer L. Marill and Marcella Lesher, "Mile High to Ground Level: Getting Projects Organized and Completed," *Serials Librarian* 52, no. 3/4 (2007): 317–322.

Mark D. Winston and Tara Hoffman, "Project Management in Libraries," *Journal of Library Administration* 42, no. 1 (2005): 51–61.

PRINCE2

U.S. libraries usually employ the traditional methodology. We encountered no article indicating the use of PRINCE2 (PRojects IN Controlled Environments) in a U.S. library. However, libraries elsewhere do make use of this public domain methodology. In the United Kingdom any publicly funded project must use it (see the sidebar below for references to some such library usages).

All the components of the traditional approach are present in the PRINCE2 method. However, the labels are different and are divided into seven stages rather than five—starting, directing, initiating, planning, controlling, monitoring, and closing.

"Starting" is rather different in this approach as it focuses on the "case" (the reason or need for the project). The need for a case probably exists in the traditional approach, in the sense a project does not begin unless someone decided there was a need for such an effort. (Essentially this is where senior management's support comes into play.) The difference is such an assessment in not usually thought of as part of managing a project in the traditional sense. Making such an assessment is certainly important, if for no other reason than that project takes time and effort from other activities. In libraries, where all resources are stretched to the "max," having resources directed away from the basic activities must rest upon a good case for doing so. A good many library projects arise from seeking and securing a grant. Presumably, the decision to seek funding occurred after some discussion of the merits of the purpose and the consequences of getting a grant.

Directing

The directing stage has some of the elements of the initiation phase of the traditional approach. Under PRINCE2, this stage addresses developing the structure of the project, for example, selecting a "Project Manager" and "Project Board" and establishing roles and responsibilities for each. The basic distinction is the Manager is charged with overseeing the daily activities of the project. A Board could be senior managers who have the authority but not the accountability of a project's success or failure. The PRINCE2 method tackles what could be a challenging situation by making it clear (perhaps even by documenting) that both parties have certain authority, responsibilities, and accountability for success or failure.

This is a good place to discuss project certification. When the project costs are substantial, when there are several interlinked projects, and/or when the project is very complex, it may be time to think about contracting with a certified project manager. There may not be too many library projects that make it cost effective to hire an outside person as manager. One possibility would be when the library plans on expanding its technological capabilities and infrastructure. Once underway it could become clear that the needs of the project require another project manager who will actually bring in the requisite power to the library in order to support the new resources.

There are several thousand such certified project managers (the Project Management Institute—PMI—is the certifying body, http://www.pmi.org/Certification .aspx) in the U.S. and the PRINCE2 Foundation also certifies such individuals (http://www.apmg-international.com/en/qualifications/prince2/prince2.aspx). Such individuals are not inexpensive to hire. It takes time and money to secure the certificate. To be considered for certification in the U.S., a person needs to document at least 4,500 hours of project management experience as well as hours and hours of classroom training in managing projects (Johnson, Liu, and Flagiello, 2016). With major projects, having a full-time person whose only obligation is the project, may well be worth the cost in professional management as well as not having a staff person trying to handle at least two more or less full-time jobs. The PRINCE2 method that makes the structuring of the project critical probably focuses more attention on real labor costs than does the traditional approach.

Initiating

The initiating segment of the process focuses on how the project is to be managed (Project Initiation Document—PID—is the phrase used for the end product). One aspect in this stage is identifying possible risk factors that would affect project activities and a means of dealing with the eventuality. Identified risks are an important section of the PID. Quality control, estimates, project resource allocations, and reporting timeframes are also components of the document. This is also where the initial scheduling takes place, using Gantt charts and critical path techniques.

Planning, Controlling, Monitoring, Closing

Under the PRINCE2 method, planning is not so much a stage in the process as an overarching ongoing activity throughout the project. Plans provide Project Directors with the information about what they need to monitor. Monitoring feedback may lead to both control activities and the plans. Closing is the same as with all the other project management approaches.

CHECK THESE OUT

The following are examples of the use of PRINCE2 in an information service environment:

Fereshteh Afshari and Richard Jones, "Developing an Integrated Institutional Repository at Imperial College London," *Program: Electronic Library and Information Systems* 41, no. 4 (2007): 338–352.

Shirley Chambers and David Perrow, "Introducing Project Management Techniques to the Robinson Library, University of Newcastle," *Journal of Librarianship and Information Science* 30, no. 4 (1998): 249–258.

Ralph Kiel, "Project Management and Cultural Change: A Case Study at the University of Western Australia," *EDUCAUSE Australasia*, 2007, https://journal.lib.uoguelph.ca/index .php/perj/article/view/1802/2493#.V2qvRKJpn2s.

Tracey Stanley, Frances Norton, and Barry Dickson, "Library Project Management in a Collaborative Web-based Working Environment," *New Review of Academic Librarianship* 9, no. 1 (2003): 70–83.

PROJECTS DO FAIL

Some years ago (2001), the Standish Group suggested that organizational IT projects fall into one of three categories—successful, challenged, and failed. A successful project ends on time, on budget, and objectives are fully met. Only 25 percent of the Standish Group's sample fell into this category. A challenged effort is one that finishes but with one or more "challenges"—overdue, over budget, lacking one or more of the objectives, or some of the original objectives were modified during the project. Fifty percent of the sample was in the challenged category. You can guess what constituted their failed category. Jenn Horwath, cited earlier, also looked at project success rates in the libraries in her research pool. Of her 86 projects, only 14 were fully successful and only 4 failures (2012, 17–20). What this suggests is, if nothing more, many people have challenges when it comes to managing a project regardless of organizational context.

There is an approach that helps remove some of the uncertainty inherit in all projects—Critical Chain Project Management (CCPM). This method draws on the traditional approach to a large degree, but focuses on finding optimum solutions. Often, the early planning in the traditional approach looks for "*a*" solution rather the best one. This happens in part because everyone wants to get it started and finished as quickly as possible. Another feature of CCPM is what is termed "buffers." These buffers (project—time, feeding—provide for critical path elements, and resources—extra resources for each step) become fallback resources for managers at this stage. Buffers provide flexibility in case the unexpected does happen.

A review of the sidebar below provides a sense of how CCPM might be useful for "accidental" project managers and when the inevitable unexpected occurs. The sidebar identifies some of the most common reasons project end in the "challenged" category.

PROJECT FAILURE FACTORS

- Inadequate communication with team members, stakeholders, or senior managers
- Failure to properly plan, to seek best solution, and/or over-estimating time required for a task(s)
- Lack of expertise in the project focus
- Lack of trained project managers
- Insufficient attention to defining project goal(s)
- Scant attention to "project creep"—additions after the start of work
- Inaccurate definition of project costs
- Absence of effective stakeholder input
- Lack of leadership
- Failure to say "no" often enough to requests for changes in the project
- Lack of an organizational culture that accepts the notion of team efforts
- Absence of true priorities or effective assessment of changing organizational priorities and objectives
- Inadequate assessment of the challenges of implementing a new approach (project management) and a new activity (project purpose) at the same time
- Scant attention to warning signs of project problems (not able to recognize what the signs might be)
- Failure to coordinate project activities effectively

We do not claim the sidebar lists all the challenges to achieving an on time, on target, and on budget project outcome. However, we do believe the list does make it clear why the success rate is low and why anyone charged with managing a project should receive solid project management training before starting on her or his first effort.

PROJECT MANAGEMENT SOFTWARE

For the "accidental" project managers, as well as the most experienced, there are a variety of software packages that aid in managing projects. Having access to software that can help avoid some to the problems listed in the sidebar above is good news. On the down side, such software will not resolve the "people" issues appearing in the table, but will aid with the technical side of project management. What such programs provide is food for thought, allow for exploring more options for organizing the activities, easy manipulation of data, guidance, and early warnings of potential problems.

Such programs are often divided into one of three categories—single project level 1 (limited capabilities, easy to use); single project level 2 (more sophisticated capabilities, can be a challenging for the novice project manager to learn); and multi-project programs (full range of capabilities, including strong graphic functions). There are a variety of types within the categories—desktop, Web, single user, collaborative, home, and visualization are frequently employed labels for program types. As the label suggests, a desktop program resides on the manger's PC hard drive of a computer and, if in a team setting, the team members' machines. Internet based programs allow access through a variety of devices and locations. Single systems operate on the assumption only one person will be inputting and/or making changes in the program. Home systems are limited in their capability while being easy to use (not too useful for library projects). There are some programs that have powerful graphic capabilities. Many of us, including the authors, can find tables of data timing consuming to work out an accurate analysis and find graphic representations of the data easier to understand and make judgments, seeing patterns, clues, and so on.

Winston and Hoffman noted there were a number of project management programs, such as "Microsoft Project, Open Plan, Primavera Software, and Turbo Project" (2005, 53), all of which are appropriate for a library setting. As of mid-2016 all the mentioned programs were available. Microsoft Project has a long history of successful use (https://www.microsoftstore.com/store/msusa/en_US/cat/categoryID.69407700?tduid=(4f0137d71774c091913df63a3d699214) (256380)(2459594)(SRi0yYDlqd0-YLwre5_Iqp6vNAAIvZJFwQ). You can read about the package's features in the 2005 article by Zhang Ying and Corinne Bishop, "Project Management Tools for Libraries: A Planning and Implementation Model Using Microsoft Project 2000" (*Information Technology and Libraries* 24, no. 3: 147–152).

CHECK THESE OUT

We did not encounter any reported use of the other packages in a library setting. You can learn more about the other programs mentioned above at the following websites:

Open Plan. https://www.deltek.com/en/products/project-and-portfolio-management/open-plan

Primavera. https://www.oracle.com/applications/primavera/index.html

Turbo Project. www.turboproject.com

What might you reasonably expect in a robust project management program? The sidebar below reflects what we believe are the minimum features you should expect in a program appropriate for library usage. Certainly there are more robust packages; however, unless the library staff are experienced project managers the additional features may cause unnecessary challenges in implementation.

PROJECT MANAGEMENT SOFTWARE DESIRED FEATURES

- Planning and scheduling
- Calendaring
- Critical path analysis
- Alternative affect analysis
- Cost variance analysis
- Early potential problem alert
- Customized reporting
- Graphic presentation

It seems highly probable that libraries will face a growing need for engaging in project management. Staffing is unlikely to expand, at least in the near term, which means staff will be stretched to carry out all the desired activities. Funding will probably increase at a very slow pace. Library users are unlikely to stop wanting expanded services as well as new ones. Finding the funding for any service enhancement will in all likelihood require seeking grants and major donations that in turn necessitate using a project approach. We believe it may be time for libraries to start building a project management orientation into their organizational culture. Having such an orientation will not reduce the "why me?" when receiving the message we noted in the chapter's opening paragraph. What it will do is reduce the stress associated with starting a project.

CHECK THESE OUT

The following are a small sample of books detailing the how, what, and when of project management:

Joseph Heagney's *Fundamentals of Project Management*, 4th edition (New York: American Management Association, 2012).

Harold Kerzner's *Project Management: A Systems Approach to Planning, Scheduling, and Controlling*, 11th edition (New York: Wiley, 2013).

Kathy Schwalbe's *Information Technology Project Management*, 8th edition (Boston, MA: Cengage Learning, 2014).

REFERENCES

Emelander, Stanley. 2014. "Project Management Challenges in Government." *The Public Manager* 43, no. 3: 32–34.

Feeney, Mary, and Leslie Sult. 2011. "Project Management in Practice: Implementing a Process to Ensure Accountability and Success." *Journal of Library Administration* 51, nos. 7/8: 744–763.

Horwath, Jenn Anne. 2012. "How Do We Manage? Project Management in Libraries: An Investigation." *Partnership: The Canadian Journal of Library and Information Practice and Research* 7, no. 1: 1–34. https://journal.lib.uoguelph.ca/index.php/perj/article/view/1802/2492#.V0hsPeRpn2s.

Johnson, Brett, Jim Liu, and Michael Flagiello. 2016. "Are Project Management Credentials Worth It for CPAs?" *CPA Journal* 86, no. 5: 11.

Revels, Ira. 2010. "Managing Digital Projects: 'Accidental' Project Managers Can Benefit from Following These Useful Tips." *American Libraries* 41, no. 4: 48–50.

Sanders, Ron. 2014. "The Difference Between Success and Failure Is Effective Project Management." *The Public Manager* 43, no. 3: 4.

Stewart-Mailhiot, Amy. 2015. "Project Management: Moving Beyond MacGyver." *Reference & User Quarterly* 55, no. 1: 18–20.

Winston, Mark D., and Tara Hoffman. 2005. "Project Management in Libraries." *Journal of Library Administration* 42, no. 1: 51–61.

Chapter 12

ADVOCACY, LOBBYING, MARKETING, AND PUBLIC RELATIONS

Libraries transform is meant to give voice to the library profession, providing one clear, engaging message that showcases the transformative nature of libraries, elevating the critical role that libraries of all kinds play in the digital age.

Nancy Dowd and Hallie Rich, 2016

In the aftermath of these early successes, leaders of the Washington Library Media Association (WLMA) quickly realized the need to expand beyond their grassroots advocacy and secure professional support by retaining a paid lobbyist.

Mark Ray, 2014

As the director of marketing at the Edmonton Public Library (EPL), I have the good fortune to work for an organization that fully embraces the value of marketing and the critical role it can play in helping ensure the success of almost any program, service, or initiative the library undertakes

Tina Thomas, 2016

Community relations. A subset of public relations, true community relations activities aim to be mutually beneficial.

Chelsea Dodd Coleman and Emily Grace Le May, 2016

Communicate, communicate, communicate. To communicate (effectively) is—or should be—one of the core traits of all managerial leaders. There are many reasons communication is so essential to personal and organizational success. We covered some of those reasons in chapter 3, and in this chapter we explore four different but interrelated concepts that are very dependent upon communication skills: advocacy, lobbying, marketing, and public relations. We also look at the role of social media in these activities.

There are some widely held misconceptions about the topics covered in this chapter. One is that marketing is inappropriate for organizations such as libraries; this was actually a strong belief of the field some years ago. Today that notion has generally disappeared and been replaced by the recognition that not only is marketing appropriate, it is essential. Tina Thomas's quotation above illustrates how the views have changed. Many large libraries of all types have at least a partial FTE devoted to marketing activities.

Another rather common misconception is advocacy is merely a grassroots activity. That may be the case for some organizations, but certainly not for libraries. Certainly, grassroots efforts are part of the library advocacy process, but only a small part. The American Library Association's (ALA's) "Libraries Transform" initiative reflects the organizational side of advocacy. Combining grassroots and organizational efforts advocacy can prove to be every effective.

Yet another common misconception is that nonprofit and public organizations may not lobby. In many circumstances it is not so. There are limitations on when and how they may engage in the activity and those limits must be observed. However, there can be ways to legally lobby regarding possible legislation or policies, if you know what they are and make use of them.

Public relations (PR) work has a negative connotation for some people who view it as a method of misdirecting public opinion. Some also think PR is simply self-serving and provides less-than-accurate information about the organization. That may be the case occasionally, but not very often. People tend to remember the exceptions rather than the usual. The concept of PR is important in the sense that it is the method for letting the world know what your organization is doing. As the Colemen Le May quotation notes above, one element of PR, community relations, is essential for libraries to use to create and maintain positive relationships.

All the concepts we cover in this chapter are independent while also being tightly intertwined. All organizations engage in these activities from time to time and certainly all of them are important for librarians to understand and employ effectively, if their libraries are to be successful. The concepts can inform, generate support, assist in showing values for monies spent, and help keep the library's existence in the minds of the service community. These concepts also rest on some basic principles and methods which require a clear articulation of organizational purpose, important issues affecting the community, solutions for challenging concerns, and how and who can address the concerns. Essentially, the concepts we cover are all concerned about improving and maintaining an organization's well-being in some manner.

CONCEPT DEFINITIONS

Advocacy: the action of advocating, pleading for, or supporting a cause, person, or purpose. (p. 32)

Lobbying: To conduct activities with the objective of influencing public officials and members of a legislative body with regard to legislation and other policy decisions. (p. 1326)

Marketing: An aggregate of functions involved in transferring title and in moving goods or services from a producer to a customer. (p. 1383)

Public Relations: The promotion of rapport and goodwill between a person, firm, or institution and other persons, special publics, or the community at large through the distribution of interpretative material. (p. 1836)

Source: *Webster's Third New International Dictionary of the English Language: Unabridged* (Springfield, MA: Merriam-Webster, 1966).

ADVOCACY

Library advocacy is relatively new (it's less than 50 years old in terms of commonplace usage). Since the 1990s, more and more library literature has included articles focusing on this or that advocacy effort. There is no doubt that such efforts have had some impact on the public's perception of libraries, almost always to the positive side of the image. If nothing more, the efforts have stopped some of the drive to marginalize and/or reduce the value of libraries and their role in society.

Libraries, at least in the United States, have a very important component of successful advocacy in their favor—trust. As we discussed in chapter 1, libraries, especially public libraries, have a high trust rating among the general public. An advocate's effectiveness is very dependent upon how trustworthy the person and the organization are in the minds of the listeners. Thus, the field has a strong "leg up" when it comes to being successful in the effort to create a positive message that's accepted by the community.

Library advocacy calls for commitment from the top down. Senior managers' support is critical if there is to be much hope of a successful outcome. It is equally important that the library's board (advisory or governing) becomes involved in the advocacy effort.

One of the strong messages that libraries can repeat again and again is that they are positive change agents. The ALA's current advocacy effort uses the phrase that libraries are "transformative" in character.

Just What Is Advocacy?

The dictionary definition only hints at how complex advocacy is and how it functions when properly implemented. Advocacy, in the sense of library endeavors, consists of taking on important social issues as well library-related issues. Libraries can be and are a type of change agent. Social change and being a change agent lies at the center of the majority of advocacy efforts. There certainly are times, especially for libraries, when advocacy is about maintaining the status quo and avoiding reductions in support. In such cases, advocacy is usually tightly linked to lobbying efforts (see the following section, "Planning for Advocacy"). There are also times when advocacy activities are part of informing the community about the value of libraries.

Being a change agent often entails addressing someone or another organization that is well established with a vested interest in the area that the advocate hopes to change. Rather often there is a reluctance to change. In cases such as this, public media is likely to view the differing opinions as "news" worth reporting. Advocates become a feature in the public's eye, which, in turn, makes it essential to have a solid campaign plan for the effort. It also means those engaging in the activity must have strong communication skills, including a degree of comfort with public speaking, and a media plan in place as a component of your advocacy plan.

Planning for Advocacy

Like all managerial activities, advocacy does not just occur. Advocacy requires commitment, thought, and careful planning to be effective. Organizational commitment to advocacy efforts is important, however, senior management commitment to the process is essential for libraries. Having board (advisory or governing) support and involvement is equally important. Board members are often very influential in the library's service community and thus play a major role in the success of the advocacy efforts.

Planning the campaign is clearly a key to achieving a successful outcome. The good news is, when it comes to planning, there are a variety of advocacy resources (templates) available on the Internet. One such resource, which is free to nonprofits, is ALA's *The Advocacy Action Plan Workbook* (http://www.ala.org/advocacy /sites/ala.org.advocacy/files/content/advleg/advocacyinstitute/Advocacy%20 Action%20Plan%20-%20revised%2001-09.pdf). An Internet search will turn up many other possibilities that are free. We recommend the ALA publication as your starting point, but also suggest some other sites that can help flesh out the 23-page workbook.

The obvious starting point is to define the purpose or goals for the venture. One good method that you may recall from workshops or courses that dealt with setting missions and goals is the acronym SMART. A SMART goal is:

- *S*pecific
- *M*easurable
- *A*chievable
- *R*elevant
- *T*imed

Many planning specialists suggest that the achievable goal should create something of a stretch for the organization. Having a goal that is too easy to accomplish fails to push the organization and its people enough to generate real benefits. Part of the goal-setting process is defining the issue, cause, problem, or purpose for engaging in advocacy as well as how to resolve the situation. Having a suggested resolution is important because people rarely respond well when a problem is raised without also suggesting a possible solution. Another aspect of the resolution is identifying who or what will benefit from a successful change.

Underlying setting the goal(s) is defining the "target audience" of the exercise: who controls the current situation, who has the authority to make changes, who has influence over the matter, and so on. Another step is identifying any potential partners. If partners exist, should they be included up front in the goal-setting process or after you have developed your approach? When identifying partners, be sure to consider how the partner would enhance your efforts. What constituencies would they most easily reach and influence? One concern with partners is deciding how to resolve differences in views about the matter in question. It is unlikely that any partner will agree 100 percent with your thoughts about the issue and what the appropriate change(s) should be.

All successful advocacy outcomes are the result of creating a well-crafted message. Such messages clearly articulate why the matter is important, good, and/or worthwhile. Effective messages contain evidence (*limited but present*). Naturally, you need to identify the benefits from doing what is proposed (that includes why it is good business and/or politics). Essentially, the message is your "story." There are some major challenges to creating a powerful effective message, such as keeping it short, interesting, easily understood, and appropriate for the audience. This all comes back to the fundamentals of effective communication we discussed in chapter 3.

An aspect of developing your message is how to best deliver it. You have three broad channels—print media, social media, and presentations. Identifying your target audience is as important as the complexity of the message. Social media can be a challenge for complex issues, given the length limitations of many platforms in widespread use. Another factor is, regardless of the communication channel, you must send out an identical message regardless of how long or short it must be. Print media also can be a challenge. When you have an article you prepared accepted for publication there is little chance the meaning of your effort will be "lost in translation." However, when you send out printed material to the media in hopes of gaining a wide audience, you have no, or at best modest, control over what the final message will look like.

Interviews with reporters and public presentation share one trait—questions will be asked. Some time and effort should go into thinking about questions that may arise and to plan several possible answers. The "gotcha" question can be embarrassing at best and, at times, can sink the best-laid plans. You may not identify all possible questions, but the more you plan the lower the chances of being taken off-guard. With reporter interviews the outcome can range from feeling great about a job well done to indignation and assertions that you "NEVER said that." While you cannot control the final version, there is no harm in asking if you can review the piece prior to publication. The reporter may say yes to a review but no to making changes. Nevertheless, just asking may keep your primary message intact.

A topic that is implied in advocacy, but not widely addressed, is the notion of opposition. If there is a need to advocate there must be, at a minimum, limited support for the matter. In most advocacy situations you have three possible target audiences—supporters, those that neither support nor oppose the issue, and those who oppose it. It takes time and effort to craft a message that can effectively address all three types of people. In terms of supporters, almost any message will maintain their enthusiasm. One way to think about the matter is as a continuum.

One end is absolute support, in the middle range the unaware and the indifferent, and at the opposite end total opposition no matter what. The questions become: How well do you understand those demographics? What is the size of the various groups, particularly the latter? Knowing the answers to such questions is essential to the process of determining the target audience.

Once the planning is out of the way, the real work begins—implementing the plan. A vital part of the implementation process is to assure the work is coordinated. Having partners in the advocacy effort makes this activity even more central to achieving success. It also means the work is more complex. With partners, it is probably a good idea to have a coordinating committee composed of people from all the allied groups.

Will all the above efforts guarantee success? Naturally, the answer is no. What the above will do is heighten the chances of success.

CHECK THESE OUT

An excellent article about ALA's "Libraries Transform" advocacy effort is Nancy Dowd and Hallie Rich's 2016 "Libraries Transform: Why ALA's New Public Awareness Campaign Is Essential for Your Library" (*American Libraries* 47, nos. 3/4: 28–30).

Jenna Nemec-Loise's 2016 "Top Ten Advocacy Myths—Busted!" (*Children and Libraries* 14, no. 1: 34–35) covers the common reasons libraries tend not to engage in advocacy.

LOBBYING

There is a common misconception that it is illegal for nonprofit and public organizations to lobby. The fact of the matter is there are some lobbying activities that are legal. Yes, there are limits to what kind of and how much lobbying is allowable, but you may be able to do so. From the library perspective you don't need to look further than ALA's Washington, D.C., office to understand libraries can influence government actions to some degree. One major reason for the office is to monitor and "inform" legislation and government policies. Another example of library lobbying appears in one of the quotations at the beginning of this chapter, from Mark Ray, where the library association in the state of Washington hired a lobbyist.

What Is Legal Lobbying for Libraries?

Most libraries, either as a standalone organization or part of a larger group, have IRS 501(c)(3) status. That status allows them to accept gifts and offer some level of tax benefit to the donor. There are rules regarding what type and level of lobbying activity organizations in this tax status may undertake. There are a variety of IRS regulations, and even a law from the 1930s, that limit nonprofit lobbying. The clearest limitation is there can be no partisan lobbying of a candidate during an election campaign. Even that limit has some degree of latitude—it is legal to "inform the public about issues" (shades of "dark money") and to encourage people to vote.

It is the IRS regulations that create the challenges for nonprofit lobbying efforts. In 1976, the Lobbying Law was enacted that helped the IRS address the "substantiality" limit in the 1934 law. There is a good deal of "maybe yes, maybe no" in the IRS documentation. For example, the page related to defining lobbying reads:

> In general, no organization may qualify for section 501(c)(3) status if a substantial part of its activities is attempting to influence legislation (commonly known as *lobbying*). A 501(c)(3) organization may engage in some lobbying, but too much lobbying activity risks loss of tax-exempt status. . . . An organization will be regarded as attempting to influence legislation if it contacts, or urges the public to contact, members or employees of a legislative body for the purpose of proposing, supporting, or opposing legislation, or if the organization advocates the adoption or rejection of legislation. . . . Organizations may, however, involve themselves in issues of public policy without the activity being considered as lobbying. For example, organizations may conduct educational meetings, prepare and distribute educational materials, or otherwise consider public policy issues in an educational manner without jeopardizing their tax-exempt status. (IRS, 2016)

When it comes to political campaigns, there is similar maybe yes, maybe no language:

> Under the Internal Revenue Code, all section 501(c)(3) organizations are absolutely prohibited from directly or indirectly participating in, or intervening in, any political campaign on behalf of (or in opposition to) any candidate for elective public office. . . . Certain activities or expenditures may not be prohibited depending on the facts and circumstances. For example, certain voter education activities (including presenting public forums and publishing voter education guides) conducted in a nonpartisan manner do not constitute prohibited political campaign activity. In addition, other activities intended to encourage people to participate in the electoral process, such as voter registration and get-out-the-vote drives, would not be prohibited political campaign activity if conducted in a non-partisan manner. . . . on the other hand, voter education or registration activities with evidence of bias that (a) would favor one candidate over another; (b) oppose a candidate in some manner; or (c) have the effect of favoring a candidate or group of candidates, will constitute prohibited participation or intervention. (IRS, 2016)

Many small- and medium-sized nonprofits that cannot really afford to pay for legal advice to sort out the yes from the no simply assume the answer is no and do not engage in lobbying. The above samples are just the tip of the iceberg; the pages cited have links to more detailed information.

What many organizations do to avoid having to decipher the legal jargon is to call their activity "liaising" or establishing legislative relations. Professional lobbyists and liaison specialists have honed the art of distinguishing between communicating to inform and communicating to influence. Engaging in the latter with government officials can violate IRS rules.

Much of your work in planning advocacy activities assists in liaison and lobbying efforts. Your message and target audience are easily identified in the latter case. The major concern is identifying the decision makers and those who are the most influ-ential. A very key concern for liaisons is creating, increasing, and maintaining the types of "connections" we covered in chapter 3.

ADVISORY BOARD EXPERIENCE

Alire maintains that once a library has an effective advocacy plan in place and operat-ing, it is time to engage frontline librarians and other library staff in *frontline* advocacy efforts. There is a role that library employees can play, at their own comfort level, in library advocacy. See ALA's Frontline Advocacy Toolkit (http://www.ala.org/advocacy/advleg /advocacyuniversity/frontline_advocacy).

MARKETING

The dictionary definition of marketing that we quoted earlier is very broad. The American Marketing Association defines the concept as "the activity, set of institu-tions, and processes for creating, communicating, delivering, and exchanging offer-ings that have value for customers, clients, partners, and society at large." (https:// www.ama.org/AboutAMA/Pages/Definition-of-Marketing.aspx). This is a tighter definition than the one provided by the dictionary, but it is still generic. Today almost all organizations, regardless of sector, engage in at least some marketing activities. For some years now, ALA has offered a generic library marketing ini-tiative (@ your library) that is billed as a public awareness campaign. The fact of the matter is, advocacy and marketing can be almost identical much of the time. Perhaps the real question is, does it really matter what you called the activity as long as it conveys a message about what libraries do and can offer?

ALA's efforts in this regard are a boon for medium- and small-sized librar-ies. Engaging in major marketing activities takes time, resources, and effort. Few libraries can afford to "officially" allocate even a partial FTE to such activities. One older survey of library marketing and public relations activities noted that almost 70 percent of the respondents who did engage in such efforts indicated that those endeavors were not part of their job description (Lindsay, 2004). Given the level of library support, especially in terms of staffing, it seems very unlikely Lindsay's data will have moved except to a higher level. Also, even though her data is related to the college library environment, we suspect a similar survey all of types of libraries today would at least match her percentages. What this means is you, as a manage-rial leader, are likely to have to engage in such efforts at least occasionally during your career.

A common method for broadly defining the components of marketing is the "4Ps"—product, price, place, and promotion. Those 4Ps are generic enough to apply to almost every organization and a sound starting point for thinking about and planning a marketing campaign. Libraries have for many years, when asked what their business is, responded with some variation of "the information busi-ness." The reality is, although information is a major component in what we do, we do have other products to offer (programming generally is less "information" focused). When we talk about libraries, comments typically focus on the free and equitable access. In both cases, those statements are not completely accurate. Yes, there is free access to a library's primary service population; however, there are costs associated with providing the access. Because libraries do cost, we must demonstrate value for monies spent just as do all organization regardless of sector. The digital world has made "place" less of an issue than in times past. However, place is still something of an issue for public libraries (think of programming activities and shut-in and handicapped individuals, for example). Clearly there is a need to promote libraries to let people know just how "transformative" libraries actually are.

Marketing professionals divide the marketing process into several steps; the number of steps taken varies from person to person. However, there is some agreement on six core steps. (You will note that there is a fair amount of crossover with the topics in this chapter.) Not surprisingly, identifying the products that you believe would benefit from a marketing effort is step one (*product definition*). Your range of options is large, ranging from the library as a whole to the library's sponsored book club. A 2016 example of a public library marketing a program appeared on page 8A in *The Arizona Republic*'s June 27, 2016, issue, where the Phoenix Public Library placed a quarter-page advertisement for its summer reading program. Newspaper ads are somewhat pricey, which suggests the library decided the cost would pay off.

Another step is to spend some time thinking about and identifying what distinguishes your product from other similar products. Before the Internet arrived on the scene, the library's main competitors were local retail stores offering print and other media items. Clearly, in today's world, there are serious competitors in many of the services that had been basic monopolies. Where do differences exist (*differential analysis*) in our activities from our competitors? The question becomes one of what makes our service of answering your question (differential analysis) better than Google or Bing or another such service? In answering such questions, you begin to address yet another step in the marketing process—identifying *a differential advantage*. These steps may take longer than you might expect; however, devoting some serious time and thought to the activities will, generally, pay off in better marketing outcomes. In the case of the Phoenix Public Library, who else is likely to offer a summer reading program for no direct user cost?

Once you have finished differentiating your products and advantages it is time to plan the *target populations* for the campaign(s). You probably already have some solid data about your service population—from environmental scanning (ES) activities and the like. For libraries, like most other organizations, the service population has a number of segments within the overall group (undergraduates, young adults, fourth graders, etc., etc.). Marketing specialists think in terms of "segments" that are homogenous or distinctive in terms of one or more characteristics and, thus, unlike the rest of the population.

Today's ILS can generate a host of demographic data about users. Environmental scanning has undoubtedly provided a wide range of demographic data you can draw upon to select a marketing target group. Obviously, what you pick is determined by what you wish to market. We think there may be a somewhat overlooked segmentation when it comes to marketing the library as an entity—heavy users, light users, and non-users. Such a grouping leads into another marketing step—*multiple marketing approaches*. Yes, you could create a broad-based marketing program. However, as we noted above, marketing endeavors do have significant costs in terms of money and effort. Thus, getting the most "bang for your buck" is a sound idea and where a targeted approach to each group or segment comes into play. Using our example of heavy, light, and non-users, a generic message is unlikely to have a major impact on any of the segments. (Marketing messages need to be even more concise than advocacy efforts.) Two of the segments already have an understanding of what the library offers, so a general message will likely generate a "ho-hum" reaction. A few non-users' awareness may increase, but a broad message will not change as many minds as would a message tailored toward non-users' lack of information about library programs and services.

Regardless of the approach, understanding what impact (*evaluation/feedback*) the campaign did or did not have is the final step in the process. Knowing what worked and what did not is essential to achieving better and better outcomes in the future.

CHECK THESE OUT

There are a number of books about library marketing; the following are some of the better titles:

Peggy Barber and Linda K. Wallace, *Building a Buzz: Libraries & Word-of-Mouth Marketing* (Chicago IL: American Library Association, 2010).

Susan Webreck Alman and Sara Gillespie Swanson, *Crash Course in Marketing for Libraries*, 2nd edition (Santa Barbara, CA: Libraries Unlimited, 2007).

Nancy Dowd, Mary Evangeliste, and Jonathan Silberman, *Bite-Sized Marketing: Realistic Solutions for the Overworked Librarian* (Chicago IL: American Library Association, 2010).

Ned Potter, *The Library Marketing Toolkit* (London: Facet Publishing, 2012).

Needless to say there are also dozens of articles on the subject as well. Two such articles are Erin Shea's 2015 piece "Taking Stock of Your Institution's Marketing Efforts" (*Reference & User Services Quarterly* 54, no. 3: 27–29) and Eva Nicole and Erin Shea's 2015 "Marketing to Faculty in an Academic Library" (*Reference & User Services Quarterly* 54, no. 4: 26–28).

Branding

We can't end a discussion of marketing without at least a paragraph about the concept of branding. Sara Gancho, Rachel Cooper, and Martyn Evans noted that "branding originated in order to differentiate products and services, and was initially related to the creation of strong and distinctive product images. . . . A brand is a living organism and invaluable as a source of promise for the consumer . . . (2016, 96). Lucille Maddalena stated, "Your nonprofit's brand is much more than its name, logo, or services it offers. It is what others think, share and feel about the organization: it is the impression people have of your work that influences their response to every message sent, action undertaken and project support by your organization" (2012, 2). Logos are a common component of organizational brand-ing, rather like the brands that cattle ranchers apply to their animals. The "@ your library" logo developed by ALA is a generic brand that any type of library may employ for its programs, services, or general purposes.

In many ways, the ALA logo reduces your work in terms of designing a brand. Your work really revolves about what aspects of the library operation you wish to brand. Certainly obvious choices are for activities that are unique to your ser-vice population and will resonate with your community. Branding those activities should have the first consideration. Protecting an organization's brand can be a challenge, especially when new competition emerges on the scene.

Brands should be distinctive, memorable, positive, and, with some luck, iconic. It is unlikely that "@ your library" will ever achieve the iconic status of the Coca-Cola bottle. However, it has some iconic potential in terms of you service population.

CHECK THIS OUT

A solid book on library branding is Suzanne Walters and Kent Jackson's *Breakthrough Branding: Positioning Your Library to Survive and Thrive* (Chicago, IL: Neal-Schuman, 2013).

Another ALA branding title is Elisabeth Doucett's *Creating Your Library Brand: Com-municating Your Relevance and Value to Your Patrons* (Chicago, IL: American Library Association, 2008).

PUBLIC RELATIONS

Our final concept for this chapter is public relations, or PR. Like advertising there is something of a cloud hanging over this process in the minds of some peo-ple. One reason people may have a negative reaction to public relations is because its purpose is often defined as "getting ink" (perhaps a better phrase today would be "getting digital notice"), with little regard for facts. Certainly the purpose of PR is to get the organization's story noticed; however, the activity does go beyond mere "puffery." PR professionals make the valid case that it is really about creating, maintaining, and enhancing relationships (think connections from chapter 3) with other organizations and people.

The overarching purpose of PR is to present the organization's perspective of its value, what it does, and promote its activities to others. Promotion of activities and events is what most people think of when thinking about PR. Another function is to announce changes and developments in the organization. A third element is to gain feedback on organizational issues. One often overlooked purpose is to handle crises or "bad press."

A primary tool of PR efforts is the press release. Some years ago Claudia O'Keefe wrote an article about preparing press releases to promote library programs (2005). Although O'Keefe's focus was promotion, her thoughts apply to almost any library PR endeavor. She identified several elements for gaining attention for library events through press releases, many of which will be very familiar to you by this point in the chapter:

- Identify the target audience.
- Select the best communication channel for the target group.
- Compose a concise message.
- Provide text and, when appropriate, visual material in the release.
- Assess the effectiveness of the effort.

O'Keefe also suggested the message should read very much like a newspaper reporter's story.

Another fact about public relations is it is closely linked to the library's community relations efforts. In a sense, every staff member who interacts with the public is a public relations representative of the library. The quality of customer service is the basis upon which the community assesses the library. The more positive those community relations are, the more effective a library's public relations will be. Thus, all staff members become a part of the library's PR efforts.

Quality customer service does not just happen. Providing the highest possible quality service takes managerial leadership and must be embedded in the organizational culture. The community may not think of the relationship in specific terms, but there are some basic factors in how a person sees the relationship. First and foremost, was the transaction outcome satisfactory? Second, was the outcome timely and accurate? Third, was the cost (time and effort) worthwhile? And fourth, was the experience pleasant? Without positive answers to all those questions the library is most unlikely to have good community relations.

CHECK THESE OUT

There are a number of books dealing with library public relations. Two such titles are Rashelle S. Karp's *Powerful Public Relations: A How-to Guide for Libraries* (Chicago, IL: American Library Association, 2002); and Lisa A. Wolfe's *Library Public Relations, Promotions, and Communications: A How-To-Do-It Manual* (New York: Neal-Schuman Publishers, 2005).

A title that explores all the aspects of customer service which underlies customer and public relations is G. Edward Evans, Margaret Zarnosky Saponaro, Holland Christie, and Carol Sinwell's *Library Programs and Services: The Fundamentals* (Santa Barbara, CA: Libraries Unlimited, 2015).

SOCIAL MEDIA

The use of social media in conjunction with the concepts we have covered in this chapter is a given today. As Scott W. H. Young and Doralyn Rossmann noted, "If there is a common thread through library social media research, . . . it ties together the broadcast-based promotion and marketing of library resources and services" (2015, 21). To be effective, library social media usage must operate on the basis of a strategic plan. Lynette Schimpf notes there are several reasons for a library to do this, beginning with the notion that a poorly executed social media effort is probably worse than not engaging in social media usage at all. As she stated, "Social media is easy to start but hard to maintain, and even harder to measure" (2014, 13). She mentions having a plan in place for handling social media helps with both the maintenance and measuring issues.

Having a social media plan or strategy is essential for publicly funded libraries, especially public libraries. There are several reasons for this, but there are two major reasons. First, as we have noted rather frequently, there is a widespread distrust of government in general and its agencies today. There is even greater doubt about the ability of government agencies to make effective use of technology generally, much less social media. (There are a host of issues, mostly related to Web usage. (Social Security, IRS, and Affordable Care Act are just a few examples of websites that have received notoriety for their less-than-satisfying user experience.)

The second major reason is almost all libraries are part of a larger organization. The larger the organization is, the more likely it is that it will have policies and guidelines regarding what subgroups may or may not do in regard to social media. It is one of your responsibilities as a managerial leader to know what those are and generate a policy that reflects those higher level directives. One example of a city government policy is from Philadelphia (http://www.phila.gov/pdfs/Social%20 Media%20Policy.pdf), which spells out in some detail what will be acceptable and what will not and includes a broad range of limitations on employees' social media usage at work. It also addresses personal usage outside of the place of employment:

> City employees have no right to privacy with respect to their personal use of social media or personal social media accounts accessed by means of City information systems, or with respect to personal social media content so accessed. They should not expect or assume privacy or confidentiality with respect to any such personal social media use or social media content. (4)

The above concern about personal social media usage touches on another reason for developing a policy; that is, residents' underlying beliefs about public employees. For example, library users tend to think of anyone working in the library as a "librarian." A personal Facebook profile that indicates the person is a library employee can set the stage for some people thinking that the views expressed are a reflection of the library's views. The Philadelphia policy states:

> Postings and user profiles on personal social media accounts must not state or imply that the views, conclusions, statements or other social media content are an official policy, statement, position, or communication of the City of Philadelphia, or represent the views of the City or any City officer or employee, unless the head of the user's agency, the CIO or designee, and the Mayor's Director of Communications and Strategic Partnerships or designee have granted express permission for that user to do so. (4)

Policy Issues

What are the major topics that you should consider in relation to any overarching policy? We will touch on several of the most important concerns—each library is likely to have some local issues to think about, especially in the absence of higher level policy. The basic and obvious question to address is, why do we want to use social media? Is it for advocacy, marketing community relations, or all of them? What is the goal or objective of this effort that will inevitably require staff time that is already likely stretched? Being active in social media just because everyone else is active in social media is a weak reason and you certainly will have difficulty when it comes to assessing value for time spent. Having one or two measureable goals is important—increased attendance at story hour programs, increased number of individuals offering to volunteer, and increased computer class size are some examples of goals that you could measure.

The question of who will handle it and what content to include are questions that are very important to think through and spell out in the policy. There should be a designated leader or monitor for the effort. Without such a person the social media postings will likely be sporadic, dated, confusing, and so on, and will do little to enhance the library's image. It is equally necessary to identify who is responsible for the content. Just thinking about these issues may suggest little or no social media activities are possible in the existing work environment. Another concern is how much monitoring will senior managers do and how often?

What are the appropriate platforms for reaching your target population(s)? How will you monitor the changing landscape of social media in your service population? Will the usage reduce some of your analog-based efforts, thus off-setting some concerns about time constraints? (In 2015 Ben Bizzle and Maria Flora wrote an interesting article about the need for and effectiveness of "traditional" methods in a "social media age" for marketing and community relations. Those methods do still work.)

We end this chapter with a quotation from Laura Solomon, in which she comments on the rather frequent false starts libraries have made in the use of social media. "Nearly all of these failures can be attributed to a lack of planning, as well as a lack of understanding about what effective social media work entails" (2013, 13). We heartily recommend her book, *The Librarian's Nitty-Gritty Guide to Social Media.*

REFERENCES

The Arizona Republic. Phoenix Public Library Advertisement. June 27, 2016, 8A.

Bizzle, Ben, and Maria Flora. 2015. "Marketing in the Real World: Using Traditional Methods in a Social Media Age." *American Libraries* 46, no. 5: 46–49.

Coleman, Chelsea Dodd, and Emily Grace Le May. 2016. "The Imitation Game: Applying For-Profit Strategies in the Nonprofit World." *Public Libraries* 55, no. 3: 34–37.

Dowd, Nancy, and Hallie Rich. 2016. "Libraries Transform: Why ALA's New Public Awareness Campaign Is Essential to Your Library." *American Libraries* 47, nos. 3/4: 28–30.

Gancho, Sara, Rachel F. D. Cooper, and Martyn Evans. 2016. "The Value and Importance of Design When Branding for Social Media: Models for a Framework Analysis." *Journal of Design, Business & Society* 2, no. 1: 95–114.

IRS. 2016. "The Restriction of Political Campaign Intervention by Section 501(c)(3) Tax-Exempt Organizations." Updated September 13, 2016. https://www.irs.gov /charities-non-profits/charitable-organizations/the-restriction-of-political-campaign -intervention-by-section-501-c-3-tax-exempt-organizations.

IRS. 2017. "Lobbying." Updated February 24. https://www.irs.gov/charities-non-profits /lobbying.

Lindsay, Anita Rothwell. 2004. *Marketing and Public Relations Practices in College Libraries.* Chicago, IL: College Library Information Packet Committee, Association of College and Research Libraries.

Maddalena, Lucille. 2012. *Branding for the Nonprofit Organization.* Philanthropic Giving Resources. http://www.pgresources.com/articles/branding-for-the-nonpofit -organization/.

O'Keefe, Claudia. 2005. "Publicity 101: How to Promote Your Library's Next Event." *American Libraries* 36, no. 6: 52–55.

Ray, Mark. 2014. "In Lobbying, Good Professional Has Amateur Help." *Teacher Librarian* 42, no. 2: 58–59.

Schimpf, Lynette. 2014. "Creating a Social Media Strategy at Your Library." *Florida Libraries* 57, no. 1: 13–16.

Solomon, Laura. 2013. *The Librarian's Nitty-Gritty Guide to Social Media.* Chicago, IL: American Library Association.

Thomas, Tina, Eva Nicole, and Erin Shea. 2016. "We Share Great Stuff Marketing Content at the Edmonton Public Library." *Reference & User Services* 55, no. 3: 210–214.

Young, Scott W. H., and Doralyn Rossmann. 2015. "Building Library Community Through Social Media." *Information Technologies and Libraries* 34, no. 1: 20–37.

Chapter 13

POLITICAL SKILLS

Politics is the process of getting along with the querulous, the garrulous and the congenitally unlovable.

> Marilyn Moats Kennedy, 1985

As the literature indicated perceived organizational politics is an important phenomenon to understand within an organization.

> Sadia Ishaq and Shazia Khalid, 2014

With the presidential election year upon us, and a spirited one at that, political talk in the office probably is inevitable. But you might want to tread lightly if you plan to engage in such banter.

> Mark Belko, 2016

"Politics" is a word that, for many individuals, brings to mind some rather negative thoughts. Descriptions of politicians include a wide range of negative words, such as "untrustworthy," "self-interested," and "duplicitous." There are times when such words—and their resulting images—are appropriate and accurate; however, not all politics and politicians are lacking in merit, nor are all of them only out for themselves. Politics are also the "art of the possible" (as the old saying goes), and these possibilities can be very positive.

As a managerial leader you must become a positive politician, if you are to be effective long term. (We expand on the notion of being a positive politician later in this chapter.) Being in the public or nonprofit sector requires an understanding of partisan politics that operate in your environment. There is also organizational politics to master, both internal—within the library itself—and external. External organizations can include those under the umbrella of a larger entity in charge of the library's funding, such as a city or county or an academic institution, or even organizations that may not have a direct impact on the library's budget, but have political power of their own and which you may find yourself partnering with, such as local schools, museums or other cultural institutions, or business groups. Finally, there are the personal political skills you must hone and employ appropriately in order to be an effective manager and grow professionally.

You may question the need for a chapter on managerial politics. There are, in fact, many instances in which "politics" becomes part of the managerial leader's activities. We have mentioned some of those in passing in various chapters. One of those instances was featured in chapter 9, on funding and the politics involved in the budgetary process. Politics also commonly arises in terms of authority and power. A related example that often involves more than the two previous issues is the politics of governing and advisory boards. We also noted that when it comes to accountability and responsibility, there often is a political aspect to where that assignment resides. For a public sector library, there is always the issue of partisan politics, which can also affect those in the nonprofit sector. A related concern is what type of political activity libraries may legally undertake. Certainly there is a strong component of politics when it comes to advocacy and lobbying efforts; politics can even come up in marketing efforts. Another time it arises, and is a major part of this chapter, is within the organization (office politics).

Your personal political skills will help or hinder you in the other types of politics when you are in the public or nonprofit sector. There is good news in terms of the necessary skills: if you are an effective managerial leader, you already possess the skills. All you need to do is learn how to employ them in a political manner.

The managerial and political processes are very similar. Why is that the case? First and foremost, both are processes that require thoughtful interaction with other people. Second, both processes rest upon how clear the vision or desired outcome is for the "constituents." And, third, success only comes as a result of others acting positively in terms of achieving the outcome. Also, to be effective in either arena, you *must* be trustworthy, straightforward, persuasive, able to build strong relationships, and perceptive—*and* adjust your behavior to the current circumstances. Add all of these to the necessity for excellent communication skills. Another common ability, in terms of positive political behavior, is being able to place the organizational "good" above personal interests.

CHECK THIS OUT

A sound scholarly book on organizational politics is *Politics in Organizations: Theory and Research Considerations*, edited by Gerald R. Ferris and Darren C. Treadway (New York: Routledge, 2012).

PERSONAL POLITICAL SKILLS

If there is so much commonality between managerial and personal politics, where do the differences lie? The differences reside in when, how, and how much you employ one or more of the characteristics we cover in the following paragraphs.

One of the most important commonalities between the two is a constant that has an impact on most situations—being trustworthy.

Trust, as we have noted several times, is a fragile thing, easily broken and very difficult to rebuild. How you build or rebuild trust rests on a foundation of the traits covered below. It is a complex process that takes time to successfully complete, and is, in fact, never truly done. Without establishing trust with your stakeholders, colleagues, staff, and the general public, you will find it almost impossible to be either a positive politician or an effective managerial leader. And we think that it goes without saying that trust should be an important component of your personal life as well.

Being authentic is one factor in building trust. There has been a lot of talk about authenticity in the current political climate, but being authentic is more than just saying what you want without regard for how it makes you look or how it affects others. Authenticity means being true to yourself and being relatable in an honest way. It is easy to see that this factor in authenticity—relatability—can be manipulated by politicians who are adept at creating a persona that fits their self-interests for a specific use. However, changing how you present yourself as the audience changes may work for a while, but in the long run people will see the variations and begin to wonder just who you really are and which message is the true belief or position. Partisan politicians have a great deal of difficulty in this area; in the workplace a lack of authenticity is an invitation to serious problems with staff.

Related to authenticity is the need to be consistent. At some point in our lives, probably all of us have had to regularly interact with someone who was inconsistent. In the workplace, be it a staff member or manager, inconsistency is highly disruptive on unit performance. Lack of consistency seems to be the stock in trade for many partisan politicians. While being so does not always have negative consequences for such individuals, it does impact how others see them and decreases their trust level. On the other hand, it is the most unusual person who is consistent 100 percent of the time. It is appropriate to adjust your behavior, attitude, expectations, and the like as circumstances change.

We have two points with the above seemingly disparate comments: first, a goal for managerial leaders is to be consistent in similar circumstances. How you responded to situation A yesterday ought to be how you respond to situation A today and tomorrow. And, yes there are likely to be some variations between those times. Thus our second point: think about your "normal" response to various common situations and consider how consistent you are in reacting to them. The more consistent you are the greater the chances of being viewed as trustworthy both in the workplace and the political arena.

"Oh what a tangled web we weave when first we practice to deceive!" (Sir Walter Scott, *Marmion*, 1808). That line is so very true in the workplace, especially for managerial leaders who are trying to build or maintain staff trust. Deception can certainly be a part of a strategy but is rarely appropriate when interacting with the staff. Being straightforward is the best way to be a trusted colleague, leader, and politician. More often than not weaving a tangled web will trip you up in time and whatever trust you have generated will be shattered.

Building positive relationships is a part of being an effective managerial leader; however, it is also a key to being an effective positive political person. All of the above personal traits are part of creating and maintaining good relations. We explored some of the major components of building relationships in chapter 3. In this chapter we emphasize the importance of building such relationships up, down, and sideways; especially when it comes to political effectiveness.

The more perceptive you are, the more effective you will be in almost all activities. Your managerial leadership perceptivity is crucial to your long-term success. That skill allows you to adjust your thoughts, reactions, and behavior quickly and appropriately both in the workplace and in the political realm. Your understanding of your EQ (Emotional Quotient; see chapter 16 for a discussion of the concept) is an important factor in assessing your, and others, state of mind and coming up with an appropriate behavior or reaction. Having and employing this skill is not inconsistent with the previous paragraphs. The key word is "appropriate;" this implies, if not directly states, that the behavior is proper for the parties concerned.

The power of persuasion, when it is used for positive outcomes, is always a useful skill to have and employ, regardless of the situation. The modifying clause in the preceding sentence is important. Think back to our discussion of bad leadership in chapter 2 to understand the powerful significance of persuasion. We also covered the ways in which you can improve your persuasive powers in chapter 3.

Perhaps the most critical component in how others see you, in terms of trustworthiness, is how they perceive what motivates your behavior. If, in the eyes of the beholders, behavior is viewed as being self-motivated rather than motivated by a desire to improve the well-being of the organization, they will be highly skeptical of your trustworthiness. Certainly there are occasions when organizational and self-interest are almost, if not completely, one and the same. On such rare occasions, it is wise to explain why there is no conflict and how the organization benefits.

CHECK THESE OUT

A short, but interesting, article on being a librarian politician is Jennifer A. Bartlett's "Developing a Strategic Mindset: Librarians as Politicians" (*Library Leadership and Management* 29, no. 2 [2015]:1–4).

A great book on the topic is Melissa K. Aho and Erika Bennett's *The Machiavellian Librarian: Winning Allies, Combatting Budget Cuts, and Influencing Stakeholders* (Oxford: Chandos Publishing, 2013). In 29 chapters these authors address all the topics we briefly cover in this chapter, as well as many other aspects of library politics and politicians.

Andrew J. DuBrin's *Political Behaviors in Organizations* (Thousand Oaks, CA: Sage Publications, 2009) is a good title for learning about how to become a good politician in almost any organization.

ORGANIZATIONAL POLITICS

Our opening quotation from Marilyn Moats Kennedy regarding office politics may be a little over the top; however, there are more than a few grains of truth in what she said. Mauricio Goldstein and Philip Read made a similar point:

> In any organizational environment, people play games. This is true of even the most enlightened companies. It is in our nature as human beings to play games when we are in groups, when stress and anxiety exist, when "prizes" (promotions, the boss's favor, funding for a project, winning a contract, and so on) are to be won and lost. (2009, 1)

The bottom line is this: organizational politics *will* occur. Your challenge, as a managerial leader, is to manage it, be somewhat involved in it, and, most importantly, understand it.

A starting point for understanding office politics is to realize that such activities are imbedded in the organizational culture (OC). (We discussed OC in some detail in chapter 7.) OC, in five words or less, is "how we do things here." In the case of organizational politics, what happens at the senior management level plays a significant role in how much game playing occurs throughout the organization. What games exist, or do not exist, at the senior level will filter down to all the staff. Thus, the fewer games you play the fewer your staff are likely to play.

Recognizing that the level of office politics and games is influenced by senior management's behavior is only a starting point for understanding those activities. There are other organizational factors that contribute to such behaviors that go beyond an individual's personality traits. In our view, it is the stress level within the organization that is the overarching factor. This, in turn, translates into different games played by staff who are fearful for their jobs: "It wasn't me!" "Nobody told me!" and backstabbing are just a few examples.

One source of organizational-wide stress is the presence of significant competition from other organizations. Failing to meet outside competition has negative impacts within the organization—fewer resources, sometimes loss of staff, and, in worst cases, closure. Today, unlike the not too distant past, libraries have serious competition when it comes to being the "go-to" information source. For-profit search engines are the first resource a person usually turns to today when seeking information.

Libraries are trying to remain a relevant information source in various ways. One example of such efforts appeared in an issue of *Public Libraries*. Brian R. Smith reported that an ILS vendor had partnered with another technology firm to develop a means of "pushing" library metadata into online search results from popular search engines (2016). He noted that "patrons already use Google and other search engines to look for information, so allowing library materials to show up in their search results is powerful not just for patrons but for libraries themselves" (39). Organizational competition, in itself, is unlikely to affect the level of stress that would then lead to more office politics. It is when that competition impacts organizational resource availability that politics tend to escalate.

In chapter 1 we discussed how public and nonprofit sector organizations lack clarity when it comes to identifying what constitutes success—they have no bottom line like profit or loss as success indicators. Lacking clarity in terms of organizational purpose frequently translates into fuzzy definitions of staff performance. When a definition of successful performance is not crystal clear, with its attendant implications for salaries and promotions, you can expect more staff game-playing.

When organizational resources are tight, you can expect budgetary politics to increase and become a factor in any effort to gain additional resources—staff, space, raises, equipment, and the like. The tighter the resource situation becomes the more politicking you can expect, and the more criticism you will receive for any expenditures. Staff will be quick to judge purchases not viewed as absolutely necessary, and will wonder why funds were used for one thing rather than another. You will need to have a calm, factual reason for why funds were used and how you made your decision.

The level and character of organizational change that is taking place will affect the amount of game-playing, especially at both the managerial and individual staff member level. When there are several changes occurring, you can expect an uptick in office politics. Think about a situation where the library is installing a new ILS or moving into new space. Anticipating how the change will impact the way the organization functions will cause a tremendous amount of stress among staff. Perhaps the most stressful change that by itself will increase library politics most dramatically is planning a new facility or remodeling the old one.

Understanding how the above issues will be reflected in a staff member's behavior is a challenge. However, the more shared work time you have with your staff the more likely you can anticipate what may manifest itself in each employee. Your overall goal is to reduce or remove the games that are disruptive to operations and engage in only modest control of those that are not interfering, keeping in mind that some game playing will take place no matter how you respond. Any form of game-playing or office politics will reduce a staff member's concentration on their work activities. Not anticipating and responding effectively to these activities can reduce morale, increase resistance to change, impair learning of new skills, and lower constructive staff interaction. None of those outcomes are positive for organizational performance.

Are office politics primarily about competition? Certainly there are times when gaining a "prize" is clearly evident. However, when you think about those instances, they are really about self-interest. Securing the prized promotion does have an element of a competitive "win," but was that the true goal? In most cases, the promotion means more money, more authority and/or power, more status, more recognition of "my value" to the organization, and so on. All those factors are about self rather than winning a prize. Our point is, many of the games played are not about competing with someone or a group but are about protecting a person's self-image from real or imagined threats. Part of understanding office politics lies in knowing that it is about more than competition.

Writers on the topic often divide organizational politics into three broad types—interpersonal, managerial, and resource acquisition. Even a cursory review of the literature will generate a list of dozens of variations of workplace games that people play. We suspect you have experienced at least one of the following from a very short list of office politics:

- The "why me?" colleague (Noncompetitive game)
- The "not my fault!" colleague (Noncompetitive game)
- The gossiper (Noncompetitive game)
- The sandbagger (Competitive game)
- The unit bully (can be either)
- The credit seeker-taker (Competitive game)
- The loose cannon (can be either Competitive or Noncompetitive)
- The staff person who promises to do it but doesn't follow through (Competitive game)
- The passive resister (can be either)
- The unpredictable monkey (can be either)
- The deflector; i.e., "No one told me!" (Noncompetitive game)
- The master Machiavellian (Competitive game)

Thinking back on those experiences, how disruptive were they for other staff members? What, if any, effort was made to reduce such behavior(s)? If such efforts occurred, were they successful? You probably noticed that when an effort was made to reduce the behavior, there would be a reduction in the behavior for a short time, but then the prior behavior would eventually return. This is not only telling about the pervasive nature of office politics, it also says a lot about human nature itself.

Why Not Try to Control Office Politics?

There are several reasons managerial leaders do not try to control the political games their staff members play. One obvious reason is they fail to recognize the behavior. Why don't they recognize the signs? When an organization is full of such game playing, the behavior is just part of "the way we do things" and not worth considering. If a person does not play such games, she or he may not see others engaging in the activity. Yet another reason can be the managerial leader is so engaged in personal games that the person has little time or interest in controlling the activity in others.

As we noted earlier, office politics will occur regardless of efforts to control them; thus, some managers see little point in trying to control, much less reduce, such activities. Further, stopping one type of game may result in something worse developing. Certainly, how office politics affect staff morale is unpredictable, making it uncertain what may develop if controls are put in place. Chances are, in an environment of game playing, efforts to reduce the games may well cause a drop in morale. On the other hand, in environments where normally games don't occur, if there is a sudden growth in office politics, morale is likely to fall and controlling efforts will improve morale. Essentially, uncertainty about controlling effort outcomes keeps some managers from doing anything about office politics.

Reducing or Controlling Office Politics

By now you know it is next to impossible to have an organization that is free of office politics. Although that is true, managerial leaders do need to address the issue to some extent. Your first step is to identify those games that are and are not disruptive to organizational or unit performance. It is best to leave the nondisruptive behaviors alone while still keeping an eye on them. What may not be disruptive today may become so sometime down the road.

How long a disruptive game has been in play is another factor to consider. The sooner you see the problem and take steps to reduce it, the more likely you are to have success. Related to the timeframe is where the games are being played—just your unit, some other units, or the entire library. Clearly the more widespread they are is the less likely you are to control matters. This becomes a time when your political skills will need to come into play to gain the collaboration of other managerial leaders.

Intervening in political games, for controlling purposes, is a form of traditional managerial counseling responsibilities related to work performance. The best practices for handling such sessions remain the same regardless of the topic. There are 5Rs for counseling sessions: right time, right place, right purpose, right approach, and right technique. Timing is a key factor in the outcome of such sessions. A good guideline is to have the session as soon as possible after the occurrence of the behavior that is in question. The right place is almost always in private unless it involves most of the staff. In the case of game playing, the first session should be private, but with the suggestion that should there be a need for a second session, it will be conducted in public or least some others will be involved.

For sessions aimed at controlling or reducing game playing, you have two primary purposes—to learn and understand why the behavior is taking place and then find means to reduce those behaviors. The learning component is the key to a successful session. There are almost always two or more people involved in the game behavior, unlike many work performance concerns. Learning requires thoughtful listening. Effective listening requires an open mind, understanding your biases, and "hot-button" words and phrases (see chapter 3 for a discussion of these topics). Feedback, on your part, will help clarify what the other person means and make it evident that you are listening and trying to understand.

Political game playing is generally complex, as is its control, and thus a full understanding of the motivations, context, and so on, is critical to finding a method that will curtail the disruptive behaviors. A sound approach is to place your emphasis on why the behavior is disruptive to work activities, morale, and effectiveness. One goal of a session is to have a fruitful dialogue (rather than a monologue). Will this always result in success? Certainly not, but it does often work. What is certain is that failing to try to control disruptive political games will cause a drop in morale, productivity, and unit and organizational effectiveness.

CHECK THIS OUT

Mauricio Goldstein and Philip Read's *Games at Work: How to Recognize & Reduce Office Politics* (San Francisco, CA: Jossey-Bass, 2009) is a good resource to consult for ideas about handling office politics.

Good Organizational Politics

Many people would say a positive or good politician is an oxymoron. H. L. Mencken's view was "a good politician is quite as unthinkable as an honest burglar" (Mencken, n.d.). Admittedly, Mencken was referring to partisan politicians rather than ones in the workplace. However, the general reaction when hearing about office politics is that whatever follows will be negative in character. In reality, there are good organizational politics. In fact, without such politics many organizations would find it difficult to function even moderately effectively. In the case of public sector organizations, politics is a basic component of their operations, both partisan and organizationally.

One obvious time you need to employ your political skills is during the budget preparation periods. Failing to understand such politics, much less being a participant in the process, will have serious consequences for your unit. Needless to say, publicly funded library managers must also understand and master the local partisan political landscape.

Another area where positive political skills are useful is in creating and maintaining relationships—upward, downward, and sideways within the organization. You will recall that earlier in this chapter we made the points about the need to be, and be viewed, as trustworthy and about what motivates your actions—self-interest or organizational well-being. Your relationship skills are the foundation for managerial leadership outcomes and success.

One effective way to build positive relationships with senior managers is to under-promise and over-deliver. Don't make promises you know you may not be able to keep just to please senior managers. Over-delivery, in a positive work environment, is relatively easy to achieve. Bringing a project in ahead of the planned date or under budget are such deliveries. The size of the difference (a day or two ahead of time or just a few dollars under budget) is less important than the accomplishment. Identifying a solution to an organizational-wide issue, especially when it is a low impact issue for your unit, is a form of over-delivery.

Building strong relationships also assists in your building "social capital." Social capital arises from your being supportive of others (up, down, and sideways) whenever those individuals may need assistance. Developing cross-training efforts that allow for more flexibility between units is one example of joint supportive efforts. Such actions generally result in those individuals supporting you (a return on your investment of "capital") when you can use such help. Essentially this type of political activity leads to greater collaboration and coordination of organizational activities and enhances organizational well-being.

Partisan politicians rarely admit to making a mistake. Positive organizational politicians are quick to acknowledge and take responsibility for their and their unit's missteps. Doing so is part of the honest, straightforward characteristics of positive leadership. It also lets the organization move forward without time spent trying to fix blame and indirectly affecting its overall well-being.

Another component of being viewed as straightforward and honest is not being a "yes man" when that is just to please the boss. When there is a question or issue about what was proposed, raising that point, respectfully, is a mark of a positive organizational politician. Doing otherwise may hurt the organizational well-being.

Perhaps one of the signature traits of good organizational politicians is sharing credit with all those who deserve the credit—even the smallest contribution should be acknowledged. That sharing builds and enhances morale, it generates a greater sense of being an effective part of a group effort, as well as increasing the willingness to collaborate. Those in turn have positive impacts on organizational performance.

The above are a few of the outcomes of being a positive organizational politician.

CHECK THIS OUT

Gerald R. Ferris, Sherry L. Davidson, and Pamela L. Perrewé's *Political Skill at Work: Impact on Work Effectiveness* (Mountain View, CA: Davies-Black Publishing, 2005) is a good book that examines all of the above discussions in more detail.

PARTISAN POLITICS

Everyone knows that partisan politics impact any organization, regardless of sector, to a greater or lesser extent. However, for public sector organizations such politics are a daily fact of work life. Shifts in political winds are a constant concern for public sector agencies as they can affect missions, purposes, programs, and goals. There can even be threats to close down an agency by party politicians. From a library perspective, there are seldom closure concerns; rather, the threat is that of being "privatized" (see chapter 8 for a discussion of what that means). The bottom line for public organizations is, they are owned, funded, and directed by a party political process.

There is a concept of political neutrality that relates to public sector organizations. The term is probably employed more outside the United States; however, the notion of not being partisan in providing public sector services is a part of U.S. public sector agencies. The basic concept is party politicians formulate policy and public employees implement those polices regardless of personal views regarding the policies. Such neutrality is rather easy to state, but a challenge to implement and enforce. The following is a model of what public agency neutrality means for most people. It also highlights why such neutrality is a challenge for public employees.

- Party politicians generate policies based on constituents' desires and public employees implement those policies faithfully.
- Public employees are hired based on their skills rather than their political party affiliation.
- Public employees *will not* engage in partisan political activities in the workplace.
- Public employees *will not* make public statements—either positive or negative about political party governance—in character.
- Public employees *will* provide full, current, and accurate information to those who formulate public policies.
- Public employees should not be held accountable for public policy decisions, but for the implementation of such policies.
- Public employees who perform their duties responsibly should be free of political pressure in those performances.

The list is not that long, but is filled with a variety of challenges for public service employees as well as society. Some of the above are reasonably straightforward, for example, the need to provide proper information to policy makers. A few are rather complex, such as the last two in our list. One of the overall challenges is the fact that just because you become a public employee does not mean you forfeit your constitutional rights, such as freedom of speech and assembly. Few people truly believe a person can be totally devoid of biases, opinions, or beliefs that in turn are reflected in their behavior. Nevertheless, there is an expectation that public employees somehow manage to totally disassociate their beliefs and values while performing their daily duties.

A common place where this dichotomy comes up is when accountability becomes an issue. There is also the fact that no one believes it is necessary for public employees to have no political party affiliation. The question is how can such membership, even at the most subtle level, not play some role in a person's work performance, from time to time, when her or his party is in or out of control of the policy making? You can understand where challenges can and do arise. (As we will discuss in the next chapter, neutrality goes well beyond political concerns.)

Balancing rights and obligations in this area is difficult. For example, outside the workplace and off duty, is a public employee free to express personal views? Can you post your political views on social media, with your name and place of employment associated with the post? Probably not a very good idea. What if that post did not have information about place of employment in it? Generally, that probably would not be a violation of neutrality. However, that does not mean there might not be blowback, especially for a senior manager who may be rather well known in the community. This is a very gray area for both public employees and service community members.

Referenda can create some interesting and challenging situations for public service staff members. It is very likely there is an ordinance, regulation, law, or governing board policy that has wording along the following lines: public employees shall not actively engage in political activities during such hours as that person is being compensated for the performance of that person's public employee duties. What creates the personal challenges is that other political campaigns do not directly involve the library. With a library referendum, every library staff member must expect that a few people using the library will ask about the referendum and perhaps even ask a question such as "Should I vote for the library's request?" The best advice is to follow the advice often attributed to the old television series *Dragnet*: "Just the facts, ma'am." Stating what the referendum is for and other facts covered in the official statement or merely handing the person a copy of the statement is not political activity.

It is the other direct question about your views that can be difficult to handle, especially when the person asking it is someone with whom you have developed a good relationship. Some library users come in so frequently that they seem like old friends and engaging in political discourse may seem natural. Even so, it is important to separate your professional self from your more casual self—you never know what the other person's political leanings are and you may be inadvertently offensive.

When a library referendum is coming up, it is probably a sound idea to have an all-staff meeting, with the library's attorney and even a public relations expert if one is available, to cover how to handle situations such as the ones mentioned earlier. It is not unknown for opponents of any referendum of a public agency, not just a library's, to try to get agency staff to violate the "no political activity while on duty" rule in hopes of creating a scandal and perhaps defeating the measure.

Intra-Staff Partisan Politics

Another thorny issue is staff members interacting with one another during a political campaign. Mark Belko's comment, one of the quotations at the beginning of this chapter, is very sound advice. He reported on the results of a 2016 survey of employees regarding their feelings about partisan political discussion in the workplace. Fifty-six percent of the respondents thought such discussions could be offensive to other employees; the balance of respondents thought such interaction would "inform" their colleagues. There was a major gender difference; 66 percent of the women thought partisan political conversations could be offensive. We wonder what the results might have been if the study were undertaken in a year when the politics were less contentious.

Although you cannot forbid, nor enforce, such a restriction on political discussions among staff members, you may set some limits. For example, banning such conversations in areas open to the public and anywhere else in the library when non-staff individuals are present would be most reasonable. It would help ensure that you are trying to maintain political neutrally. Another reasonable limit would be that the staff confines such talks to break and meal times and in the staff lounge or other non-public areas of the library.

You might want to suggest some guidelines for staff members who do wish to engage colleagues in political discussions, especially when the campaign is highly contentious. You might start with a reminder that the library is expected to maintain political neutrality. If necessary, outline what that concept means as well as making it clear this in no way means a person cannot have a position on whatever the election may be about. Rather, such views cannot be expressed while on duty and interacting with the public. Your second focus should be on the need to maintain performance quality and service to users.

One obvious guideline for the workplace is to not have election material on a desktop. Having such material in view on a public service desk would clearly violate political neutrality. In the case of private office spaces, such material could be offensive to other staff members, which in turn can impact work performance. Also, a private office where the public may occasionally visit to discuss some matters cannot have campaign material in plain view and still claim the library is politically neutral. Another guideline is to communicate with staff that any discussion, political or otherwise, that becomes an argument, noisy, or contentious, is no different than any other type of work disruption and it would be treated as such with potential disciplinary action.

Other guidelines would be more difficult to implement, but still worth suggesting. Such ideas as keeping the discussions low-key, non-confrontational, and two-way (where no one person dominates the discussion) are suitable topics. Lectures and uninvited one-way "presentation of the facts" would be detrimental to staff morale and work performance. Such topics are also reasonable subjects to bring up.

Organizational politics are a fact of work life, whether they are positive or negative. Partisan politics tend to play a greater role on the operations of public and nonprofit sector organizations than they do in the for-profit sector. Thus, managerial leaders, especially in the public sector *must* study, understand, and become skillful in the political area. As you will read in chapter 15 about ethics, many of the issues covered in this chapter are broader than just politics.

REFERENCES

Belko, Mark. 2016. "How to Handle Political Discussion at Work." *Arizona Daily Sun*, May 8, C4.

Goldstein, Mauricio, and Philip Read. 2009. *Games at Work: How to Recognize & Reduce Office Politics*. San Francisco, CA: Jossey-Bass.

Ishaq, Sadia, and Shazia Khalid. 2014. "Job Satisfaction, Commitment and Perceived Organizational Politics in Employees of a Public Sector University." *Journal of Behavioral Sciences* 24, no. 2: 69–82.

Kennedy, Marilyn Moats. 1985. *Office Warfare: Strategies for Getting Ahead in the Aggressive 80s*. New York: Macmillan.

Mencken, H. L. n.d. "H.L. Mencken Quotes." In *BrainyQuote*. http://www.brainyquote.com/quotes/quotes/h/hlmencke157553.html.

Smith, Brian R. 2016. "New Product News." *Public Libraries* 55, no. 4: 38–39.

Chapter 14

LEGAL ASPECTS

The people's good is the highest law

Cicero, 106–43 BCE

There is no escaping the political nature of the director's job. No matter if it is a city library, small rural county, or large urban system, library policies and practices will run into the political process at some point.

Douglas Crane, 2015

When we consider how much of our web content comes from outside vendors, we may feel like we don't have much control over our users' experience. That is simply not true. My library has chosen not to subscribe to certain platforms because they were not ADA-accessible and the vendor had no plans to change that.

Meredith Farkis, 2016

The most challenging part—but in many ways the most important—is to make sure you are in compliance with the law relating to public screenings of films.

Kati Irons, 2015

By now you know laws, regulations, and the like play a role in library operations. The quotation from Cicero above sums up the legal environment for public and nonprofit sector managerial leaders. Organizations in those sectors exist because of some law or regulation.

Nina McHale highlighted why we included a chapter on legal aspects: "Colorado Library Law (C.R.S. 24-90-101 et seq.) dictates much of what we need to know about how to run our libraries" (2011, 1). We decided to structure this chapter along the lines suggested by McHale's comment. That is, we look at six areas where laws and regulations impact library activities:

1. Organization and structure
2. Services
3. Operations
4. Users
5. Staff
6. Collaboration

A person could write an entire book on the aspects of laws and regulations that affect library activities; this is simply a brief chapter. Essentially, we will highlight a few examples of how legalities come into play in terms of library activities.

Every library employee is aware of at least one legal issue that affects libraries—copyright. That awareness often goes no further than that; knowing that copyright exists and never wondering why, if it's an issue, we supply copy machines without worrying about the nature of the copying. Experienced librarians know that the issue extends beyond some public access copy machines. Public service staff members are aware of at least one other legal issue—liability. They know that especially when the weather is bad—rain, ice, or snow—it is time to get out special floor mats and signs about slippery floors. Again, they may have no further understanding of the legal ramifications than knowing that something should be done before someone slips. In both of the above cases, it is important that at least one managerial leader have a good grasp of the basic legal concerns in order to protect the library from unwanted legal wrangles.

We doubt that many in our profession thought they might need to have almost a paralegal background upon becoming a supervisor or manager. By the time you finish reading this chapter you may think you need to enroll in a few law school classes. That is probably unnecessary and not worth your time and effort, especially as the laws and "regs" constantly change, get deleted, get expanded, and so on. Your goal is to keep up to date about those laws and regulations that affect the library. The good news is there are some websites that will help you in that endeavor, such as http://librarylaw.com/, which covers all the major legal concerns facing libraries, and a related blog can be found at http://blog.librarylaw.com/.

We hope that if nothing else, your take away from reading this chapter is the notion of "if in doubt about the law, seek legal advice." Doing something and seeking forgiveness later may work for some managerial actions or decisions, but taking this approach when there are legal implications is an invitation for trouble. *Nothing* in this chapter is intended as legal advice beyond the advice to consult with an attorney if there is the slightest doubt.

FORMING A LIBRARY

Libraries don't just appear because some people think they would like to launch a library. Almost all academic, public, and school libraries have some legal basis for their existence. Academic libraries are part of an organization that exists because of legislation or charter. Rarely does the legislation or charter spell out details of the organization's component parts, such as having a library. However, almost every academic library has nonprofit status in order to aid in its fund raising activities. That status, as you know, arises from meeting a variety of Internal Revenue Service (IRS) regulations, which are modified from time to time by legislative action.

Public and school libraries are only formed in compliance with state laws. The range in how much legal control exists varies from state to state. California's "library laws" run many pages (224 pages in the PDF document available online at California Library Laws 2016, https://www.library.ca.gov/publications /2016CaliforniaLibraryLaws.pdf). Wisconsin Statutes' Chapter 43, "Libraries," is 13 double-column, tightly packed pages (http://docs.legis.wisconsin.gov/statutes /statutes/43.pdf). In both instances, they reflect the libraries legal status as of late 2016. One example of establishing a library district, from Michigan, is a 15-page document spelling out the steps required, entitled "Michigan District Library Law" (http://www.michigan.gov/documents/mde/LM_Michigan_District _Library_Law_329703_7.pdf). Most of such laws spell out tax rates (*millages*— see chapter 9 for a discussion of mil rates), budgeting processes, and library boards for example.

The following is an example of a specific law from *Virginia Administrative Code*, authorizing the formation of a school library, which appears to mandate such libraries:

A. Each school shall maintain an organized library media center as the resource center of the school and provide a unified program of media services and activities for students and teachers before, during, and after school. The library media center shall contain hard copy, electronic technological resources, materials, and equipment that are sufficient to meet research, inquiry, and reading requirements of the instructional program and general student interest.

B. Each school shall provide a variety of materials and equipment to support the instructional program. ((8 VAC 20–131–190 (2014))

It is the rare for a librarian to be involved in forming a new library. The primary reason for discussing the topic is most of the legislation regarding the establishment of a library goes well beyond that process.

Almost all such legislation contains statements about governance and other structural matters. For example the Michigan District Library Law, mentioned above, states:

This publication covers three major areas of district libraries: (1) **establishment** (including the selection of participating municipalities, board structure, the district library agreement, proper filing with the Library of Michigan, and other miscellaneous considerations), (2) **funding** (including various options such as districtwide millages, local millages, local appropriations, and bond issues), and (3) **district library boundaries** (including adding a participating municipality, withdrawing, and district consolidation).

Another example from Wisconsin Statutes highlights what powers a library board may exercise:

> **2)** Every public library shall be free for the use of the inhabitants of the municipality by which it is established and maintained, subject to such reasonable regulations as the library board prescribes in order to render its use most beneficial to the greatest number. The library board may exclude from the use of the public library all persons who willfully violate such regulations. (9)

That document also allows for a library to acquire library services from library services in other states (similar to OCLC). Without that authorization the library would not be allowed to use public funds to pay for services such as those offered by OCLC and the like. A final example from Arizona is an example of how the laws can impact operations:

> A city or town may levy annually, in addition to all other taxes, a tax not to exceed one and one-half mills on the assessed value of all property in the city or town, exclusive of the valuation of property exempt from taxation, for the purpose of establishing and maintaining therein free public libraries and reading rooms, for purchasing books, journals and other publications, and erecting and maintaining such buildings as may be necessary therefor (A.R.S. § 9-411 Tax levy for library purposes).

We suggest you check the library laws whenever you take up a new position. We often have a tendency to think about changes to make upon starting a new job. There are times when laws may impact the way something is done, rather than habit. In any case, getting the "lay of land" before being a new broom is always a wise decision.

Reciprocal borrowing service is a fairly common library practice for all types of libraries. Such programs are usually voluntary and may place restrictions on what can be borrowed and for how long, and the like. The nature of the system is in part influenced by laws and regulations related to spending money across jurisdictional boundaries. It is almost a given that there will be overdue fines and lost or damaged items. Who and how to pay for those events varies. For example, the Alaska State Library "has an 'insurance fund' to help partially compensate libraries if materials are not returned by reciprocal borrowers. An advisory committee monitors the program and recommends how the 'insurance fund' is used" (The text of the Alaska Libraries' Reciprocal Borrowing Program can be accessed at this website: http://library.alaska.gov/recipborrow/home.html). In other programs, the library where the material is returned collects and keeps any such fees; that arrangement removes the problem of cross jurisdictional payments and assumes the collection of fees will balance over time. Some programs, such as the Reciprocal Borrowing policy as the Tampa Bay Library Consortium, have requirements such as "Individual libraries are responsible for insuring that their staffs are aware of, and adhere to, statutory requirements concerning confidentiality of public library users' registration and circulation records as required by Florida Statute 257.261" (https://tblc.org/programs-and-services/reciprocal-borrowing/).

IMPACT ON SERVICES

You may be surprised by the number of library activities that are, at least in part, affected by legislation or regulation. Some activities are library specific and others apply to any organization that provides services to the general public.

One example of a law that applies to any organization is the Americans with Disabilities Act (ADA). This law states that it is illegal to discriminate "on the basis of disability in the full and equal enjoyment of the goods, services, facilities, privileges, advantages, or accommodations of any place of public accommodation" (42 U.S.C. § 12182(a) 2000). This broad statement applies to both physical and intellectual access to library facilities and services.

Meredith Farkis's opening quotation suggests how the ADA might come into play in terms of a service (2016). Needless to say, the issue extends beyond what a vendor does or doesn't do. A library providing Internet access must have connected machines that will allow a visually impaired or wheelchair-bound individual to have easy access to the service. Then there are questions about the library's collections—how accessible are they, especially for those with vision issues? Does the library have to spend as much on resources for visually or physically challenged individuals as it does on material for the general service population? Would an allotted percentage be acceptable, based on the service population with such challenges? The answer probably is that it depends on what a court might decide should a lawsuit be filed. (Keep in mind the difference between "equal" and "equitable".) The percentage approach probably is a safe one and even if the court were to rule it wasn't adequate there would be little chance of facing penalties—there was a good faith effort made to comply with the law.

Access to the library's facilities covers just about everything—entrances, width of aisles generally and in the stacks particularly, restrooms, drinking fountains, and access to multistory facilities are a few examples. Since the passage of the ADA (in 1990), libraries existing at that time have faced fiscal challenges to move their facilities toward compliance. Remodeling older buildings is always costly and often the only funds available are maintenance accounts. Choices are often difficult to make, especially given limited funding. Should we modify windows to be more energy efficient, replace damaged roof sections, or remodel restrooms to be ADA compliant? The fact of the matter is, making the decision to be compliant may not end the matter. From time to time, requirements change as a result of court cases. [Check out the LibraryLaw Blog (http://blog.librarylaw.com/librarylaw/disability_access/) to review some recent decisions.]

Meeting rooms in many publicly supported libraries can produce some long-term issues. Perhaps the biggest challenge relates to who may use the space for what purpose. A monthly meeting of the garden society poses few concerns. The same is true for a service club or a variety of other social organizations. When it comes to political and religious organizations things can get murky. The notion of separation of church and state can be a major concern and balancing political activities can create another conundrum regarding political and ethical neutrality. To allow or not allow such groups to use the space can be tricky.

Over the years libraries have been sued for various decisions to allow or not to allow an event to take place. Perhaps one of the longer running cases involved the Contra Costa County, California, Library system's rejection of a request by a religious group to use a meeting room. The court case involved almost five years of staff time and legal fees. The final resolution occurred when the U. S. Supreme Court refused to hear an appeal of the Circuit Court's decision that ruled in favor of the library system (for a summary of the complex and appealed court case, see Leonard Kniffel's "Supreme Court Won't Hear Meeting Room Appeal," *American Libraries* 38, no. 10 (2007): 18).

An example of a political case that reached the professional literature took place in 2006 in Montana (Goldberg, 2006). In this case, the ACLU wanted to screen a film and have a discussion of the Patriot Act. Someone complained, after the program was announced, that there was no speaker in support of the Act—political neutrality was missing. The program eventually took place but in a different publicly supported library. The important difference and the point to take away from this section is to have a carefully prepared room use policy approved by the library board and vetted by a lawyer in place long before who can use the space for what purpose becomes an issue.

One of our opening quotations for this chapter (from Kati Irons) touches on another aspect of law that has an impact on library activities—film programs and performance rights. Libraries of all types must address performance rights from time to time. Even when the film or video is publicly screened and no money changes hands, there is the potential for violating the law. Having a film program that is open to the public has the potential for legal challenges if the library did not acquire performance rights when it purchased the film or video (such rights almost always entail a higher cost for the item). Academic and school libraries face issues regarding the use of such material for "reserve" use by an individual student, classroom use, or for streaming to a classroom. Performance rights usually take the form of a license agreement that goes into some detail what you may and may not do. We explore contracts and licenses in the next section.

IMPACT ON OPERATIONS

We all sign contracts occasionally with little thought or full understanding of what we are signing. Think of cell phone or car rental agreements, and even insurance policies, as examples of contracts we sign quickly to "get on with our lives." Probably 99 percent of such signings never become an issue. It seems likely the most common problems are related to what was and was not covered by your insurance policy. As the saying goes, "contracts and policies are written by lawyers for lawyers." The general public has little chance of truly understanding such documents without the assistance of a lawyer. Libraries have a number of contracts and leases that are tied to their operations and services. Libraries should not sign such documents without a full understanding of the terms.

What are some of the common contracts? The library's ILS is usually contract based and spells out performance requirements as well as fee structures. Then there are contracts with vendors such as book or other media firms and security sys-tems providers. Some libraries have a contract for janitorial services. Then there are license agreements (different than contracts) for allowing access to online data-bases, as well as the leases noted above for performance rights.

Does it matter what the document is called? In one sense, they all have the com-monality of being a legal document. There are some important differences. Con-tracts are a "voluntary, deliberate, and legally binding agreement between two or more competent parties. . . . Each party to a contract acquires rights and duties relative to the rights and duties of the other parties" (http://www.businessdictionary .com/definition/contract.html). Licenses are a "revocable written (formal) or implied agreement by an authority or proprietor (the licensor) not to assert his or her right (for a specific period and under specified conditions) to prevent another party (the licensee) from engaging in certain activity that is normally forbidden (such as selling liquor or making copies of a copyrighted work)" (http://www.businessdictionary .com/definition/license.html).

The major concern in the language of such documents is that a layperson has little chance of being able to grasp the full meaning of the clauses. The best advice is to secure input from an attorney on a first-time agreement, regardless of its label, and periodically review the agreement.

Library agreements contain some limits on the library's liability for misuse by its users. The operative phrase in that statement is "some limits." Without careful review and adjustments to the final agreement, the library can find itself fully liable of any misuse, even after the user leaves the library. "Full liability" is a very common component for the first draft of such documents.

CHECK THIS OUT

The American Association of Law Libraries has laid out some principles online for handling licensing agreements with database vendors that are useful for all types of libraries in its Procurement Toolkit and Code of Best Practices for Licensing Electronic Resources (http://www.aallnet.org/mm/Publications/products/procurement-toolkit.html).

There are operational activities that may be affected by some laws or regulations. For example, how the library may handle, or whether it can even have, fines for overdue items may be circumscribed by a law. The California State Library has limits on what it may do regarding unreturned materials; there are laws that impose such limits on other types of libraries.

Sec. 19333. Suit for unreturned books.

The State Librarian may bring suit in his or her official capacity for the recovery of any book, or for three times the value thereof, together with costs of suit, against any person who has the book in his or her possession or who is responsible therefore. If the department has purchased a duplicate of any book, it may bring suit for three times the amount expended for the duplicate, together with costs of suit. (California State Library, 2016)

There are also regulations regarding how active a library may be in its "collections" efforts (fines and fees that are unpaid). As the opening quotation from Perry Neal noted, fines can have negative consequences long term and, we would add, can decrease trust and/or respect for the library.

Public and school libraries face an ongoing operational issue—collection space is finite. Academic libraries have somewhat similar issues; however, they do have an option that rarely exists for public and school libraries—off-site storage. Weeding or deselection of materials is a standard library operation regardless of type. The activity also generates the question of what to do with the pulled weeds. Whether you can sell the items, give them away, or get permission to dispose of the items are questions the answers for which may be found in laws or regulations. Often the laws and regulations regarding "surplus items" purchased with public funds are very generic and often do not take into account differences in costs. It is wise to know what your options really are. Generally there are few problems, even if the disposal method may not be directly addressed in a law or regulation. However, it takes just one person to become upset and do some checking to generate a kerfuffle for the library. One belief that some people hold about books is they are special, almost unique, and must be preserved at almost any cost. Combine such a belief with the desire to never waste taxpayer money and you have the potential for a problem. Be sure about what you can and cannot do with your weeds.

Our final example could have gone into the next section (users). We placed it here because it is a combination of factors that are both operational and user in impact. It is also an example of how a library can unknowingly get itself into a potentially serious legal tangle.

Libraries often establish "standard" operational procedures and frequently copy one another's practices. Most of the time doing so causes no difficulty, legal or otherwise, for the library. In addition, those activities may continue for years before anyone realizes there is a problem. So it was for the following incident. The events took place long ago; however, it does illustrate just how subtle legal issues can and how problems can arise even when a library makes every effort to be lawful.

In the past, public libraries with branch operations employed a budgeting model that included a usage factor for branch operations. A branch's budget was augmented by its usage data. Certainly a reasonable approach; heavily utilized branches with heavier workloads and more patrons seeking services could more effectively employ additional funds than lesser-used branches (greatest good for the greatest number). It is a rational approach and one that became the basis for a city attorney to state that the library system was in violation of the equal protection clause of the U.S. Constitution, the U.S. Civil Rights Act, the Federal Revenue Sharing Act, and equal protection provision of the California State Constitution (McDermott, 1975). There were a variety of factors that came into play well beyond the funding model that created the potential and real illegalities.

As people moved from "the inner city" to new suburban communities, the library built new branches in those areas (almost always larger and better staffed than the inner city branches). Budget challenges for the library system made funding all branches difficult. Collections created to serve a particular population remained in the older branches even as that population disappeared. Lack of funds made it more and more difficult to replace those collections with new material that reflected the interests of the new residents. The result was a drop in usage of the older branches with a declining budget base. All in all it was the perfect storm that, with some political factors tossed in, led to the city attorney's findings. The good news was no court case arose as the library had acted in good faith and made efforts to redress the problems identified. [You can learn more about this incident in G. Edward Evans and Margret Zarnosky Saponaro's *Collection Management Basics*, 6th edition (Santa Barbara, CA: Libraries Unlimited, 2012), 45–52.]

The bottom line is when undertaking major operational changes it is important to spend some time thinking carefully about the long-term outcomes and potential legal concerns. Part of that thinking should take into consideration in changing political winds.

IMPACT ON USERS

There are some well-known user-related laws, such as those dealing with confidentiality and privacy concerns. There are many others that come into play because libraries fall under the legal heading of "public forums." That is, they are facilities, regardless of type, that have open access, unless they are private and have established a controlled access policy before restricting someone's entrance. Certainly libraries that are publicly funded must be accessible. Being accessible can create some interesting issues for the library regarding behavior, usage, and the like.

One challenging issue about being a public forum is what can a library do about unattended children? This is, in part, a societal problem, but also one that academic and public libraries must deal with from time to time. In 2014, Melissa Higely wrote about the challenges unaccompanied children can present for libraries:

> Children are often left unattended in the library, dropped off by parents for a few hours, or simply "latchkey" children—children that come to the library while parents or guardians are at work or not at home. Most libraries have policies regarding at what age children can be left unattended, how long children can be left unattended, or what areas of the library unattended children can visit. These policies vary from library to library, but most librarians would agree that this is an issue in public libraries today, especially with the increase of working parents and single-parent homes.

The basic question in regard to such children is, "Who is responsible for the child's well-being?" Another question is, "How can the library be liable for the child?" The answers are more complex and legal in character than you might expect. There are laws related to child protection that exist at many levels of government and are, at times, contradictory. The best way to work on the issue is with the board and an attorney to develop a policy that clearly and legally sets forth what the library is responsible for and when it may ask for assistance (from child welfare officials or the police, for example). Below are some options that may be available depending on a library's location:

- Bar children without parental supervision
- Create programs for such children

- Establish timeframes for calling child welfare services or police to assist, especially if at or near closing time
- Establish, and post, the maximum time a child may be left unattended

---

CHECK THIS OUT

The following example of an unattended child policy is from the Flagstaff–Coconino Public Library System in Arizona. It was crafted by the supervisor of the youth services department and the city's legal department and was in response to increasing instances of children being left unattended:

http://www.flagstaffpubliclibrary.org/services/youth_services/parents_and_educators /unattended.html.

A Web search will produce a host of other examples.

Service Animals

Another, perhaps surprising, area of legal constraint, and one that has arisen from being a public forum, is with service animals. We are familiar with seeing-eye dogs and recognize their importance as service animals. However, do you really want a miniature horse in the library? How about a ferret, parrot, or a squirrel? You might doubt that any of those could be an issue, much less that someone would argue that one of them was a "service animal." They can be and legally are so in some states, as long as they meet certain assessment factors. Because the ADA covers service animals (though it only covers dogs and miniature horses) and organizations open to the public, libraries are not alone in handling the issue when it arises (https://www.ada .gov/service_animals_2010.htm). The following is a link to one library's policy on service animals: http://libraries.ucsd.edu/about/policies/library-service-animals.html.

Keep in mind that other jurisdictions may have broader definitions of what constitutes a service animal. The ADA provides some guidance for developing a local service animal policy that addresses issues such as when the service staff or users may have an allergic reaction or a fear of the animal (see the above link). To be a service animal it must be trained to perform a function that directly relates to the person's health issues—comfort and emotional support, if the sole role of the animal, does not qualify as service. You also have the right to have the animal removed if it is not housebroken. Again developing a written posted policy is a wise action to take.

Disruptive Behavior

Needless to say, service animal issues are uncommon. What is common is user behavior that is disruptive. The list of potentially disruptive behaviors can be rather long. A challenge in formulating a user behavior policy is when you encounter disagreements over what exactly constitutes a disruption, along with a number of legal considerations. Is loud talking disruptive? It is, more than likely, for many people—users and staff alike. Can you force a loud talker to leave? Perhaps, perhaps not. A person with a hearing impairment may be a loud taker as result of the impairment and thus have some expectation that ADA would offer protection from forcible removal. There are a variety of behaviors that are disruptive beyond obvious criminal behavior (such as drug use, assault, and arson), but that are open to questions from a legal perspective. For example, menacing behavior (often it is in the eye of the beholder), verbal abuse (again subject to one's point of view), and gang activity are behaviors that may occur and, in the absence of clear guidelines, leave staff in awkward and stressful positions.

The fact that most libraries are public forums does mean the law may play a role in how you formulate policy in terms of "behaviors." Just what can you do regarding guns in the library? Can you simply ban them? Can you ban them if you make provision for their storage while the person is in the building? The fact of the matter is what you can do legally today may be illegal tomorrow. This is true of all types of disruptive behavior. Homeless advocates often challenge policies that they say unfairly affect the homeless; for example, limiting the number of items a person with no fixed address may borrow (see "Homeless Residents Sue over Borrowing Restrictions," *American Libraries* 37, no. 7: 18; and "Stir Raised by Dallas over Body Odor Rule," *American Libraries*, 37, no. 2: 11). Court decisions in such cases become part of case law, an interpretation of the law, and an extension of the law. Legislative bodies make new laws and amend old laws with regularity; thus, a policy made is never set in stone.

CHECK THIS OUT

You can read a more detail discussion of disruptive behavior that looks at user and staff interaction in *Library Programs and Services: The Fundamentals*, 8th edition, by G. Edward Evans, Margaret Zarnosky Saponaro, Holland Christie, and Carol Sinwell (Santa Barbara, CA: Libraries Unlimited, 2015), 313–316.

User Privacy and Confidentiality

Privacy and confidentiality are two common words that people often employ interchangeably. They are, from a legal perspective, different but interrelated. The following demonstrate both the differences and interrelationship.

Privacy

The constitutional right to privacy protects the liberty of people to make certain crucial decisions regarding their well-being without government coercion, intimidation, or interference. Such crucial decisions may concern religious faith, moral values, political affiliation, marriage, procreation, or death. The federal Constitution guarantees the right of individuals to make these decisions according to their own conscience and beliefs. (http://legal-dictionary.thefreedictionary.com/privacy)

Confidentiality

The legally required process of keeping identifying or other significant information secret; the principle of ethical practice which requires social workers and other professionals not to disclose information about a client without the client's consent. (http://legaldictionary.lawin.org/confidentiality/)

From the library's standpoint, privacy is more of a user's responsibility while confidentiality is an obligation of the library; libraries must not make the user's information available to others without consent. There are some exceptions to a library's responsibility regarding confidentiality, which we explore below.

Every public service staff member knows, or should know and be well acquainted with, the confidentiality and privacy issues related to users' information and borrowing and searching activities. Most states have some form of confidentiality law, for example, California (Cal Civ Code § 1798.3, 2014), Colorado (C.R.S. 24–72–204, 2013), Illinois (75 ILCS 5/1–7, 2014), and New York (NY CLS CPLR § 4509, 2014). Like most laws, the various legislations do not go into all the possible scenarios that can and do arise. Also, there is case law related to confidentiality concerns that broadens or narrows the scope of the legalities that exist for the library.

The most widely discussed situation is when a law enforcement officer arrives and asks or demands information about a person's library records. When that happens between 8 a.m. and 5 p.m. on a weekday, the staff member has the option to pass the request up the chain of command. If it happens at night or on the weekend, it is important that the staff understand the library's privacy policy and resist the request unless the officer has a subpoena (staff must comply in that case). Will you know what the local subpoena looks like? Having a sample of that document as an attachment to the policy will be a great help for the staff.

ALA has some guidance for how to formulate an effective policy in this area. See the following:

> "Confidentiality and Coping with Law Enforcement Inquiries: Guidelines for the Library and Its Staff" (http://www.ala.org/Template.cfm?Section=ifissues&Template =/ContentManagement/ContentDisplay.cfm&ContentID=21654).
>
> "Privacy: An Interpretation of the *Library Bill of Rights*" (http://www.ala.org/ala /issuesadvocacy/intfreedom/librarybill/interpretations/privacy.cfm).
>
> "Privacy Tool Kit" (http://www.ala.org/advocacy/privacyconfidentiality/toolkitsprivacy /privacy).

AUTHOR EXPERIENCE

The authors know of a situation where, at one library, the police showed up asking for a list of books that a particular user had checked out. It was the officers' hope that the list of books would provide evidence regarding the location and activities of the user. Luckily, the staff person who encountered the officer was aware of the library's policy and didn't provide the information, but instead informed the officer that he would need a warrant.

Libraries collect a surprising amount of personal data that most people regard as private—the items borrowed and Internet searches conducted, for example. In order to borrow materials from the library a person is required to give at least a name and address; some libraries require proof the address is where the person actually lives—for example, a driver's license or a utility bill. The library's circulation system records what a person checks out. While it is true that most ILS break the link between the user's ID number and the item's bar code upon the item's return, there still is a record of a person's borrowing information for a long time—in backup files kept on the library's servers.

Do parents have the right to request information about their minor children's library usage? As is so often the case, it depends on your library's home state, as there are many variations in if, how, and why parents want the information. ALA's guidance in this area is murky at best: it states "extend to minor patrons the maximum allowable confidentially and privacy protections" while also stating that "parental responsibility is the key to a minor's use of the library" (*Questions and Answers on Privacy and Confidentiality*, http://www.ala.org/advocacy/intfreedom /librarybill/interpretations/qa-privacy). The second sentence might be interpreted as saying that a responsible parent has the right to information about their children's library activities.

CHECK THIS OUT

A Web search will turn up many library privacy and confidentiality policies. One we like is a document from Mill Valley, California. It clearly outlines what data the library gathers about its users activities and has a section on the library's approach to minor children's privacy: http://www.cityofmillvalley.org/Index.aspx?page=581.

There is one area where libraries have limited ability to protect user privacy and confidentiality—online activities. Angela Maycock suggested, "The ease of communicating in the digital age has changed the way we live, work, and learn—often in wonderfully exciting and positive ways. But the capacity of . . . databases to collect and store personal information presents growing challenges to individuals' privacy" (2013, 34). Library online services and database vendors do collect data about the individuals who use their services. In 2010, Trina Magi wrote that "the Web 2.0 environment . . . poses new challenges for librarians in their commitment to protect user privacy, as vendors of online Library databases incorporate personalization features into their search-and-retrieval interfaces, thereby collecting personally identifiable user information not subject to library oversight" (254). Online library product vendors frequently have a tab that offers the opportunity for the user to create a personalized search approach. Some examples are EBSCO's "MyEBSCOhost," Emerald's "Your Profile," and ProQuest's "My Research." Many users are unaware that their "profiles" become a potential asset for vendors.

There is a difference in the motivation between libraries and online vendors once you go beyond the notion that privacy and confidentiality is an important issue. Librarians are motivated and/or compelled to strive for maximum user privacy and confidentiality. Vendors' bottom line is profit and online services tend to view user profile data as a potential revenue stream. In mid-2016, Todd Carpenter published an article that reported on new National Information Standards Organization (NISO) consensus privacy principles. Parties to the agreement were libraries, publishers, and "software provider systems" representatives. Carpenter noted, "As a situation is developing or when the risks are modest, recommended practices are called for. But when community practice is just being formulated, when issues are still being assessed, or when an agreement is proving difficult, lighter consensus or white papers can be used to advance common practice and trust" (26). In the article Carpenter also provides a list of the 12 consensus principles (28).

In 2015, Ken Varnum, a member of the editorial board for the journal *Information Technology and Libraries*, said about the NISO principles: "This new consensus framework sets a series of guidelines for us to consider as we begin to move into this uncharted (for libraries) territory. If we are to record and make use of our users' online (and offline, for that matter) footprints to improve services, improve the user experience, and justify our value, this document gives us an outline of the issues to consider" (3).

The consensus principles may help, but there are still serious differences. What might libraries do? We agree with Trina Magi's statement: "Don't assume users know anything about how a third-party database works and puts their privacy at risk; tell them" (2013, 39). Informing users at least provides the individual with knowledge upon which to decide how much to share. The opening quotation from Meredith Farkis suggests another, if more drastic approach: cancel the service. Perhaps the best approach is to start a discussion with the service vendor(s) about how to better inform users regarding the data collected and how the vendor uses the data.

CHECK THESE OUT

The following items explore in more detail the issues of privacy, libraries, and digital environment:

John W. W. Cyrus and Mark P. Baggett, "Mobile Technology: Implications for Privacy and Librarianship," *Reference Librarian* 53, no. 3 (2012): 284–296.

Yong Jin Park, "Digital Literacy and Privacy Behavior Online," *Communication Research* 40, no. 2 (2013): 215–236.

Theresa M. Payton and Theodore Claypoole, *Privacy in the Age of Big Data: Recognizing Threats, Defending Your Rights, and Protecting Your Family* (Lanham, MD: Rowman & Littlefield, 2014)

Alan Rubel, "Libraries, Electronic Resources, and Privacy: The Case for Positive Intellectual Freedom," *Library Quarterly* 84, no. 2 (2014): 183–208.

IMPACT ON STAFF

Needless to say, there are some legal issues that relate to staff and staffing. The hiring and retention processes are filled with legal aspects. Many of those aspects are both federal and local in character. You probably know the major employment laws that cover some aspects of employment from recruitment to retirement and dismissal. In addition to those laws, there is the ADA, which may both affect hiring as well as existing staff who become disabled.

There is also the Occupational Safety and Health Administration (OSHA). If you are acquainted with OSHA it is most likely due to a staff member having an accident or another work/health issue. The other common time when an OSHA officer visits the library is when a staff files a complaint with their office about some perceived health or safety problem.

Any formal complaint related to the above will take time, effort, money, and a fair amount of stress to resolve. There will be meetings, with and without attorneys, which eat into your time for "normal duties." It takes some effort to stay focused on the job as well as on the legal issue. There is likely to be some direct or indirect cost for the library; if nothing else, lost staff productivity as a result of resolution processes. Any solution of an OSHA or ADA complaint is likely to result in a direct library cost arising from fixing the problem. The most common OSHA issue for a library is ergonomic workstations and equipment. These can be expensive to fix, especially when doing so involves a number of staff workplaces. Repetitive motion (bending, stooping, pushing, etc.) injuries are common library health issues, with carpal tunnel injuries not too far behind.

Progressive Discipline

Beyond the rather well-known areas of legal concern with regard to staff discussed above, there are several other potential legal pitfalls. Perhaps the one area that you may know something about is staff discipline ("progress discipline" is a common label). Most introductory management courses cover the concept as do courses on human resources. You rarely have a situation where you implement the full progressive discipline process, but when it does occur it eats into your time, effort and productivity. You are wise to talk with the HR department early in the process to be clear what and when to do what. During the later stages the chances grow that lawyers will become part of the process. A topic that does not get as much attention as might be useful is "The Fairness Doctrine."

The Fairness Doctrine may not be a law as such or even a regulation, but lawyers for the plaintiff will draw upon the features of the doctrine when a court sits in judgment. The following is a definition of the concept:

> Fundamental fairness doctrine is a rule that applies the principles of due process to a judicial proceeding. Fundamental-Fairness is considered synonymous with due process. The due process guarantees under the Fifth and Fourteenth Amendments to the U.S. Constitution Clause provide that the government shall not take a person's life, liberty, or property without due process of law. (http://definitions.uslegal.com/f/fundamental-fairness-doctrine/)

HR departments will emphasize the need for due process during progressive discipline but rarely discuss the elements of the doctrine.

There are 10 elements to the doctrine and you may be surprised how far back in time the elements go. The first component goes back to the first orientation period—was the expected performance or issue covered at that time? It also covers ongoing training for all new performance areas. The second element is particular to a performance concern—is the performance expectation reasonable? The third element can be a pitfall for an organization—what is the basis for the expectation? Is it based on test results with a range of acceptable performances? Few organizations truly test for what is deemed satisfactory performance. Having an expectation based on a test is not enough on its own. The question will be how well the expectation was or is communicated and understood by the person. The fifth element is related to reasonableness; that is, is the expectation an industry standard or based on best practices? We rarely think about checking this out when implementing a new procedure/activity with a performance expectation attached. The question, are *all* employees assigned to the activity as the person being disciplined, meeting the expected performance? That is the sixth element in the doctrine. Element seven raises such questions as, is the basis for the discipline tainted by a personality clash or bias, and has a neutral party investigated the matter? The next element relates to the preceding element, did the supervisor's supervisor look into the matter prior to the process starting? Number nine questions whether the process was discriminatory in some manner—all the usual suspects can come into play here. The final element is, does the punishment fit the crime?

You can see how some of the elements are part of progressive discipline, but with a slightly different slant. You can be sure, if it becomes a court case, the plaintiff's lawyer will drill into those elements. In some cases, the library may not have solid answers. Checking over performance expectations and getting them in line with the above, well before the lawyers arrive, is our best advice. These elements also apply to the next several sections: create policies, have them approved by the appropriate board, communicate those policies to staff, and finally, provide staff training in what those policies mean in terms of expected performance.

Sexual Harassment

For such a short word, sex has a surprisingly large role in organizational life. From a managerial leadership perspective there are two interrelated issues. One is by far the biggest challenge: sexual harassment. The second much smaller and less common challenge is workplace romances. The biggest issue with the "romance" situation is they can and do sometimes morph into bitter break-ups with the potential, especially if the couple was in a reporting relationship, for a sexual harassment charge.

Title VII of the 1964 Civil Rights Act includes sexual harassment as being potentially discriminatory. By law organizations *must* investigate any claim of sexual harassment—keep in mind a person of any gender may make such a claim. By now, you understand any such investigation takes time, builds stress, and reduces productivity. Thus, it is not surprising that managerial leaders have a concern about relationship or behavior issues within the staff. When a work relationship falls apart and a claim is lodged, don't be surprised to find yourself pulled into the investigation. If it happened on your watch, what you did or didn't do to protect the library from involvement is a question that may well arise.

As is true of so many workplace activities and behaviors, the starting point to address them is to develop a clear policy that addresses harassment, in any form, as well as the position on romantic relationships. It is best to include a full description of how a claim is to be investigated and what the outcomes(s) may be should the claim be upheld. All of the Fairness Doctrine elements can come into play, especially if there is no or a weak policy in place—"I/We did not know about this" can impact the findings.

Organizations have come to realize there is little chance of their being able to effectively enforce a no fraternization policy. A number of organizations now require a "romance contract:" essentially, an agreement that makes it clear the relationship is consensual. Having such a document makes it almost impossible for a person to make a later claim of harassment. One obvious drawback is knowing if a relationship exists when the couple is discrete. One likely way is from other staff members who have greater opportunities to observe the behavior. They may report the relationship, especially if one of the parties is married.

The last sentence touches on something that tends to receive less attention in discussion of sexual harassment—a third party can file a claim on the basis of a "hostile work environment." (It has and does happen, as one of the authors can attest.) Another wrinkle in terms of sexual harassment is any person connected to the workplace—vendor, patron, service personnel—may be factor in a claim.

Substance Abuse and More

Life is full of personal challenges that have nothing to do with our work. How we go about handling those issues is highly personal, and often we try to cope without help from anyone. Sometimes our approach works, or at least seems to allow us to get through the days and nights without much difficulty. Sometimes we cope with a mechanism that, in the long run, is harmful. In any circumstance, regardless of what we believe, we do bring our issues to the workplace. Most of the time our coping approach does not affect our performance to the point that our supervisor needs to talk to us about the performance. Being late occasionally or taking a "mental health day" may not seem all that significant; however, from an organizational point of view such actions add up to real productivity losses. Some writers suggest nationally the cost of such behaviors cost billions of dollars a year.

Many of today's organizations offer employee assistance programs (EAP) designed to help with various non-work issues that can become performance problems. Such programs are not a legal or a regulatory requirement; however, long-term performance problems can translate into disciplinary action. In that case, the Fairness Doctrine may well become a factor.

Originally, EAPs focused on alcohol abuse programs—still a significant problem—but over the years they have expanded to help with such problems as financial difficulties, domestic violence, gambling problems, legal needs, and social services. Some programs even offer training of supervisors and managers in how to identify possible problems and how to go about offering help. (Note: not all employees are receptive to getting help even when acknowledging the problem exists. This is where the organizational protection is clearly apparent.)

<table>
<tr><td>

CHECK THIS OUT

A detailed discussion about one type of EAP intervention is Genevieve M. Ames, Joel B. Bennett, and Christopher Spera's 2011 article "Prevention Intervention of Alcohol Problems in the Workplace: A Review and Guiding Framework" (*Alcohol Research and Health* 34, no. 2: 175–187).

    The journal *Supervision* has from time to time over the years published a column "Labor Law for Supervisors." Some of those columns cover, in more detail, all the above topics and many more. It is worth taking the time to review the columns occasionally.

</td></tr>
</table>

IMPACT ON COLLABORATION

Where would libraries be today, in terms of offering online resources, if consortia did not exist? Certainly the offerings would be more limited than they are, as most libraries do not have the financial resources to acquire what they have available as an independent entity. There are other programs and services that are cross-juridical in character, for example reciprocal borrowing. The operative phrase is cross-juridical; often there are limits to what a library may transfer, especially public monies, to another jurisdiction without some form of legislative approval. The following provide examples of how one state (New York) goes about authorizing such activities:

New York State's *Interstate Library Compact.* "Because the desire for the services provided by the libraries transcends governmental boundaries and can most effectively be satisfied by giving such services to communities and people regardless of jurisdictional lines, it is the policy of the state's party to this compact to cooperate and share their responsibilities; to authorize cooperation and sharing with respect to those types of library facilities and services which can be more economically or efficiently developed and maintained on a cooperative basis, and to authorize cooperation and sharing among localities, states and others in providing joint or cooperative library services in areas where the distribution of population or of existing and potential library resources make the provision of library service on an interstate basis the most effective way of providing adequate and efficient service. . . . .

Article IV. Interstate Library Districts, Governing Board

(a) An interstate library district which establishes, maintains or operates any facilities or services in its own right shall have a governing board which shall direct the affairs of the district and act for it in all matters relating to its business. Each participating public library agency in the district shall be represented on the governing board which shall be organized and conduct its business in accordance with provision therefore in the library agreement. But in no event shall a governing board meet less often than twice a year.

(b) Any private library agency or agencies party to a library agreement establishing an interstate library district may be represented on or advise with the governing board of the district in such manner as the library agreement may provide. (NY CLS Unconsol Ch 111-B § 1 (2014))

Most consortia involve a membership and often a contract designed to protect all of the involved parties. Consortia contracts with a vendor present some interesting legal issues, if they are not properly reviewed by all the parties. Most joint purchasing collaborations involve a contract between the vendor and the membership *group*—not with individual libraries. Member libraries may have a voice in the negations but ultimately it becomes a group decision to accept or reject the terms. What if a library's attorney suggests the contract is not in the best interest of the parent organization? Worse, if the vendor files a claim against the group who covers any settlement costs? Would the library that had doubts about the contract have any liability? The best approach is to have the group incorporated as a nonprofit; the articles of incorporation, the bylaws, and membership agreement then become the legal basis for the group activities.

CHECK THIS OUT

For a good article that looks at a purchasing group in New York State and highlights some of the development and operation issues that may arise during the start-up of a new collaborative effort see Sheryl Knab, Tom Humphrey, and Caryl Ward's 2016 article "Now Streaming: A Consortial PDA Video Pilot Project" (*Collaborative Librarianship* 8, no. 1: 41–54).

LIABILITY

Public sector library liability is relatively new; in the past there was no or limited liability as a governmental agency. The concept of liability is complex, as reflected in the following definition:

> [Liability is] a comprehensive legal term that describes the condition of being actually or potentially subject to a legal obligation. Primary liability is an obligation for which a person is directly responsible; it is distinguished from secondary liability which is the responsibility of another if the party directly responsible fails or refuses to satisfy his or her obligation. (http://legal-dictionary.thefreedictionary.com/liability)

As you see, the concept involves actions taken as well as actions not taken and includes a hierarchy of responsibility. The most common liability concern for libraries is injury to someone—either staff or visitor. Tort law is the legal realm where injury claims fall. A key element in court cases of that sort involve the notion of negligence. Its legal definition is:

> **Negligence**, failure to exercise the care toward others which a reasonable or prudent person would do in the circumstances, or taking action which such a reasonable person would not. Negligence is accidental as distinguished from "intentional torts." (http://dictionary.law.com/Default.aspx?selected=1314)

All libraries with entryways directly to the outside face a common issue that can lead to an injury and possible lawsuit—a slippery floor.

Broadly thinking, there are three interrelated issues related to negligence, or a mental, emotional, or physical injury. *Negligence* requires the existence of three conditions: that the cause of the injury is a person (not an act of God), that the person causing the injury has responsibility or a duty to the injured party, and that the duty may be one of warning or one of action. There are a variety of possible outcomes to the slippery floor scenario, from no negligence and liability to full liability. The best option is, be sure to put out signs at the first hint of moisture, in clear view, and leave them there until it is completely dry. It pays to be watchful of any hazard on the library property—such as a broken sidewalk or a light out in the parking lot—as any associated property is open to negligence claims.

Malpractice

What about malpractice? Is it likely a librarian could lose a malpractice suit? Probably not, unless there was clear proof the librarian failed to provide proper professional assistance. Any lawsuit, if a lawyer would accept the case, based on the fact the information provided was defective in some manner, is unlikely to succeed. Librarians are viewed as experts in locating information; it is up to the information seeker to assess the usefulness or accuracy of the information.

CHECK THIS OUT

Paul D. Healey's book, *Professional Liability Issues for Librarians and Information Professionals* (New York: Neal-Schuman, 2008), covers a host of liability issues for librarians. Healey's background as a practicing attorney and a librarian makes his material very credible.

By this point you can understand why we believe laws and regulations play a rather large role providing library services. We recommend you read Stephanie P. Newbold's essay "Understanding Your Liability as a Public Administrator" in *Handbook of Public Administration*, 3rd edition, edited by James L. Perry and Robert K. Christensen (San Francisco: Jossey-Bass, 2015), 616–635. It provides a broad overview of public sector liability and administrators. In our view, it also has applications for those in the nonprofit sector.

CHECK THESE OUT

The following are some resources to consult regarding libraries and archives and the law:

   Menzi L. Behrnd-Klodt's *Navigating Legal Issues in Archives* (Chicago, IL: Society of American Archivists, 2008).

   Charles Oppenheim's *No-Nonsense Guide to Legal Issues in Web 2.0 and Cloud Computing* (London: Facet Pub., 2012).

   Mary Minow and Tomas A. Lipinski's *The Library's Legal Answer Book* (Chicago IL: ALA, 2003).

When an incident occurs that has a hint of legality issues, our advice is document, document, document! Paper trails are very important; develop the habit of making notes and keeping them.

REFERENCES

Americans with Disabilities Act of 1990, as Amended. n.d. https://www.ada.gov/pubs/ada.htm.

Arizona Library Law. n.d. azleg.gov/ars/9/00411.htm.

California Library Law. 2016. Section 19333:9.

California State Library. 2016. California Library Laws. http://www.library.ca.gov/publications/2016CaliforniaLibraryLaws.pdf#page=1&zoom=auto,-73,792.

Carpenter, Todd A. 2016. "Respecting Privacy: Consensus Is Reached on NISO Privacy Principles." *Computers in Libraries* 36, no. 5: 25–29.

Cicero. n.d. *De Legibus.* The Quotations Page. http://www.quotationspage.com/quote/24317.html.

Crane, Douglas. 2015. "May I Ask You a Question? Lessons Learned from Interviewing Public Library Leaders." *Public Libraries* 54, no. 6: 34–38.

Farkis, Meredith. 2016. "Accessibility Matters: Ensuring a Good Online Library Experience for All Our Patrons." *American Libraries* 47, nos. 9/10: 54.

Goldberg, Beverly. 2006. "Montana State Library Pulls ACLU Film Screening." *American Libraries* 37, no. 4: 12.

Higely, Melissa. 2014. "Unattended Children in the Public Library: Trends and Issues." http://unattended-children.wikispaces.com/.

Irons, Kati. 2015. "Screening Legally: Film Programming for Public Libraries." *American Libraries* 46, nos. 1/2: 38–41.

Magi, Trina J. 2010. "A Content Analysis of Library Vendor Privacy Policies: Do They Meet Our Standards?" *College & Research Libraries* 71, no. 3: 254–272.

Magi, Trina J. 2013. "A Fresh Look at Privacy—Why Does It Matter, Who Cares, and What Should Librarians Do About It?" *Indiana Libraries* 32, no. 1: 37–41.

Maycock, Angela. 2013. "Privacy, Libraries, and Engaging the Public: ALA's Choose Privacy Week Initiative." *Indiana Libraries* 32, no. 1: 34–36.

McDermott, John E. 1975. *Report on Legality of Branch Library Funding Disparities.* Los Angeles, CA: Office of City Attorney.

McHale, Nina, 2011. "Who Says I Have to Wear Shoes in the Library?" *Colorado Libraries* 35, no. 4: 1–2.

Varnum, Ken. 2015. "Editorial Board Thoughts: Library Analytics and Patron Privacy." *Information Technology and Libraries* 34, no. 4: 2–4.

Virginia Administrative Code. n.d. 8VAC20-131-190. Library Media, Materials and Equipment. http://law.lis.virginia.gov/admincode/title8/agency20/chapter131/section190/.

Chapter 15

ETHICS IN THE WORKPLACE

[Today's] realities create a setting that is ripe with temptations that can obfuscate and darken pathways for consistent ethical action. Such inconsistency has a corrosive effect on public trust and public confidence.

Brian N. Williams, 2015

Everyday ethics is about guiding the decisions and actions at your library according to principles that ensure that everyone is treated fairly, that governing the library does not happen in secret, that library users have access to all types of information, and that confidentiality is respected.

Pat Wagner, 2013

Ethical interventions have, for the most part, failed, and will continue to fail because they fail to recognize the *moral hypocrisy* that occurs when individuals' evaluations of their own moral transgressions differ substantially from their evaluations of the same transgression committed by others.

Michael Macaulay and Surendra Arjoon, 2013

Moral good is a practical stimulus; it is no sooner seen than it inspires an impulse to practice.

Plutarch, 46–120 CE

We concluded a previous chapter with the statement that many of the issues we covered are broader than politics. Ethics in the workplace create some of the same issues as office politics in the sense of personal versus organizational values and expectations. Brian Williams's opening quotation for this chapter highlights why ethics are critical for public, as well as nonprofit, organizations—trust.

Trust is a word that appears often in this text because any public or nonprofit sector organization not thought of trustworthy has little chance of long-term success. Ethical actions and behaviors are key components in creating, building, and maintaining trust. Ensuring that operations are ethical is a responsibility of a managerial leader and is rather complex to carry out.

The complexity arises, in part, as a result of several sets of beliefs, values, and expectations that the organization and the employee hold, as well as society. For example, from a library perspective and looking at library functions, there can be differing views about what constitutes equitable procedures, equitable access, quality equitability, and equitable outcomes. A key point to keep in mind is "equitable" is not identical in meaning with "equal." The American Library Association's (ALA's) Code of Ethics (http://www.ala.org/advocacy/proethics/codeofethics /codeethics) only uses "equitable."

While equitable and equal are related, and in some peoples' minds identical, no library, or many other public agencies, perform all their functions at equal levels; they simply do not have the resources to do so. The dictionary definition of *equitable* reads: "characterized by equity: fair to all concerned: without prejudice, favor, rigor entailing under hardship" (*Webster's*, 1966, 769). You can see how that definition applies, or should, to any public or nonprofit sector organization. You can also see how it is possible for an individual employee to have some difficulty in reconciling her or his personal views with the need to be equitable. Your job as a managerial leader is to make such situations less difficult while ensuring the service receives equitable treatment. In this chapter, we focus on the managerial leadership issues for creating and maintaining ethical operations.

CHECK THIS OUT

For an in-depth discussion of specific programmatic and service ethical issues see chapter 14, "Ethical Aspects," in *Library Programs and Services: The Fundamentals*, 8th edition, by G. Edward Evans, Margaret Zarnosky Saponaro, Holland Christie, and Carol Sinwell (Santa Barbara, CA: Libraries Unlimited, 2015).

MORE NUANCED THAN YOU MIGHT THINK

The starting point for creating a workplace environment in which ethical behaviors are so much the norm is by understanding just how varied your challenges may be. We touched on the complexities in the above section—values. The fact of the matter is values are just a small component of why achieving ethical work habits is not easy. Let's assume you have a library staff of 50 people. The odds are very high you will have staff divided into at least three political party points of view (Democrat, Independent, and Republican—there could even be several more), who hold differing values, beliefs, biases, positions, and so on, about social issues that rarely are congruent. The Independents are rather unpredictable as to what their position may be on a specific issue.

With the above staff of 50, chances are there will also be several religious faiths represented, including atheism. In today's diverse library workplace you are likely to have the major U.S. groups present—Catholic, Protestant, and Jewish—with some of their subdivisions for good measure. Those broad groupings are just the tip of the iceberg when it comes to the varying values and beliefs of religious groups. You most likely have seen news reports of someone in public employment challenging the obligation to perform a task on religious freedom grounds. Such events are rather rare but they do suggest there may be biased behavior taking place more often than we recognize.

Beyond the political parties and religious faiths, the staff also are likely to have grown up in different parts of the country, with at least a few distinctive values and biases. The educational level as well as place of education will be a variable. The librarians are likely to have degrees from several different schools with varying areas of emphasis on professional ethics. Some support staff may have some course work, paraprofessional library functions, degrees, or even a certificate. That in turn will have an effect on their awareness of desirable library ethical actions.

Needless to say, cultural heritage differences are probable in today's diverse library workforce. In the past, there was the notion that the United States was, and should be, the world's great melting pot, absorbing people with varying cultural backgrounds and molding them into "Americans." Clearly that did not actually happen and evidence of former cultural values, beliefs, and morals remain. Today we make efforts to celebrate the heritages and their differing contributions to our society. The strengthening and valuing of differences can add to a public sector managerial leader's challenges to create and maintain an ethical workplace.

PERSONAL VALUE SYSTEM

Our initial values and beliefs form as we interact with our parents, relatives, and care givers as small children—a small universe of values to draw upon but very powerful in terms of influence. With exposure to a wider world of values, as a result of education and associated interactions, we begin to see that what we thought of as fixed values are really less fixed and highly variable. In the process of encountering differing beliefs, we begin to formulate a personal moral code. That process is rarely something we do while seated quietly, pondering our value system, much less while making decisions about what we should believe; rather it is an ongoing subconscious process about which we rarely think. Over the years, our personal set of values may bear little resemblance to our initial version. However, some of those early values are still there in the subconscious and can come to the fore unexpectedly.

It is unlikely that many applicants for a public sector job give much, if any, thought to possible ethical or moral decision conflicts that might arise because personal values conflict with a public sector organization's obligation to be equitable and ethical in its actions. There are a number of newspaper articles available about public sector employees refusing to act in a legal, ethical manner. (A recent widely reported example was regarding the legalization of gay marriage and a public official who refused to issue marriage licenses to same-sex couples on the grounds it violated the employee's religious beliefs.) What we don't read about are the probably hundreds of daily occurrences when people act in compliance with workplace ethical guidelines that run counter to their personal belief systems. Over time, those "small" actions can begin to generate stress, tension, and performance issues and the person may not be able to identify the stress source.

ETHICAL CONCEPTS

Ethical issues arise from having to make decisions and choices about what course to follow. Most work decisions come with at least two choices—act or not act. Generally, not acting is a poor choice. The more common situation is there will be a number of options, each with some difference in outcomes, costs, and/or effectiveness, and ethical implications on occasion. How to choose the option to implement—make the "right" choice—is not always the most ethical or straight-forward. For example, you have an obligation to the funding authorities to operate your library as cost effectively as possible—a moral obligation. Selecting the option that best achieves that outcome may restrict access for some of the user population. You also have an obligation to that group. There are some methods that will assist you in making the choice—that's the good news. The bad news is they will not make the choice; you have to do that and live with the outcome.

There are several schools of thought that can be helpful in selecting the option to implement and taking ethics into consideration. Some are philosophical theories, making their direct application to organizational decision making less easy. There are theological moral and ethical codes that may apply, at least in part, to public sector decision making (do unto others as you would have done to you, is one example). Other approaches use applied ethics such as bioethics and business ethics. Table 15.1 provides a very simplified overview of some of the most widely employed approaches when seeking guidance on organizational ethical actions.

There are challenges for any of the above approaches as Table 15.2 suggests.

In today's busy world, at least at work, you don't have much spare time, much less spare time that can be specifically devoted to pondering philosophical approaches to ethics and their application. We offer some questions that may help speed your ethical decision making activities. The obvious first question should be is there an ethical concern? When there is a concern, thinking about the following questions can assist in sorting through what your options and alternative actions are for addressing the concern:

- Does the outcome conform to professional codes, standards, or guidelines?
- Does the outcome provide a social benefit?
- Does the outcome provide assistance for those in need?
- Does the outcome provide assistance for those who might be able to achieve the outcome independently?
- Does the outcome harm any person or any group?
- Does the outcome provide benefit for the decision maker?
- Does the outcome violate any laws, rules, or regulations?
- Does the outcome conform to current standards of fairness?

- Does the outcome restrict a person's or group's moral rights or freedom unnecessarily?
- Does the outcome have the potential for being misinterpreted or viewed as a deception?
- Does the outcome degrade social responsibility?
- Does the outcome provide equity for all concerned?

Table 15.1.

Common Organization Approaches to Ethical Decision Making

Method	Major Focus
Common Good	Balancing individual and common goods (Aristotle, Jean-Jacques Rousseau)
Contextualism	Making choices dependent upon situation (Michael Williams, Keith De Rosa, and David Lewis)
Cost-Benefit	Making choices that generate the lowest cost and greatest benefit
Kantian	Treating people as the ends not the means (Kant's non-consequential theory, also known as Deontology)
Moral Obligation	Basing choices on the public good (social contract)
Moral Rights	Making choices that respect everyone's rights (20th century, John Dewey, Roscoe Pound, Louis Brandies)
Theological	Making choices that follow doctrine
Universalism	Choices reflect universal principles of right actions (the Golden Rule, for example)
Utilitarian	Basing choices on the greatest good for the greatest number (Jeremy Bentham, John Stuart Mills, and Henry Sidgwick)

Table 15.2.

Interpretation Challenges

Concept	Challenges
Common Good	How does one define "common" and "good," and who defines each?
Contextualism	An attitude of "it depends" can lead to at least the appearance of inconsistency and loss of stakeholder trust.
Cost-Benefit	Can/should dollars always be the basis of ethical decisions?
Kantian	In the case of public sector decisions/actions, people are always a means as well as the ends.
Moral Obligation	Are there differing "moral obligations" to different groups that create dissonance for the decision maker as to what to prioritize?
Moral Rights	Are all moral rights of equal weight and do those rights differ from group to group?
Theological	Can a public sector organization rightfully employ any religious doctrine in a pluralistic religious society?
Universalism	Who identifies the universal rules of ethical behavior and can more than a very few truly be universal?
Utilitarian	How can the greatest good for the greatest number be fair to all in a pluralistic society?

As we noted above, most decisions have several potential actions. It is probably obvious that different alternatives will have different answers to ethical questions (such as the above). Again, the answers will not make the decision, but they will help in making the final choice.

Perhaps Michael Harmon (1990) best summed up the challenges in making ethical choices when he wrote, "The public sector environment is pressure packed and ripe with conflicting, competing, and countervailing values, expectations and responsibilities coupled with the ever-present, politically inspired cry 'to do more with less'" (584). In today's partisan political world, probably any of the ethical options will make someone or some group unhappy. The bottom line is, make the best ethical choice, given what you know, and then live with the outcome.

CHECK THIS OUT

John M. Budd's chapter, "What's the Right Thing to Do?," offers some sound insights into ethical philosophy and library ethics in his book *Self-Examination: The Present and Future of Librarianship* (Westport, CT: Libraries Unlimited, 2008), 111–146.

PROFESSIONAL ETHICS CODES

Most professions have a code of ethics in one of two broad categories: enforced and unenforced. We believe most codes are of the unenforced variety, like those you encounter in librarianship. Thus, they are guidelines rather than injunctions regarding the rights or wrongs of an action or decision. Why do those codes lack an enforcement provision? The primary reason is the groups and associations that formulate such codes involve voluntary membership, unlike associations where if you practice the profession you must become a member of the association and thus everyone in the profession is bound to follow the code. If you would like to review ALA's statement on why there is no enforcement of its ethics code, visit http://www.ala.org/advocacy/proethics/explanatory/enforcementfaq.

While there is certainly an expectation that public and nonprofit sector organizations will act ethically, in many cases there is no clear statement that they must do so. In point of fact, an organization cannot be either ethical or unethical; only the people within that organization determine whether the organization does or does not act ethically. Thomas R. Wotruba, Lawrence B. Chonko, and Terry W. Loe noted that "the ethical climate of an organization is a composite of formal and informal policies of that organization as well as the individual ethical values of its managers. In this context, an ethics code as a formal policy would be one building block of the organization's ethical climate, representing a statement of corporate ethical values" (2001, 60). Thus, there is room for personal values and beliefs to come into play, especially in a field where there is no enforcement of a code of ethics.

Given there is no enforcement behind library association codes of ethics, there is room for individuals to exercise personal values and beliefs without fear of formal sanctions. Looking at ALA's Code of Ethics (which takes a very broad-brush approach to ethics, in part a function of needing to accommodate a diversity of perspectives) you see there is ample room to mold your actions in a variety of ways. The first point of ALA's code employs the word "equitable" in reference to services and access issues. "Equitable" can be very much a matter of personal interpretation. Point two addresses intellectual freedom, and again there are several versions of what that means (this is reflected in the many court cases that litigate what that word does or does not mean). You get some guidance in Statement III regarding privacy and confidentiality. However, in both of those areas there are laws that come into play when it comes to actions or decisions that make the issue less about choice. In Statement IV the old issues of copyright and intellectual property are mentioned. Each of the code's points is one sentence in length, which also gives rise to variations in interpretation.

There is a complicating factor in terms of library ethical decision making and actions and looking to ALA for guidance. That is, there are a variety of guidelines, resolutions, position papers, and the like, on almost all the issues covered by the Code of Ethics. What follows is a sampling of such documents.

Library Bill of Rights

(http://www.ala.org/advocacy/intfreedom/librarybill)

Freedom to Read

(http://www.ala.org/advocacy/intfreedom/statementspols/freedomreadstatement)

Freedom to View

(www.ala.org/advocacy/intfreedom/statementspols/freedomviewstatement)

Developing a Confidentiality Policy

(http://www.ala.org/bbooks/challengedmaterials/preparation/developing
-confidentiality-policy)

Intellectual Freedom Principles for Academic Libraries

(http://www.ala.org/advocacy/intfreedom/librarybill/interpretations/intellectual)

ALA and Filtering

(http://www.ala.org/Template.cfm?Section=litoolkit&Template=/ContentManagement
/ContentDisplay.cfm&ContentID=50652)

CHECK THESE OUT

One good book that explores library ethics in great detail is Jean L. Preer's *Library Ethics* (Westport, CT: Libraries Unlimited, 2008).

Two other solid texts are Robert Hauptman's *Ethics and Librarianship* (Jefferson, NC: McFarland, 2002) and Amy L. Besnoy's *Ethics and Integrity in Libraries* (New York: Routledge, 2009).

Two older, but thought-provoking, items are Douglas J. Foskett's *The Creed of a Librarian: No Politics, No Religion, No Morals*, Library Association Occasional Papers no. 3 (London: Library Association, 1962) and David McMenemy's 2007 "Librarians and Ethical Neutrality: Revisiting *The Creed of a Librarian*" (*Library Review* 56, no. 3: 177–181).

There are times when it seems that public sector employees face two masters—their profession and the public. You might think there can't be such a problem for libraries—clearly the public is the only master. Richard Kravitz noted, "When the demands of the profession's two matters conflict, whom are we to serve?" (2016, 80). For libraries, there are indeed two masters: the profession and the service community. Take a minute to ponder the question of how much of a role community standards play in a library's efforts to provide equitable programs and services. Is it right or ethical to exclude items, access to services, and so on, based on what the community values? Perhaps the most widely known instance within the profession is reflected in Marjorie Fisk Lowenthal's study, *Book Selection and Censorship* (1959). This study covered California public libraries during the Joseph McCarthy era amid concerns about the spread of communism. Although the McCarthy era has passed, there are still a variety of social issues today that can come into play when community standards are the yardstick for determining library activities.

ADVISORY BOARD EXPERIENCE

As we have mentioned several times the ALA's Code of Ethics is very general. The following highlights the fact that as you move from one type of library environment to another you may need to adjust your thinking about workplace ethics. Sachi Yagyu noted the following regarding her shift from an academic library to a corporate library environment: "The move required a recalibrating of some ethical considerations. One of those modifications related to the notion of user confidentiality. The new environment called for sharing who had what material. The reason relates to the fact that only employees may check items out of the library and that there is a heavy emphasis on report writing and speed is a critical factor in organizational success. Thus, you need to share some user information with colleagues, unlike in a university setting."

WORKPLACE ETHICS AND VALUES

What are some of the areas where library staff members' personal values and beliefs create stress when having to act in accordance with professional library codes of ethics? A longstanding library function where personal values, beliefs, preferences, and so on, come into play and are likely, on occasion, to be deemed unethical is collections development. In 2009 Debra L. Whelan published the article "A Dirty Little Secret: Self-Censorship Is Rampant and Lethal," looking at how collection development staff engaged in censorship, albeit often unintentional. A frequently employed exam question in collection development courses is to discuss the difference between selection and censorship. It is easy to rationalize the decision not to add something to the collection—lack of money is always an answer that has some truth to it. A tougher question to answer is, "Are you *really sure* it is not, in part, you imposing your value system on the decision process?"

Another library function where it is difficult to assess ethical behavior is the reference assistance process. Librarians are, more often than not, viewed by the public as experts in finding information. As a result, users generally have a high

---

AUTHOR EXPERIENCE

Some years ago Evans conducted a small research project to explore the question of how balanced academic library collections are (differing points of view on controversial issues present in the collection). A sample of 200 titles dealing with controversial topics with different perspectives was checked against the holdings of six colleges (public and private or religiously affiliated institutions). All of the sample titles had at least two positive published reviews. One interesting finding was no library held more than 72 percent of the titles.

The primary focus of the research was to explore why titles were missing. The individuals responsible for collection decisions were interviewed to assess the reasons for the absences. Not surprisingly "not enough funds" was the most frequent reason given. The second most common response was "there was a better title available." "No one asked for it" was another frequent answer. What may surprise you was the occasional "I don't think that author is a writer" and its opposite sentiment "the author really does understand the issues." You could think those who made statements such as the latter were ethical, by their standards, if perhaps less so in terms of professional ethics.

We suggest that as a managerial leader you occasionally undertake something like the above to check on the equity level in terms of differing perspectives on controversial topics in your library's collection.

---

level of trust that the information identified by the librarian is accurate, complete, and unbiased—although it is unlikely users think in those exact terms. Rather, users count on the authority of the librarian and trust what they are given. This also means that it is possible, on occasion, that personal values may unintentionally come into play and color the results. This situation could be viewed as unethical. Certainly there is ample opportunity for intentional efforts to skew the search results. In either case, it is almost impossible for you to identify such outcomes when they are rare events.

A slightly different but related possibility is with filtering Internet access. Libraries, in order to get a low-cost Internet connection (e-rate), are required to filter public access computers in a way that limits search results. School libraries must use filtering software in order to get the rate and because it is the purpose of the law to protect children from inappropriate material on the Internet. Additionally, public libraries qualify for the e-rate if they also employ filtering software; however, there is a provision that allows an adult user to request unfiltered Internet access. In this case the user asks the library to turn off the software and allow access and the library turns it back on when the person finishes her or his searching. One question is, how ethical is it for a public library that does filter to not prominently post signage indicating adults may request unfiltered access?

The above is a small sampling of potential areas of conflict for employees between their belief systems and the requirements of ethical public service. Part of your responsibility as a managerial leader is maintaining an effective workforce. One component of that maintenance is to keep the work environment as stress free as possible. One source of public sector workplace stress is the need to disassociate personal values and beliefs from work performance. That is often not a problem but can be on occasion, as we illustrated above.

A first and critical step to building an ethical environment is modeling ethical behavior. Your actions do play a role in how staff understands the organizational culture (OC) and performance expectations. Just as senior management sets the tone in terms of office politics, it does the same in setting the ethical tone. One way to gain staff trust and model ethical behavior is to never speak poorly about one staff member to another staff member. While it may feel necessary at times to vent, avoid doing so. The manager-leader who feels compelled to gossip infects the entire organizational environment and creates an atmosphere where trust and honesty are lacking.

Dave Anderson offered some suggestions for modeling ethical behavior. The first point is an obvious one—consider the outcome(s) of your actions. His second point also seems obvious and easy to do—"tell the truth at all costs (literally!)." That is not always so easy, for his article is about "little white lies." He suggested that there are four words at the start of a sentence that may suggest you are not being fully honest and/or ethical—"Just tell them that . . ." Most of us have said something like this more than once and in doing so we are pulling someone else into the mix; essentially we are asking another person to pass on a message that is at best mixed rather than the full truth. As he stated, "White lies are like the gateway drug to bigger offenses. Get away with them and you're tempted to tell ever bigger ones" (2011, 22).

Bennett Tepper noted, "A compelling body of empirical research evidence suggests that it is disturbingly easy for authority figures to put their direct reports in positions where unethical choices are preferred over ethical choices" (2010, 592). Some of the empirical studies that support Tepper's point are Stanley Milgram's *Obedience to Authority: An Experimental View* (New York: Harper & Row, 1974); Thomas Blass' *Obedience to Authority: Current Perspectives on the Milgram Paradigm* (Mahwah, NJ: Lawrence Erlbaum Associates, 2000); and Kerry Patterson, Joseph Grenny, David Maxfield, Ron McMillan, and Al Switzler's *Influencer: The Power to Change Anything* (New York: McGraw-Hill, 2008). As was noted in *The Economist* in reference to being asked to do something you think unethical by your boss, "Standing up for yourself can be bad for your career" (2016, 70).

Beyond setting the tone you might consider taking time to think about what you have observed about staff member performance in terms of potential ethical stress points. Over time and shared work experiences, staff members, at all levels, have some sense of one another as individuals. Thus, some thought about potential stress points may help you think of ways to help reduce them should they arise. One method that allows you to indirectly address possible stress points is during staff development activities. Many libraries have an annual training day when a session on ethics could be offered. During this session, staff could have the opportunity to discuss this or that library ethical concern. Perhaps divide the staff into small groups to discuss the same case or ethical conundrum and then bring the groups back together to review ideas and issues that were raised. There are a variety of resources that offer either such situations or ideas for creating one of your own. Certainly the books on library ethics, cited above, provide many ideas for a case.

One article that provides eight ready-made situations is Helen R. Adams's 2009 "Reflection on Ethics in Practice" (*Knowledge Quest* 37, no. 3: 66–69). Another way to create an ethical work atmosphere is to periodically review ALA's Code of Ethics and/or some of its guidelines, position papers, and the like that have ethical implications at a staff development program.

In addition to full-day staff trainings, it is also important that a discussion of likely ethical scenarios and possible responses be part of every employee orientation. Many library staff are not professional librarians and may never have seen the ALA's Code of Ethics. Even if the presentation lasts less than 15 minutes that point will be made. Showing them that a code exists and having them read it will, at the very least, provide a foundation for future discussion should they ever be faced with an ethical conflict at work. You should also review your state's statutes regarding libraries and have staff become familiar with these as well.

AUTHOR EXPERIENCE

One librarian we know worked at a library that had the uncomfortable experience of having law enforcement show up asking for a specific user's library records. The staff member who dealt with the police officer didn't know that it went against state statute to divulge records without a court order—a warrant—and simply thought she was doing her civic duty. This episode was used as an opportunity for staff training later.

Beyond being an ethical role model and having discussions of ethics at staff development programs and during orientation, what can you do to create and maintain an ethical library? Earlier in the chapter we suggested it is unlikely many applicants for public sector positions give much, if any, thought to potential ethical challenges or even the need to set aside their values while performing the job they are seeking. We suggest it may be useful to bring up the topic during interviews with applicants. Doing so probably will result in a comment such as "Oh, no problem for me." Given they are hoping to get the position, no other response is likely. What it will do is at some level inform the successful candidate that ethics is important. In essence, it highlights from day one that there is an expectation that personal views will not color work performance.

You can further highlight its importance by occasionally bring it up in staff meetings, especially when there is a recent news article about ethical challenges in the professional literature. Another option is to distribute the "Code" to staff once a year, rather like the conflict of interest forms that are required for board members.

Exit interviews can also help identify possible ethical stress points, assuming you get the topic into the interview schedule. Often such interviews are performed by the Human Resources department, in part to gain clues about operational issues that trigger resignations. One way to handle this, in an environment where ethical actions are a solid component of the organizational culture, is to have the departing employee's supervisor chat with the person about their experiences in reference to ethics.

Professional ethical codes must be broad in scope and with little detail, such as the ALA Code of Ethics. Given the generalities in the code, many people have difficulty translating it into something that applies to what they do at work. One approach to addressing this is to have the staff develop a local code of ethics. This will not only make it more relevant to their personal work, it will also create a sense of buy-in from staff. We suggest getting some members of the library's board involved in the process as well. If nothing more, doing this will suggest to the staff that the issues do have importance. An easy way to get the process started is to use the ALA's code as the skeleton for the local code.

Keep in mind the Statement V of the code is about ethical treatment of staff. You may expect this to raise some sticky points, perhaps along the lines of librarian/support staff relations. It may also bring up the ethics of accepting meals or other gifts from vendors. Some people believe even accepting a small holiday box of candy for the staff from a vendor is unethical. We think the degree of influence exerted by a meal or box of candy on library decision making is small but worth thinking about. It might be the small "gift" is that gateway event to ever bigger transgressions (like little white lies). Perhaps this is a matter for the library board to resolve.

If you do develop a local code, hanging it on the staff room wall will serve as a reminder that the library does care and value ethical service and treatment of people. A local code will carry far more weight than would posting the ALA Code of Ethics on the wall as it is a product of the people who work there and is indicative of the organizational culture. Further, the process of developing the code will stimulate staff into thinking about the issues and embed the code into the organizational culture.

A quotation from Renée Jefferson and Sylvia Contreras sums up the ethical challenges that exist for library staff, especially for librarians:

> It is evident that the professional ethics and principles of an organization may often conflict with societal and personal ethics. In fact, professional ethics and principles often have internal conflicts. These conflicts are interwoven into the professional responsibilities of information science professionals. (2005, 66)

CHECK THIS OUT

A very detailed book on ethics in the public sector is Carol W. Lewis and Stuart C. Gilman's *The Ethics Challenge in Public Service: A Problem-Solution Guide*, 3rd edition (San Francisco, CA: Jossey-Bass, 2012).

REFERENCES

Anderson, Dave. 2011. "Leadership and Little White Lies." *Public Management* 93, no. 10: 22.

The Economist Staff. 2016. "Cross the Boss: Religion, Ethics and the Workplace." *The Economist* 418, no. 8981: 70.

Foskett, Douglas J. 1962. *The Creed of a Librarian: No Politics, No Religion, No Morals.* Library Association Occasional Papers No. 3. London: Library Association.

Harmon, Michael M. 1990. "The Responsible Actor as 'Tortured Soul': The Case of Horatio Hornblower." In *Images and Identities in Public Administration*. Edited by Henry D. Kass and Bayard L. Catron, 151–180. Newbury Park, CA: Sage Publications.

Jefferson, Renée N., and Sylvia Contreras. 2005. "Ethical Perspectives of Library and Information Science Graduate Students in the United States." *New Library World* 106, nos. 1/2: 58–66.

Kravitz, Richard H. 2016. "Serving Two Masters: A Challenge for the Profession and Planners." *The CPA Journal* 86, no. 9: 80.

Lowenthal, Marjorie Fiske. 1959. *Book Selection and Censorship: A Study of School and Public Libraries in California*. Berkeley: University of California Press.

Macaulay, Michael, and Surendra Arjoon. 2013. "An Aristotelian-Thomistic Approach to Professional Ethics." *Journal of Markets and Morality* 16, no. 2: 507–527.

McMenemy, David. 2007. "Librarians and Ethical Neutrality: Revisiting *The Creed of a Librarian*." *Library Review* 56, no. 3: 177–181.

Perry, James L., and Robert K. Christensen, eds. 2015. *Handbook of Public Administration*. 3rd edition. San Francisco, CA: Jossey-Bass.

Plutarch. n.d. "Plutarch Quotes—page 3." AZ Quotes. ww.azquotes.com/author/11735 -Plutarch?p=3.

Preer, Jean L. 2008. *Library Ethics*. Westport, CT: Libraries Unlimited.

Tepper, Bennett J. 2010. "When Managers Pressure Employees to Behave Badly: Toward a Comprehensive Response." *Business Horizons* 53, no. 6: 591–598.

Wagner, Pat. 2013. "Everyday library Ethics." Siera: www.sieralearn.com/everyday -library-ethics-series/.

Webster's Third New International Dictionary of the English Language: Unabridged. 1966. Springfield, MA: Merriam-Webster.

Whelan, Debra Lau. 2009. "A Dirty Little Secret: Self-Censorship Is Rampant and Lethal." *School Library Journal* 55, no. 2: 26–30.

Williams, Brian N. 2015. "Embracing Ethical Principles for Public Action." In *Handbook of Public Administration*. 3rd edition. Edited by James L. Perry and Robert K. Christensen. New York: Wiley.

Wotruba, Thomas R., Lawrence B. Chonko, and Terry W. Loe. 2001. "The Impact of Ethics Code Familiarity on Manager Behavior." *Journal of Business Ethics* 33, no.1: 59–69.

Chapter 16

UNDERSTANDING
ONESELF AND OTHERS

Good words are worth much and cost little.

George Herbert, 1651

When people talk about corporate culture, they're typically referring to *cognitive* culture. . . The other critical part is what we call the group's *emotional* culture: the shared *affective* values, norms, artifacts, and assumptions that govern which emotions people have and expressed at work and which ones they are better off suppressing.

Sigal Barsade and Olivia A. O'Neill, 2016

Gifted bosses don't just hire employees, they acquire allies. Great employees don't have jobs, they have talents.

Dale Dauten, 2011

The best known proponent of a new-model, meritocratic civil service was Max Weber.

The Economist, 2016

We concluded chapter 9 (Fiscal Matters) saying, "From a library's point of view, we believe money is the second most important thing. In first place, by a considerable distance, is a staff of collaborative people who are committed to providing the best possible service using the available resources." Having such a staff is not a given; you must put forth a serious effort in order to achieve that outcome. All good managerial leaders understand and implement the ideas expressed in our opening quotations.

Dale Dauten's comment quoted above about great leader-managers is very sound in terms of staffing. He makes it clear there is interdependence between you and your staff. The stronger that interdependence is the more likely everyone, including the library and its users, will benefit. In our view, in order to create the type of work environment described in the first paragraph, above, you must start by an understanding of yourself.

Thinking you know yourself and understanding yourself are rather different. We all think we know ourselves; however, how others see us can be very different. In chapter 2 (Leadership), there is an extended discussion about assessing yourself in terms of your interest in becoming a leader. Those "assessment tools" are also part of coming to grips with self-understanding. Especially useful is the comparison between your abilities and how others, such as colleagues, view your capabilities. Another good self-assessment method is using some of the personality-workplace tests, such as Meyer-Briggs (http://www.personalitypathways.com/type_inventory .html) or 16 Personalities (https://www.16personalities.com/free-personality-test).

Another part of self-assessment is to ponder how you prefer to work. When you become a manager you must shift your thinking about working relationships. As an operational staff member, you had a superior, as well as work colleagues, to consider. As manager you've added a third relationship—subordinates. All of these relationships are important to your long-term career success, and how you worked in the past probably will not be effective in at least some managerial situations. Former work colleagues may be left behind, either because you left your old library or because your new role requires it. Some colleagues may even have become your subordinates—this can be a major challenge. You will also find you have fewer colleagues at your new level; there are simply not that many managers in libraries and those that do exist all have different areas of responsibility, making for less commonality beyond that of being managerial leaders.

One of your most important new relationships to develop is with your supervisor. Although you had a supervisor in your former position, the relationship is much different as a manager. We mentioned some of the most common challenges facing managerial leaders in chapter 2. You and your supervisor must work together if the library is to be effective and succeed. We recommend having a meeting with that person as soon as possible after starting in your new role. This also applies when that person moves on and is replaced by a new supervisor.

The purpose of the meeting is to start establishing a sound working relationship. Each of us has a preferred style of working. Getting a grasp of one another's preferred style is a major first step in developing a good relationship. Part of our style is based on our goals and expectations regarding the work. Don't be surprised if these turn out to be slightly different between yourself and your supervisor. Another part of our style relates to communication, how much (full details or just the major points) and how often should routine communication take place, and what is the preferred mode of communication (in person, email, telephone, written memo, etc.). Yet another important topic is the normal expected response time to a question raised in a message. Perhaps a key issue relates to your and your supervisor's approach to managing—from micromanagement to "big picture." Certainly a single meeting will not resolve everything; only time will make clear what needs improvement. These are issues you should also clarify with your staff—what do you want to know, when, and how, and so on.

Here are some tips for building and maintaining a good working relationship with your superior.

- *Never* blindside the person
- Under promise and over deliver
- Be proactive rather than reactive to situations
- Provide some recommendations for problem situations
- *Never* mislead the person about the magnitude of a situation, if anything over-emphasis is better than understating the issue
- Stay within your budget
- If you see a problem, don't just inform your supervisor, have a ready solution
- Be loyal
- Never lie
- Your supervisor is your boss, not your friend
- Always provide information; never hide information
- Don't denigrate your supervisor to others
- Never have an affair or be romantically involved with one of your reports

It is equally important that you share your preferred work modes with those who report to you as well as with managerial colleagues. Preferences such as whether you have an open-door policy or you'd rather have scheduled discussion times are important matters to discuss. How do you handle emails and voice mails (deal with them as they arrive or check on them once or twice a day) are also things to consider. Do you prefer handling most issues through discussions or memos? Many of the issues you worked out with your supervisor are just as important to work out with your staff.

EMOTIONAL INTELLIGENCE

People who have a high Emotional Quotient (EQ) have the ability to recognize their emotions, what effect emotions can have on their own performance, and the impact emotions may have on those they supervise. Debate has centered on whether EQ is a part of a personality that can't be changed or if, with the right kind of training, it can be developed. Research suggests that EQ, or emotional intelligence, can be split into three categories:

- Enablers (sensitivity, influences, and self-awareness)
- Drivers (motivation and decisiveness)
- Constrainers (emotional resilience, conscientiousness, and integrity)

It is argued that the drivers and constrainers form enduring elements of an individual's personality and are therefore more difficult to change. However, the enablers can be developed—for example, self-awareness can emerge through interpersonal skills training. The drivers and constrainers are best handled with coping strategies; for example, those with low emotional resilience should avoid highly stressful situations (Dulewicz and Higgs, 1999).

Creating self-awareness is the first step. Reading can help, and receiving coaching or participating in a training program will help you develop recognition of personal strengths and how they contribute to a high EQ. It is notable that men and women have been found to have significantly different profiles when tested for EQ. Women generally have much stronger interpersonal skills than their male colleagues, while males demonstrate a significantly higher sense of self and independence.

CHECK THIS OUT

An excellent book covering libraries and emotional intelligence in some detail is Peter Hernon, Joan Giesecke, and Camila A. Alire's *Academic Librarians as Emotionally Intelligent Leaders* (Westport, CT: Libraries Unlimited, 2007). Although the title indicates the focus is on the academic library environment, the content on emotional intelligence and library leaders applies to any library environment.

An interesting journal article is Daniel Goleman and Richard Boyatzis's 2008 "Social Intelligence and the Biology of Leadership" (*Harvard Business Review* 86, no. 9: 74–81). A fairly recent (2016) journal article on the subject that is library oriented is Jason Martin's "Emotionally Intelligent Leadership at *30 Rock*: What Librarians Can Learn from a Case Study of Comedy Writers" (*Journal of Library Administration* 56, no. 4: 345–358).

STAFFING DIFFERENCES ACROSS SECTORS

Human resource administration is both similar and different in the three organizational sectors. All of the differences can and do affect how you perform, or should perform, your managerial duties. There are a host of federal, state, and even local employment laws and regulations that all organizations must address (from recruitment to retirement). Certainly, there are differences in how those laws and regulations are implemented in each sector. For example, public employees have a higher degree of job security than those in for-profit organizations and public sector union members have less freedom of action than do those in the for-profit sector.

The public and nonprofit workforces, combined, represent about one-third of the total U.S. workforce (Maciag, 2011).. One result of that relatively small percentage is that less workforce research occurs in those two sectors. Even apparently neutral research (motivation, team building, etc.), has something of a for-profit bias. For example, in terms of motivation, for-profit managers have greater flexibility in both rewards and sanctions. The same flexibility also exists when thinking about when, how, and where to employ teams. It is important to keep the bias in mind when reading workforce literature.

There are several very basic differences between public sector hiring and the other two sectors. One such difference lies in the purpose of hiring and what is being sought. Private sector staffing focuses on an understanding of the profit motive and how that affects the organization's "bottom line." Public sector hiring seeks to hire individuals with a strong service motivation. Neither sector is always successful in achieving such goals, but they do try. Private companies expect and demand loyalty, while the public sector emphasizes ethics, integrity, and accountability.

Perhaps the most significant difference resides in the selection process. Our opening quotation from *The Economist* highlights the difference: merit. The federal personnel system is a civil service system—mandated by law. Most states also employ some form of civil service—there are many variations in the what and the how from state to state. A great many county and local governments also use such systems. A merit or civil service approach attempts to select people based on what they know rather than who they know or how much money their family does or does not have. Thus, these systems almost always start the selection process with a test of some type. In many instances, the testing carries on into the promotional system as well. *The Economist* article employed the word "meritocracy" as the broadest label for civil service systems. Beyond making the point that more and more countries are using some form of the concept, it suggested that the system reduces corruption, saves money, and even appears to promote economic growth.

The initial test is generally written, taken at a scheduled time and place with a group of individuals "sitting" for the exam. Those who pass the test are listed, or ranked, by their test score(s). They are considered "eligible" for employment. An eligible list can be in effect for some time (until a new examination takes place).

Unlike their counterparts in non–merit system organizations, public managers working in a merit system have a limited "pool" of people to review or interview. Such systems usually place a limit on how many eligible candidates a manager may interview (three to five is the most common number). It is possible to reject the first set of people, with a very solid reason, and then interview another set. However, it takes time to prove your rejections were valid and the vacancy remains an issue for the work unit. In addition, those candidates almost always have to be at the top of ranked eligibles. Thus, the top three or more people after the examination have the first opportunity for employment. As the top people are employed or are no longer interested, the list becomes shorter and shorter until it is deemed time for another examination.

You might think that such a system means the test score determines the ranking. Sometimes it does, sometimes it does not. Many systems have "preference points" that get added to the test score (two of the cost common preferences are military veterans and prior work experience in the field of the examination). Thus, it is possible for someone not having a passing test score still to be on the eligible list due to the person's preference points. Which makes it clear why achieving Dauten's ideal expressed in the quote at the beginning of the chapter is so challenging in the public sector merit system.

AUTHOR EXPERIENCE

Evans's first library job (as a part-time page in a public library) came about as the result of passing the "page exam," the physical (required in those days), and an interview with the librarian in whose library he was to work. The examination took half a day and there were several hundred test takers.

Later in his career he served on a number of library promotional interview panels. Rather like the written test, the interview was highly structured, including who would ask which questions and when to pose the question. There were *no* unscripted questions.

The entire hiring process is filled with potential legal land mines. There is a very large body of court cases that in one way or another impact the process. Often the cases grew out of requirements that were not clearly associated with successful job performance. Asking for something that may not be essential, at least at the time of hiring, can lead to legal problems. Another example that has arisen rather too often is employing imprecise statements such as, "the successful applicant will have a lively personality." We don't know which would be more difficult to prove: (a) that a lively personality was essential for successful job performance, or (b) what factors are present in a "lively" personality. A better way of getting at what the writers of such statements were looking for would be to seek individuals with a "demonstrated ability to work effectively with customers and staff in a highly service-oriented environment." Although more "wordy," it is much clearer about what the library is seeking and less open to question. Another example would be that instead of using the phrase "good speaking ability," use something like, "make oral presentations of technical material in such a manner as to be easily understood by a non-technical audience."

Before moving on to other staffing issues, there are two issues we should mention that relates to job descriptions. The first is that almost all Human Resources (HR) departments distinguish between jobs and positions. Every employee in the library has a position (full- or part-time full-time equivalents—FTEs). In all but the smallest libraries, there will be fewer jobs—from the HR point-of-view—than there are positions. A clear example is reference librarians. For HR, there is the *job* category of reference librarian and the library may have ten *positions* in that category. Within the library, at least for librarian positions, there is not too much concern regarding this distinction, for support staff it may matter a great deal.

The reason for HR's distinction is that the public sector organization will have many people in many departments performing basically the same type of work, for example clerk-typists or secretarial work. (This is particularly the case in merit systems.) One of HR's responsibilities is to achieve a high degree of comparability in compensation, benefits, and so on, for work that is equivalent or nearly so. That means that clerk-typists, across the organization, receive similar compensation when the skills, experience, and tasks are similar. Clearly, that means how you define the job can have an influence on what a person's salary and benefits will be.

You might have guessed what the second issue is—requests or even demands that "my position be reclassified." As a manager, you are likely to be the first to hear such requests. Handling the matter effectively can be a challenge. The person making the request will give a number of reasons why this should happen. HR departments are inclined to act slowly on such requests unless you have assigned additional duties. In that case, you probably should have thought about such a request before actually assigning the new duty(ies) and made a case for such an adjustment with HR. The person may not accept "no" as an answer, even when it comes from an HR officer. Threats of legal action are not unheard of and can be carried out.

Position equivalencies can come up with librarian positions as well. One example is academic—public and school district libraries have branch locations. Is the head of a branch equal to a main library department head or that of the senior library managers? You can make a case for either point of view and perhaps even that branch heads are not equal to either group.

AUTHOR EXPERIENCE

Evans still recalls the furious debate that arose when he started his professional career over job categories and compensation equivalencies. The statewide personnel system for the library where he worked issued a new set of guidelines grouping jobs into broad equal compensation groups. (This took place not long after the Equal Pay Act was passed by Congress.) Why a furor? Librarians were grouped with hog farm managers. You just never know when the job description will come to the fore.

CHECK THESE OUT

The following are just four of a great many titles that will provide more in-depth information about the hiring process:

Mary J. Stanley's *Managing Library Employees: A How-To-Do-It Manual* (New York: Neal-Schuman, 2008) is a good starting point to gain an overview of various aspects of working with library staff.

Patricia Tunstall's *Hiring, Training, and Supervising Library Shelvers* (Chicago, IL: American Library Association, 2010) although focused on shelvers, it does provide insights into the library hiring practices in general.

Geoff Smart and Randy Street's *Who: The A Method for Hiring* (New York: Ballantine Books, 2008) is a reasonably comprehensive look at hiring practices.

The United States Merit Systems Protection Board's *Prohibited Personnel Practices: A Study Retrospective: A Report to the President and Congress of the United States* (Washington, DC: U.S. Merit Systems Protection Board, 2010) is a review of hiring and other personnel practices you must avoid.

WORKPLACE BEHAVIOR, STAFFING, AND MANAGERS

Seth Silver in writing about manager-employee work relationships, suggested that between 25 percent and 40 percent of all U.S. employees are dissatisfied with their jobs and would like to leave their current employer (2008). He went on to say,

> Even our fictionalized accounts of work life, seen in such comedies as *Office Space* or *The Office,* portray life at work as frustrating, trivial, and, at times, demeaning. These depictions hit close to home, otherwise they would not be funny. . . . In other words, despite all the books, seminars, and training on how to improve the work environment, the basic problems remain—at lot of people go home at night and complain about their boss, their colleagues, and their jobs. (64)

Work and personal lives are intermingled, like it or not.

One of your major goals as a manager is to work hard to avoid having your staff become part of the group about whom Silver was writing. Undoubtedly, this is the goal of almost every manager. Unfortunately, many do not succeed. If Silver's 25 percent of unhappy workers is the case, then a goodly number of those well-intentioned managers are not coming close to achieving that goal.

Scholars working in the area of workplace psychology and motivation identify five personality characteristics of leader-managers that have a positive effect on followers' work attitudes—emotional stability, extraversion, openness, conscientiousness, and agreeableness. (For an example, see Alan Smith and Jonathan M. Conger's 2004 study "Effects of Supervisor 'Big Five' Personality on Subordinates Attitudes" [*Journal of Business and Psychology* 18, no. 4: 465–481].) This is not to say exhibiting those five characteristics will guarantee managerial success; however, they certainly will provide an important component in achieving a positive and productive work environment.

New managers, although pleased to have secured the position, are often unsure of their managerial skills and would like some assistance from senior managers during the early days on the job. Phaedra Brotherton listed six problem areas which new managers expressed concerns about senior managers' behavior (2011). What is interesting about that list is that it applies just as much to managers and their staff's common complaints about them. The items were:

1. Not listening
2. Not providing adequate transparency for decisions taken
3. Not providing adequate advance warning for changes
4. Not having realistic workloads and performance standards for staff
5. Not providing adequate motivation and incentives
6. Not providing adequate training or real growth opportunities

This is a good list of what you must work on avoiding throughout your career.

Avoiding the above issues and exhibiting the five personality traits will go a long way toward achieving long-term leadership and managerial success. However, you will have to navigate a number of rocky shoals in which the above will only be of minor assistance. One of the most dangerous and difficult shoals are the personal-professional relationships with your staff when it comes to personal life and work life.

People glibly talk about the need to separate personal or home life from workplace life. When sitting around a table drinking coffee with colleagues it is easy to make grand statements about the issue. When it comes to everyday reality, you know that isolating the two lives is almost impossible over the long term. Issues at home can and will spill over into the workplace and impact performance and vice versa. One person's problems often, directly or indirectly, affect that person's work colleagues. You are faced with the responsibility of handling the overall performance of your unit and the question of how personal to get with a staff member when trying to resolve a work performance problem. How you answer that question will be very personal and may vary from time-to-time. There will be times when some personal information comes out during a meeting that is more than you are comfortable knowing. It may be about a health concern, domestic partner issue, or economic problems, for example, and you may not be sure how to respond. A sound starting point is to seek input from your HR department about your options and dos and don'ts.

Occasionally a person suggests that managers need to know that one of their roles will involve becoming something of a psychologist. Still others say managers should not underestimate the importance of knowing who is sleeping with whom. Although they make such statements somewhat "tongue in cheek," there is a real grain of truth in these statements.

All of us respond to life's challenges in different ways that reflect our psychological makeup. What the challenge is—health, personal relationship, economic, and so on—generates some response on our part and that response will come to work with us. As long as the coping mechanism does not affect our work performance, only our closest friend(s) at work will likely to be aware there is a problem. When it does become a performance issue managers must begin to think about taking action. Sorting out lack of skill or knowledge of the tasks being performed from personal life issues takes time and sometimes a fair amount of discomfort for both parties.

The authors and advisory board members all faced one or more of the issues discussed below at some point during their careers; in the case of long careers there were several such occurrences. We agree with Reginald Bell's comment, "There is possibly no management responsibility more frustrating than having to tell a long-term employee, with whom you have a good interpersonal relationship, to 'straighten up your act'" (2010, 3). We'd go farther and say it is hard to say that to any staff member. And, it becomes even more frustrating and difficult when there are strong elements of home or personal life troubles playing a role in the poor performance.

Perhaps one of the most common personal behavioral coping mechanism that arises in the workplace is alcohol or other substance abuse. The odds are you will have this come up at least once during your career. Why is that the case? Ames and Bennett reported that 8.8 percent of all full-time employees self-reported they were "heavy drinkers" (2011). In 2009, T. L. Stanley indicated that there were more than 13 million heavy drinkers in the workforce. (A heavy drinker is defined as a person who consumes five or more drinks on one occasion on five or more days during the past 30 days.) Also, keep in mind that the data is self-reported; thus, the actual numbers are likely to be higher.

You may be surprised (or not) to realize there are legal issues that do keep popping up. It is wise to learn some legal considerations associated with handling substance abuse as well as other workplace behavior issues. When it is a matter of illegal drug abuse the matter is straightforward—it is illegal. Prescription drug abuse is more complex and is on the rise. Alcohol consumption is legal and that makes handling the matter rather difficult. Dwoskin, Squire, and Burdick noted,

> Handling problems of substance abuse and abuse at work are some of the most challenging issues confronting employers. Not only does the law impose on employers the obligation to provide a safe, healthy and productive work environment to employees, but it also requires that employers accommodate the needs of substance abusing employees, often the very same individuals who may be causing the health and safety problems. (2012, 32)

Failing to address employee workplace behavioral issues will, in a rather short time span, lead to performance and morale issues for you and the other staff members. Staff may begin to doubt your managerial leadership skills if they believe you are doing nothing about the problem. Related to behavioral issues is another challenge—confidentiality. More often than not, you may not tell others what is being done to resolve the situation—at best all you can say is "It's being worked on" and even that may not be acceptable. Staff may accuse you of keeping secrets, even when you are legally unable to disclose information. They often don't know the legal ramifications and respond negatively if they feel they're being kept out of the loop.

Unfortunately, substance abuse is not the only behavioral concern that may impact your staff. Carol Milano, in writing about unhappy homes and unhappy workplaces, reported a sad statistic, "One in five full-time workers—both male and female—has experienced domestic violence. In a major study, 20% of those victims surveyed had been abused by a domestic partner while at work" (2008, 42). We have no data to support that thought, but suspect that those numbers would be higher if one included more than domestic partners in the abuser category—such as someone who has a grudge against an employee. From a legal point of view, workplace violence goes beyond the physical aspect; it includes such behaviors as harassment, intimidation, and disruptive behavior.

Almost every library has a policy regarding user behavior. All parent organizations of libraries have an employee behavior policy. While the library staff is likely to know the key elements of the library user behavior policy, they are not as likely to know the employee behavior policy of the parent organization; that is, until a problem erupts. You should take some time to review that policy so you are better prepared to handle a problem when it does happen.

Given the broad definition of workplace violence you can probably envisage a situation in which "violence" is taking place but you are unaware it is happening. An unhappy person invading a workplace brandishing a gun and injuring or killing one or more people makes the news. Such occurrences are rare. The more typical situation is when an employee receives harassing telephone calls or emails throughout the day or a person manages to get the employee into a less public area and engages in intimidating behavior. Perpetrators employ a variety of ruses to gain workplace access, such as "I'm her husband and she forgot her lunch." An even harder form of harassment or violence to spot is when two or more employees are involved.

Earlier we mentioned that employers must provide accommodations for employees who have workplace behavioral issues. Milano noted that in terms of violence, failing to give, much less dismiss, "a victim requesting time off to obtain a protective order, or heal from injuries, may, violate the federal Family and Medical Leave Act" (2008, 44). There are a variety of other accommodations that may be required for other unacceptable behaviors under federal or state legislation.

Given the complexity of these issues you might imagine organizations, usually through their HR departments, create systems to assist in managing the inevitable mixing of personal and work life issues. The most common label you will find in the literature for such efforts is employee assistance programs (EAP). This is the program you may be referred to when you initially seek assistance in handling an employee's performance problem that goes beyond the skills and knowledge sets required to do the work. Typically, these programs offer assessment services, short-term counseling, and referral services for long-term issues. Some programs include health-related counseling, limited legal assistance for all employees, and even services to employee family members.

One can make a strong case that one of the most frustrating, emotionally charged, and disruptive workplace behaviors for the staff is the "workplace romance." Certainly some of these relationships end up in marriage. Whatever that percentage is, however, those relationships that fail are likely to cause you, as manager, frustration and substantial effort to keep the disruption to a minimum.

When the couple is young and single, staff members often think the relationship is "sweet" and hope for the best for the couple. From your point of view, the relationship is a danger to work unit performance. Two scenarios are all too real possibilities: one, the couple begins to forget their work responsibilities and focus too much on one another during work times. This is most easily addressed when both are in your work unit. When one is in another department there may be some coordination issues and potential fallout that will affect more library staff. Another possible outcome is a failed relationship. That can cause challenges that are harder to address. There is likely to be some bitterness on one or both party's part, other staff may begin to take sides about the breakup, work time will be disrupted, and productivity will fall—none of these are easy to handle or quickly correct.

The above is the least difficult "romance" to handle. The more complex relationship is when one or both of a couple is married to someone else. There is unlikely to be any on the staff who thinks such relationships are "sweet," and somehow such relationships have a way of becoming widely known very quickly. Earlier we mentioned there are times when co-workers may engage in intimidation or harass one another—this type of relationship is one in which such behavior may come up. You now have two issues to consider. Intimidation in the workplace is illegal no matter why it is taking place, and there is the added challenge of keeping staff focused on their work rather than the relationship.

"Fraternization," as HR often refers to the above, is sometimes covered by the parent organization's employment rules and regulations and thus you may have a resource to help in resolving the challenges that arise. Some organizations try to ban any such workplace relationships. These policies are easy to state but almost impossible to enforce; if the couple keeps a very low profile they may get away with the relationship. If that relationship ends in marriage and the organization does nothing about what happened, lawyers for another couple who is caught and disciplined have extra fodder for their case. A more common policy is to ban relationships within the same work unit. A few for-profit companies have a "love contract" approach whereby the two people wishing to have a relationship sign a contact stating the relationship is consensual and the company will have no legal responsibility for what does or does not happen. (We are unaware of any library parent organization that employs this approach. However, it is relatively new and may find its way into libraries. The concept is especially useful when the couple is in a workplace superior–subordinate role.)

For all of the issues discussed in this section, before you begin to address the issue with the employee, we recommend that you seek information and/or assistance from your HR department. You cannot be expected to know all the potential pitfalls that may arise in these sensitive areas. However, you can be faulted for not seeking some guidance beforehand. Also, while it is always wise to maintain a paper trail for all your managerial actions, it is imperative to do so in sensitive instances. You should document all meetings, what you said and did, and your understanding of what other participant(s) said and did.

Keep in mind the person causing the problem may not want or be willing to face the situation. Getting HR involved from the very beginning is the best insurance you have for avoiding major problems. Joan Pynes identified seven outcomes from failing to take action on any of the above:

1. Decreased morale
2. Increased stress
3. Decreased trust among coworkers
4. Decreased productivity
5. Increased turnover
6. Decreased trust in management, and
7. Increased absenteeism (2013, 31)

LABOR UNION AND COLLECTIVE BARGAINING ISSUES

Library labor unions are not all that common. According to an ALA/APA 2005 report, only 35.8 percent of 2,040 academic and public libraries responding to a survey had some or all of their staff in a union (ALA/APA Staff 2006). The percentage would probably be higher if school libraries were included in the data as most school library media specialists are certified teachers and elementary and secondary teachers are very often represented by a union.

Why do we include this topic? The reason is, if you are a manager in a union-ized library—regardless of what percentage of the staff are members—your relationship with the staff will be governed to a greater or lesser extent by a union contract. Carla McLean commented that "contrary to commonly-held conceptions, wages and benefits are *not* the primary issues brought forward in the vast majority of public employee organizing drives. Employees desiring a union instead want: (1) to gain an effective voice in the workplace, (2) to be treated with dignity and respect and be proud of their work, and (3) to create a better work environment" (2005, 11).

We can't speak to what percentage of contract negotiations focus on her three points; however, we do know that almost all contracts do contain material about working conditions beyond salary and benefits. As such, there will be contract sec-tions that impact what you can and cannot do as a supervisor. We also know there is evidence that there is a marked difference in salaries and benefits of unionized and non-union members. The *Congressional Digest* (2009) reported that the median weekly salary for union members was $886 and for non-union members it was $691. (It is important to note the foregoing figures are for all union members, not just library employees. A 2006 study of academic librarian salaries and unioniza-tion by Lee, Rogers, and Grimes suggested the difference may be substantially less within higher education.)

Perhaps the most common contract provisions, beyond salary and benefits, relate to work schedules and promotions. Your scheduling will be a tad more complex and personal preferences and special needs become harder to accommodate. Promotions, at least within the covered employee categories, may have to take place on the basis of seniority rather than merit. There is likely to be a provision that forbids merit increases for union members—finding other means to reward exceptional perfor-mance of a union member is a challenge. Needless to say, such provisions can lead to tension in the staff as well as for yourself, especially when the union exists in a right to work state. In such cases, you may have some staff, in a unionized category, who are union members and others who are not. This can cause considerable tension.

Even if you are working in a non-union library it does not mean unionization issues will not arise. They can. When a union organizing drive is underway you will face a number of challenges regarding what you can and cannot do. Even modest performance corrections, of a person who supports unionization, can get blown up into a major issue—an unfair labor practice. As a manager, you will, most likely, not be eligible for membership and will have three groups to keep in mind dur-ing the "drive"—organizers (either outsiders or library staff), library employees in general, and your employer. There are sets of operating rules for each group that are established by the National Labor Relations Board (NLRB) for the duration of the drive. Alleged violations (unfair labor practices) often lead to substantial attorney fees.

We cannot possibly address all union rules, but will touch on a few to illustrate the complexity of the process. Organizers may not engage in organizing activities on the employer's property except in "public" areas unless the employer allows it. Libraries, where most of the spaces are public, tend to find it easier to allow access throughout the building. Things become muddied when the drive is for a class of employees across the library's parent organization. In such cases, often the decision is to enforce the public area only access rule—it is easier to enforce rules the same way in all locations.

Staff members may campaign for the union doing working hours—both in public and workspaces—but only during their break and meal times. If these times were not strictly enforced prior to the drive, strict enforcement during the drive can cause an NRLB hearing and all that entails. Management can campaign against unionization and even require all employees attend a meeting at which an anti-union message is the topic. Any retaliation against pro-union staff is forbidden. The definitions of what is and is not retaliation can become a matter of "in eyes of the beholder" and becomes yet another NRLB issue to resolve.

AUTHOR EXPERIENCE AND ADVISORY BOARD EXPERIENCE

Evans was in charge of a university branch library during a unionization drive that would, if successful, unionize a variety of university employees, including all the support staff in the library system. The university held a series of mandatory managers' meetings. The library managers' meeting lasted eight hours, with presentations by the university's general legal counsel, its labor law attorney, the university president, and both the university-wide HR department head and the library's HR person. Other than a brief (20-minute) presentation on why the university opposed such a union the rest of the day covered the dos and don'ts for managers during the drive. At the end of the day each manager received a 75-page notebook that would "provide more details regarding the topics covered during the day."

Mika, as an assistant director in the library at an academic institution, was placed within the bargaining unit by the NLRB, and he eventually became the union president on his campus. His opinion is that sometimes unions are not inherently bad, and sometimes there is a good reason for staff to unionize.

As Mary Kathryn Zachary noted, "Supervisors and other managerial employees should be extremely cautious with respect to their statements and employment decisions made during employee union organizing efforts" (2007, 26).

CHECK THIS OUT

An informative set of essays about libraries and unions appears in a 2002 issue of *Public Libraries* (41, no. 3: 135–142). The essays provide both positive and negative points of view regarding labor unions and libraries.

MOTIVATING STAFF

Everyone needs motivation, both the staff and yourself. This is especially true at times of economic stress. Managers at every level must create the right environment and motivation to ensure their staff can work in an efficient and effective manner. Motivation plays a role in retaining staff. (Keep in mind, high staff turnover is often the sign of poor leadership.)

Part of being an effective leader-manager and motivating your staff is understanding what motivates you and how you operate. What drives you does not drive everyone else. However, we sometimes forget that and try imposing our views on those we work with and do so without being aware of what we are doing. Periodically thinking about our preferences in the workplace and looking at how we are interacting with our staff is a useful exercise.

You can begin to gain insight into your preferred values and temperament by taking the Keirsey Temperament Sorter (http://www.keirsey.com/sorter/register .aspx), developed by David Keirsey in 1998 to determine different types of personalities. The Keirsey test is available online, with an option for purchasing a more detailed analysis. Are you an idealist, a guardian, a rationalist, or an artisan?

Artisans are perceptive, adaptable, athletic, cheerful, realistic, impulsive, and easily bored; they seek adventure and an adrenaline buzz, love impact, have a mechanical aptitude, and pride themselves on finesse or skill. They work best in stimulating, varied environments and need the freedom to act. *Idealists* are enthusiastic, humane, subjective, imaginative, crusading, and up in the clouds; they seek identity, love integrity, pride themselves on empathy, and value friendship. They work best in expressive personal environments and need an appreciation of their uniqueness. *Guardians* are dependable, factual, thorough, routinized, and painstaking; they seek security, love obedience, pride themselves on dependability, value regulations, and insist on others following rules. They work best in organized secure environments and need responsibility and a place. *Rationals* are thinking, abstract, exacting, intellectual, logical, inventive, and terse, they appear arrogant, seek insight, love justice, pride themselves on competence, and value technology. They work best in innovative intellectual environments and need competence and success.

Keirsey applies the description of each temperament to leading, parenting, and mating, and then indicates how each temperament will probably get along with each of the others. It is an interesting test to take, and you may find the results are surprising. But remember that while personality tests are helpful, they can reflect your mood at the time you took the test. And don't cheat—be honest with yourself. A good crosscheck on the test results is to have your mentor or someone who knows you well to compare the results against their perception of your temperament.

Spend some time thinking about what you learned in Psych 101 as an undergraduate, assuming you took such a course. It you didn't, almost all introductory management textbooks have a chapter on motivation. Also, review your understanding of the theories about work motivation. Much of the literature is based on the theories derived from Elton Mayo's Hawthorne studies (1933), and the writings of Keirsey (1998), Herzberg (1959), and Skinner (1953).

Herzberg examined workplace motivation in the late 1950s and, building on Maslow's hierarchy of needs, developed a two-factor theory that distinguished between hygiene factors and motivation factors. He found that managers need to provide the hygiene factors to remove sources of dissatisfaction, but once this has been settled, staff are only motivated by motivation factors (Herzberg, 1959). The hygiene factors consist of:

- Organizational policies and procedures—the rules, privileges, and grievance procedures
- Supervision—methods to ensure that the tasks are performed well
- Salary and benefits—pension plan, health insurance, vacation time, and study leave
- Interpersonal relations—staff relationships with colleagues and bosses, and opportunities to mix at tea and coffee breaks
- Working conditions—heating, air conditioning, ventilation, lighting, cleanliness, freedom from building hazards, privacy of workstations
- Status and privileges related to the position held.

The motivation factors are:

- Achievement—a feeling of accomplishment
- Recognition of achievement by colleagues and managers
- The work itself—its degree of challenge and satisfaction
- Responsibility—for the work allocated, especially increased responsibility
- Advancement—opportunities for promotion
- Access to information—about the job and the organization—being "in the know" or "in the loop"
- Involvement—participation in decision-making

The first five of these factors are the most important. However, not everyone is motivated by the same factors, and people may be motivated by different factors at different stages in their career. For example, study or family leave time may be important at an early stage in a career, while a person close to retirement may be more interested in a salary rise to boost their pension or a reduction in working hours to avoid a sudden change in lifestyle.

Two theories help to explain why people behave the way they do—they are Expectancy Theory and Reinforcement Theory (Vroom, 1964; Skinner, 1953). Expectancy Theory indicates that managers should:

- Get to know what rewards are valued by employees, and provide them if possible
- Link the rewards to specific behavior or tasks
- Inform staff of what is expected of them, and what the outcome will be when expectations are met
- Ensure that staff are capable of performing the tasks that are required of them
- Work to increase the skills and knowledge of staff so that their competencies can be extended

In writing about motivation, Levant identified 5 key steps to ensure desired performance:

1. Define the expectations
2. Demonstrate how the job is valuable to the organization

3. Make the work assignments achievable
4. Give regular feedback
5. Reward employees when they meet expectations

When times are difficult and monetary rewards are limited, remember that, above all, people want to be recognized and valued.

Many recognition programs operate across the library's parent organization. Programs may be of the "employee of the month" type, based on overall performance, or may focus on specific areas such as diversity, cost saving suggestions, and public service. While some people crave recognition, others prefer to remain unidentified. A public award may motivate many people, but some others might find it a source of self-consciousness or embarrassment.

Motivation and Retention

Earlier we noted that staff turnover is a management issue. There are several reasons a manager should be concerned when there is rapid turnover. First, the hiring process is costly in terms of time and money. Second, the vacant position is not doing anything to help the unit's productivity. Third, the lost productivity will have some negative affect on user service, however slight. Fourth, hiring and training the new person requires some of your, or a staff member's time—more lost productivity. And finally, it can be a signal that there is something amiss with the work atmosphere. That is a negative reflection on the manager. Turnover problems can also create organizational instability. One way to prevent or minimize these problems is creating the right atmosphere. Determining what atmosphere is "right" involves studying what helps to retain staff.

Some information about the work atmosphere can come from your conducting an "exit interview" with the departing person. You are likely to receive a more honest assessment of the workplace environment now that the person is not a subordinate. Many HR departments also conduct such interviews—they are thus gaining a picture of managers' performance. You can request feedback from HR when they are learning of the problems—they may not share such information unless you request it.

Another important retention factor is trust. Managers create a good atmosphere when they demonstrate that they have trust in their staff. Building a climate of trust requires a foundation of well-developed interpersonal skills that demonstrates:

- Excellent listening skills;
- The ability to withhold judgmental comments;
- Expression of a sincere concern for individuals; and
- A display of empathy.

These factors assist in creating a bond between managers and their staff by encouraging the sharing of concerns, problems, aspirations, and information.

Building trust extends beyond the immediate work team. Trust must exist between managers and their superiors, other managers, and service staff within the organization. We concur with John Hamm's comment: "If your employees don't trust leaders, they won't feel safe. And when they don't feel safe, they don't take risks. And where there is no risk taken, there is less innovation, less 'going the extra mile,' and therefore, very little unexpected upside" (2011, 8).

Here are some tips for building a strong positive working relationship with your staff:

- Develop and maintain mutual trust; this trust must be two-way.
- Demonstrate your appreciation for what they do. It does not have to be something major; even little "victories" should be celebrated just as much as big ones.
- Give staff ample opportunities to grow and develop work skills, even those that may lead to a person leaving for a better job.
- Allow staff to experiment with new approaches and ideas without the fear that failure will be punished. Innovation thrives only in a fear-free environment.
- Talk with them, from time to time, about nonwork subjects. You can take an interest in each person without being "friends." Not showing an interest often leads staff to feel that they are just cogs in some machine and that kills motivation.
- Define individuals' roles clearly and indicate how each role is essential to everyone's success.
- Seek their input into decisions that will impact on their work. Seeking input should not imply that the final decision will necessarily reflect the input; when that is the case, take time to explain why that is so.
- Select people for their positive attitude as well as their skills and experience.

CHECK THIS OUT

An interesting article about motivation, tough economic times, and libraries is Donna Dziedzic's 2011 "Staffing in Times of Crisis" (*ILA Reporter* 29, no. 2: 4–6).

WHEN AND HOW TO DELEGATE

One way to achieve trust is to delegate tasks. On a purely practical level, managers cannot do everything themselves without having a breakdown. Delegating tasks indicates trust in and regard for the abilities of staff members. A manager checking everything the staff does is the quickest way to demoralize the group, as well as being a major drain on the manager's time and effort.

Keith Jackson, although writing about project managers, made a point that applies to any manager, "project managers simply can't be on-site 24/7. And, if proper planning doesn't take place beforehand, that time away from the project can lead to all kinds of problems—even project failure" (2012, 64). In a library setting, being away for a little time is unlikely to lead to unit failure; however, his "all kinds of problems" can indeed arise. (Note: Too much time away, especially at the most senior levels, can result in serious problems for the library and, occasionally, the person who has been absent.)

Delegation is a key component in the "proper planning" for time away. Such time away is inevitable, so planning for such times is just common sense. Two given times away are vacations and sick time. (We most strongly recommend that you take most, if not all, of your annual leave time. Not doing is likely to increase your stress levels and that is likely to affect how well you lead.) Jackson's article title, "Who's Minding the Store?" is important. If the answer is no one, serious problems are much more likely to come up in your absence. With planning and proper delegating the likelihood of serious problems are reduced significantly. Even then it is possible a major issue will occur, but the consequences are likely to be lessened.

Striking a balance between too little and too much delegation is a challenge and one that can affect your stress level. The "you can always reach me at _____" statement is necessary for almost any leader-manager. The key to keeping stress levels low for everyone is for everyone to know when to and when not to reach the person. We offer the following ideas for how to achieve proper delegation, for any purpose, and keep stress to a minimum.

Effective delegation involves:

- Anticipating tasks and responsibilities that can be delegated—not leaving them to the last minute.
- Determining what needs to be accomplished and who might be the best person to do it.
- Delegating a little more than you are comfortable with—without overwhelming the person taking on the task.
- Working through the implications and making time available for the task to be accomplished.

For the person taking on the task, a careful and thorough briefing is vital. The more time you spend on this process, the less likely there will be problems for yourself and the person who has the delegated duties.

- Allow sufficient time for the briefing, and arrange to meet away from the person's workplace, preferably in your office.
- Ensure that the person possesses the necessary skills to carry out the assignment, or can easily acquire them.
- Provide sufficient information about the task(s), especially if the person is new to the task.
- Don't overload the person.
- Encourage the person to come up with new ideas and approaches.
- Discuss and set down the objectives, agreed targets, timeline and deadlines, resources required, and expected outcomes.
- Make sure the person understands what is required.
- Set down the expected outcomes in writing and exchange copies—this protects both the person undertaking the task and yourself.

You must provide appropriate information to everyone involved; your staff and your supervisor must know the plan. In the case of the supervisor, his or her input and approval is also important, especially when you first take over a unit. That person may have knowledge or information about the environment that you may not yet be aware of. Thus, inform the following:

- The person who has the delegated task
- Those in the immediate work unit
- Your boss(es)
- Other departmental managers who may need to be consulted

There are two other key elements in effective delegation that sometimes are overlooked. Remember, you must delegate the appropriate authority for the person to carry out the task(s) delegated. In addition, ensure the person will have the necessary resources to perform the task(s). A final point to always to keep in mind is you can delegate tasks, resources, and authority but you can never fully delegate the responsibility for what takes place. You are always ultimately responsible for what takes place in your unit, just as are the senior library leaders responsible for everything that occurs, or doesn't occur, in the library.

In the next chapter, we explore two essential components of having a high performing unit and/or library. The first is implementing a sound training program for your staff. The second is doing what you can to develop your staff. (While the two are somewhat related they are in fact different.) We also devote some space to the concept of teams. The reality is any high performing organization operates as a team, whether or not the team concept is implemented.

REFERENCES

ALA/APA Staff. 2006. "Library Staff Covered by Collective Bargaining Agreements." *Library Worklife* 3, no 6. http://ala-apa.org/newsletter/past-issues/volume-3-no-6 -%E2%80%A2-june-2006/.

Ames, Genevieve M., and Joel B. Bennett. 2011. "Prevention Intervention of Alcohol Problems in the Workplace: A Review and Guiding Framework." *Alcohol Research and Health* 34, no. 2: 175–187.

Barsade, Sigal, and Olivia A. O'Neill. 2016. "Manage Your Emotional Culture." *Harvard Business Review* 94, nos. 1/2: 58–66.

Bell, Reginald L. 2010. "A Three Step Process to Save Troubled Employees From Themselves." *Supervision* 71, no. 11: 3–6.

Brotherton, Phaedra. 2011. "New Managers Feeling Lost at Sea: New Survey Finds That Most Managers Enter the Role Without Formal Training." *T+D* 65, no. 6: 25.

Congressional Digest. 2009. "Union Membership: 2008 Data from the Bureau of Labor Statistics." 88, no. 3: 71, 96.

Dauten, Dale. 2011. *The Gifted Boss: How to Find, Create and Keep Great Employees*. Revised edition. New York: William Morrow.

Dulewicz, Victor, and Malcom Higgs. 1999. "Can Emotional Intelligence Be Measured and Developed?" *Leadership & Organization Development Journal* 20, nos. 4/5: 242–253.

Dwoskin, Linda B., Melissa Bergman Squire, and Jennifer L. Burdick. 2012. "Substance Abuse in the Workplace: ADA and FMLA Issues to Consider—Part II." *Employee Benefit Plan Review* 66, no. 8: 32–38.

The Economist Staff. 2016. "Civil Servants: Mandarin Lessons." *The Economist* 418, no. 8980: 57–58.

Hamm, John. 2011. "Trustworthy Leaders: Why Building a Culture of Trust Will Boost Employee Performance." *Public Management* 93, no. 9: 6–9.

Herbert, George. 1651. *English Poems, Together with His Collection of Proverbs Entitled Jacula Prudentum.* London: T. Garthwait.

Herzberg, Frederick. 1959. *Motivation to Work*, 2nd edition. New York: Wiley.

Jackson, Keith. 2012. "Who's Minding the Store?" *PM Network* 26, no. 7: 62–65.

Keirsey, David. 1998. *Please Understand Me II: Temperament, Character, Intelligence.* Del Mar, CA: Prometheus Nemesis Book Company.

Levant, Jessica. 1998. "Motivation." In *Gower Handbook of Management Skills*. 3rd edition. Edited by Dorothy M. Stewart. Aldershot: Gower.

Lee, Deborah O., Kevin E. Rogers, and Paul W. Grimes. 2006. "The Union Relative Wage Effect for Academic Librarians." *Industrial Relations* 45, no. 3: 478–484.

Maciag, Mike. 2011. "Census: Government's Share of Workforce Varies Greatly Among States." *Governing* Magazine. September 29. http://www.governing.com/news/state/2010-census-public-employees-workforce-among-states.html.

Maslow, Abraham H. 1954. *Motivation and Personality.* New York: Harper.

Mayo, Elton. 1933. *The Human Problems of an Industrial Civilization.* Salem, NH: Ayer.

McLean, Carla. 2005. "The Not-So-Odd Couple: Libraries and Unions." *Alki* 21, no. 2: 11–12.

Milano, Carol. 2008. "Unhappy Home, Unhappy Workplace." *Risk Management* 55, no. 11: 42–46.

Pynes, Joan E. 2013. *Human Resources Management for Public and Nonprofit Organizations: A Strategic Approach.* 4th edition. San Francisco, CA: Jossey-Bass.

Silver, Seth. 2008. "Transforming Professional Relationships." *T+D* 62, no. 12: 62–67.

Skinner, B. F.. 1953. *Science and Human Behavior.* New York: Macmillan.

Stanley, T. S. 2009. "Good Substance Abuse Programs Can Make a Big Difference." *Supervision* 70, no. 8: 15–18.

Vroom, Victor H. 1964. *Work and Motivation.* New York: Wiley.

Zachary, Mary Kathryn. 2007. "Labor Law: Union Organizing Efforts Fraught with Legal Pitfalls." *Supervision* 68, no. 4: 22–27.

Chapter 17

TRAINING AND DEVELOPING STAFF

Libraries face a host of new challenges, among them finding ways to be relevant in the Information Age. Libraries are required to do more with less, and the skills library professionals need continue to evolve.

Erin Davis and Kacy Lundstrom, 2011

Although the importance of developing people is growing, many managers lack the knowledge, capability, and organizational support they need to put the right pieces in place.

Preston "Tim" Brown, 2010

Virtually all leaders believe that to stay competitive, their enterprises must learn and improve every day. But even the most revered for their dedication to continuous learning find it difficult always to practice what they preach.

Francesca Gino and Bradley Staats, 2015

Profound changes in the workforce are making teams trickier to manage. Teams work best if their members have a strong common culture.

The Economist, 2016

Every organization is facing a rapidly changing operating environment; libraries are not alone in this regard. As a result, ideas for handling the training and development challenges come from a variety of organizations, regardless of sector. Adjusting appropriately to changes often calls for new or different levels of skill than existing staff possess; this is particularly true for public and nonprofit organizations where staffing is almost always extremely tight.

Especially in the public sectors managers face the toughest training and development challenges. With budgets cut almost to the bone, if not into the bone, they have little funding for training beyond what is absolutely critical; few have any funds for staff development. The ongoing "slow growth" economy makes it difficult, if not impossible, to secure a new full-time equivalent (FTE) to bring the new requisite skills into the organization. For libraries this is almost always the case. Perhaps the library can rewrite a job description when a person resigns in order to bring the new skill set into the staff. That option is likely to mean the library loses some other necessary skill set(s). And, that option may not be available in the foreseeable future. Thus, you need to identify other possible options. Your best option is to look for a staff member who is suitable for further development in the area of the required skills.

For most of today's libraries, retention of their best people is a concern. The concern is due to hiring freezes and sometimes the loss of a vacant position. Certainly since 2008, employers have been quick to let staff go. In many ways, that has caused many of the best and brightest to think, "Why should I have any loyalty to the organization, if it has none for me?" For many, all it takes is a hint of staffing changes, real or imagined, or something else perceived as a threat to them, to get staff looking for other employment. With underlying "loyalty" weak at best, having programs that give ample opportunities to grow and develop is an important factor in long-term retention of the best and brightest people. You have two basic training and development areas to consider: specific job-related skills and career development competencies and opportunities.

CHECK THIS OUT

Louis Uchitelle, a *New York Times* reporter, published an interesting book in 2006 about the loyalty question: *The Disposable American: Layoffs and Their Consequences* (New York: Knopf).

DIFFERENCES BETWEEN TRAINING, COACHING, AND DEVELOPING

Many people use these terms interchangeably, with few problems arising from that usage. However, there are some important differences that may help or hinder your obligation to handle these concepts effectively. In a sense, Preston Brown's comment, in one of the quotations at the beginning of this chapter, about managerial lack of knowledge may reflect, in part, a lack of understanding about the difference between training, coaching, and developing staff.

Training focuses, or should focus, on making certain each staff member understands what the library expects the person to perform in her or his job (job in the Human Resources sense of the word—see chapter 16 for a discussion of "jobs" and "positions"). Training is generally a one-on-one activity and commences on the day a person begins work. All new employee orientation plans include some training elements. The amount of training a person may require in the job will vary to some degree based on the person's education, knowledge of the required tasks, and prior library experience. Even a highly experienced person will need some training in how your unit does things. Although all libraries perform a set of core functions, they all have variations in how those functions are carried out. Training can occur throughout a person's employment, no matter how long they have been in their current position. For example, when something totally new is added to that person's employment job requirements, training may be appropriate to assure the person can carry out the new duty(ies).

Coaching lies between training and developing. Few of us are perfect in everything we do; even if we are proficient in some activity we can improve our performance when we have good coaching (there is a field called "executive coaching"). As with training, coaching is individual focused and attempts to identify existing areas of performance where some adjustments, large or small, can produce better outcomes.

Developing is more group focused—think staff development days. This activity should be forward looking in the sense of what the library may need in the future. It can, and should, also be individualized in terms of long-term career goals.

Given the above differences you can see how each term calls for slightly different plans and approaches to providing staff with growth opportunities and job satisfaction. Effective programs in these areas can, in fact, help with staff retention.

IDENTIFYING CURRENT TRAINING NEEDS

Identifying training needs should be relatively easy. Start with the job descriptions (JDs) if you don't recall the position details. If they were carefully prepared, you have a ready-made list of most of the training needs for every job in your unit, at least as they were at some point in the past. Those documents are the starting rather than ending point for your thinking about training needs. A JD is job specific and your unit is likely to have unit-wide issues that affect all the jobs and are not addressed in the JDs. One example may be the relationships and workflows between your unit and other library units.

Performance appraisals (PAs) results can provide some additional data about training needs. Certainly PAs are less useful than are the JDs because they tend to focus on overall performance rather than specific activity performances.

Your coaching needs may be partially identified from PA data. However, the JDs will provide the best starting point. Those two sets of documents are what you can use to ponder what aspects may require more or less coaching and which areas may require greater training. A major coaching area to think about is non-job specific concerns, such as working relationships and team building. You may be surprised how much coaching you need to do in such areas. Another thing you can count on is new areas popping up that will require your best coaching skills.

Development needs will be the most complex to identify. One reason is developmental activities can, and should, be both individualized and group based, for example, future needs for the library. On the personal side you can begin to identify long-term work-related goals during the PA process. Ending that process, a process that neither the rater nor ratee particularly enjoys, on some positive note can be useful. Discussing the person's career goals and what you and/or the library might be able to do to assist the person in reaching her or his goals tends to be a positive activity.

In terms of group needs, you can draw upon information gathered during the PA discussions to identify areas of commonality that you and the library could address on a group basis. You might conduct an informal survey of all your staff to determine what they think would be a good topic(s) for a unit staff development activity. Some libraries have a standing committee that is charged with planning a library-wide staff development day. Such committees frequently solicit suggestions for topics of high interest. Finally, you should periodically take time to think about trends and development in your unit's functional area that may impact what skills your staff may need sometime in the future. Such skills would be additional fodder for staff development activities.

General Training Needs

A new employee's first few days on the job set the tone for what follows. "Glad to see you; go to work" is not the best method for getting a new person to become a productive employee. By planning a formal orientation process, you create a solid beginning for both the person and the library.

The first day for the new person should be a combination of orientation, training in the job, and some time with Human Resources (HR) to take care of all the new employee paperwork. Possible events for the first day might include:

- Sending an email to the staff letting them know a new person is starting and to please welcome the individual.
- Informing the individual to start at the HR office to complete the hiring and payroll process.
- Allowing some time for the person to ask any questions they might have about the HR process that they were reluctant to bring up with the HR staff. Two likely areas are health insurance and retirement-related issues.
- Escorting the new employee to the work area and reintroducing the person to her or his colleagues and supervisor—if different than yourself.
- Allowing time for the new employee to put away personal items at her or his desk or workstation.
- Providing a tour of the library and introducing the new person to staff members, giving a short summary of what the new person will be doing.
- Returning with the employee to his or her department for an overview of its activities.
- Providing a demonstration of duties and activities the person is to perform, with both a supervised and private practice period.
- Completing a review session with the employee.

During the training time, the person should receive information about the significance of her or his duties. Early and frequent praise helps to develop a good working relationship and attitudes. New employees generally find the first several days confusing and somewhat unsettling. Spreading orientation out over several days helps make the new information, people, and duties less overwhelming. Your training plan should be flexible in order to adapt to various learning speeds as well as the person's prior experience (one size should not fit all).

A new person's past work experience may influence the way in which the person reacts to training. Experienced professional or supervisory personnel may require only an explanation of objectives, policies, practices, and potential problems. Beginning professionals should know the fundamentals of any starting position, though they will need to learn the local variations from general practice. In any event, some monitoring will be necessary during the first month or two for beginners.

Some ideas for making the training smoother:

- Prepare a training kit and checklist for each job category.
- Policies are just as important to have in the kit as are the actual job activities—such as personal use of telephones, break and lunch times, and when, where, and from whom to get needed supplies, for example.
- Involve some of your staff in the training—it helps the new person get to know their workmates and provides a more balanced perspective of the unit's culture.
- Have an online manual for each job in your unit—such manuals allows a person to check on something without worrying that older staff might think them slow to grasp their new duties.
- Make certain your expectations for work performance/outcomes are clear and understood—doing this orally and in writing in the manual will help ensure the message gets across.
- Make a plan for how to handle different learning styles—something for the traditional learner and for more visual learners at a minimum.

TIP

Pairing up a new person with a person who is at their level in the workgroup will provide a point of reference for any matters that require clarification, without the new employee feeling that she or he might be asking a supervisor a silly question. It helps the mentor by giving recognition and the motivation to check over those points that are often taken for granted.

Ongoing Training

Libraries face a rapidly changing technological environment. Keeping staff current with the changes related to their activities is a major challenge, especially in times of "steady state" or declining budgets. Failure to maintain staff skills results in users receiving poorer service, which in turn leads to dissatisfaction with the library. You face a dual technological challenge: acquiring and upgrading the technology and finding training and development funds in order to make effective use of the technologies.

Online training opportunities can also assist in meeting staff training needs. Many vendors have their system manuals online. Certainly, you will want carefully to review such manuals to be certain there are no conflicts with your library's usage, assuming the system allowed for a degree of customization on the library's part. Also, some vendors' manuals are easier to use than others; a hard-to-follow manual can waste a good deal of staff time.

There are online services that help with basic skills in various work activities—application software, business writing, and more. Connie K. Haley's 2008 article "Online Workplace Training in Libraries" is a good starting point for thinking about what such services may offer. A quick search of the Internet will turn up thousands of such services. We advise checking with colleagues in other libraries to determine what, if any, experience they have had with such firms. Finding training and development funding is too hard to come by to waste a penny.

Coaching and Monitoring

You will have two types of coaching to address as a manager—fine-tuning and under-performance. They do call for slightly different approaches and, of the two, handling under-performance is the most tricky and complex. That is also the area where you will have to engage your best diplomatic people skills.

Under-performance is an issue that is easy to put off handling. Such coaching sessions can be awkward for both you and the employee. It is natural to not want to deal with "that" today. Putting off the session is a poor idea for at least two reasons. First, the longer you wait to discuss the matter with the person the more difficulty the person will have in seeing the issue as a problem—"You never mentioned it before. Why now?" is a very common reaction. They do have a point: why today and not when you first noticed the issue? There may be a good reason for not addressing the problem immediately, such as having obligations away from the library for a few days. Our point is, address the problem as soon as possible; it may be awkward but it *will not* get any easier with time.

The second reason is your department's morale. Others will begin to wonder if the lack of correction is the "new normal" for the unit or if the person is a "teacher's pet" or some other reason. They *will* notice—don't think they won't. It doesn't matter what the issue is—quality or quantity of work, taking overly long breaks or meal times, being tardy to work, and so on—it will cause staff members to talk and wonder.

When you decide it is time to have a meeting regarding under-performance, take at least a few minutes to plan the session. Some things to keep in mind: listen more than you talk, consider if you have prejudged what the issue(s) may be (has your thought been "my way or the highway"—not too conducive to getting improved performance), and plan an approach that will allow the person to "solve" the issue(s) rather than telling them how to do so. Of course, you must decide what the consequences will be if things do not improve. Coaching sessions ought to include the following elements:

- Begin by agreeing on what the purpose of the session is about (this is often not all that easy to accomplish).

- State your perception of the issue—be as neutral in tone as possible and avoid accusing the person when possible.
- Ask for and *listen* to the person's view of the situation.
- Discuss the differences in perceptions—chances are good that there will be more than one difference.
- Explore the possibility that outside factors may be playing a significant role in the under-performance—e.g., lack of timely resources, too many duties, conflicting imposed goals, and demands from another unit.
- Seek a series of small steps rather than one grand solution with reasonable timelines.
- End with an explanation of the consequences, if there is no improvement.

These steps can assist in keeping an uncomfortable session from escalating too much. The steps will not solve everything but they will help.

There is one additional step to finish the coaching process for under-performance. Write up what took take place—again, try to keep to the facts but do include what both of you said and, hopefully, upon what you both greed. We recommend that you give a copy of the summary to the person. We offer the following tips for any type of coaching effort:

- Timing of coaching is critical—provide feedback promptly for both good and not-so-good performance.
- Thinking and planning before coaching, like most all other managerial activities, is important.
- Coaching should be discrete and confidential.
- Asking staff to self-evaluate their performance can provide clues to where coaching may be appropriate.
- Providing suggestions for improving performance is a better practice than directing ("I might do . . ." is usually more effective than "You should do . . .").
- Encouraging two-way discussions tends to be more effective than giving one-way directives.
- Asking if there is anything standing in the way of a person's performance that you might be able to address tends to build more solid working relationships and performances.
- Keeping any commitments you've made is critical to maintaining solid performance.
- Asking if you had to do it over again, "what would you do differently?"

STAFF DEVELOPMENT

Beyond training, there are developmental activities that should be provided for individuals moving into supervisory positions or other promotional opportunities, for keeping staff current with changing professional standards and technological issues, and for library-wide activities such as handling "problem users," disaster and emergency procedures, library security, and changing legal issues affecting the library.

Julie Todaro and Mark Smith had the following to say about training and development, "As library directors, we know that a single well-planned and executed training session can have a tremendous effect and is often all that is possible" (2006, vii). The concept is that at least some in-house effort is better than nothing at all. Perhaps the biggest challenge to implementing staff development on an ongoing basis is it generally requires shutting down public services for some time, perhaps closing the entire library for a few hours. Some governing boards, senior (non-library) leaders can take a dim view of closing services for almost any reason (even after major natural events such as an earthquake—yes, that has happened to the authors).

One solution to the "never close" situation is to split the activity into two or more identical segments and with only a few staff in attendance at any one time. Such an approach would allow at least the public service points to remain open with some staff. Another possibility is to hold the event on a day when the library is not open to the public; as you might expect that is not a popular option with the staff. However, you might be able to make it more acceptable if attendees received "comp time." That would, of course, require prior approval from a higher authority.

To be effective, a staff development day (SDD) requires a good deal of planning and some resources to support the activities. Some libraries have a standing committee for planning such days. Others have a staff association with the responsibility to plan any such event. One of the first tasks, for whatever group is to handle the SDD planning, is to identify one or two potential topics for the day that will appeal to a large cross section of staff members. This is not always an easy task and one of the reasons that effective SDD planning takes several months of effort. A successful SDD is the result of months of assessment, planning, and implementation.

Assessing involves taking a long look at what did and didn't work for prior events and identifying staff interest for a future event. Planning obviously focuses on program content but also securing the resources to make the day happen. There may the need to plan for food—anything from catered meals to a potluck or a break-time snack. There may be some decorations for the meeting space to provide a more welcoming and less of a "this is work" atmosphere. There may be the need to do some vetting of potential speakers and what each might charge. (A possibility for handling the "Don't close the library" policy is to ask if the presenter would be willing to allow a recording of the presentation so staff members unable to attend might view the program.)

CHECK THESE OUT

Marcia Trotta's *Staff Development on a Shoestring: A How-To-Do-It Manual for Librarians* (New York: Neal-Schuman, 2011) is an excellent resource that focuses on the very real challenge of limited funding.

Two good articles are Ben Bizzle's 2012 "eReader Training: Supporting the Digital Patron" (*Arkansas Libraries* 69 no. 2: 18–19); and Lisa Johnston's 2012 "Tech Expo: A Model for Emerging Technology Education for Library Staff" (*Journal of Library Innovation* 3, no. 1: 66–85).

AUTHOR EXPERIENCE

Evans was involved in something akin to what Lisa Johnston's article describes—a "vendor day" for e-resources and other companies that offer library-related technologies. In this case, Evans's academic library served as the host site for the annual event. One of the campus buildings had 34 "smart classrooms" and four 25-seat computer labs. Initially, it was a one-day program for the membership of a library consortium (currently operating under the legal name State of California Electronic Library Consortium, SCELC—originally it was a Los Angeles–based regional organization). The last event Evans was involved in was in 2005 when the program had grown to two days—one day for the vendors and one day for staff development activities, committee work, and the organization's annual meeting. The event had also long outgrown its members-only focus (the 2005 program had over 250 library staff members in attendance from all types of libraries).

Vendors each had a smart classroom, with all the technology, and six one-hour time slots to present new features, handle Q&As about their existing products, and get feedback on what librarians did and did not like about their product(s). The four computer labs were available in one-hour slots for training purposes in some of the more widely held products. The program was not just limited to database vendors, although they made up the majority of the presenters. Services such as serial management, online reference, and electronic reserve services vendors were frequent participants.

Many member libraries sent both librarians and support staff to the event. For Evans, the program was great for keeping the staff current with library technology issues as staff could drop in and out of programs while keeping the library open. It also meant that the library's staff development day could focus on non-technology issues.

Obviously this was a special situation, if not perhaps unique. However, it is an example of something you might be able to organize, on some scale, with consortium partners.

We offer some thoughts regarding challenges for planning SDD events:

- Begin planning early and book your venue as soon as possible.
- Find topics that will appeal to the majority of staff members and ones that will benefit the library in the long run.
- Make the event enjoyable, worthwhile, developmental, and informative.
- Ensure quality while not breaking the SDD budget.
- Limit the number of topics to a reasonable level while addressing the variety of topics the staff would like.
- Have a program that is both practical and forward-looking at the same time.
- Provide food! You can't underestimate the appeal of a good meal and its effect on staff morale.
- Provide nametags so attendees can network during the event.
- If you're bringing in outside speakers, make sure that you have previewed their content to ensure quality and relevancy.
- Collect vendor "freebies" during the year and at the SDD draw names for the "freebie" prizes.
- Check out the hot topics and well-attended programs at ALA, PLA, and ACRL conferences and replicate those for the staff at the SDD.

Your staff may have difficulty seeing the value of development activities unless you demonstrate enthusiasm and commitment to the idea. One tactic for showing your commitment is to have mini-developmental activities within the unit. You could get the staff together for a half hour or so to have them brainstorm about some topic related to the department's functional area—perhaps how a trend in the field may impact the unit. A variation, and one that you would need to spread over a long series of such meetings, is to begin to develop some scenarios for the unit's future. Although scenarios are generally viewed as a forward-looking planning process, they also can be employed as a developmental tool. As Jennifer Church-Duran and Deborah Ludwig stated, "constructing scenarios requires substantial intellectual engagement and a thorough analysis of trends and driving forces" (2012, 12). You may not be able to create much in the way of scenarios for your unit in short bursts of effort; however, if nothing else, you have the staff started on thinking about the future and what they may need to know and do.

HR offices, at least in larger organizations, offer some institution-wide development and training programs that a library may find beneficial, such as basic supervision, improving writing skills, or communicating with customers and colleagues. One drawback to these programs is that, except for the very largest organizations, such programs seldom are available more than once a year and may not cover a topic the library staff needs. Another issue is institution-wide programs tend to be very general in order to draw enough participants to make the program successful for the organizers.

Professional associations are an excellent source of development opportunities. Unfortunately, there are very few such organizational opportunities for support staff. The primary reason is that support staff members have few opportunities for paid travel, and their salaries are substantially lower, making it almost impossible for them to pay for such programs on their own. As more educational institutions and professional bodies extend the range of distance education programs, such opportunities ought to increase.

School library media specialists usually have mandatory development requirements on some regular basis. In most cases, they have the same continuing education requirements as the teachers in their state. They face the same issues of time and money for such activities as do other types of librarians, but they know there are consequences for not doing what is necessary. For the rest of us, development is a matter of self-motivation. Being short-staffed, as most libraries are, makes it more challenging to take several days off to attend a workshop or conference. We may know we should, but find it hard to justify the effort. It becomes even more difficult if there is no financial support from the library. Nevertheless, such activities are critical if you hope to move ahead in your career.

Training, coaching, and developing staff is never cost-free. Such activities always require time away from the "real duties." This is a real cost: developmental activities more often than not cost time and money. With limited staff, it becomes difficult to have staff off at a program for any length of time. Some jurisdictions are so shortsighted that they refuse to give time off to attend such programs even when the staff member is willing to pay for the program—shortsighted because over time the library becomes less and less effective.

Finding real dollars to devote to staff development has been a significant issue in most libraries for many years. Given the recent economic conditions, the funding challenge has become even greater than in the past. Managers must be the advocate for the unit staff especially when it comes to staff development efforts and needs.

ADVISORY BOARD EXPERIENCE

Alire worked hard to engage support staff in training and development. She not only encouraged staff members to join their respective paraprofessionals' interest groups within the respective library associations locally, statewide, and/or nationally; but she also provided funds for travel, registration fees, and administrative leave for the library paraprofessionals to be involved. Her philosophy was that the more the support staff got out and networked with other paraprofessionals, the more the library would benefit in terms of morale, updated skills, and "Our library isn't so bad after all" attitudes.

Evans was fortunate to have enough training funds to allow for each support staff member to have up to $500 for attendance at work-related workshops, seminars, and so on; these funds were in addition to funds for the professional staff.

Evans also was able to assist those support staff members who were interested in pursuing library degrees. It was relatively easy to fund coursework that directly related to the person's current job duties. The person could also use the $500 for course fees. And, almost always near the end of the fiscal year, there was a pool of unused staff development funds, especially those for support staff, which could be reallocated to the person seeking an MLS. In the past, that worked only when the library was near a library school. Today there are many online options for earning an MLS.

LEARNING ORGANIZATIONS

Learning organizations attempt to generate, acquire, and pass on information and knowledge with the goal of adjusting their activities, based on "new" knowledge, to create a more effective organization. As a manager, you have an important role to play in creating and maintaining a learning organizational environment. You need actively to bring new ideas to the staff and the library at large. Actively removing barriers to sharing new ideas is one technique for reducing the "silo" effect that often afflicts units in large organizations. ("Silos" are units that tend to think of themselves as independent units within a larger organization.)

Learning organizations, as a concept, are part of organizational development (OD), which in turn is an element within the field of organizational theory. Some people raise the question, "Is the learning organization just one more management fad, such as quality circles, TQM, and participatory management?" We do not believe it is, unless you consider having staying power for more than 40 years a passing fad. Chris Argyris (a name that you may remember from reading about workplace motivation) and Daniel A. Schön published the first book on the topic

(*Organizational Learning: A Theory of Action Perspective*, 1978). However, it was not until Peter Senge published *The Fifth Discipline* in 1990 that the concept gained wide attention.

Senge's "cornerstone" discipline in the *Fifth Discipline* is systems thinking, which leads to a holistic approach to organizations and the people who work in them. His five "component technologies" of a learning organization are:

- Systems thinking—This refers to thinking about the organization as an interrelated whole. It should do away with the silo thinking that we mentioned above.
- Personal mastery—This refers to each staff member taking "ownership" of learning for the organization's benefit.
- Mental models—This refers to how the staff and the organization assume how the organization operates and its values. The notion is those "models" ought to be challenged from time to time.
- Building shared visions—This idea was discussed in chapter 2, Leadership.
- Team learning—The importance of teams is discussed later in this chapter.

Senge's approach is a method for helping managers improve organizational performance in either a traditional or team setting, and often employs a consultant to facilitate the change process. While the consultant assists in program development and may provide training, facilitate discussions, and act as something of a mediator, at the end of the day the consultant leaves and it is up to the people in the organization to make the plan work or fail.

The learning organization emphasizes the idea that everyone in an organization needs to be involved in the learning process. A learning organization is one in which "people continually expand their capacity to create the results they truly desire, where new and expansive patterns of thinking are nurtured, where collective aspiration is set free, and where people are continually learning how to learn together" (Senge, 1990, 3).

CHECK THESE OUT

If you'd like to learn more about the learning organization concept, we recommend the following as good starting points:

Joan Giesecke and Beth McNeil, "Transitioning to the Learning Organization," *Library Trends* 53, no. 1 (2004): 54–67.

A themed issue of *Library Trends*: "Organizational Development and Leadership," edited by Keith Russell and Denise Stephens (53, no. 1, 2004).

Creating a Continuous Learning Environment

Realistically, you cannot implement the learning organization in just your unit; it must be library-wide to be effective. What you can do is take some of some of its concepts and develop an environment that encourages lifelong learning. Earlier in this chapter, we discussed demonstrating your commitment to staff development. Certainly, such development is a part of ongoing learning; however, we believe that life-long learning goes well beyond job skills and knowledge.

Perhaps Jaclyn McLean summed up the value of continuous learning in her article "How to Manage Managing: A Guide for New Librarians." She wrote, "The most valuable lesson I've learned lately has been that learning never stops—I have spoken with librarians at different stages of their careers, and they are all learning something and continuing to develop as professionals and as people, too" (2012, 66). We would like to emphasize her last point. Yes, we do need to grow and develop professionally. However, we believe it is equally important to have a sound life–work balance. Part of that balance is continuing to grow on the personal side just as much as professionally. We believe it is also important for you to encourage both types of ongoing learning among your staff. Showing an interest in each person's outside interests can, when carefully done, encourage them to expand those interests and, hopefully, allow them to have a sound work-life balance as well.

Getting to know some of each person's outside interests is a delicate process. You do *not* want to appear to be prying. You want to be friendly, but not a friend—remember our caution about friendships. You will need all your people skills to begin to ascertain staff outside interests. One starting point could be by simply asking, "How was your weekend?" This may give you some clue(s) about the person's interests. Don't expect this to be a quick process; if you force it there will be a strong implication of your trying to spy on the person for some unknown reason. Any such suspicion is likely to destroy a large amount of trust, if not all of it, which you built up over time with the person.

Once you have some idea about a person's interests, take some time to learn something about those interests. You could say something like "I was reading [or watching] about X and was a little confused about Y. I think you said you knew something about that subject, if that is correct, could you help me better understand Y?" Whatever approach works for you, the point is to show an interest in the person. By showing some knowledge about the current "state" or new facet of the topic you can indirectly demonstrate the need to continually learn.

If you do something along the lines of the above, it can prove useful in at least two ways for both you and your staff. First, and foremost, it helps make the point that you recognize staff as individuals and that they each bring a variety of skills to the workplace, including non-work-related knowledge and interests, and are more than mere cogs in the library's machine. Second, it can encourage lifelong learning in both professional and personal areas.

CHECK THIS OUT

Bernadine Goldman described how her library defines itself as a learning organization in "Transforming Your Library into a Learning Organization" (*Public Libraries* 50, no. 3 [2011]: 20–21).

OPTIONS FOR SAVING LIMITED TRAINING AND DEVELOPMENT FUNDS

Handling training and development activities with limited financial resources is a challenge. We offer some suggestions for stretching the funds you do have. One obvious resource is the Internet. Although many virtual training and development options usually carry some cost, they can save you travel and per diem expenses. They can also allow more staff to benefit from the sessions. One starting point for identifying such offerings is the home of the Kentucky Department of Libraries and Archives, which lists free programs (http://kdla.ky.gov/librarians/staffdevelopment /Pages/OnlineClasses.aspx). Another resource is OCLC's Web Junction (http:// www.webjunction.org/), under the tab "Find Training." Yet another virtual site to explore is Info People (https://infopeople.org/). This site offers a variety of training opportunities. A very nice feature is its calendar of future training sessions. The best feature is most sessions are free.

ALA, library schools, and state library associations provide continuing education and staff training programs at low or no cost. The same is true of state libraries. The challenge of these resources is when do/will they offer something from which your staff will benefit.

CHECK THIS OUT

Erin Davis and Kacy Lundstrom provide a useful case study for establishing an SDD group in their 2011 article, "Creating Effective Staff Development Committees: A Case Study" (*New Library World* 112, nos. 7/8: 334–346).

MENTORING

Mentoring is useful for both you and your staff. Here we focus on the mentoring of others. Not all of us make good mentors. Tami Echavarria Robinson made the point "Mentoring seems to come naturally to some of us. We teach, we guide, we encourage. In some libraries were I have worked during my 25-year career, there were few of us with that inclination" (2011, 13). Why some of us are not naturally inclined to mentor is unclear. However, we can all develop some of the appropriate skills, just as we learned leadership skills.

The starting point for developing mentoring abilities is to understand the difference between coaching and mentoring. Coaching focuses on current work related issues and tends to be highly structured. Mentoring, on the other hand, is about the whole person (in and out of the workplace) and should be driven by the mentee's life goals. Essentially, mentoring is about relationships and is not skill-focused (although skills may become part of the picture, if they are relevant to the mentee's long term goals). Strong mentor-mentee relationships arise from being open and honest with each other, and a willingness for both to ask questions, challenge views, and even disagree at times. Another important feature of mentoring is distance— that is, it ought not be a direct reporting relationship. What that means is you are unlikely to have occasion to mentor one of your staff. However, you can be a mentor to a staff member in another department. It is also possible to become a mentor to a volunteer in your unit—perhaps a student who might have an interest in becoming a librarian. That is also a possibility for someone on your staff who has a long-term goal of becoming a professional, in which case you may provide as much guidance as possible.

What do mentors do? They work with a mentee by:

- Listening
- Modeling
- Supporting
- Sharing
- Guiding
- Networking

Effective mentors can provide real-world perspective that a mentee may not have considered, provide alternative ideas for the mentee act upon. What a mentor does not do is make the mentee's decision for her or him. Mentors are advisors, supporters, and an informed sounding board. They may provide networking leads that prove useful over time. Mentees need to hone their listening skills and understand a key part of the mentoring process is to learn and expands one's horizons. Another skill that can be improved in a sound mentoring environment is the mentee's ability to evaluate situations and advice of others. None of the mentoring activities are out of the ordinary and they are basically what you do normally as an effective manager. Nevertheless, some individuals hesitate to undertake mentoring or do not do it at all.

All of the above are attributes and abilities you could provide to someone else. The major issue is motivation and a willingness to do so. Perhaps the most common reason for not mentoring is time. We all face increasing demands on both our work and personal time. (Certainly the higher up you go as a leader-manager the less time you seem to have.) There is no doubt that being a good mentor does take time, and occasionally lots of time. Senior leaders also have the most varied experiences and thus have more they could share with younger leaders.

Another common reason for not mentoring is thinking you have nothing to offer in the way of useful advice or guidance for anyone else. If you have been in practice for several years, you are likely to have much more to offer than you think. Further, it is always possible "to test the mentoring water" on a small scale. Formal mentoring does not unusually involve a contract; relationships begin and end through mutual agreement. If things do not work out for either person, they can end the effort.

A third rather common reason for not being a mentor is feeling uncomfortable with the idea behind mentoring—assisting someone else with regard to their work issues and perhaps career plans. "What if I give bad guidance or advice?" That is certainly a possibility; however, keep in mind it is the mentee who is responsible

Table 17.1.
Mentoring Approaches

Direct	Indirect
Making suggestions	Listening
Giving feedback	Reflecting back
Discussing and debating	Paraphrasing
Sharing technical knowledge	Summarizing
Offering guidance	Asking questions to raise awareness
Questioning a position/view/opinion	Drawing out mentee's ideas
Reviewing mentee's progress	Providing alternative views

for what she or he decides to do or not to do. We are not suggesting that is okay to give poor advice. Rather as mentor, especially if you are in a different library than the mentee, you cannot know all of the issues that exist in the mentee's library. If you are uncomfortable with the prospect of something like the above, it is probably best not to try mentoring.

To be a good mentor you need the desire to assist others in their work and career goals; to have a broad understanding of current professional practice and an interest in trends; strong communication skills, especially in listening; to have a positive outlook about the profession as it currently stands and its future prospects; and be a good time manager (and having a good sense of humor doesn't hurt).

Keep in mind that mentoring is *not* a one-way process; you gain some benefits as well. One important benefit is mentoring trends to sharpen our interest in developments and trends in the field and pondering their implication for the profession as a whole, not just in our specialty. You can also learn from your mentee's experiences. It is possible you will gain insights about another professional area and/or how another library operates that proves useful for you. There is a good likelihood that you will improve your communication skills. Then, of course, there can be the satisfaction of seeing the mentee progress in her or his career.

There is no right or wrong approach to the mentoring process. There is just what works and that will vary by time and circumstances, even with a single mentee. There are two main approaches—direct and indirect.

What determines your approach is the mentee's personality, the issue under consideration, the urgency of the matter, and current circumstances.

One important skill to develop in a mentee is an understanding of the difference between tactics and strategy and why those concepts are significant for one's managerial activities as well as career. Very often newcomers have difficulty seeing "the big picture" and are likely to see their unit's situation as the only one that matters. The notion of giving a little now in order to have big gains later is rather foreign to their thinking.

To summarize mentoring:

- Mentoring is about guidance and facilitation.
- Mentoring must be mutually satisfying.

- Mentoring requires open honest communication.
- Mentoring a direct report is generally not a good idea.
- Mentoring requires time, thought, and effort to be effective.

CHECK THIS OUT

Nicole Saylor, Jen Wolfe, and Paul Soderdahl explored the benefits of mentoring in their 2100 article "Mentoring, It's a Good Thing: What We Learned Partying with Student Librarians" (*C&RL News* 72, no. 10: 566–570).

TEAMS

Why have a discussion of "teams" in a chapter focusing on training and development? First and foremost, effective teams require both training and development, even when the members are all millennials (millennials are often more team experienced than older cohorts). Also, unless you are thinking of implementing a team structure for the entire library, staff members not on a team will need some orientation/training to what and how a team functions.

It wasn't that long ago when "teams" were the hot managerial fad. However, as the quotation from *The Economist* at the beginning of the chapter suggests, teams can be a major managerial challenge. That essay quotes Leigh Thompson (a professor in the Kellogg School of Management) as saying, "Teams are not always the answer—teams may provide insight, creativity, and knowledge in a way a person working independently cannot; but teams may also lead to confusion, delay, and poor decision-making" (*The Economist*, 2016, 71).

Teams are very good for projects (short- or long-term), assuming they have effective guidance to avoid the confusion, delay, and poor decision-making mentioned by Thompson. Virtual teams are often essential for accomplishing organizational objectives. Teams can bring together skill sets and knowledge that might not otherwise be combined in another approach and produce outstanding results. Using the concept judiciously is the best approach, in our view. It is our belief that all successful organizations are, in the broadest sense, great teams, regardless of what label the organization employs for its structure.

So what types of training do team members require to be effective? Two related areas are negotiation and compromise; all members must understand the need for and how to engage appropriately in both. Group decision-making is a related area where the team may need development. Organizational teams are somewhat different from other teams—"taking my marbles and going home" threats are pointless. Engaging in "my way or the highway" behavior will destroy team trust and cohesion. While some of that behavior may have worked in other settings it very rarely leads to anything but the unemployment line in an organizational setting. Truly effective team performance is rarely a naturally occurring phenomenon; it takes training to bring good teams into being.

To be truly effective, there should be cross training of team members. That is, two or more members are capable of performing any team task. Such training means sick days and vacation leave will not disrupt team activities. Getting the right mix of members can be challenging both in terms of team member interests and team requirements. Another area where training is almost always necessary is group accountability. Even individuals who played team sports experienced less team accountability. When a professional sports team has failures, more often than not, it is the coach rather than the entire team who becomes accountable. Accountability and team usage is a significant managerial challenge.

CHECK THIS OUT

For a more detailed discussion of teams and e-work issues, including e-teams, see G. Edward Evans and Patricia Layzell Ward's *Leadership Basics for Librarians and Information Professionals* (Lanham, MD: Scarecrow Press, 2007).

Coaching, developing, and training staff is a basic managerial responsibility. Doing it effectively is often a challenge, not for lack of knowledge but a lack of finances. For many organizations, large and small, when funding is tight, cutting back or deleting training and development monies is an easy decision. It is akin to deferring maintenance of the physical facility. Both are easy decisions to make at the moment, but the long-term costs for the organization are often far greater than the money saved. In such tight funding situations your coaching skills will be in high demand.

REFERENCES

Argyris, Chris, and Daniel A. Schön. 1978. *Organizational Learning: A Theory of Action Perspective* Vol. 1. Reading, MA: Addison Wesley.

Brown, Preston. 2010. "Having Their Backs: Improving Managers' Skills in Developing Others." *T+D* 64, no. 4: 60–64.

Church-Duran, Jennifer, and Deborah Ludwig. 2012. "Bringing Scenario Planning Home to KU." *Research Library Issues: A Quarterly Report From ARL, CNI, and SPARC* Issue 278: 12–16.

Davis, Erin, and Kacy Lundstrom. 2011. "Creating Effective Staff Development Committees: A Case Study." *New Library World* 112, nos. 7/8: 334–346.

The Economist Staff. 2016. "Schumpeter; Team Spirit." *The Economist* 418, no. 8981: 71.

Gino, Francesca, and Bradley Staats. 2015. "Why Organizations Don't Learn." *Harvard Business Review* 93, no. 11: 110–118.

Haley, Connie K. 2008. "Online Workplace Training in Libraries." *Information Technology and Libraries* 27, no. 1: 33–40.

McLean, Jaclyn. 2012. "How to Manage Managing: A Guide for New Librarians." *Feliciter* 58, no. 2: 65–67.

Robinson, Tami Echavarria. 2011. "Mentoring Aspiring New Librarians: One-on-One Relationships That Matter." *ALKI* 7, no. 3: 13–14.

Senge, Peter M. 1990. *The Fifth Discipline: The Art and Practice of the Learning Organization.* New York: Doubleday/Currency.

Todaro, Julie, and Mark L Smith. 2006. *Training Library Staff and Volunteers to Provide Extraordinary Customer Service.* New York: Neal-Schuman.

Chapter 18

COLLABORATION

Models of partnerships and collaborations can help today's organizations shift their viewpoints to find new ways of working and providing services.

Joan Giesecke, 2012

Never before has the imperative to cooperate and collaborate been so clear or so urgent.

Paula Kaufman, 2012

Collaboration is clearly still at the heart of what we do.

Jill Emery and Michael Levine-Clark, 2016

Man is not the creature of circumstances, circumstances are the creatures of men.

Benjamin Disraeli, 1804–1881

Collaboration, when you think broadly, is a very common behavior; that is, interacting with others to achieve a common goal. And while it may be common, it certainly is not always easy or straightforward. There will be times when, faced with a deluge of differing opinions, you may wonder "why did I get into this?" Despite this, it is one of those human behaviors we don't think about very often; it is somewhat akin, in a sense, to talking and listening: we take these activities for granted as part of our everyday lives. Additionally, the skills we exhibit in all of these are often not as strong as we think they are. With all this being said, we believe there are at least three subcategories within the broader theme of collaboration: personal, workplace, and organizational. Our focus here will be on the workplace and organizational categories.

As suggested above, just because it is commonplace does not mean that everyone collaborates effectively or that people engage in positive collaborations routinely;

it simply means that collaborating with others is a fundamental requirement for functioning in society. Despite this, there are times when there is active resistance to being cooperative.

Overcoming resistance to collaboration requires an understanding of the collaborative process. This is especially true in the workplace. Most of the time, people will make an effort to get along with one another and work together to accomplish a desired outcome. This can be done even when there is a personality clash or when people don't like one another; the shared goal(s) is the force that binds them together.

A Google search for "collaboration in the work place," for example, generated more than 56 million results in late 2016. Obviously, the topic and its impact on the workplace, especially in terms of productivity, are relevant and timely. Before we discuss how to create a truly collaborative environment and the best practices, it is necessary to define what, exactly, collaboration is. "Many words—consortia, cooperatives, partnerships, alliances—are used synonymously and interchangeably" (Kaufman, 2012, 54). Because of this, a simple definition may be the most useful. We like the one offered on Study.com: "Collaboration in the workplace is when two or more people (often groups) work together through idea sharing and thinking to accomplish a common goal. It is simply teamwork taken to a higher level" (Hill, n.d.). Collaboration can occur between two people or two organizations, and every size group in between. In the *Handbook of Public Administration* (2015), Rosemary O'Leary defines collaboration "as the process of facilitating and operating in multiorganizational arrangements to solve problems that cannot be easily solved by single organizations" (528). Collaboration allows organizations to find new ways of providing services, and offers up opportunities for new services that better reflect the needs of both the organization and the people it serves.

While seemingly an easy notion, collaboration is not simply two people or groups working together. As stated above, the goal must be agreed upon and each member must contribute something unique to the collaboration; in other words, each contributing party must offer something that wouldn't be possible for the others to offer on their own. This exchange of valuable expertise, products, resources, and ideas are what then results in a superior product.

The Disraeli quotation at the beginning of this chapter indirectly suggests that the opposite of collaboration is competition. And indeed competition is an important factor in when, how, and if collaboration occurs. Factors that drive competition are factors that impede collaboration, and in today's fast-changing environment, it is more important than ever to engage in collaboration.

Collaboration allows for an exchange of ideas and expertise and, when done effectively, maximizes each member's strengths and skills, resulting in a more robust and effective product. It is also unlikely that every individual always has all the information and skills needed to complete a task; nor does every institution or organization have all the content and resources available to meet every need. In these cases, collaboration allows for a more effective exchange and sharing of information.

WHY COLLABORATION IS A NECESSITY IN TODAY'S WORLD

In 2015, Barbara Crosby, Mellissa Stone, and John Bryson made the case for public sector organizations engaging in collaborative efforts, "public administrative scholars and practitioners increasingly assume that partnering across organizational and sectoral boundaries is both a necessary and desirable strategy for addressing many of society's most difficult public challenges" (38). One way to think of effective organizational collaboration is as a continuum from no cooperation to a merger of organizations with increasing collaboration in between.

In an era of declining resources, of all types, as Geri Stengal noted, effective collaboration can:

- Save costs by sharing infrastructure (resources) and administrative expenses.
- Strengthen programs.
- Expand the value proposition for both organizations.
- Improve efficiency.
- Tap complementary skills and abilities.
- Increase leadership skills. (2013)

With these potential outcomes as inspiration, it is easy to see why collaboration has become such a buzzword for nonprofit and for-profit organizations alike. Using the definition given above, the question then becomes, "how do we get collaboration to a higher level?"

As suggested above, today's environment is a driver of collaboration. Some years ago Fred Emery and Eric Trist described the impact of different environments on organizational behaviors and planning (1965). One of those environments they defined as "turbulent." A turbulent environment is one in which there is a high rate of change, uncertainty, and even a danger to ongoing viability. Perhaps the viability component is lacking in today's libraries, but the other characteristics are very much present.

The current environment, fed by constant news feeds, rapidly evolving technology, and an overabundance of information coming from every possible direction, can be overwhelming. This environment can also create "a tsunami filled with obstacles as well as with potentials, a tsunami that is striking so forcefully and so quickly that often it is difficult . . . to reflect on what being in that storm of whirling ideas and concepts may mean for us in the future" (Kaufman, 2012, 57). Collaborating with peers and leaders in the profession, as well as with those outside of it, can help create a mutually beneficial environment that will allow you to not only reflect on, but to adequately address the "tsunami"; it can create an eye of calm in the storm.

Today, one of the major drivers of increased collaboration is fiscal in nature (not that money was unimportant in earlier collaborative activities). In the present environment, almost every public and nonprofit organization is strapped for cash and seeking supplemental funds from granting organizations, making competition rather fierce. Combining forces makes good sense from various points of view. From the library's perspective, multi-library grant proposals tend to receive extra attention and multi-type proposals get even more consideration. Management and programmatic factors are also drivers. Sharing expertise or labor may provide better, more, or longer service for the end users—think 24/7 reference service as an example. That outcome, in turn, can translate into stronger community ties/relations.

Library collaboration is nothing new. What is different is the extra pressure to increase those activities. Sharing collections between libraries occurred as early as the creation of reliable postal delivery. As Paula Kaufman noted, "librarians in the late nineteenth and early twentieth centuries seized opportunities to build the infrastructures necessary to share some collection items through a system of inter-library lending. Capitalizing on newly available technologies when possible, their successors shared catalog records; shared access to online catalogs, first to single libraries, then to groups of libraries, and ultimately to a large group of the world's libraries; . . . and so much more" (2012, 60). This notion of sharing content and resources allowed librarians to meet the challenges of low funding with ingenuity and creativity, skills every successful librarian must possess.

Creating a Collaborative Environment

In thinking about collaboration, it is important to remember there is a plurality of environmental settings. There is the personal environment—family, friends, and social groups. Another is your place of work. A third is inter-library activities. Yet another environment is cross-sector efforts. Without doubt they share some commonalities; the differences arise from the degree of emphasis on some of the commonalities.

An example of a difference in emphasis is group decision making. When spending time with family and friends, there is inevitably some group decision making occurring: should we have pizza tonight or Chinese take-out, what time should we eat, do we need to get something without gluten and without meat for Bob, who's paying, and so on. Within these negotiations, there is a degree of involvement from everyone but within a limited range of options. It is also often clear that there is one ultimate decision maker (the family matriarch or patriarch, for example). In work or inter-library environments, the decision will be group-based, often on a consensus basis, and one or more of the parties are able to opt out of taking part in the chosen process.

Creating a truly collaborative environment is not an easy task, especially in the workplace. Taking into account people's varying personalities and workloads, getting everyone to work together and staying on task can be challenging (it's challenging enough with people you love or know really well; with colleagues it's even more so). It's also not uncommon for one person to feel as though they are getting stuck with the bulk of the work. In an attempt to combat these issues and others, it is important to proactively identify potential stumbling blocks and create a respectful, mutually beneficial environment.

Establishing good working relationships with people is always desirable, but not always easy. Work life with its varying challenges is rife with comedic possibilities; this is reflected in the ongoing popularity of films like *Office Space* or television shows like *The Office*. These comedies "portray life at work as frustrating, trivial, and, at times, demeaning. These depictions hit close to home, otherwise they would not be funny" (Silver 2008, 63). Knowing that work can be, and often is, frustrating and stressful, does not mean that one should just be resigned to being miserable—there are tips and tricks that can be used to ease one's suffering and can, in fact, help with both fostering good work relationships with colleagues and lead to successful collaborative endeavors.

So how do you go about lessening various work annoyances (and dealing with those pesky colleagues) *and* creating a collaborative environment? Luckily, many of the characteristics that create successful collaborators are the same characteristics that can help foster a balanced home and work life and a healthy workplace environment. Good collaborators "treat others as equals regardless of rank and look out for the welfare of network members" (O'Leary 2015, 538). We think it goes without saying that treating others as equals is a good tactic, regardless of circumstance. Another fact is good collaborators share most of the traits of a positive politician (see chapter 13 for a full discussion of the traits). The traits are:

- Trustworthiness
- Consistency
- Perceptiveness
- Straightforwardness
- Authenticity
- Persuasiveness

There is yet another key trait for being a great collaborative partner: seeking the common good rather than personal gain. Effective collaboration rests on the idea that compromise is a necessary part of the group's activities. Yes, you seek the best outcome for your library but recognize that you will rarely get everything to go your way—it is a matter of give and take. Collaboration cannot be a zero sum game if it is to succeed in achieving the common goal. Compromise requires a high degree of trust by all the partners.

Successful collaborators also work on developing good communication skills—including writing well, speaking well, and listening well. They must learn to listen to "not only the actual words being said but the underlying message being conveyed. They legitimize anger while addressing the frustration that people often feel" (O'Leary 2015, 538). This ability to empathize while still getting things accomplished is yet another skill that will serve you well in many areas of your life.

In order to create the most fully functioning, collaborative team, it is also necessary to agree upon a shared goal. This may seem obvious, but how often have you been called into a meeting without really knowing what the meeting would be about or even why you were invited? Communicating the purpose of establishing the team at the onset and continually reviewing this purpose throughout the process will help ensure that the goal is not forgotten or altered into something unrecognizable.

Effective collaborators are more interested in seeing a triumphant project come to fruition than having their own contribution hailed. In order to achieve this, they "must be self-confident, decisive risk takers with a passion for outcomes" (O'Leary 2015, 538). Allowing others to shine and giving them opportunities to contribute will also pave the way toward creating an environment of trust and mutual respect—two characteristics that are a necessity in any collaborative environment.

Barriers to Collaboration

Interlibrary and cross-sector cooperative efforts usually involve senior managers, if not the most senior person, at least at the outset of the effort. That also means they have substantial authority at their home institutions. Further, they may not be used to having their views questioned, much less rejected. Position and ego both can be barriers that are difficult to surmount, especially during the initial stages of the group effort. It takes time and commitment to the group's goal to sort out the issues and reach a working relationship.

Consensus decision making, based on equal authority/power, is also something that some individuals have trouble coming to terms with, as it is somewhat of a novelty for them. Consensus building takes time, at least more than many managers are familiar with in their home institutions, and many can become impatient with the "talk, talk, talk" that is a requisite for good group decision making.

Yet another barrier is the "my turf" mentality, especially when it comes to cross-sector cooperation. In some cases the "turf" is not because of member concerns as such, but rather a matter of parent institution (jurisdictional) rules and regulations or legislation. More often than not these can be overcome, but undoubtedly it will add to the time necessary for reaching a group decision. One example of such a problem is when an academic library group purchases a program in which there are differing fiscal years and rules regarding any pre-payments for services. Other library types may also face the pre-payment issue; however, that one is relatively easy to resolve by receiving an exception ruling from the parent organization. The budget year concern can be significant as few institutions are willing to change that cycle just for the library. (This is not to say institutions don't change their budget cycle, they do. One of the authors worked at one organization that changed its cycle three times in a space of seven years. That wreaked havoc on the library's consortia buying activities.) Joint efforts with afterschool programs that cross sectors offer may also have some major challenges with rules and regulations.

Certainly, as noted earlier, organizational cultures are special, if not unique. This translates into each collaborative partner bringing to the group table a different culture. Part of those cultures relate to "how we do things." What that means, in the best cases, is that the group begins to create its own culture that draws on all of the different cultures. Not doing so will make success harder to achieve as individuals try to do it "my way."

It may seem like an obvious statement: collaboration will only be effective if there is trust between the parties collaborating. While seemingly a no-brainer, establishing trust is not always an easy task. In any professional endeavor, it is often necessary to work with people from different backgrounds and with different approaches, work ethics, and personalities. All these personalities must somehow come together to form a cohesive team that has in common a specified goal.

A fundamental component of building trust requires that individuals approach the task with an open mind. According to Rosemary O'Leary, "the primary skill of the successful collaborator is an open mind, specifically being open to new ideas to change and to help others succeed" (2015, 537). Being open to change and being able to tout the accomplishments of others will help your team—even if it's just one other person—see that you aren't out only for yourself. This acknowledgment will help you gain the trust of your colleagues, and will form the foundation for an environment where each individual participant isn't afraid of being undermined or not getting credit. When this foundation is strongly in place, all team members will learn to support, encourage, and trust one another.

Collaborating in Your Library

Collaboration will only be effective and meaningful if it is supported by the larger organization. If your library doesn't provide the time or guidance needed to create effective work teams, collaboration is a nearly impossible task. With that being said, if your organization does strive to create and support collaborative environments, it can open up a wealth of opportunities for your library.

Depending on the format of your organization, the collaborative possibilities will differ. For academic librarians and libraries, the opportunities to collaborate with each other are varied, from the long-standing ILL system to 24/7 reference services. OCLC, the giant and critical part of how today's libraries offer services, began as a cooperative cataloging service for some Ohio academic institutions. You never know just where you collaborative efforts may go in time.

There is an area where libraries might be more effective in their internal collaborations: making certain there is an effort to ensure all the staff has opportunities to participate in projects and activities. There are times, especially in large academic library operations, when a division exists between the "professional" staff and the rest of the staff and has become part of organizational culture; this division discourages teamwork and diminishes trust. Michael Perini, in writing about librarian support staff collaboration, noted that "barriers also existed due to attitudes and perspectives of librarians toward classified staff, as well as a lack of understanding of capabilities" (2016, 157). Professional staff may take on an attitude of, "this is my project, and my project only," and others will likely feel devalued.

AUTHOR EXPERIENCE

Evans has been involved in a number of collaborative projects over the years, some highly successful and some that failed.

Two of the successes grew from local endeavors into multistate programs. One started as a small regional private academic cooperative buying group for electronic resources. It slowly grew to be a statewide operation and multi-type library consortia. Finally, it crossed state lines and continues operating today. The second success was a resource-sharing program for academic libraries that expanded to a multi-type undertaking. The progress for either success was neither fast nor easy: turf, jurisdictional issues, and building an organizational culture were all challenges they had to address.

One failure was international in scope. It was an effort to merge two similar publications, but different in content, that served an academic field worldwide but produced in two countries. The effort came close to success but in the end organizational and country cultures were too much to overcome. Cross-jurisdictional or sector efforts, even with the strongest of wills, can be hard to implement. Below we offer an example of how they can also succeed.

If you are part of a public library that is governed by a city government, you may find it beneficial to collaborate with colleagues in different divisions within the city. There are many areas of library work, including programming, circulation, and reference, that can benefit from collaboration with other areas. For those of you who may be put in charge of scheduling and hosting informational and/or entertaining programs and workshops for the library, collaborating with your colleagues in other departments may prove to have both financial and professional benefits. For example, reaching out to those who are aware of city developments in the areas of economic growth may result in a popular program designed to educate patrons about upcoming developments in the city. If your city has a department focused on sustainability, it may be a good resource for a series of workshops aimed at informing the community about recycling and other green initiatives. Forming collaborative relationships with your non-library colleagues is also an opportunity to market library resources and services: an endeavor that is unceasing in your library career.

Collaborating with other city departments may benefit your circulation departments as well. Perhaps your library can offer a hold delivery program, where staff who work in areas outside of the library can request to have their holds delivered to their office. This can increase your library's circulation statistics and provide a service that can create positive PR for your library. You may also partner with managers in other city departments and get a list of new employees every quarter and offer them a library card as one of the perks of their new position.

Cross-Sector Collaboration

Not only is it important to collaborate with others inside your organization, it is also critical to look outside your like-minded peers and forge collaborative relationships with outside organizations. These types of relationships have the potential to result in large gains for your library; meeting with and learning from those who may have a similar mission can create opportunities for your library and the people you serve.

At Pima County Public Library (PCPL) in Arizona, librarians saw firsthand the deleterious effects of the economic downturn. They saw an increase in their numbers of homeless and those suffering from mental illness, and were looking for ways to address it and "better serve . . . patrons with exceptional social service" (Johnson, Mathewson, and Prechtel, 2014, 32). As they were looking for solutions, they learned that the San Francisco Public Library had partnered with the San Francisco Department of Public Health to employ a social worker. This model inspired librarians at PCPL to look at forming their own collaboration, and they approached their local health department.

Through the collaboration the librarians initiated with the Pima County Health Department, PCPL hired a public health nurse (PHN). Both organizations agreed to co-supervise the position while PCPL would manage the program. Both organizations were involved in interviewing and selecting the candidate. The resulting program was so successful that they ended up needing to hire additional PHNs.

Pima Library's success is just one example of how collaborating with outside agencies can help in addressing gaps in service or new services altogether. From a professional standpoint, collaboration can provide many rewards. Collaboration via a consortium with database vendors, for example, can result in real savings for your library. These types of relationships can mean even more content at a lower price. Interlibrary Loan is yet another very common and long-standing form of collection sharing and collaboration. Many libraries that are part of a large county receive significant cost savings by purchasing access to digital resources for all libraries within that county.

Although working collaboratively can provide rewards for both the organization and the individual employee, it is not without critics. According to a 2016 article in *The Economist*, employees are often "forced" to "share large noisy spaces" or are "bombarding them with electronic messages," all under the guise of collaboration. Open-plan offices and the increase in electronic communication that often coincide with collaborative efforts can create an environment rife with frequent interruptions; these interruptions can "increase the total time required to complete a task by a significant amount." The article also argues that while many cite the many benefits of collaborating, managers may "fail to measure its costs."

Costs involved in collaboration include the increase in staff workload, including the additional time required for more meetings (either virtually or face to face). Schumpeter argues that "employees are spending so much time interacting that they have to do much of their work when they get home at night" (2016, 63). This can take a toll on the employee, and may result in burn-out and disillusionment. Additionally, the "deep thinking" that is often required to do a major task is incredibly difficult to accomplish in this sort of environment, and organizations need to not only give employees the opportunity to collaborate with one another, but they must also "give them time to think" without interruptions.

There are six keys to successful collaborative efforts:

1. A strongly held shared vision
2. An environment of open and honest communication
3. A very high level of mutual trust
4. An atmosphere of compromise
5. An environment of shared leadership
6. An organizational culture unique to the group

E-Collaboration

In today's digital world, you may be expected to collaborate with individuals whom you have never met. It's becoming increasingly more common to form professional relationships with people you may never meet in person. If, in fact, you do have an opportunity to connect with your fellow professionals at a state or national conference, you will have the benefit of already having formed virtual relationships; this can make it much easier to strike up conversations.

Public and nonprofit sector organizations have become ever more dependent upon the e-environment to both provide services and in order to interact with their "communities." We have mentioned, at various points in this book, the idea that libraries are seeking to become "participatory." The primary driver for doing so is the Internet and social media. As Ines Mergel noted, such "technologies allow government to partner with the public throughout the decision-making process, from identification of the problem, to the development of alternatives and identification of preferred solutions" (2013,151). Later Mergel made the point that, "The most difficult-to-address challenge is creating a collaborative culture that respects the existing hierarchical knowledge-sharing culture deeply established in any government organization" (207). We will discuss social media's impact on collaboration more in the next section.

For libraries, collaborating with digital vendors is critical in today's age of e-books and downloadable audio. Librarians are key players in negotiating and advocating with both publishers and authors. In response to publishers' concerns that supplying e-books to libraries will diminish their financial returns, libraries have pointed out "that libraries help create customers by introducing our patrons to an author's work for free, and then, once they get hooked, they go on to purchase additional titles" (Coffman 2012, 20). *Library Journal* even came out with a survey showing that e-book borrowers "are also active book buyers who make many of their purchasing decisions based on the authors or books they first discover in the library. In fact, over 50 percent of all library users go on to purchase books by an author they were introduced to in the library" (Bowker 2011). There is no doubt that giving away content for free is an important driver of e-book sales.

A Book Industry Study Group (BISG) report from April 2011 indicates that receiving a free or promotional sample chapter was the leading reason people cited for purchasing an e-book. More than 30 percent of the respondents stated that they had purchased a book on this basis, while 25 percent said they bought an e-book after receiving a free or promotional e-book by the same author. Free e-books are a major component of the digital marketplace; in November 2010, the BISG reports that 48 percent of all e-books downloaded were free; by January 2011, that number had grown to 51 percent. This data would seem to vindicate the contention of librarians that giving away material for free helps drive sales (Coffman 2012, 20).

In addition to this cost, e-collaboration presents its own unique set of challenges. Good writing is an art, and having only this medium to convey your message can be a challenge. Additionally, it can be easy for others to misread your intended message or, even worse, take offense at some tone or brusque manner that they may have perceived through your written word. A way to help combat this is to not rely solely on written communication. Using software programs that allow for all users to log in to a shared meeting space at once can be useful in helping establish a team environment and for users to get to know one another (GoToMeeting and WebEx are great platforms for online meetings and are free with a limited number of participants). These types of platforms allow users to communicate face-to-face, hear one another's voices, and get a deeper sense of the person (other than just through email or a shared online document).

If getting everyone to meet at the same time isn't possible and the collaborative effort must solely be done via chat, email, or a shared document drive like Google Docs or iCloud, create a user profile—even if it's simply a personal headshot—that will allow others to get a better sense of who you are. Even having a picture associated with written communication can go a long way in fostering a sense of familiarity.

Collaborating via Social Media

We'd be remiss to discuss e-collaboration without mentioning social media and its impacts. Social media and public sector organizations are still somewhat strange bedfellows. There is no doubt about the role the Internet has played in creating e-government and the manner in which it has changed citizen-government interactions. There are several reason that social media is less well integrated into public sector activities.

At the most fundamental level, there is the pluralistic character of the system of government in the United States that has the U.S. Constitution as the base—federalism. While there is the national (federal) government, there are state and local governments that can expand or limit federal control. Perhaps the best way to illustrate this approach to governing is in terms of marijuana laws—as of 2017 it is still an illegal drug at the federal level yet legal in some states. Essentially, there is a rather high degree of freedom of action even within a jurisdiction, which also includes freedom for agencies within a jurisdiction. Add to that mix the notion of separation of powers and you can see why social media utilization does not exist evenly across agency lines within a single jurisdiction.

There are also turf issues at play that often limits information sharing between agencies. Rarely is there a mandate to share information, even for such mundane concerns as what social media platforms have worked for us in terms of these issues. Of course there is some sharing on a person-to-person level, but rarely interagency efforts. That often results in the implementation of platforms the individuals use personally, which may or may not the most effective choice for the library.

A term some writers on organizational behavior use for the lack of sharing is "silos." Silo mentality makes collaboration difficult or impossible. Generally the silo effect begins at the top rather than with the front line staff, which further limits opportunities for collaborative efforts.

Other challenges for public agencies deployment of social media, as a normal part of their activities, resides in the general public's expectations regarding social media. Perhaps the biggest expectation is almost instantaneous response or interaction. Instantaneous response is not a notion that comes to mind when thinking about public sector organizations' actions. Given that much of the public sector's social media application is the result of one or two "Lone Rangers" who have a range of other duties that are part of their job description; it is not surprising that quick response is rather uncommon.

Another expectation is that social media is personal/individual in character. Libraries, like other public sector organizations, exist to serve a population that is generally highly diverse in needs, interests, and values. That in turn makes it unlikely that many single social media posts will be effective for the entire service population: one message rarely fits all.

Some years ago Mary Lynn Pulley and Valerie Sessa wrote about some paradoxes that exist for e-organizations that seem to be rather applicable to public and nonprofit social media implementation:

- Swift vs. mindful
- Individual vs. community
- Top down vs. bottom up
- Big picture vs. detail
- Flexible vs. stable (2001)

Clearly, the first paradox applies to social media and public sector usage where being mindful is important and being swift is the expectation. You can achieve mindfulness fairly quickly, but even in work situations you are familiar with, the "gut response" is not as often beneficial to your career as is a mindful one. Mindfulness takes a little time at a minimum.

The second paradox relates, to some degree, to the service community diversity issues mentioned above. Social media posts tend to be broad in scope and certainly are not tailored to an individual. Composing effective individual messages takes time and thought that may be needed for other duties.

Libraries, like other public sector organizations are, to a greater or lesser degree, hierarchically structured. That almost always translates into a pattern of top-down control—decision making, planning, and so on. The one notion behind social media is grassroots can and should drive actions/decisions; in fact, that is a user expectation.

Social media posts are generally big-picture in nature. One reason is many platforms limit the size of a single posting. Another factor is users are accustomed to short posts. From a government perspective the big picture is fine for attention getting, but as some say, "the devil is in the details." The typical outcome of the need to make details available is a PDF (Portable Document Format file), not a social media post.

The final paradox, flexibility vs. stability, is perhaps more than a paradox. Public sector organizations can and do change, however slowly that may occur. Flexible government is something of an oxymoron, or perhaps an invitation to chaos. A constantly and rapidly changing public sector is unlikely to be acceptable to anyone other than anarchists. Nevertheless, social media users have an expectation of flexibility.

We are *not* suggesting libraries shouldn't engage their service populations through social media, far from it. What we are suggesting is it is important to assess the various platforms in terms of what they can do for your library and what you wish to accomplish. Further, you'll be able to better understand the above paradoxes and employ the media judiciously.

Nowadays, most libraries have a presence on social media in one form or another, whether it's on Twitter, Facebook, Instagram, or another one that most likely came into popularity since this book was written. These platforms, along with others designed to allow users to share documents and ideas in a single location—blogs and Google Docs, for example—have created a number of new opportunities for collaboration; they also can come with a few challenges.

Social media is, by nature, highly dynamic and, at its best, can be an incredibly responsive tool for engagement. Additionally, although using it is relatively easy, it still requires a "strategic approach . . . and a novel way of thinking" (Kietzmann et al. 2011, 250). This "novel way of thinking" encourages the use of social media to engage and interact with shareholders in a collaborative way. Organizations can use social media "explicitly to tap into their [community's] brainpower and energy. They ask customers and followers to participate in brainstorming with them so they can learn how to be a better company, offer better products and services, or support the values and issues of the community" (Moore, 2011). Savvy users of social media understand that ideas can come from anywhere, not always from within the organization. Within the environment of social media, the "direction

---

CHECK THESE OUT

A pair of detailed articles in 2002 on collaboration management are G. Edward Evans's "Management Issues of Co-operative Ventures and Consortia in the USA. Part One" (*Library Management* 23, nos. 4/5: 213–226 and nos. 6–7: 275–286); and "Management Issues of Co-operative Ventures and Consortia in the USA. Part Two" (*Library Management* 23, nos. 6/7: 275–286).

A recent book that provides an in-depth look at library consortia is Valerie Horton and Greg Pronevitz's *Library Consortia: Models for Collaboration and Sustainability* (Chicago, IL: American Library Association, 2015).

of information flow changes, roles interchange and become parallel. Information democratizes, the one-way communication model shifts towards a more complex, two-way model" (Bányai, 2009, 242). If utilized correctly, this two-way model can be an incredibly effective way to work collaboratively.

We end with the following quotation from Hal Rainey: "However one might distinguish between networks and collaboration and other concepts related to political power and public policy process, the vital role of networks and collaboration is clear. Public managers and policy makers need the skills to engage effectively in networks and collaborative situations" (2014, 144).

REFERENCES

Bányai, Edit. 2016. "The Integration of Social Media into Corporate Processes." *Society and Economy* 38, no. 2: 239–259.

Boughzala, Imed. 2016. "Social Media and Value Creation: Exploring the Perception of Generation Y Toward Corporate Social Networking Applications Use." *Journal of Organizational and End User Computing* 28, no. 2: 107–123.

Bowker Staff. 2011. "Library Journal Releases Patron Profiles Detailing Who Uses Libraries and Why the First Issue Is Titled Library Patrons and Ebook Usage." http://www.bowker.com/news/2011/290243381.html.

Coffman, Steve. 2012. "The Decline and Fall of the Library Empire. *Searcher* 20, no. 3: 14–47.

Crosby, Barbara C., Mellissa M. Stone, and John M. Bryson. 2015. "Governance in an Era of Partnership." *Handbook of Public Administration*. 3rd edition. Edited by James L. Perry and Robert K. Christensen. New York: Wiley.

Disraeli, Benjamin. n.d. "Benjamin Disraeli Quotes." In *BrainyQuote*. https://www.brainyquote.com/quotes/quotes/b/benjamindi121418.html.

Emery, Fred E., and Eric L. Trist. 1965. "The Causal Texture of Organizational Environments." *Human Relations* 18, no. 1: 21–32.

Emery, Jill, and Michael Levine-Clark. 2016. "Same as It Ever Was: *Collaborative Librarianship*'s Future." *Collaborative Librarianship* 8, no. 1: 1–2.

Giesecke, Joan. 2012. "The Value of Partnerships: Building New Partnerships for Success." *Journal of Library Administration* 52, no. 1: 36–52.

Hill, Aaron. n.d. "What Is Collaboration in the Workplace? Definition, Benefits & Examples." Study.com. study.com/academy/lesson/what-is-collaboration-in-the-workplace-definition-benefits-examples.html.

Johnson, Kenya, Amber Mathewson, and Karyn Prechtel. 2014. "From Crisis to Collaboration: Pima County Public Library Partners with Health Department for Library Nurse Program." *Public Libraries* 53, no. 1: 32–35.

Kaufman, Paula. 2012. "Let's Get Cozy: Evolving Collaboration in the 21st Century." *Journal of Library Administration* 52, no. 1: 53–69.

Kietzmann, Jan. H., Kristopher Hermkens, Ian P. McCarthy, and Bruno S. Silvestre. 2011. "Social Media? Get Serious! Understanding the Functional Building Blocks of Social Media." *Business Horizons* 54, no. 3: 241–251.

Mangold, W. Glynn, and David. J. Faulds. 2009. "Social Media: The New Hybrid Element of the Promotion Mix." *Business Horizons* 52, no. 4: 357–365.

Mergel, Ines. 2013. *Social Media in the Public Sector: A Guide to Participation, Collaboration and Transparency in the Networked World*. San Francisco, CA: Jossey-Bass.

Moore, Karl. 2011. "From Social Networks to Collaboration Networks: The Next Evolution of Social Media for Business." *Forbes*, September 15. http://www.forbes.com/sites/karlmoore/2011/09/15/from-social-networks-to-collaboration-networks-the-next-evolution-of-social-media-for-business/#2b3f89ee76ea.

O'Leary, Rosemary. 2015. "Becoming and Being an Effective Collaborator." In *Handbook of Public Administration*. 3rd edition. Edited by James L. Perry and Robert K. Christensen. New York: Wiley.

Perini, Michael. 2015. "Conceptualizing Classified Staff as Collaborative Partners." *Collaborative Librarianship* 7, no. 4: 150–159.

Pulley, Mary Lynn, and Valerie I. Sessa. 2001. "E-leadership: Tackling Complex Challenges." *Industrial and Commercial Training* 33, no. 7: 225–229.

Rainey, Hal G. 2014. *Understanding and Managing Public Organizations*. 5th edition. San Francisco, CA: Jossey-Bass.

The Economist Staff. 2016. "Schumpeter; The Collaboration Curse." *The Economist*. January 23. http://www.economist.com/news/business/21688872-fashion-making-employees-collaborate-has-gone-too-far-collaboration-curse.

Silver, Seth R. 2008. "Transforming Professional Relationships." *T&D* 62, no.12: 62–67.

Stengal, Geri. 2013. "Nonprofit Collaborations: Why Teaming Up Can Make Sense." *Forbes*. April 9. http://www.forbes.com/sites/geristengel/2013/04/09/nonprofit-collaborations-why-teaming-up-can-make-sense/#3ad4de694c2c.

Chapter 19

NEGOTIATION

Negotiating is an art. It is complicated. To become an exceptional negotiator traditionally requires years of practice, but that doesn't mean that most people couldn't quickly and easily learn good negotiating practices if someone shows them what to do.

Steven Babitsky and James J. Mangraviti, 2011

By approaching a pending negotiation as a problem that needs to be solved rather than as a televised boxing match, you can not only manage your emotions at the table, but you can also free up mental bandwidth to think better on your feet.

Karen Cates, 2016

Conflict is a part of our daily and work lives. Functional and dysfunctional conflicts are different, but they both crop up in human organizations.'

Golnaz Sadri, 2012

The efficiency of negotiation is often hampered by a lack of sufficient information about each other's priorities.

Ho-Won Jeong, 2016

Negotiation. It is not a very long word, but it is one loaded with implications. Not only is skillful negotiation a necessity in order to get what you want; it's also necessary in order to keep the people you manage. Negotiation is rather like communication; we all do it, but not always effectively. And, like with communication, we can learn to be more effective.

The fact is that we all have been in almost daily negotiations all our lives. As children we negotiated with our parents, although we were not aware that we were negotiating—"Can I take the trash out later?" "Can't the dishes wait until—?" or "Can I go to—?" are just a few examples. In adulthood, we negotiate with spouses, family, friends, colleagues, and in some instances, even salespeople. We are rather like Molière's Monsieur Jourdain, who was surprised to learn he spoke prose, when we learn we "do" negotiation.

Employees engage in negotiations in the workplace just as much as they do in their personal lives. "Can we switch nights this week? I'll be glad to—, if you can do that for me" or "I have a favor to ask" are pretty common transactions in the working world. One of earliest, if not the first, negotiations to occur in the work context is about your starting salary and/or benefits. The higher you go as an administrator, the more likely your starting salary negotiations are to be complex and somewhat drawn out.

Managerial life would be a little easier if the only negotiations you had to handle related to salaries. That is not the case, as you probably know. The fact is you will need to develop and hone your negotiation skills as well as another skill—managing conflict. You are lucky if you have had some training in these areas prior to becoming a middle manager. Many of us had to learn through the school of hard knocks, not a very pleasant experience for ourselves or the other people involved. Our advice is, seek some assistance early on in your managerial career in these two areas, be that guidance from a mentor, workshops, or a course or two. The time effort spent developing the skills will pay dividends over the years.

AUTHOR EXPERIENCE

There are times when you may reasonably expect heated competition for a very scarce resource—a new library position. On one occasion Evans was told early in the budget process that the library would receive one additional professional position and that the library could decide where to deploy the position *after* it was granted. (This is rather unusual as generally you have to build a case for a new position and submit that case for approval. The library was being rewarded for some special achievements over the preceding five years.)

Needless to say, word got out and soon every unit head was meeting with Evans making a case for why their unit should get the FTE. After several meetings with individual unit heads, Evans thought the situation could get too heated and, especially if he made the decision, all but one unit head might think the "winner" was a favorite. His solution was to announce there would be a joint unit head meeting, scheduled for 3 hours, with the sole purpose of allocating the new position to one unit. Each unit head would have 15 minutes in which to make her or his case. After that, the remaining time would be for discussion and making the final decision.

Much to Evans's surprise, the meeting lasted less than 20 minutes. Later, he learned that the unit heads decided they ought to come to the meeting having already negotiated among themselves who would receive the FTE. What could have been a long-lasting conflict environment was avoided by eight people thoughtfully negotiating with one another.

CONFLICT MANAGEMENT

Organizational politics are fact of work life, like it or not. It is also a source of conflict that can seriously disrupt library activities if left uncontrolled. Not to mention, as observed by Maggie Farrell, "Leaders are encouraged to surround themselves with individuals who are different and bring a variety of strengths to a team. But face it, there are people that we sometimes just don't like" (2014, 501). Your negotiation and conflict management skills will be essential components in keeping that disruption from happening.

Conflict can be destructive, but it can also be harnessed to help improve unit performance. Two types of conflict can emerge in any work unit. In the first, feelings are so strong that discussion gives way to personal attacks. In the second, useful debate emerges, with criticism directed at the substance of the discussion, rather than individuals. Each can present challenges for you, because in both situations the disagreeing parties may divide unit staff into winners and losers. Your goal is to resolve the conflict and, when possible, make it a positive for your unit and the library.

Your beginning point is to understand the common approaches people employ when encountering a conflict situation. Such approaches apply equally to personal and work conflicts. Most people have a preferred method for handling conflict regardless of the situation. The five most common methods are:

1. Avoidance
2. Accommodation
3. Confrontation
4. Compromise
5. Collaboration

There is no right method as each is appropriate from time to time as circumstances vary.

CHECK THIS OUT

There are a number of quizzes and other resources available online to help you learn more about conflict management strategies and techniques. One site that lists a number of handouts and tools for negotiation and conflict management is the MIT Open Courseware "Negotiation 101" site: https://ocw.mit.edu/courses/sloan-school-of-management/15 -667-negotiation-and-conflict-management-spring-2001/study-materials/. Of note are the "Negotiation Styles/Strategies" and "Conflict Styles" handouts.

A useful way to think about conflict is as a continuum with "confrontation" (fight) at one end and "avoidance" (flight) at the other extreme. In between are three common possibilities ("accommodation," "compromise," and "collaboration") that are sometimes referred to as "flow" because the methods tend to keep things moving forward. We believe there are differences, if slight, between the three middle ground approaches. We place "accommodation" closer to "avoidance" than the other two approaches. When you look up "accommodation" in a thesaurus you find such words as "bow," "defer," "submit," and "yield" under the heading related words. Those words, as well as "accommodation," suggest giving up something without much struggle rather than attempting to retain it—close to but not exactly fleeing. Compromise suggests a give and take (negotiation) where the goal is to reach some middle ground resolution with each side giving up some initial goal(s) or position(s). Collaboration suggests an even greater effort to reach a common goal that the sides recognize from the outset and only differing slightly over "how to do it."

TRY THIS

Write down the first five words that come to your mind when you hear the word "conflict." Ask several of colleagues to do the same. When you compare lists, don't be too surprised to find a high degree of commonality on the lists. You will also find commonality with the words we use in this chapter to discuss conflict and resolve conflicts between colleagues, words that are frequently listed by participants in Evans's workshops on conflict management.

Although we all probably wish it were not true, the fact is that conflict is a part of life. It has been said that conflict is a growth industry, and, unfortunately, we believe that is correct. Today's economic environment, pressure to do more and more with less and less, the fear of losing one's job if you can not do more, job loses, and so on, all create worry, stress, fear for everyone. One likely outcome of those concerns is less tolerance for perceived "slights" on someone's part and a conflict situation can develop.

Models of conflict are based on two axioms: conflict invariably involves more than one person, and it involves a negative intersection/interaction of values, beliefs, and so on. Some years ago, Ken Jones wrote the following:

> Conflict with others is the strongest and most disturbing way in which organizational change may be experienced, and its successful resolution appears as one of the most intractable and difficult problems. Objectively, conflict appears as a disagreement about what should or should not be done. Subjectively, and less consciously, it is experienced either as a threat and challenge to the needs, status, authority and even sense of identity of oneself or one's group, or as an opportunity for stronger self-confirmation. The significance and relative force of these two facets of conflict will, of course, differ from one situation to another, but they are as integrally related as the two sides of this page. (1994, 235)

Although his focus was on change and conflict, Jones's points apply to any conflict situation.

Why should you take an interest in staff members' interpersonal relationships that are less than friendly? First, even small interpersonal tensions have the potential to damage unit productivity. Second, other staff members will be aware of the issues and, if you don't intervene, the unit's morale can drop and that too will impact productivity. Beyond those two reasons the situation can lead to ever-greater stress and even burnout.

Another potential concern is absenteeism. When you become aware of staff members preferred method for handling conflict, you can, potentially, spot an early sign of "underground" conflict. This is possible when one or more staff members who are, by inclination, conflict "fleers." One easy way to avoid stressful, conflict, work frustrations, and so on, is to take sick leave at the first hint of an ailment. Unusual sick day patterns are a signal something is amiss in the unit. It may or may not be conflict that is the cause, but in any case you should pay attention and start looking for the cause. Certainly, there are times when the flu is rampant and staff cannot avoid it. When one or two people appear to be taking more than their typical sick leave and there is no widespread illness making the rounds, it may be a work-related issue rather than a true medical problem.

One major cause of underground workplace conflict is the widespread notion that open expression of frustration, irritation, anger, and so on, is inappropriate at work. Almost every staff member knows such expression can lead to disciplinary action—reprimand, unpaid leave, and even immediate dismissal for certain behaviors (see chapter 16 to review common reasons). The result is people tend to suppress their stronger reactions to work conflict, frustrations and stress. There is also an increasing concern and fear among staff when someone does become highly emotional or confrontational. The fear comes from the fact that there are more and more examples of real violence in the workplace. The fear is, to use a popular term, that the person is "going postal." Libraries are not immune to killings, murder, and other physical violence; admittedly, most often it is often between users, but not always.

Managing conflict rests on two simple principles: gathering information and acting on that information. Like so many things in life that are "simple," neither principle is easy to implement. What follows is presented in terms of your *not* being a party to the conflict. We will touch on that type of situation at the end of this section.

Before starting your information gathering remind yourself that most conflicts are driven by self-interest and desire to gain control. Both factors tend to cause the participants to see matters as black and white, right or wrong, my way or the highway, either/or, and so on. There may be times when things are that clear-cut, but, in our opinion it is relatively rare. There may be some black and some white in the situation, but there will be a host of shades of gray. It is those grays that offer the best opportunities for finding some middle ground resolution. We don't suggest finding such middle ground will be easy, but it is critical to success.

Once you have identified the "disputants," your first step in information gathering is to *bring them together*. (Note: for ease of discussion we prepared the text as if it is a two party situation; however, what follows applies to multiple-party conflicts as well.) That might appear to be counterintuitive; however, it is the best approach. Why is that so? When your first step is to talk to them individually, you set up a situation wherein the second party can, and is likely to, think you have already taken sides. You may not have done so, but the person's perception is real and will make finding that middle ground more difficult than it needs to be. Also, there is chance that you may have, subconsciously, done so. Another risk factor in meeting individually with the parties is it can escalate the situation has the parties begin creating "facts," exaggerating the events, seeking out of allies to support "my case" for example. Thus, drawing in other staff members and further complicating the situation.

We believe the greatest risk in the individual "interview" approach is you are essentially taking ownership of finding a solution. The participants are likely to assume you are acting as a judge and will make someone the winner and the other the loser, whatever solution you put forward. Worse yet, in the event you propose a middle ground resolution, neither party is likely to put much effort into making it work. After all it was your solution not theirs.

Before bringing the parties together, do think about how the participants, including yourself, tend to handle conflict. There is no question that the meeting will be stressful, tension filled, and probably confrontational. Your primary challenge will be the "avoider." Such individuals are likely to be uncommunicative and tend to agree to almost anything just to get out of the meeting. That may not be the best option for your unit's well-being. If you suspect you have such a situation, spend some time thinking about how you will effectively draw the person into the session.

Maintaining control of the session is critical and a "fighter" will work hard to gain control of the session. Thus, either of the extremes of the conflict-handling spectrum will be challenging. Having two middle-spectrum parties is rather rare, as they probably would have worked the matter out by themselves.

Many of the ideas for handling staff counseling and progressive discipline sessions apply here as well. Start quickly, firmly, set the ground rules, and do not allow discussion of long past grievances to distract the session from the current concern. However, once the session has started we recommend being as indirect as possible—you don't want to fall into the trap of "I'm the boss" and "I have the authority to sort this out." That will make it clear you are acting as the judge and jury. By holding the session in your office you establish something of a "being called to the principal's office" atmosphere. The office itself will handle the message regarding authority; you don't need to emphasize the power.

If possible, set up the meeting space with just chairs—"no barriers" between the participants. You take the center chair and direct the participants to their chairs. You should almost be in the middle between the parties. Such an arrangement makes easier for you to control the session.

Setting the "ground rules" for the session is essential. Some variation of the following works well: "We are here for me to gain an understanding of what has occurred. Each of you is to talk to me, not to one another. You are to remain silent when the other person is speaking. What I want to learn from this meeting is how each of you views the current situation. I'm not interested in hearing about past differences, we are to focus on the current situation." Such ground rules will not stop some bickering and interruptions, but will go a long way toward keeping them to a minimum and maintaining control of the session.

It is important not to visually or verbally agree, disagree, or sympathize with any party's statement. Doing so immediately provides a signal to the other party(ies) you have taken a side, at least in their minds. It rather common for each of the parties to try to draw you to their side; don't let that happen. A frequent tactic for doing this is asking you a question. "Wouldn't you do the same?" "What else could I do?" "Wasn't that reasonable?" are examples of the ploy. Your best approach is do not answer the question, you can ignore it, turn back to speaker by asking a question, and so on.

Maintaining control of the session can be difficult. Don't hesitate to say something like "I told everyone not to interrupt" or "Let's get back to the topic." You will know it is time to conclude the session when the parties repeat and repeat the same statements. Your ending segment should illicit from the parties what they think should be done. End the session by summarizing what you have heard with an emphasis that it is a summary of what was said—not who won or lost.

Once the session is over you may or may not have enough information to make a decision on what to do. Again you may have to engage in more information gathering from other sources. When you do have all the information you are likely to get, it is time to take action. Your action options are varied but limited in a sense—do nothing more, give an order, explore moving or transferring one or more of the parties, reassign work duties to separate the parties, discuss with Human Resources (HR) the possibly of leave (paid or unpaid) for one or more of the parties (a cooling off period), start mediation (yourself or having a professional mediator), possibly refer one or both parties to HR for possible referral to some specialist, and, in rather rare instances termination.

The above may appear to be a laundry list of possibilities. It is long; however, the reality is very few cases actually offer the entire list. Termination is very rare—in most cases where it is an option, the behavior would call for immediate termination rather than the process outlined above. Transferring and reassignment of work are only available occasionally. Leave with or without pay is likely to be available only with very serious situations. Referral to an outside specialist is even more rare. Giving an order is always possible but places you back in the position of establishing the solution which neither party will work very hard on carry out. Doing nothing more is, rather surprisingly, not a bad option in many cases. From the list of possibilities, mediation is probably a sound choice. The sidebar below reviews some options for resolving conflicts between colleagues.

RESOLVING CONFLICTS BETWEEN COLLEAGUES

- Do *not* take sides.
- Get the facts and confirm the information gathered.
- Clarify points of view.
- Get both parties to explain what they want.
- Do not give the impression you will have the solution; to make it work it needs to be their solution.
- Summarize the situation.
- Agree on a solution, how it can be implemented, and how to evaluate its success.
- Evaluate the outcomes with both parties after an agreed-upon time period.

We now turn to conflict situations in which you *are* a party. It is almost inevitable that as a middle manager you will become a party in some conflict situations. There will be disagreements between yourself and your staff members for a host of reasons—performance evaluations, changes in procedure, scheduling issues, and so on. You may have to address upset users, if you work in public services. Vendors can become upset with some library policy or practice. Even a non-user from the general public may challenge some library service, program, or policy. Your personal approach to handling conflict will be important in just how difficult dealing with each situation will be. Our advice is to practice being somewhere in the middle of conflict handling continuum, especially if your natural inclination is at one end of the scale. It is expected leader-managers will approach such situations with the goal of keeping things flowing. We acknowledge that looking for middle ground is often easier with non-staff members than when it is with staff and it can be difficult to go against your natural inclinations.

As noted earlier, your negotiation and mediation skills will be essential in resolving conflicts. There is another useful trait to develop or hone—assertiveness. "Assertive" is a word that, for many people, carries a negative connotation. We suggest there are positive and negative forms of assertiveness. There is a positive value of being able to calmly, firmly, and clearly state a position (assertive). Being overbearing, unreasonable, authoritarian, or even threatening are negative forms of assertiveness. We further suggest, middle managers should engage in positive assertiveness. One advantage of positive assertiveness in conflict environments is it helps set clear limits for the matter. Also keep in mind assertiveness is *not* the same as aggressiveness, although some people do not see a difference.

If a situation arises outside of your office with you as participant, your best first step is to move the "discussion" to a more private space. Taking the person to your office may be the only option, but keep in mind the office carries an air of authority that might not be best at that moment. Finding a neutral space is a better option. Keeping clam is critical and may be very difficult to achieve, the move to a more private space may give you a few moments to regain control of your emotions. Once in the private space use some of the techniques for handling conflicts between other people—tell me again what the issue is so I can better respond, paraphrase the person's statement to clarify their issue(s), and so on. Remember you are negotiating, not mediating, in the sense of trying to have a mutual understanding of the issue(s). Also, remember you are not a neutral party and therefore perhaps less inclined to be objective.

There will be times when you realize that there is a need to get a neutral third party involved in order to resolve the matter. Your first option may be to go to the senior leader-managers for this purpose, and often this would be almost mandatory; however, the staff member is unlikely to accept the idea they are truly neutral. After all, you are one of "them" and "they" will support you no matter what. You can reasonably expect the staff member to go the parent organization's HR department to complain and seek a real neutral party. They may do this immediately, but are likely to be asked, "Has this been discussed with your supervisor's supervisor?" If the answer is no, the person more often than not is informed that is a required step before HR becomes involved. We have had situations in which a supervisor and staff member could not resolve the matter even with the assistance of HR. That is when a professional mediator may be called upon.

FOR FURTHER THOUGHT

Think about some of the work conflict situations you have been in. Which mode is your typical response? As a person called upon to act as a third party, how would your typical conflict mode impact your efforts to reach a resolution?

MEDIATION

Mediation is the preferred approach to resolving conflict, regardless of its source. The meaning of the word mediation carries a very specific legal connotation in the United States. There are individuals who make their living as professional mediators. While you do not have to develop the skills of a certified mediator, some understanding of the way professionals handle the process may save the library a substantial amount of money. (A professional mediator's fees are typically in the range of $5,000 per day; the fee quickly escalates with the complexity of the situation.) Mediation, while having a legal meaning, is not a legal process. Its goal is to facilitate rather than impose solutions through having the parties to find a mutually agreeable resolution. The key to successful mediation is the neutral third party who works with the disputants in finding a mutual solution.

When the matter is between two staff members you may be able to serve as a mediator—a less costly option than having a professional called in. That still may happen, but it is often worth an effort on your part. It will only work if the disputants truly believe you are and will be neutral. When it involves a number of people or even most of your staff, it is best to explore getting a professional mediator.

Professionals in the field agree that every mediation "case" has three starting components. Indeed the actors and the specifics vary, and each case is special in many ways, but the starting point is always the same. That fact is, those three starting components exist in each conflict you handle.

The first component is each party, regardless of the number involved, will present a very *personal* version of the events leading up to the mediation. That version will place the individual in the best possible light (innocent of causing the situation). The second component is a description of how "bad" the other party(ies) really are and how they are responsible for creating the need for mediation. The last component is a presentation of what needs to be done to resolve the matter and that always requires the other party(ies) to change with no changed required on the part of the speaker. To summarize, the three components are:

1. I am innocent.
2. You are guilty.
3. You change, not me.

WORTH CHECKING OUT

The following titles are some of the many available in the area of mediation and are well worth a look:

Kyle Beardsley, *The Mediation Dilemma* (Ithaca, NY: Cornell University Press, 2011).

Margaret S. Herrman, *The Blackwell Handbook of Mediation: Bridging Theory, Research, and Practice* (Malden, MA: Oxford: Blackwell Publishing, 2006).

Kimberlee K. Kovach, *Mediation in a Nutshell*, 3rd edition (St. Paul, MN: Thomson/West, 2014).

Ellen Waldman, *Mediation Ethics: Cases and Commentaries* (San Francisco, CA: Jossey-Bass, 2011).

You can see the participants view the proceedings as judgmental, with the mediator as the judge and jury. Which is the last thing that mediator is, whether professional or yourself.

Effective mediation takes place in a "neutral" setting, which should be as pleasant a physical environment as possible. This should rule out using your office—it carries too much authority and raises at least subconscious doubts about your neutrality. Obviously the space must be private and if possible away from the library. It is best not to have a telephone available, and participants should be told to turn off any cell phones—the idea is to have uninterrupted time with the focus solely on the issues in dispute. This also means that supervisors of the parties must not, to every degree possible, impose work deadlines that overlap with the meeting times.

The typical mediation process consists of several elements. The obvious first element is gaining the participants' perspective of the issue(s) in the case. Another element is to get the parties to reach a mutual agreement as to what is the problem that needs resolution. This step requires the mediator to continually point out to the participants the similarities of their points of view (the mediation term for this is "mutualizing"). Doing so helps them start thinking the problem is solvable. Another aspect of the process is to remind participants the problem(s) is not unique, in fact it is rather common (mediators call this "normalizing"). Again the idea is to suggest a resolution is possible because it is not unique in character. A fourth step is to get everyone thinking about the future, not the present and past ("futureizing"). That is, the solution lies in the future, not the past or immediate present. Mediators employ such past/future words as *solution* rather than *problem*, *goals* rather than *complaints*, *fluid* not *fixed*, and *change* instead of *unchangeable*. Again, the goal is to get the participants thinking positively about the future.

A successful mediation normally results in a written memorandum of understanding, even if only the parties to the dispute have copies. The memorandum should cover:

- Who is to perform which tasks;
- What specific performance is expected;
- When the performance is to occur;

- How the performance is to be handled;
- How much is expected; and
- What outcome will result from failure to perform.

The above are only highlights of the process; reading about the subject is recommended (see the sidebar below). You are simply using some of the techniques that may keep the situation from escalating to the point of requiring the full process or a professional mediator.

NEGOTIATION SKILLS AND THEIR VALUE

Deborah Kolb and Judith Williams echoed the comments of Steven Babitsky and James J. Mangraviti in one of the opening quotations for this chapter when they wrote, "Negotiation was once considered an art practiced by the naturally gifted. . . . but increasingly we in the business world have come to regard negotiation as a science" (2011, 39).

Library frontline staffs do not have many opportunities to develop negotiation skills other than the few they develop from working with unhappy users. Even then, policies and rules limit the range of options for the staff. All staff will engage in "negotiations" with their supervisors over work schedules and perhaps performance assessments, and with colleagues about switching holiday, evening, or weekend hours. However, all these "negotiations" are highly informal and do not call on the skill set needed for formal negotiations, although such skills will still come in handy.

Negotiations take on several forms in a service environment. Customer relations and intradepartmental negotiations are two important areas in which negotiation skills are essential. Almost any collaborative project with other organizations will involve some negotiating. Middle managers may negotiate with vendors on a daily basis, senior managers negotiate between the library and governing boards and/or funding agencies, and there will be union contract negotiations in some settings.

CHECK THIS OUT

One title that is worth reviewing to learn more about the art of negotiation in a library setting is *The Librarian's Guide to Negotiation: Winning Strategies for the Digital Age*, by Beth Ashmore, Jill E. Grogg, and Jeff Weddlem (Medford, NJ: Information Today, 2012). It is well worth a look.

You must understand the differences between influence, negotiation, and coercion. Influence employs a strategy of shared power; negotiation employs the strategy of trading power; and coercion uses power imposition. While the first two methods are most common and desirable in the library environment, there are a few times when managers must resort to coercion.

Negotiation is useful when trying to reach an agreement between two parties that have some interests in common and some in opposition. Keep in mind that it is people, not organizations, that negotiate; successful negotiations are more dependent on the negotiators than on the parties they represent. Misunderstandings, intended or not, often trigger emotions or reactions that sabotage a negotiation, so it is essential to know the others as much as possible and to ensure shared understandings of terms and concepts.

You should think of negotiation as a six-step process:

1. Preparing,
2. Opening session,
3. Conducting the negotiation,
4. Moving toward agreement,
5. Reaching an agreement and.
6. Following up

Naturally there are steps within the steps.

Preparing has two major components—developing your plan and planning what the other party may do. Planning on your side starts by mustering all the facts and issues that support the position. You should lay out what goals and objectives are for the negotiation, what can be conceded easily (creating an atmosphere of "let's make a deal"), what are possible to give up when an impasse appears likely, and those that can not be forfeited. Developing several strategies for handling the negotiation and plan for when you might want to change the strategy is also part of your planning process.

CHECK THIS OUT

Karen Cates, in her January 2016 article "Negotiating Effectively" (*AALL Spectrum* 20, no. 3: 25) advocates the use of a planning document or grid when preparing for negotiations. Cates's document allows you to think ahead about what areas of common ground may exist between you and the other party, as well as knowing what you want and what you are willing to give up in order to facilitate a positive outcome. The article and the grid are worth a look.

The preparing component focuses on thinking about the opposing side's goals and objectives and what might be common to your own. A fairly typical library negotiation activity that can be used as an example is negotiating a contract with a database vendor. In those cases, the library wants access to the database and vendor wants the library to have access (the common goal). The issues are how to reach that goal. Perhaps there is a library concern regarding how much data the vendor may collect about individuals accessing the database and what the vendor may do with that data (user privacy rights). Cost is always a consideration. Cost concerns include how does the vendor typically set the price (per users, potential users, etc.), and are alternatives available? What happens if the library has to cancel the license sometime in the future, will the library still have access to the information it paid for during the time the license was in force? You can gain some insight into such issues if you know other libraries that negotiated with the vendor. Checking with those libraries may also provide other information about the vendor's negotiation tactics. The old saying "forewarned is forearmed" certainly applies to negotiations. With such information in mind, you are ready to create your final plans, and think about potential "sticking points" how to get past them.

In this case, your opening gambit should be to outline areas of mutual issues and goals (we both want the library users to have access to the database; how can we make that happen?). Sometimes that is all it takes to get to a mutual solution, it is rare but does happen. What is more likely is such an opening creates a positive atmosphere in which the negotiations can take place. After that you can begin to address those possible sticking points you identified.

This is the point where negotiations actually begin and your preparation will pay off. It may be a slow process and take more than one session. It is matter of proposal and counter-proposal as well as a high degree of patience and emotional control. Reaching the agreement is a matter of give and take. It is when the time you took to plan what to give easily and reluctantly comes into play. Remember to ask for what you need. As noted by Cates, "Fear of getting a 'no' in response to a request can feed anxieties. However, if you don't ask, the other party isn't going to read your mind. You have to tell him or her what you want" (2016, 26).

Once you achieve agreement it is essential to immediately document what was agreed upon. In our example of the database negotiations, the vendor will have a standard license and the agreement reached is likely to call for changes in that document. That may require the vendor negotiators to have the new terms signed off by the firm's lawyers. It may also require the library's lawyer to review and approve the document. Having a document covering the agreed terms reduces the chances of the "he said, I said" arising and forcing another round negotiations.

The final step is follow-up. This is very important when the negotiators have to check with other parties. Be certain to carryout any tasks you agreed to in a timely manner. Keep the other side informed, as much as possible, about progress and delays in getting the final approvals. You want to maintain the positive atmosphere that hopefully existed at the time of the agreement.

The ability to see, think, and feel, the issues as though you are on the other side, is as valuable to negotiation as facts and figures. Getting all relevant emotions out in the open is essential, as unexpressed feelings become barriers to the process. Defeat the problem, not one another. What are the skills and characteristics of an effective negotiator?

- Patience: Take your time. Negotiations have an element of conflict as well as uncertainty, and many people try to deal with these factors quickly because they are uncomfortable. A patient negotiator has an advantage.

- Preparation and knowledge: Work to understand your needs and issues and those of the other side.

- A good sense of organization: Know the implications (funds, people, time, etc.) for your side and the requests the other side is likely to make.

- Tolerance for conflict, uncertainty, and ambiguity—Be willing to leave an issue unresolved and move on to another issue when necessary, and remember that resolutions you make will affect those unresolved issues. The negotiator who is best able to handle these factors has an advantage.

- Willingness to take some reasonable risks: Know that every negotiation or agreement involves a greater or lesser degree of risk. Being unwilling to take some risk almost always results in a failed negotiation.

- Ability to relate to the people "on the other side of table."

- Good listening skills.

- High self-esteem: Possess a sure sense of your abilities and be able to take on personal responsibilities without allowing the other side to gain something your side did not want to concede. Wanting everyone to like you is not a good trait for an effective negotiator.

- A sense of humor.

- Integrity.

- Physical and mental stamina: Have the mental and physical stamina to handle long negotiations and avoid making mistakes. Dealing with labor contracts or the purchase of new software can take 15 to 18 hours at a time.

- Persistence: Know when to continue and when to walk away. Many people are not persistent enough in negotiations, either taking the first rejection as final, or conceding something too soon.

In summary, a successful negotiator should:

- Differentiate between wants and needs for both sides;
- Ask high and offer low, but be realistic;
- Make it clear that he or she was not "giving in," but that the object conceded was of value; and
- Strive for a profitable agreement for both sides.

An agreement that is completely win-lose is unlikely to last for any length of time.

TRY THIS

Think about a negotiation you've recently had that reached the agreement stage; if you haven't been involved in one, find a colleague who has been. Think about that negotiation and ponder the following questions:

- What did you do that appeared to be effective?
- What did you do that was less successful?
- What would you have done differently based on hindsight?
- What might have been done to reach an agreement more quickly?

It is also useful, when possible, to have the other party in that negotiation say what their assessment of the process was.

REFERENCES

Babitsky, Steven, and James J. Mangraviti. 2011. *Never Lose Again: Become a Top Negotiator by Asking the Right Questions*. New York: Thomas Dunne Books/St. Martin's Press.

Cates, Karen. 2016. "Negotiating Effectively: Getting to Win-Win." *AALL Spectrum* 20, no. 3: 23–27.

Essex, Louellen, and Mitchell Kusy. 2008. "Playing the Office Politics Game." *T+D* 62, no. 3: 76–79.

Farrell, Maggie. 2014. "Playing Nicely with Others." *Journal of Library Administration* 54, no. 6: 501–510.

Jeong, Ho-Won. 2016. *International Negotiation: Process and Strategies*. Cambridge, UK: Cambridge University Press.

Jones, Ken. 1985. *Conflict and Change in Library Organizations: People, Power, and Service (Looking Forward in Librarianship)*. London: Clive Bingley.

Kolb, Deborah M., and Judith Williams. 2011. "Breakthrough Bargaining." In *Harvard Business Review on Winning Negotiations*. Boston: Harvard Business Review Press.

Sadri, Golnaz. 2012. "Conflict's Here. What Now?" *Industrial Management* 54, no. 3: 20–25.

Chapter 20

LONG-TERM CAREER SUCCESS

Severe emotional and physical strain along with the lack of positive feed-back leads to exhaustion, cynicism, and decreased performance. Dissatisfaction with work is also an important determinant of burnout.

Zsuzsa Gyorffy, Diana Dweik, and Edmond Girasek, 2016

Working life often seems like an endless sequence of tiresome meetings. Catch-ups, kick-offs and reviews litter the calendars of most professionals. Effectiveness around the conference table can determine success in almost every career.

The Economist, 2015a

Women leaders often blame the glass ceiling for their lack of success, but there can be other reasons for not reaching leadership potential. One reason may be inadequate skills in public speaking. A leader must be able to convey ideas and information clearly. Thus, a critical skill for a strong leader is effective presentation.

Ingibjörg B. Frimannsdóttir and Barbara Whiting, 2011

For new professionals, creating and presenting a conference session can be very daunting, especially if one is not actively involved in a research project or pilot program.

Tanya Lisa Rogoschewsky, 2011

Building a long-term career takes self-awareness, a dedication to lifelong learning, a desire to succeed, and a good deal of effort. It also involves knowing your strengths and weaknesses. We touched on the topic of self-awareness in chapters 2 and 16; here we look at how that understanding interacts with other elements in building a rewarding career. How well you handle your combination of strengths and weaknesses will determine your long-term managerial leadership career. Your combination will be specific to yourself, if not in fact unique. However, there are some areas that a great many people share and we will address some of those commonalties in this chapter.

Before exploring those topics, we thought it useful to remind you of the substantial list of people and conceptual skills we have at the end of chapter 2. Table 20.1 repeats that list to help you assess strengths important for any managerial leader. Keep in mind the list is far from comprehensive. Also, while self-perception is the starting point, how others see you in your managerial leadership role is equally important. Consider having your mentor or a candid colleague rate you on the items on the list. In addition to these trusted resources, there are many resources available online that can help guide you toward greater self-perception. We mentioned some of these in previous chapters, such as the Meyers-Briggs self-assessment (there are many free online versions; one good one can be found at https://www.16personalities.com/free-personality-test).

Having a clear idea of your personal strengths and weaknesses can help guide you in your career as manager and will only help you both personally and professionally. Keep in mind, too, that recognizing areas for improvement does not mean that you won't be an effective manager. In fact, acknowledging personal weaknesses while striving to improve upon them can make you more empathetic and more accessible to the staff you supervise. Nobody wants to feel as though their manager couldn't possibly understand their various trials and tribulations at work, or that their manager wouldn't want to hear varying points of view or ideas because he or she is "perfect" and "already knows everything."

If your future career goals include a managerial role, also consider the team of people you work with from day one. Establishing and building good relationships and rapport is invaluable and will only help you if, in fact, you are eventually promoted—either within your current library or elsewhere. We'll talk about networking and collaboration in later chapters, but the point we want to make sure to

Table 20.1.

Keys to Managerial Leadership Success

People Skills	Conceptual Skills
Effectively coaching and training	Creating a vision
Supporting teamwork	Assessing issues
Communicating openly and honestly	Making rational decisions
Collaborating with others	Accepting reasonable risks
Managing conflict	Thinking strategically
Driving cultural competency	Managing funds effectively
Addressing user needs	Employing a big picture perspective
Creating trust	Writing thoughtfully
Motivating others	Listening with an open mind
Demonstrating flexibility	Developing realistic plans
Championing change	Learning throughout life
Assessing performance fairly	Seeking to improve processes
Recognizing/supporting talents in others	Showing initiative and innovation

convey is that it is incredibly challenging to adopt change within a team if there is not first a well-established atmosphere of trust.

COMMON AREAS FOR IMPROVEMENT

Stress management is an essential skill to develop and maintain regardless of your status as a manager as well as in your personal life. One type of stress that is more common than you might expect for public and nonprofit managers arises from when one or more board members pushes you to "operate like a business." This can be particularly stressful when the board is a governing body. More often than not the pressure comes from individuals who own businesses (think back to the quotation that opened chapter 1 from Herbert Simon). Library managerial leaders often do not know the research literature that documents the many differences between the private sector and the other sectors. In our view, the critical difference lies in the purpose of for-profit organizations (maximize profit) and the other two sectors (public good).

In terms of spelling out the differences in purpose, a frequently cited and in-depth assessment of the concept of public good is Mark Harrison Moore's *Creating Public Value: Strategic Management in Government* (Cambridge, MA: Harvard University Press, 1995). It is a work that has been widely translated and has gone through at least seven printings over the years. Moore provides a thorough assessment of how public good/values arise from the efforts of public sector activities. Almost all of his points, in one way or another, apply to nonprofit sector efforts as well. Some for-profit organizations espouse social responsibility, but none claim their purpose is to provide a public good. Another title that provides additional useful material is John M. Bryson, Barbara C. Crosby, and Laura Bloomberg's *Creating Public Value in Practice: Advancing the Common Good in a Multi-Sector, Shared-Power, No-One-Wholly-in-Charge World* (Boca Raton, FL: CRC Press, 2015).

CHECK THIS OUT

Although it examines the difference in decision making between public and private organizations, the references in Paul C. Nutt's 2005 "Comparing Public and Private Sector Decision-Making Practices" (*Journal of Public Administration Research and Theory*) provide a fine assortment of research material on various differences (http://faculty.cbpp .uaa.alaska.edu/afgjp/PADM610/Comparing%20Public%20and%20Private%20D -M.pdf).

Will knowing some major differences between sectors help you keep the pressure to operate more like a business from occurring? Of course not; however, it will help you effectively counter and resist the pressure. We like to think the various chapters in this book will help you as well.

Another common area where managers, regardless of sector, can improve is in creating and maintaining a healthy balance between their work activities and personal lives. There is no doubt that you will have more work-related obligations as you advance to higher levels of management. That fact makes it ever more important to achieve a healthy balance and find effective ways to manage your stress. As our opening quotation in this chapter states, stress can be a critical factor in work performance. Although the quote is from an article about burnout and stress among female physicians, the statement applies to managers in any sector.

We believe there is a work–life balance continuum that ranges from total work focus to total personal life focus. Clearly managers, at least the vast majority of managers, are somewhat short of the total work focus and rather far from the total personal life focus. Finding the right mix is a personal matter. However, the closer you are to the total work focus end of the continuum, the higher the risk becomes for burnout. As Pamela Babcock wrote, "it's important to 'help people recognize when the stress they are experiencing has become unhealthy' and impacted different aspects of their personal and affects professional lives" (2009, 68). We agree, and that means you have a dual role in helping your staff avoid burnout along with effectively avoiding it for yourself.

Perhaps stress has always been an issue but it seems an even greater one at present. Each of us faces the stress of personal and family issues, community and society issues, as well as work-related issues. If we could face only one set of stressors at a time it might not be so difficult, but all too often we must attempt to handle all three simultaneously. Few of us are capable of setting aside personal stressors upon going to work and leaving work stress behind when we go home.

AUTHOR EXPERIENCE

Shortly after Evans started his first full-time library job, his director suggested he purchase a punching bag and hang it by the garage door, saying, "Punch it out before getting in the car to come to work and beat the devil out of it before going into the house." The director's advice had some scientific merit—physical activity can be a significant tension and stress reducer. Unfortunately, physical activity is not always an option; nor is it the sole solution.

Evans did not buy such a bag but found the advice about physical activity helpful. As a director, each year Evans would buy the library staff association a holiday gift of some type for the staff lounge. One year it was a variation of the boxing punching bag (a "Bop Buddy," an inflatable, freestanding type of punching bag). It lasted two months before it was punched to pieces. Another year it was a dartboard with Evans's picture attached to the bullseye. Not too long after he learned the university president's face had replaced Evans as the target. The picture approach had to stop, but Evans learned the replacement was verbal comments before throwing the dart.

Our point is there are some ways to assist the staff in releasing some of the frustrations and stress of the workplace that are rather easy to provide.

What are some of the major sources of workplace stress? In the Unites States, workplace stress is such a critical issue that the National Institute of Occupational Safety and Health (NIOSH) has identified six categories of risk factors: workload and pace, work schedule, role stressors, career security, interpersonal factors, and job context. The following are more specific triggers that may affect information professionals:

- Lack of professional autonomy
- User expectations that constantly rise and need to be met
- Role conflicts, such as those between professional and paraprofessional staff
- Lack of control over service operations
- High idealism
- Perfectionism
- Over commitment
- Technology that doesn't work as expected

A strategic use of the word "no" is probably one of the best techniques for reducing stressors. The judicious balancing of "yes" and "no" will go a long way toward reducing stress and keeping the workload reasonable while maintaining a reputation of being a highly effective performer.

Take some time to learn a few short- and long-term relaxation techniques. One problem the authors have noted that their younger colleagues have is that they have to learn to take time off. Vacation or leave time exists in organizations for the benefit of both the individual and the organization. In U.S. libraries, as well as in other organizations, you hear people talking about "taking a mental health day." It is usually said in jest, but the reality is that people do require time away from the job or they will "burn out."

Having a good support network inside and outside of work is another mechanism for reducing stress, even if it is only three or four individuals you can "vent" to about work, who understand the environment and who may even have some useful suggestions. Stress and burnout are very real concerns.

CHECK THIS OUT

A study of the problems that arise when the organization expects an employee to be a 24/7 employee (no personal life) is Erin Reid and Lakshmi Ramarajan's 2016 "Managing the High Intensity Workplace" (*Harvard Business Review* 94, no. 6: 84–90). Although libraries are far from having a Silicon Valley environment and expectation of employees, the issues these authors discuss are just as real for library employees.

Two interesting Web pages that discuss burnout are "Burnout Self-Test: Check Yourself for Burnout" (https://mindtools.com/pages/article/newTCS_08.htm) and "Tell Tale Signs of Burnout: Do You Have Them?" (https://www.psychologytoday.com/blog/high-octane-women/201311/the-tell-tale-signs-burnout-do-you-have-them).

MEETINGS—THE SEEMING LIFE BLOOD OF ORGANIZATIONS

As suggested by the opening quotation from *The Economist*, a managerial fact of life is that meetings are inevitable and frequent. It is also true that you are, in part, judged by how you handle the meetings you call. Yet another fact is not all meetings are created equal. Some seem pointless, others make you wonder why you had to be present, still more drag on and on, and some are pithy, pointed, and productive. What makes the difference?

We believe the difference lies in how well the person calling the meeting applies three of the communication Ps—planning, preparation, and presentation. Those three are essential if you are to connect with and persuade people. Thinking about the various types of meetings you have been involved in and those that were relevant or useful are likely to be those that were pithy and pointed. What were the factors that made them effective?

Too often we don't spend enough time planning and preparing for our meetings. In part, this is due to the fact that a number of them are regularly scheduled and seem routine. For example, departmental meetings or a regular meeting with our supervisor we tend to think of as "routine" and require little pre-planning. Certainly such meetings require less planning and preparation than many other types of meetings because much of the basic planning has been done. It is also true that even with extensive planning and preparation a meeting can fail to be productive; however, the chances of that happening are greatly reduced when you do put time in on those two Ps.

Planning starts with thinking through exactly what you hope to accomplish from a meeting. The vast majority of library meetings fall into one of several broad categories—information sharing, decision making, problem solving, planning, coordinating, or training. Each category calls for slightly different approaches and no two meetings, even in the same category, are identical.

Even before you begin to plan your approach, take a moment or two to consider if a physical meeting is actually necessary. Could the matter be effectively handled electronically? Handling an issue with email will save all of the potential participants some time. Anything that just requires a vote is a potential candidate for an electronic rather than a face-to-face resolution. Matters that you know are even somewhat contentious probably can be more quickly resolved with a physical meeting. While your meeting activity may only consume 30 minutes, the total time involved will almost always be longer. There will be some "social time" before, perhaps during, and certainly after the meeting. A 30-minute meeting may well cost the library 45 minutes or more in staff time per attendee. Think long and hard about which approach is most appropriate.

Another step is to carefully consider who *must* attend and also those who might *like* to attend. Keeping the number of participants as low as possible will allow the meeting to move more quickly. In terms of those who might like to attend, can you think of an approach that will let them know the meeting's purpose and its outcome without their physical presentence? Don't let the needs of the "like to" category impact the meeting time and purpose. Our suggestion is to contact those who must be present to determine their availability, set a time on the basis of their needs, and inform anyone else with an interest about the when and where of the meeting. Your inquiry regarding available times should include the meeting's topic, purpose, place, tentative agenda, and length. In some cases, you may need to supply attendees with information to review ahead of time. Keep such material to the absolute minimum; everyone has more than enough to read without unnecessary padding. You may need to ask one or more of the attendees to lead a portion of the discussion. Handle such matters prior to the meeting; you will lose valuable time doing this during the meeting. If you think there may need to be several meetings in order to achieve the purpose, you might want to state that expectation.

Time is a significant issue in meetings. We have all attended meetings that seem to drag on and others that seem too rushed. Thinking through the timing is critical to having a successful session. Information sharing should be as short as possible. Developing a new policy is likely to require more than one meeting. Meetings dealing with decision making and coordinating activities are likely to be intermediate in length. Most scholars suggest 30 to 60 minutes as the average for a productive session. Longer periods tend to lead to some loss of focus by attendees as fatigue sets in and other work pressures tend to intrude on their attention.

There are some additional preparations to think about; some of which are handled without much thought when it is a regularly scheduled meeting time and place. For other meeting types spending a little time in advance handling "logistics" can provide more time for having a productive session.

Something as simple as the meeting room size can play a positive or negative role in meeting success. Selecting the appropriate space will help assure success. Rooms too large or too small can create a negative environment. In most cases, your options certainly will be limited in a library, but you will likely have at least two options—your office and some type of all-purpose meeting room. Trying to crowd a number of individuals into your office can cause people to focus more on the crowded conditions than on the meeting topic. There are times when seeking a meeting space outside the library is worth the expense. Topics such as strategic planning (or other "retreat topics") often benefit from being held away from the library—fewer work distractions and, if nothing else, a change in atmosphere. It is unlikely you can hold more than one such meeting away from the library to discuss such issues; however, it can start the effort on a very positive note.

Another "environmental" issue can be the temperature of the meeting space. A space too hot or too cold can shift attendees' focus to the temperature rather than the meeting's topic. The temperatures of infrequently used meeting spaces are often kept at energy efficient levels to save money—rarely are such levels people friendly. Checking an hour or so ahead of the meeting time can allow you to get the room comfortable—sometimes this may require the assistance of someone else (some organizations have locked covers over room thermostats). Having to deal with the issue of the space being too hot or too cold during the meeting disrupts the attendees' concentration and costs time.

Yet another issue is visual—will there be a need for technology or even just simple flip charts or a white board? From a technology point of view think about sight lines, light control, and whether there is readily available technological support if needed. Think about how to handle recording information on flip charts, white boards, and so on. Doing this yourself will slow the session down; trying to get a volunteer to do this at the meeting also uses up time—recruit someone ahead of time. Do the same in terms of taking meeting minutes.

How you manage the meeting is a "presentation" on your part. The attendees may not be aware they are doing it, but they are making judgments about you as a manager. How you handle the meeting will make an impression on the participants. Their judgments will be similar to those that arise when you give a formal presentation. In the case of a meeting, some judgments will focus on the importance of the meeting's topic and who you identified as necessary to be at the meeting. Perhaps a more significant judgment will be about how well you handle the meeting, especially when there are differing views about the meeting's topic.

One important element in effective meetings is to assure everyone participates— why have a person attend if their thoughts are not needed? Some individuals tend to be less outgoing in meetings and you may need to get them involved by asking their opinion on this or that point. At the opposite end of the spectrum you have the challenge of the individual who begins to dominate the session with such behaviors as nonstop talking, interrupting others, "putting down" or disagreeing with another person in a personal manner. Again, you need to take action to modify such behavior or you will lose control of the meeting. One tactic for handling a "talker" is to step in, thank the person for her or his thoughts, and say something like "Let's hear what the others have to say." For the interrupter ("I'm the only one that knows about this"), you may have to be comparatively blunt—"Please, do not interrupt, you can speak after X has finished their thoughts on the matter." "I value all points of view and would appreciate it if you waited until I call on you." Will such tactics always work? Of course not; however, they will help reduce the behavior and other attendees will be grateful for your efforts to control the situation.

Keeping the meeting on topic, listening to a variety of views, and getting resolution on agenda items will enhance your reputation for being an effective manager. People will be more willing to attend your meetings. People dislike ineffectual meetings. People like to have a feeling of accomplishment that arises from having a productive meeting. Well-run meetings will help you achieve such goals. The sidebar below provides a list of steps to take for presenting effective meetings.

STEPS FOR EFFECTIVE MEETINGS

- Create an agenda.
- Share the agenda ahead of time with participants.
- Start on and end on time.
- Outline meeting's purpose and time limit.
- State any "ground rules" for the meeting.

- Review the agenda items and any associated time limits.
- Ask if there are any suggestions for reordering the item sequence.
- Introduce/confirm minute taker and recorder, if appropriate.
- Open the discussion of the first agenda item and ask for comments (prepare some opening thoughts in case there is silence).
- Listen thoughtfully to others before stating your views (if you begin the discussion you may cut off other ideas because attendees may assume your view is all that matters).
- Elicit comments from everyone (use direct questions if necessary to get shy individuals to speak up).
- Integrate/summarize comments to determine if there is consensus.
- Outline action items (who will do what and how soon).
- Set next meeting time, if appropriate, and close meeting.
- Share the minutes of the meeting with participants and any interested parties.

FORMAL PRESENTATIONS

In a sense, how you handle the presentations in the meetings you call reflects on your managerial leadership skills. However, there are a number of other presentations that you will be required to perform in your role as manager; in fact, you may be somewhat surprised by how often you will be called upon to give public presentations. The presentations can range from describing a proposed change in your unit to colleagues to giving a speech at a national conference. Most of the presentations will be within the library or to local groups such as the library's friends group or to the library's funding body during budget request times. Often because we are familiar with the subject matter and know the individuals in the "audience," we tend to treat the matter in a casual manner. Doing so does a disservice to the topic and to the listeners.

Public speaking is not an activity that many people are totally comfortable doing. Even those who make their living giving speeches have at least a tad of anxiety prior to the start time. The standard wisdom is that, if you don't feel a little anxious, you don't really care enough about your topic. We can't say if that wisdom is accurate, but what we can say is that after years of teaching and public speaking, we still have some nervousness before starting a class session or formal presentation.

Public speaking worries are common enough to have a label—glossophobia. Only a few of us suffer from the phobia to the degree we cannot or will not speak publicly. Most of us can master the fear to a greater or lesser degree. Again, there are three Ps that can assist in dealing with such fears—planning, preparation, and practice, lots of practice. Practice for a speech involves rehearsing and more rehearsing. In other cases, such as teaching, careful preparation and thoughtful review of the material several times prior to the start of session can reduce the normal anxiety. A person with information literacy instruction experience whose training included the development and delivery of presentations has "a leg up."

One common fear when it comes to public speaking is of making a mistake during the presentation. This is not about content; you can control that aspect, but rather

---

COMMON CHALLENGES IN PUBLIC SPEAKING

- Not being prepared
- Not practicing beforehand
- Speaking too fast
- Running words together
- Using fillers such as "um" or "like"
- Using visual aids that don't add to the presentation (e.g., a PowerPoint presentation that reiterates all of the speaking points without offering any additional or pertinent information)
- Lacking pace
- Exhibiting nervous tics such as inappropriate laughter or clearing one's throat
- Speaking too softly, or, less often, too loudly
- Giving too many details too rapidly
- Jumping back and forth between main topics
- Having a poor structure of the presentation
- Speaking in a monotone
- Employing poor body language and gestures
- Misusing/misgauging the timeline for the presentation

---

is about stumbling, or getting distracted by something going on in the audience. Even the most experienced public speakers, including those who make their living from such presentations, occasionally make a mistake. The more often you do speak in public, the less likely you are to experience a mistake. Also, keep in mind that 99.9 percent of your audience is seeking information, insights, entertainment, and the like, *not* perfection in presentation; they will overlook a mistake or stumble. And, usually, you will be the expert on the topic, not them.

The Pesky Ps

You probably remember the six Ps from chapter 3; they are critical for effective presentations. The obvious starting point for the planning process is your presentation's purpose. Is your purpose to inform, convince, gain a consensus, entertain, or something else? The purpose becomes your infrastructure for the presentation. Another element is audience composition. Will it consist of library peers? Will it be people who do or don't have an understanding of your library? Is it intended for professionals, laypeople, or a mix? Answers to such questions will help you plan your content as well as the structure of the speech.

Yet another factor is the timeframe. A budget request presentation may be as few as 10 or 15 minutes, often delivered to listeners who have been listening—more or less—to a number of other similar presentations. On the other hand a keynote speech to a large audience might be 45–60 minutes. Most of your presentations will fall somewhere in between those extremes. Whatever your allotted time is, it will force you to structure the content to fit the timeframe. The shorter the time, the more you have to prioritize what you cover and the less useful the general guidelines will be for creating an effective speech.

For most presentations, other than very short ones or staff meetings you call, the following are general elements that help you in creating a sound structure:

- Tone setter/attention getter
- Background
- Overview of key points
- Key points
- Supporting material
- Implication—why does it matter, what to do
- Transition
- Summary

With a structure in place you can begin the preparation phase. Getting an audience's attention is clearly essential. Doing so is especially critical when your presentation time is short and you are just one of many doing so to the same group during a day or evening. Getting the group's attention, being pithy, concise, complete, and so on, is a challenge and one you often have to address as manager during budget preparation periods. If anything, these sessions take much longer to prepare for effectively than do other sessions that last longer, at least in our experience.

Sometimes, but not always, starting with a joke helps get the group's attention and helps put you into a comfortable mode of presentation. Jokes for joke's sake are not all that effective. Having a joke that links to the topic of the speech is more effective. One of this book's authors has something of a "shaggy dog" joke about a "perfect person" that can to be tailored to almost any topic. It serves as a tone setter and quickly highlights the speech's topic. If you can come up with such a joke, keep it in your presentation toolkit and don't be afraid to use it, even if some of the audience may have heard it in several incarnations. Such jokes let you move into the background and overview discussion naturally. The old adage, "Tell them what you are going to tell them. Tell them. Tell them what you've told them" has merit.

"Telling them" the key points is where you provide the supporting information regarding each point. Try to keep those points to as small a number as possible while covering the topic. Having too many "key" points can cause your listeners to lose track of the overall message you are trying to convey. Not filling the time available is not always a bad thing. Allowing time for a Q&A session is often as important as the speech itself. If there are few questions, there is usually no harm in ending the session earlier. Few people object to getting out of meeting sooner than expected.

You have a number of options when it comes to how to structure your main points. Problem solving is where you pose a problem, provide a potential solution, and describe the benefits of your solution. Moving from the simple to more complex is a long standing method of structuring a presentation. Another tried-and-true approach is chronological. A dramatic approach is effective (building to a climax), but not always an available option, depending on the topic. Outlining a series of propositions and their potential benefits is another possible structure for your presentation. However you structure the main body of your presentation, be careful to include enough, but not too much, detail to match your anticipated audience's knowledge, or lack of knowledge, of your topic. Too much or too little detail will likely result in your losing the audience's attention.

Visual Aids

With the content structured you can think about the use of visual material as a part of the presentation. Visual aids should be just that, aids, and not a substitute for content. Certainly visuals can help you stay on track and help reduce your concern about making a mistake and other associated public speaking fears. Becoming too dependent on the visuals can lead to a situation in which you might be more effective by writing out your thoughts and distributing them rather than speaking. At a minimum, use visuals to provide an overview of your main points.

One of the standard visuals is some variation of the ever-present PowerPoint slide. There are other options for such visual material, for example, Google Presentation (https://docs.google.com/templates?category=2&type=presentations&sort=hottest&view=public)or Keynote (http://www.apple.com/apps/iwork/keynote), or Prezi (http://prezi.com/). Regardless of the software, you create "slides." We have all sat through such presentations, some we liked and some we didn't, and our reasons may not have anything to do with the content.

When creating each of your "slides," we recommend keeping the following factors in the forefront of your thinking:

- Content—not too much;
- Color—reds and yellows tend to be hard to read when projected;
- Background—light or dark with the opposite for the text;
- Font—san serif fonts tend to be easier to read when projected;
- Size—text should be 12 points or larger to be read in a large room;
- Animation—use with care, it can be distracting;
- Text—use bullet points rather than full sentences; and
- Charts and diagrams—keep them as simple as possible, complex forms are hard to read.

The top five peeves of audiences in which presentation software was featured are:

1. Presenter reading the slides to the audience
2. Full text rather than bullet points
3. Unable to read slides due to small font size
4. Color choices make slides difficult to read
5. Overly complex charts and diagrams (David Paradi, 2011, p.19)

CHECK THIS OUT

An interesting website that may help you improve your visual presentations is "Think Outside the Slide" (http://www.thinkoutsidetheslide.com/).

A fine book that will help you make better use of visuals in your presentations is Stephen Michael Kosslyn's *Better PowerPoint: Quick Fixes Based on How Your Audience Thinks* (New York: Oxford University Press, 2011).

Practice Is the Key

Practice may not make perfect, but it will improve a performance. How much practice is necessary depends on your self-confidence, experience, and the importance of the event. And remember that just because a timeframe is short does not mean less practice is needed. In some cases, the shortest session requires the greatest amount of practice.

While the following points may not reduce the stress felt at the prospect and at the time of delivery, they will help ensure that the presentation is well structured. For many people, just knowing this is a stress-reducer. The key is preparation; the more time spent on preparations, the more likely the presentation will be good. Following the checklist is no guarantee of success, but it will enhance the chances.

ORAL PRESENTATION CHECKLIST

- Define your objective—write a single sentence about your goal.
- Define your audience—analyze their level of knowledge of the topic, likes and dislikes, and what they expect from the presentation.
- Define your approach—write a single sentence describing the thought or message that best leads into your topic.
- Develop your opening—you have 30 seconds to grab your listeners' attention; does your opening lead to your objective, relate to your audience, relate to your approach, and does it have both verbal and visual impact?
- Develop the body—does it explain the point(s) you want to make, describe what you've done, use language appropriate for the audience, and deliver the message in the fewest possible words?
- Develop the closing—does it summarize your point in two or three memorable sentences and ask for the action you want from the audience in terms of specific steps and a timeline?
- Create visual aids—are they related to your point, helping you make your point, readable from all points in the room, and compatible with the time allotted?
- Time the presentation—is it 10 percent shorter than the time allotted?
- List dreaded questions—have you developed a list of potential difficult/dreaded questions and thought about how to answer them?
- List general questions—have you listed expected questions and your answers to them?
- Check the room layout—are the room and expected audience size compatible?
- Check the lectern—is it the right height for you, and is there a glass of water?

- Consider other distractions—have you checked lighting, temperature controls, and possible noise sources? Are there any trailing cables to avoid?

- Check PowerPoint/projectors/visual equipment—if you are using equipment, have you checked it in terms of operation? Is there backup in case of failure, and do you have a number to call for technical assistance, if required?

- Rehearse—have you rehearsed the presentation a number of times from start to finish, using your visual aids, if appropriate?

- Develop choreography—have you thought about how you will move to and from the visuals?

- Plan audience participation—is there an element where you can gain audience participation in the presentation?

- Plan questions for the audience—are there questions you could ask the audience during the presentation, and have you factored into your timing their involvement or lack thereof?

- Plan handouts—are there handouts that you want the audience to have, and have you planned when their distribution should take place—before, during, or after the presentation? If the distribution is before or during, have you considered how that might impact your timing or verbal presentation?

- Consider attire—if in doubt, tend toward the conservative, but have a bright scarf or tie that is visually attractive. Check in a mirror before going to the room.

- Analyze post-presentation—after the presentation, analyze, with a participant if possible, what worked, what didn't work, and presentation time versus rehearsal time.

CHECK THESE OUT

Two books that can assist you in managing your glossophobia are Scott Berkun's *Confessions of a Public Speaker* (Sebastopol, CA: O'Reilly, 2010); and Melody Templeton's *Public Speaking and Presentations Demystified* (New York: McGraw-Hill, 2010).

Written Presentations

While there are many similarities between oral and written presentations, there are several important differences. The obvious major difference is that in written presentations you lack the face-to-face element of oral presentations. You can gauge an audience's reaction to your oral efforts—bored, confused, with you, and so on. With an oral presentation, be it a committee meeting or keynote speech, there also is a time factor that limits how much detail you can include. There are fewer limits for your written efforts, although there are practical limitations if you wish to hold the reader's attention.

Perhaps the most significant difference between the two is the longevity of the presentation. Unless your oral presentation is recorded, your exact words, gestures, emphases, and non-verbal behaviors are lost and gone forever. Not so for your written words. More than 2,000 years ago the Roman author and poet Horace had an insight as to the long-term implications of the written word when he wrote, "Let it be kept till the ninth year, the manuscript put away at home: you may destroy whatever you have not published, once out, what you've said can't be stopped" (*Oxford Dictionary of Quotations* 1980, 258). All you have to do is think about confirmation hearings for government posts to know something written years and years ago can come back to haunt a person.

It is unlikely that you will ever have to face confirmation scrutiny, but what you write today may well impact your long-term career. The reality is, in today's e-world, you don't have to publish your thoughts in the traditional sense to have them "preserved" in some form almost indefinitely. Almost 100 percent of your work related e-communications is stored somewhere long after you have deleted the files from your work hard drive. Between backup tapes and forensic computer specialists, most files can come back into play, even from your hard drive, unless you reformatted the drive.

Do you use social media? Do you tweet? You are undoubtedly aware of the privacy concerns and growing concern about employers requesting social media passwords from employees and even prospective employees. There was a short news note in 2016 that indicated 36 percent of reporting Human Resource (HR) departments disqualified a job candidate due to social media postings (*Arizona Republic*, 2016). Did you ever consider your tweets might live on indefinitely and be available to almost anyone? You may be surprised to know that, as of January 2013, the Library of Congress archived all 170 billion (it is a "b" not an "m") tweets that were posted on Twitter since the firm started operations and the Library of Congress (LC) will continue to archive new tweets (http://blogs.loc.gov/loc/2013/01/update-on-the-twitter-archive-at-the-library-of-congress/). Not only will LC archive the billions of probably unplanned thoughts and spontaneous reactions, but it will also make them available to users. If you go to the above address you will also learn LC collects other Web resources. Horace's thoughts might take on more meaning for those of us who do use social media. You may think LC's congratulatory statement regarding the preservation of your 140-character tweet should have been a condolence. The archiving of tweets also suggests that the first of our Ps (planning) becomes ever more important.

Clarity of purpose is the key to effective, persuasive, and meaningful communication, be it oral or written. Lacking a firm purpose you can muddle through preparing a message, but don't expect your reader to figure out what your purpose was—they won't. There is a reason for that line that often appears on printed memo forms—"Subject." If you can't write out your basic purpose in a dozen words or fewer, preferably three or four, you really do not have a good handle on your purpose.

As is the case with oral presentation, audience composition is central to planning the most effective message. With purpose and audience in mind, you can think about how to structure the document as well as what delivery channel to employ—electronic, paper, and so on. Often your intended audience will be a major factor in deciding what channel(s) you employ.

Writing for Non-Work Audiences

It is reasonably easy to master the art of business- or work-related writing. You quickly learn the ins and outs of communicating with your staff and other library staff members. The ongoing work relationships reveal what channels and styles of writing are most effective. When it comes to writing for those outside the library the process takes time, effort, and probably a few mistakes along the way before you can be reasonably confident your written message(s) will be effective.

When writing to an outside audience, there are other considerations to keep in mind. There are many more variations that exist than when you write to your library peers. You will write for some outside groups on a more or less regular basis—library users, library governing board, library funding agency, library support groups, and so on. Over time you will gain an understanding of the individuals in each group and can tailor your content to their preferences. For example, the funding agency may be like Sergeant Joe Friday on the old TV series *Dragnet*—"Just the facts, ma'am." That group may not be interested in a flowing narrative or fine turn of phrase; it wants facts and figures. Perhaps the library governing body may enjoy a fine narrative filled with anecdotal material, while the library's support group (Friends of the Library, for example) may want a mix of facts and stories about successes. It takes a few efforts to identify a group's interests as well as what some of the most influential individuals within the group want—keeping in mind those can be very different approaches. Another challenge is the members of such groups change from time to time, requiring you to identify new preferences.

Professional Publishing

"Writing offers an opportunity for librarians to reflect on their practice. It is potentially a powerful tool to help identify where we have come from, where we are now, and how we want to develop" (Fallon, 2010, 35). You may or may not agree with Helen Fallon's sentiment but she was correct that such writing does reflect on a person's professional practice.

Needless to say, topic selection is the starting point for a writing project. A standard recommendation is "write about what you know." That is fine advice up to a point, although if you don't explore new topics you will not grow. One type of writing project that allows you to dig into a new area is the literature review or state-of-the-art essay. Another possibility is writing about some library program or activity that is somewhat unusual. Occasionally, especially for academic librarians employed at institutions that have faculty rank or status for librarians, a research project is a good candidate for publication.

Regardless of topic, doing a literature review is important. One reason is it helps to know what has already been published on the topic and that information may well impact how you structure your presentation. Not doing a literature review will likely result in the material coming back to you with a strong suggestion you should include such information, if you wish the publisher to accept the piece. That will happen when the publisher has an editorial board or employs peer reviewers. Professional journal editors want to publish the soundest articles possible and try to work with authors to achieve that end. Most of them provide feedback to the author(s), even for material they reject. They want to encourage authors to keep improving and submitting material.

Writing for publication is a matter of drafting, editing, drafting, and editing, over and over, at least for most of us. Once you have a draft you are reasonably comfortable with, ask your mentor or trusted friend(s) to give you feedback on content, style, grammar, and so on. Take the comments to heart and revise your manuscript. This step will enhance the chances of your work being accepted by the first publisher you send it to. Do keep in mind to send it to one publisher at a time; making simultaneous submissions to multiple publishers is not acceptable.

Also, do your homework prior to submitting the material; blind submissions rarely succeed. Once you have identified the most likely best fit of your topic and journal interest, check out the journal's guidelines for submission and style (do you need an abstract of fewer than 100 words, use footnotes vs. endnotes, etc.) and rework your paper as necessary. Such attention to detail improves the chances of acceptance.

When or if you are motivated to attempt a book-length manuscript, the process is a little different, at least in terms of professional books. The vast majority of such projects, including new editions of an existing title, commence with the prospective author submitting a book proposal—either on her or his own initiative or at the suggestion of a publisher. Most proposals have more or less standard components.

BOOK PROPOSAL CONTENT

- A narrative describing the project and the need for such a book
- A description of the intended audience
- An indication of the anticipated manuscript length
- A proposed table of contents, in as much detail as you can provide
- A completed sample chapter—essential for first-time authors
- A discussion of special or unique features (photographs or illustrations, etc.) of the proposed title
- A discussion of how the work differs from other competing titles
- A discussion of the potential market
- A timeline for the delivery of the completed manuscript
- A résumé of the author's (or authors') qualifications for writing the book

---

A successful book proposal results in a contract. It is rare for someone to complete a professionally oriented manuscript without having a contract. If nothing more, the contract deadline helps keep the author working on the project. Writing takes time and effort. There are days when you lack motivation to write or find you have written yourself into a box; these and other things make it easy to set the project aside and do something else. The authors of this book have had occasional days when washing the windows seems more appealing than writing.

A contract does *not* guarantee publication. Essentially, the contract gives the publisher "first refusal rights." Your completed manuscript will be read by at least one of the publisher's editors and probably by one or two outside experts in the field of the book's subject. Just as with a submitted journal article, you may receive suggestions for changes, additions, deletions, and so on, that even experienced authors find annoying, at least on first reading. Again, the suggestions are intended to make the book stronger. The reality is, if you don't make those changes the publisher may decline to publish the book. It is also possible, though not too likely, the publisher may reject the manuscript after you make the changes. In that case, you are free to take it to another publisher.

AUTHOR'S EXPERIENCE

Evans has had years of experience on all sides of the publishing table—as an author, a managing editor, and a member of a journal editorial board (*Library Management*).

   He is always sad when he has to say the manuscript is not ready to publish or is unacceptable. He is sad because he is well aware that the manuscript is almost always prepared on the author's personal time. The person(s) gave up some evening and weekend hours and, sometimes, vacation time to complete the manuscript. Undertaking a writing project is challenging, sometimes frustrating, but also rewarding. Do think about giving it a try.

As noted earlier, some academic librarians don't have an option regarding publishing; they are under pressure to publish or otherwise engage in "scholarly activity." They face an additional publication challenge, not just making the time to write something and get it published, but also of writing for the "best" type of publication.

There is an unwritten "pecking order" within academia, at least in institutions that place an importance on publishing research. It is primarily among those types of institutions that have faculty rank or status for librarians. It also important to understand that although there are "three legs" to the tenure stool (teaching, research, and service) one of the legs far outweighs the importance of the other two—research. And, for research to really count, you must publish the results.

You might be able to guess what some of the "lower level" publications are in terms of weight when it comes to tenure or promotion. Publishing a review of an item a library might or might not acquire is very useful for librarians; however, it is at the bottom of the weight list. State-of-the-art articles are slightly weightier, but not by much. Third from the bottom are anthologies that have little or no commentary by the complier; the publication carries more weight with the decision makers if it includes commentary or analysis. Textbooks carry only slightly more weight, but only if they contain new information or insights. A case study article (perhaps some activities you undertook) and a chapter in a book are of about equal weight depending upon how much new analysis they contain. At the top of the list are research articles and monographs. Even the publisher carries some importance—publishers that employ peer review for their publications are viewed as more important than those who do not.

Those weights may at first appear pretentious; they are in one sense, but not in another. The reason for this difference rests on the fundamental reason for academic research. That is, research should advance human knowledge and well-being, and provide benefits to society and the like. Peer reviewing is considered a measure of the accuracy and value of the material in a publication.

Social Media as Presentation

Libraries and librarians have steadily increased their use of social media, in part to make connections with the younger users who are almost constantly connected. Marketing and public relations are other reasons for using social media. Although focused on the public library environment, Hanna Carlsson's comment applies to any library type: "Inspired by the utopian Web 2.0 discourse and the popularity of social media, current trends in public library services development have been described as an attempt to create a Library 2.0, combining ideals of increased user participation with the implementation of social media technologies, such as blogs and social networking sites" (2012, 199).

In today's e-world, libraries are almost compelled to make use of social media. Libraries and librarians should keep two facts in the forefront of their thinking about employing social media professionally. First, social media postings are presentations. Second, such postings are becoming ever-more-permanent reflections of the library's or librarian's image. Just because you deleted a posting does not mean it is no longer out there in the virtual world. Earlier we noted that LC is archiving tweets and plans to continue to do so. Facebook's "Timeline" means that some silly photo or shared message from years ago is still available. Some libraries are attempting to archive government websites for future researchers. Many libraries that fall under a city municipality also must archive all of their social media postings in order to comply with record retention laws governed by the state.

TIME TO SAY GOODBYE

Our concluding section of this final chapter is about the inevitable need to say goodbye to a managerial post. Such goodbyes can be happy or sad occasions, and once in a great while, can be an unwanted goodbye. Retirements generally are a mixture of happiness and sadness. Moving on to a new post is generally a happy occasion, while having to leave due to health or other personal reasons is sad. Timing of such departures and the attendant transitions is almost always difficult. That is why spending some time thinking about the "hows" and "whens" of departures is a good idea (often referred to as "succession planning").

Succession planning is a concept that is more often discussed than it is effectively implemented. In the for-profit sector, such planning is thought to be essential for the long-term managerial leadership success of an organization. Essentially, the notion is the organization needs to plan for the inevitable changes in leadership, at least at the senior level. The ideal plan starts with the hiring of the best possible people for entry and mid-level positions and then developing the best of the best to take over senior positions sometime in the future as the need arises. That ideal rarely lives up to expectations, in large part due to time. "Sometime in the future" is a problem. Top-flight people are highly sought out and opportunities for a top position frequently arise long before the "sometime" in their current organization. If the concept rarely fulfills its promise, why devote space to its coverage?

Our answer is, because there will be transitions—they are like death and taxes—so at least thinking about how to address that fact is a sound idea. Although such planning is a major for-profit concern, public sector organizations also consider the need to have smooth transitions. For example, in 2014, James Larue wrote "Directors come and directors go. And now, the long heralded retirement of one generation of leaders (Baby Boomers) and the rise of two others (Gen-Xers and Millennials) is finally materializing" (14). In early 2015, *The Economist* also commented about senior managerial leaders stepping aside or stepping down: "Staying in a post too long greatly increases the chances of making a calamitous error or becoming stale" (2015b, 64). The March 2016 issue of *Public Management* included a discussion of succession planning by three city and county senior managers. Although these pieces focus on senior management, the issue of leaving applies to any level of a managerial position.

Timing of the "event" is the key to a successful transition. Other than for health and personal reasons, there can be some type of planning for departures. Even in the case of health issues, some transition time is often possible. One challenge to getting the timing "right," from an organizational point of view, is the emotional aspect we noted in the opening paragraph of this section. Often the "right" timing is different for the leave taker and the organization.

There are what we think of as the five Es from which stem the differences in timing perspectives: empowerment, emotion, expertise, experience, and ego. Empowerment (having power) can be a major impediment to achieving a mutually agreed-upon transition point. We opened this chapter with a discussion of the value of having a balanced work life as well as the notion that there is a continuum from all work to all personal life. Our sense is the closer a person is to the all work end of that spectrum, the harder it is for that person to step aside or step down. Much of the person's sense of being rests on being a manager and having the attendant powers of such a position. From an organizational point of view, such individuals can either be an asset or a liability when it becomes necessary for the person to step down.

Expertise and experience, while related, are different. Both are valuable and necessary traits in all staff members for an organization to be successful. Long-term managers are very likely to possess both traits and certainly have a vast knowledge of the institutional memory that helps direct activities. Again, the work-focused person may overvalue her or his skills and knowledge in these areas and believe he or she must stay. The view of organization or board may be that there are other staff members equally qualified in those areas and who are equally energetic and younger. The reverse can also be true; in either case those views will complicate the timing issue.

As noted above, emotions will be part of the timing considerations. The person involved may be either eager or reluctant to leave and the same is true for the board or organization. Either way it may be difficult, if not impossible, to find a time that is truly agreeable for both parties. Above all there is an ego factor on the part of the individual. For public institutions, in particular, it can be difficult to encourage or push a "reluctant dragon" into a departure. Yes, when there is a governing board, there is the power to dismiss a director (it does happen); however, that action tends to be messy. It can be a nightmare from a public relations point of view; especially if there is a hint that age may be a factor. Encouragement, rather than dismissal, is the usual board approach (offering extended benefits, a significant one-time tax-free contribution to the person's retirement program, etc.).

Regardless of the timing, the library or board must address the question of who will take over. With a full-blown succession plan in place that question is moot. However, all other situations will most likely, in a library environment, translate into the need for an interim manager. In the public sector, the hiring process can be a long, drawn-out affair, even with the expectation that there is a most likely internal candidate. The timeframe from departure to the first day on the job for the replacement can be many months and even more than a year in some instances.

That timeframe can be very challenging for both interim appointee and the organization. Given that there is likely to be some fluidity in the timeframe the uncertainty about what the interim appointee can and should do, beyond maintaining services, presents issues for the interim manager, the staff, and board members. Can or should major decisions take place? How should budget preparation be handled, should the interim appointee still be in place? Even minor decisions can add to uncertainty for people. What if the interim person decides to become a candidate for the permanent appointment?

Being an interim manager is not easy. For libraries, having some type of formal legal agreement is probably the best option for handling such a situation. That way, expectations and limitations can be spelled out. In the case of the interim being an internal staff member, it is especially important to specify compensation. There is also the issue with internal candidates about that person's old duties. Is it realistic to expect or demand that both jobs be fully carried out? It may be possible for one person to handle all the duties for a short time before burnout causes a disaster for the person and the organization. Realistically some reduction in duties is in everyone's best interests.

CHECK THIS OUT

We highly recommend James Larue's 2014 article as it provides many insights into the issues related to interim appointments written by three individuals who experienced that role: "Executive Transitions: The Interim Director" (*Public Libraries* 53, no. 6: 14–19).

After a long managerial career you can look forward to retirement. If you maintained a sound work-life balance, those retirement years can be as rewarding as the work years. For those who tended too far toward the all work end of the continuum, retirement can be a challenge. Not having non-work interests can make it difficult for some people to enjoy their newfound free time. We hope this book will assist you in having a long, balanced, and rewarding managerial career as well as a wonderful retirement.

REFERENCES

Allen, Erin. 2013. "Update on the Twitter Archive at the Library of Congress." Library of Congress Blog, January 4, 2013. http://blogs.loc.gov/loc/2013/01/update-on-the -twitter-archive-of-the-library-of-congress.

Babcock, Pamela. 2009. "Workplace Stress? Deal with It!" *HR Magazine* 54, no. 5: 67–68, 70, 72.

Bryson, John M., Barbara C. Crosby, and Laura Bloomberg. 2015. *Creating Public Value in Practice: Advancing the Common Good in a Multi-Sector, Shared-Power, No-One-Wholly- in-Charge World.* Boca Raton, FL: CRC Press.

Carlsson, Hanna. 2012. "Working with Facebook in Public Libraries: A Backstage Glimpse into the Library 2.0 Rhetoric." *Libri* 62, no. 3: 199–210.

The Economist Staff. 2015a. "Free Exchange: Meeting Up." *The Economist* 415, no. 8943: 72. http://www.economist.com/news/finance-and-economics/21647680-new-research -hints-ways-making-meetings-more-effective-meeting-up.

The Economist Staff. 2015b. "The Last 90 Days." *The Economist* 414, no. 8924: 4. http:// www.economist.com/news/business/21642181-successful-bosses-end-almost -important-beginning-last-90-days.

Fallon, Helen, 2010. "And So It Is Written: Supporting Librarians on the Path to Publica- tion." *Journal of Library Innovation* 7, no. 1: 35–41.

Frimannsdóttir, Ingibjörg B., and Barbara Whiting. 2011. "Dynamic Presentations for Strong Leaders." *Delta Kappa Gamma Bulletin* 77, no. 4: 31–37.

Gyorffy, Zsuzsa, Diana Dweik, and Edmond Girasek. 2016. "Workload, Mental Health, and Burnout Indicators among Female Physicians." *Human Resources for Health* 14, no. 1: 12–20.

Larue, James. 2014. "Executive Transitions: The Interim Director." *Public Libraries* 53, no. 6: 14–19.

Moore, Mark Harrison. 1995. *Creating Public Value: Strategic Management in Government.* Cambridge, MA: Harvard University Press.

Paradi, Dave. 2011, "What Annoys Learners Most About PowerPoint?" *T+D* 65, no. 12: 19.

Public Management. 2016. "On Point: Succession Planning." 98, no. 2: 4.

Rogoschewsky, Tanya Lisa. 2011. "Developing a Conference Presentation: A Primer for New Library Professionals." *Partnership: The Canadian Journal of Library and Informa- tion Practice and Research* 6, no. 2: 1–7. https://journal.lib.uoguelph.ca/index.php/perj /issue/view/112/showToc.

INDEX

About the Authors

G. EDWARD EVANS, PhD, is a semi-retired, award-winning author and Fulbright Scholar. He holds several graduate degrees in anthropology and library and information science (LIS). Throughout his career, he has been an administrator, researcher, teacher, and writer. As a researcher, he has published in both anthropology and LIS and held a Fulbright Fellowship and a National Science Foundation Fellowship. His teaching experience has also been in both fields in the United States and the Nordic countries, in particular at the Graduate School of Librarianship and Information Science at the University of California, Los Angeles. Evans has substantial administrative experience at private academic libraries such as Harvard University and Loyola Marymount University. He retired from full-time work as associate academic vice president for libraries and information resources at Loyola Marymount University. Evans spent the early years of semi-retirement looking after the Museum of Northern Arizona library and serving on the Foundation and Friends of the Library boards for the Flagstaff City–Coconino County Library System.

HOLLAND CHRISTIE, MLS, is the Public Services Manager at the Flagstaff City–Coconino County Public Library. Christie manages the Reference, Circulation, and Youth Services departments and is responsible for collection development, creating policies and procedures, and supervising Library programming. She received her MLS from the University of Arizona and a bachelor's degree in English from Northern Arizona University. She has worked in both public and academic libraries, and has a diverse work history outside of the library world. She has also worked as contributing editor on several fiction and nonfiction titles. Her most recent book project was as co-author of *Library Programs and Services: The Fundamentals* (Libraries Unlimited, 2015).